CONTEMPORARY HINDUISM

Religions in Focus
Series Editor: Graham Harvey, Open University

The *Religions in Focus* series offers a radical new venture in the study of religions: textbooks that introduce religions as they are actually lived. Books in the series examine contemporary religious activities and communities and the varied ways in which texts and traditions are employed in the evolution of religions.

Contemporary Hinduism

Edited by
P. Pratap Kumar

ACUMEN

First published in 2013 by Acumen

Acumen Publishing Limited
4 Saddler Street
Durham
DH1 3NP, UK

ISD, 70 Enterprise Drive
Bristol, CT 06010, USA

www.acumenpublishing.com

ISBN: 978-1-84465-689-9 (hardcover)
ISBN: 978-1-84465-690-5 (paperback)

British Library Cataloguing-in-Publication Data
A catalogue record for this book is available from the British Library.

Typeset in Gentium.
Printed and bound in the UK by CPI Group (UK) Ltd, Croydon, CR0 4YY.

Contents

List of illustrations

Acknowledgements

As the editor of this book, I wish to first acknowledge the hard work put in by all the contributors in shaping their chapters and making them suitable for the readership intended for the *Religions in Focus* series. All chapters in this book have been thoroughly peer-reviewed by scholars in the field. I particularly wish to acknowledge the assistance of Jeffery D. Long for his painstaking review of many chapters. I also thank the publisher's anonymous reviewers for their many helpful comments. This book could not have materialized without the help of Graham Harvey, who conceived the series and gave shape to this book as the first in the series. Obviously no book sees the light of day without the hard work of a group of experts in the publisher's office, such as reviewers, copy-editors and a host of others. I wish to thank all of them, especially Tristan Palmer, my editor, for working closely with me. I have had great pleasure in working with all who have contributed to the final shape and content of *Contemporary Hinduism*, and I thank all of them and hope that this book will prove a real contribution to the understanding of Hinduism today.

P. Pratap Kumar

A note on terminology

Every author in this book brought his or her own narrative style. As the editor, I have allowed such diversity of narrative style as it also makes the very point about the diversity of Hindu practice. However, some points need clarification. In presenting their narratives most authors limited themselves to a minimum of Sanskrit or regional vernacular words, but there are still a fairly large number of key non-English terms in use across the chapters. We have used the glossary section at the end of the book to provide brief definitions of most of these key terms in an easily accessible manner. The foreign words that appear in the glossary have been highlighted in bold at their first occurrence in the text. While Sanskrit words have been placed with diacritical characters to indicate correct pronunciation, some vernacular words have been left without diacritical characters as some scholars who used them anglicized such spellings. As the editor, however, I am satisfied that the foreign words are easily pronounceable by non-expert readers with or without diacritical characters.

P. Pratap Kumar

Introduction

P. Pratap Kumar

Being a Hindu can be removing one's shoes before entering a temple; or offering worship to **Gaṇeṣa** at the start of a wedding ritual so that it all goes well; or in the diaspora such as Trinidad and South Africa Hindus might mark their homes with flagposts (***jhandis***); or in other diaspora locations the Hindu priests might creolize the worship by accommodating even Orisha spirits; or Hindus might parade their deities in the streets as part of an annual festival; or, as in Nepal, Hindus can combine in one festival the celebration of a Vedic god Indra with a local goddess Kumārī and Bhairav; or elsewhere female ***sādhus*** might engage in devotional worship with householders; or devotees may simply read the collection of discourses (*Vachanamrut*) prepared by their ***gurus*** as it happens in the case of the Swaminarayan devotees; or some may offer selfless service to **Kṛṣṇa**, which is how Pushtimargis express their Hindu devotion; or some might tattoo the name of Rām on their forehead to express their devotion to their deity, Rām; or other Hindus find the dalliances of Kṛṣṇa with his female devotees sacred and sweet; or highly educated women will engage in the worship of snake goddess; or in places like Kerala the orthopractic **Nambūtiris** and Ayyappan devotees practice their respective traditions side by side and neither feels less Hindu; or seeing the deities in images of stone and metal and offering service to them can be a profound Hindu experience; or, for some Hindus, accessing their personal deity in the temple on a hill top can be as fulfilling as receiving deep intellectual knowledge of God; or in some cases Hindu ascetics can be militant political activists.

Any of the above, or a combination of the above, or all of the above could form authentic Hindu practice. With so many ways, Hindu practice is not always drawn from elite versions of texts, but from perpetually evolving regional traditions that are expressed in vernacular languages. It is this diversity that this book aspires to achieve. In dealing with contemporary Hinduism, the distinctions of great and little, classical and popular collapse and there is no need to privilege the textual tradition over the ordinary Hindu religiosity, as some scholars of Hinduism tended to do (e.g. Flood 1996: 6–7).

Not only within south Asia, but also in the diaspora context we find such vastly diverse Hindu practices. Hindus are today all over the world and have established their traditions in the many host countries in which they have chosen to reside. There is a plethora of Hindu traditions that are available in the diaspora today. Some have attained unique local versions of what they might have brought from the subcontinent; others are more recent plantations of present-day temple traditions in India. And these diaspora Hindu traditions have today become the first line of contact for many a modern person. At the same time, in the subcontinent of India, Hinduism has continued to evolve and diversify, exhibiting a variety of fascinating forms. The primary focus of this book, therefore, is the lived experience of Hindus spread not only across the subcontinent, but also throughout the world.

Introducing contemporary Hinduism is therefore about looking out for two aspects – to carefully document what people do in their daily religious life; but also to locate those descriptions in the regional and vernacular narratives, and to desist from essentializing those descriptions in line with the idealized elite versions. For so long the study of Hinduism has focused on the idealized elite versions that are often construed as a monolithic, single and continuous narrative. Focusing on contemporary Hinduism fundamentally calls into question such presumed unity in Hinduism. It forces us to look at such a wide variety of traditions that are not necessarily tied to a single narrative drawn from the privileged textual sources. Besides, traditions that are so far flung from each other across India and the diaspora locations are sometimes marked by their differences more than their similarities. Attempting to force unity among them can only result in a lack of appreciation for the rich diversity in form, structure and content of those narratives. As C. J. Fuller (2004: 28) rightly says, it is "mistaken to overstate the unity of Hinduism". Even when unifying factors are felt to be necessary for a common understanding of Hinduism, such unity need not be built on the basis of how popular traditions are related to the elite Brāhmanical traditions, but rather the other way around is also possible. I shall discuss the methodological implications of such shifting of focus and attention in the Afterword. For now, let me not delay the reader from absorbing and appreciating the rich diversity of narratives that we have included in this book.

Before introducing the plan of the book, let me first outline some of the broad themes and ideas presented. The first aspect I wish to underline is the discovery of many commonalities and distinctions in religious experiences among Hindus both in India and abroad often across the specific religious boundaries. These commonalities and distinctions form part of the larger narrative of Hinduism. Every essay included in this book presents opportunities to find some common features, and yet opens up a vista of distinct ways in which Hinduism is practised in specific regions. For instance, the chapters on the snake goddess (Chapter 14) and the goddess in Śrī Vaiṣṇavism (Chapter 16) offer conflicting implications of goddess worship for female devotees as well as for our scholarly analysis of feminine notions of divinity in Hinduism. Or the very same goddess in Sri Venkateswara temple can evoke different religious sentiments for Hindus and Muslims – she may be Padmavati for Hindus, but she is Bibi Nanchari for

Muslims (Chapter 17). A second aspect that I wish to underscore is the fluidity with which the many different Hindu traditions often coexist and intersect with each other. They do so by organically and naturally appropriating the others' texts and traditions for enriching their own religious experiences. Of particular significance is the fluidity that exists between not only different Hindu experiences, but also between Hindu, Sikh, Jain and Muslim traditions. A Jain text is used for a Hindu wedding (Chapter 2); a Hindu shrine and a Muslim one can seamlessly exist next to each other (Chapter 15); in Jhule Lal not only Sindhi Hindus but Sindhi Sikhs and Sindhi **Sūfis** (Muslim) can find meaning (Chapter 8); a Sindhi wedding can follow both Vedic and Sikh conventions. These are some of the broad themes and common ideas that the reader is invited to explore.

Plan of the book

The chapters in this book are not organized hierarchically but as regional representations. In the course of reading them we want to highlight the important themes and motifs that Hindus across the subcontinent and around the world can relate to in their practice. For the sake of convenience, we have divided the book into three parts. The first part deals with the diaspora Hinduism. We chose to begin with the diaspora because the conversation about Hinduism and its diversity arises not necessarily in the subcontinent, but as Hindus become globalized and interact with other cultures, invariably Hindus encounter people asking them about their religion. Thus, it might be useful to begin our presentation of contemporary Hinduism from the diaspora context.

Throughout the world, Hindus from first generation to fifth or even sixth generation live and actively practice the traditions that they have dutifully carried with them. In order for us to understand the significance of contemporary Hindu practice, we need also to focus on the diasporic representations of it. There is a plethora of literature available on south Asian diaspora, and a good deal of that literature covers Hindus in the diaspora substantially (e.g. Jacobsen & Kumar 2004; Rukmani 2001; Kumar 2006, 2013). In this book, therefore, we want to offer a sample of the diaspora Hindu experiences. We chose two examples of Hindus linked to colonial experience (Trinidad), and three from non-colonial experiences (USA and Norway). It is hoped that between the colonial context and the more recent diasporic experiences, the reader will have a reasonable account of the Hindu practice in the diaspora. An example from the African continent would have added value to this book. However, since an essay on South African Hindus was already published in the same series of *Religion in Focus* (P. P. Kumar 2009), we omitted that region and invite readers to consult that book should they be interested in the South African narrative of Hinduism. There is also a strong presence of Hindu diaspora in south-east Asia and east-Asia. Fascinating comparisons could be made between the south-east Asian and east-Asian Hindu diaspora and the North American Hindu diaspora, particularly with regard to the Sindhi community in North America, Indonesia and the Philippines. Steven W. Ramey's essay in this book offers such an opportunity (Hutter 2012 has similarly made such comparative study between Indonesia, Philippines and Germany in the case of Sindhi community).

As we begin Part I, we will first look at the first-generation diaspora Hindus who are still connected to their land of origin very strongly through their religious affiliations. The Indian community in North America in general and in the USA in particular dates back more than 150 years. The early Indian immigrants to North America were those who entered the USA and Canada from Mexico and the Caribbean countries. The next wave of them came from Punjab. This group included Hindus and Sikhs who sailed from Calcutta via Singapore and Hong Kong. Some of the Punjabi Sikhs and Hindus were in fact part of the British Indian army who were stationed in London. After their assignment, some of them made their way to Canada and the USA between 1897 and 1899 and settled in British Columbia and California (Muthanna 1982: 86). Since then, throughout the twentieth century mostly students and educated Indians made their way to the USA in search of lucrative careers in science, technology and other fields. The result of these immigration waves generated substantial number of Hindus living in various parts of the USA. In the last thirty years several famous Hindu temples have been built on US soil. Hindu temples in Pittsburgh (Pennsylvania), Bridge Water (New Jersey) and Malibu (California) are good examples of some well-known Hindu temples in the USA.

The story of Hinduism in Europe is somewhat different in that in countries such as Britain it is closely connected to the impact of British colonial experience, whereas in continental Europe, Indian immigrants arrived there both as refugees and in recent times as professionals in various science and technological fields as well as business families. With such a variety of immigration experiences, Hinduism in North America and Europe reflects both the first generation orthodoxy as well as the changing practices of new generation Hindus. While there is plenty of material available on Hinduism in Britain (e.g. Kim Knott 1986), due to limitations of space we could only accommodate one essay from continental Europe (Chapter 5). Similarly due to space constraints we could not provide some account of Hinduism in Australia, and we refer the readers to excellent studies already available in this area (e.g. Bilimoria 1989). With these few reservations, let me offer an insight into the first part of the book.

In Chapter 1, Jeffery Long introduces us to three temples in the USA. The first temple that he refers to serves as a place of worship for a variety of subgroups within the Hindu community and not surprisingly even the Jain and the Sikh communities as well. Long's comment in this regard illuminates the nature of diasporic Hinduism – "if we are accustomed to thinking of religion as an exclusive, either/or affair, we may be puzzled to find figures associated with these two traditions in a place of honour in a Hindu temple". In contrast, although the Washington Kali Temple welcomes all Hindus, Long points out that it "does sustain a distinctively *Bengali* atmosphere and cultural environment". He nevertheless hastens to add that most Bengali families are members of both temples, and as such the two are not at cross-purposes. The third one, the Vedanta Centre, is inclusive of all Indians, and typically attracts more non-Indian members than the other two temples cited above. In a sense, the three places of worship and meditation are attempts by Hindus in the diaspora to make Hinduism as universal as possible seemingly with a view to include both Indians and non-Indians. What is significant about Long's chapter is that it raises some thorny issues relating to when Hinduism is practised outside its homeland (e.g. the issue of whether ethnic Hindus are more Hindu than the non-Indian Hindus). Surely this issue will continue to be debated in the Hindu diaspora for a long time to come.

Chapter 2 relates to Nepali Hindus in the USA. Deepak Shimkhada explores the extent to which the Nepali Hindu diaspora struggle to maintain their ancient culture that they practised back home. Using the ancient form of wedding ritual as a means to illustrate this point, Shimkhada explores questions of why diaspora Nepali Hindus continue to practice this ritual in which young girls are married to a "fruit" in order to deal with the harsh treatment to which women are subjected to when they become widows. He also offers insight into the pragmatic nature of Nepali Hindu practice in the diaspora (e.g. being willing to accept someone without priestly background to conduct weddings). It is interesting to note that the perpetuation of their Hindu practice is intrinsic to their sense of identity and survival in a foreign culture. For them this sense of identity is derived largely by following their daily customs and rituals rather than intellectual philosophy such as **Vedānta**, as Shimkhada points out.

From first-generation diasporic Hindus we move to places where Hindus lived for many generations away from their land of origin. In Chapter 3 Paul Younger introduces us to the background in Trinidad where, in the relatively sheltered villages that the Indians created for themselves during the colonial period, they practised their religion through various festivals and rituals. In this chapter Younger discusses the role of the **Ārya Samāj** and the Hindu Maha Sabha in reorganizing Hinduism in Trinidad and the identity issues that the younger generation faced in practising their religious traditions. As such, his chapter introduces us to the various socio-political situations in which Hindus appropriated each other's traditions across the north Indian and south Indian divide (e.g. the south Indian appropriation of goddess **Kālī** in place of **Māriyamman**). However, Younger notes that as people moved away from the villages to the urban areas after the Second World War, the north Indian Hindus especially tended to follow more Brāhmanized Hindu rituals. What is significant about the Trinidadian Hinduism is that many of its practices have migrated to North America as more and more Trinidadians re-migrated to other western countries in search of new opportunities.

Against the broad background offered by Younger, it would be useful to look closely at one particular example of Hindu practice. Indrani Rampersad

(Chapter 4) offers such an example of the significance of *jhandi* (a flag commemorating a Hindu deity) among the north Indian Hindus of Trinidad. She notes that this practice of observing the annual ritual of hoisting the *jhandi* in the courtyard of every north Indian home in Trinidad goes back to the time of the indenture labour. Through this ritual, Rampersad offers an insight into the family tradition. Over the many years of Indian presence in Trinidad, the flag served both as a marker of sacred space, but significantly it also served as an identity marker. Rampersad offers an insight into the politics of this practice. Locating this practice within the tradition of Rām-Vaiṣṇava worship, she also alludes to the various other deities worshipped in contemporary Hindu society in Trinidad.

Chapter 5 closes Part I by dealing with the establishment of Tamiḻ Śaivism in Norway. Knut Jacobsen offers an insight into the Tamiḻ festivals associated with Murukaṉ, a son of Śiva, and how Tamiḻ Śaivism arrived in Norway. The narrative of the arrival of Tamiḻ Śaivism in Norway is replete with heroic stories of the early immigrants. Jacobsen offers details of the festival processions, temple rituals and the establishment of their religious calendar applicable to local situations in Norway. He points to the larger significance of these religious activities in Norway when he says:

> [I]n the Tamiḻ Hindu temples in Norway, it is primarily the ritual world of the temples of the country of origin that is attempted to be recreated. Such recreation makes religion seem authentic and the foreign place seems like home. But the diaspora situation often leads to an increased focus on the temple as a place for the preservation and generational transfer of culture and as a place to confirm identity, and the temple often becomes the single most important cultural institution of the group.

In this sense, the Tamiḻ Hindus seem to have found a niche in Norway.

Part II introduces chapters from the north Indian region. Here also we could not be as comprehensive as we would have liked. Nevertheless, we tried to bring focus to some of the major regions in the north: Punjab, Sindh, Rajasthan, Gujarat, Maharashtra, central India and Bengal. We also included Nepal here as we believe it offers some unique experience of Hinduism, although in a sense we stepped out of the Indian political boundaries.

Chapter 6 begins this second part by looking at Nepal. One of the most interesting ways to see contemporary Hinduism in Nepal is through the many festivals that are celebrated there. Here we have selected one such festival that permeates the entire Nepali society. Michael Baltutis wonderfully describes and explains the festival of Indra in Nepal. It is a festival that seamlessly links the classical with the popular, Hindu priests with the Buddhist ones, and places Indra, Śiva and the goddesses in a complex ritual performance that has both sociological and political significance. It offers an insight into the practice of caste, and the shifting focus of the ritual from the royal family to the elected government structure. As such, the Indrajatra festival continues to be relevant to the Hindus of Nepal beyond the monarchy. It does so by the ritual's multi-faceted focus on the king on the one hand, and as Baltutis points out, on the "local divine king Bhairav, the royal Kumārī, and the city's ancestors as it is to the ancient Hindu god Indra and the political leader of Nepal". It is a window into contemporary religious practice in the Nepali Hindu society.

Chapter 7 is from Rajasthan, a very colourful and vibrant region with intense devotional traditions. Devotion ordinarily brings to mind the ecstatic devotees and their intense devotional affinity to the temple deities to whom they are devoted. In this chapter, however, devotional Hinduism and ascetic Hinduism come together in that we are introduced to a new form of asceticism that is steeped in devotion. Antoinette E. DeNapoli points out that the ascetic practitioners that she met in Rajasthan rooted in the vernacular tradition:

> experience and express asceticism differently than the ways that it is predominantly imagined, constructed, and interpreted in the classical Sanskrit texts and academic scholarship. The kind of asceticism that these *sādhus* articulate in their practices identifies a phenomenon that is communal and positive, rather than individualistic and negative.

This ascetic practice, unlike the conventional one that is removed from day-to-day society, is expressed in daily group singing of devotional songs of **Kabīr**. DeNapoli characterizes this phenomenon as devotional asceticism and these female *sādhus* come together as a community to help each other, as exemplified in the life of the female *sādhu*, Ganga Giri. It is a sort of asceticism in which relationships and friendships are significant. Here we are offered a different model of asceticism, in which even liberation "constitutes a relational-devotional experience of love between devotee and deity" that is rarely present in the texts.

It is interesting to note how many different forms the offering to the deity takes in the context of devotional rituals. In Chapter 8, Steven W. Ramey takes us in to the depths of the Punjab and Sindh regions where devotional practices among the Sindhi Hindus for whom the Sikh sacred text known as **Guru Granth Sāhib** represents a "reformist Hindu tradition". It is profoundly significant to see how differently Hinduism can be circumscribed by so many different formations. In the practice of Sindhi Hindus what is practised as Sikhism is indeed another form of Hinduism. It is another example of how systemic reifications of religions can become problematic in real society. As such, the Sindhis have no difficulty in incorporating Sūfi elements into their practice. For them Sufism is beyond any single religion. As Ramey notes, "Sufism for many Sindhi Hindus is an extreme expression of devotion to the divine that is not exclusively associated with one religion. A person can be a Christian Sūfi, a Buddhist Sūfi, or a Hindu Sūfi." It is against this background that Ramey introduces us to the religious life of Sindhis that oscillates between their Persian connections and the Hindu traditions as well as geographically overlapping between Punjab and Sindh. Conversion was therefore not only irrelevant for them but it was in the context of the pressure from the Muslim rulers that they seem to have invented their new god known to them as Jhule Lal. For this reason their religious practice is inseparable from politics on the one hand, and Hindu–Muslim relations on the other. Jhule Lal, thus, is not only a Hindu god; for Muslims he is Khwaja Khizr. It is in this broader context of relations that one has to see their devotion to the Guru Granth Sāhib as a sacred text and manifestation of divinity.

From the Punjab and Sindh region we move to the western part of India into Gujarat. In Chapter 9, Hanna H. Kim takes us through the journey to introduce us to the Swaminarayan devotees and their devotional and ritual practices in Gujarat. With the humble beginnings of the temple back in 1907, the Swaminarayan community today is flourishing throughout the world with over 700 temples. While the Gujarati ethnicity and language circumscribe the tradition, its devotees attempt to transcend these limitations through their daily rituals that underline the finitude of their material body and the eternality of their soul (***ātman***). It is with the firm belief that their soul, as Kim notes, "upon the death of her physical being, be in a state of offering loving devotion to **Purushottam**, far away from the unpredictability of rebirth" that they offer their daily rituals. An abstruse philosophical idea of the soul becomes real in the daily lives of these devotees of Purushottam. The ideal is not to leave the world in search of their spiritual existence, but rather "to be able to live in the world without being derailed by bodily and mundane desires". The daily ritual is a constant reminder of this larger ideal. Kim's tactful narrative leads us through the intricacies of their relationship with the divine, the *gurus* of the tradition and themselves. It is in this relationship that the ritual takes central place around which their entire life revolves.

Staying in north India, we experience another form of devotional Hinduism that understands devotion in terms of service to God. Devotion often insists on exclusive loyalty to the deity. In Chapter 10 Shandip Saha illustrates this exclusive devotional practice in the lives of what is commonly known as Puṣṭi Mārga followers in north India. In the lives the Puṣṭi Mārga followers this devotion is expressed as service to Kṛṣṇa as a comprehensive response that includes daily rituals, moral actions, and use of their material wealth – all of it to attain the consciousness that everything is the manifestation of Kṛṣṇa. However, what is significant is their association with the image manifestation of Kṛṣṇa and the residence (*havelī*) in which the images are located. Saha notes that when the devotees enter the residence and stand in front of the inner sanctum or what is referred to as the real sacred space (*nijmandir*) they "feel that they are leaving their mundane (*laukik*) surroundings to enter into the realm of the sacred (*alaukik*) where they are to come into the immediate presence of their beloved lord Kṛṣṇa". For this reason, the seeing of Kṛṣṇa takes on a very detailed ritual act in this tradition such that Saha identifies eight different visualizations of Kṛṣṇa during their elaborate ritual daily. Finally, this devotion is not only an individual one, but a corporate one, which is expressed in their food offerings.

In Chapter 11 we are taken on a pilgrimage to Viṭṭhal temple in the town of Pandharpur in Maharashtra. Jon Keune introduces us to the pilgrimage tradition of Vārkarīs in west-central India. Balancing between his role as a scholar documenting this tradition and at the same time as a pilgrim along with hundreds of Vārkarīs, he takes us into the heart of this community's "fascinating and bewildering aspects". In describing the absence of hierarchy in the community, the lack of rigid boundaries between traditions on the one hand and practices such as the **Brāhman** men sitting down to eat, as well as the etiquette of waiting for the preliminary rituals to bless the host are done before eating, Keune intricately weaves together details that offer us a picture of a tradition in its dynamic nature. Through these minute details Keune brings together the caste practice and caste deviation among the Vārkarīs of Maharashtra. If the pilgrims are on their way to see God Viṭṭhal in Pandharpur, the local villages along the way see in the pilgrims the very same God, as did the old woman in Keune's narrative.

From Maharashtra, Ramdas Lamb (Chapter 12) takes us into the region of central India, where he explores the **Rāma** devotion and the significance of various associated festivals among the low-caste people. It is clear that festivals mark the most significant form of religious life among the urban low caste people in the central Indian region. On the other hand, in the rural areas of this region three distinct religious groups belonging to the low caste appear prominently – the **Kabīrpanth**, the **Satnāmi Samāj** and the **Rāmnāmi Samāj**. All three groups are distinguished by their rejection of caste, image worship and its associated rituals. However, Kabīrpanth is more syncretistic in nature, while the other two are rooted in the Rāma ***bhakti*** tradition. The tribal communities in the region on the other hand have a range of female deities whom they worship. Lamb points out that their beliefs have become intermingled with the Sanskritic ones and as such some of their original deities obtained features of Brāhmanical goddesses. Because of their belief in spirits that could be both benevolent and malevolent, the role of the ritual officiant known as ***Baigā*** is crucial.

From this central region we enter the eastern shores of India, where Abhishek Ghosh (Chapter 13) offers another example of Vaiṣṇava devotion in the region of Bengal. Contextualizing within the context of priest centred Hindu practices that emphasized ritual purity on the one hand and engaged in left-handed ritual practices that involved ritual sex and meat eating, Ghosh details the origin, development and philosophical subtleties of Gauḍīya Vaiṣṇavism in Bengal. It is a tradition that emphasizes a utopian alternative reality "where every step is a dance and every word a song", but at the same time "can also manifest within our phenomenal world for a sincere and qualified practitioner of *bhakti*". Seeing Kṛṣṇa in his image form, living in the company of devotees, and dwelling in holy places together with a life-style that is conducive for spiritual wellbeing are practices that "would inevitably help her to come out of the 'spiritual amnesia' and remember her real position in the realm of Kṛṣṇa". It is this intensely other worldly consciousness and at the same time rooted in worldly engagement that seems to appeal to thousands of people. As Ghosh puts it:

> whether it was a village in Bengal or downtown Manhattan, Gauḍīya Vaiṣṇavas more or less have some core beliefs, values and practices: For them Kṛṣṇa is the supreme personal being and each and every individual is a minute part of him, like sparks from fire; the natural state of every being is to engage in his loving service, *bhakti.*

In Part III we enter south India, where we are introduced to a range of devotional expressions of Hinduism that are generally treated as part of rural and illiterate folk. But challenging such stereotypical representations, Amy Allocco (Chapter 14) offers us an insight into what classical anthropologists and religionists alike relegated to the periphery. Focusing on women, she narrates the story of snake worship in Tamilnadu. What is interesting is that her account challenges the general tendency to treat popular religious practices such as village goddesses as the preoccupation of illiterate lower strata society in rural India. Allocco's narrative of Susheela, who is a scientist and of Brāhmin caste, is particularly significant in this regard as this worship of the snake goddess takes place in the urban centres of Tamilnadu. Her skilful narrative points out the special significance that this worship tradition has for women, especially those who suffer what is known in Tamilnadu as the "snake blemish": the inability of a woman to conceive. However, she also offers a counterpoint to this partisanship toward women by offering the narrative of a young man who she encounters while offering his worship to the snake goddess on behalf of his family. Either way, the worship of the snake goddess is structured around a mutual relationship between the goddess and the devotees. She therefore suggests that:

> it is common for an individual worshipper to make a vow (***vēṇṭutal*** or ***pirārttaṉai***) to formalize this devotional pact with the deity; such vows may be instrumental (that is, the vow serves as a means for the devotee to get something s/he wants), prophylactic (meaning that the vow is undertaken to ward off some undesirable occurrence, such as illness) or offered in thanksgiving (meaning that the vow is discharged in gratitude after a wish is fulfilled).

The material relationship that characterizes this tradition of worship is often ignored in philosophical Hinduism. Here temples play a central role in shaping Hinduism that connects us to the significance of vows, gender and caste.

Chapter 15 introduces us to the religious life of Kerala. Using two distinct traditions as vantage points, George Pati offers an insight into the complex ritual practice through which the Nambūtiri Brāhmans live their religious life and the intense ascetic lifestyle observed by the devotees of Ayyappan. Between these two – the ritualistic life of Nambūtiris and the ascetic life of the Ayyappans – two distinct religious and cultural traditions come together in Kerala, where we are introduced to the non-dual philosopher **Śaṅkarācārya**, caste divisions, Muslim participation in Hindu ritual and, more significantly, the weaving together of two distinct religious orientations of **Viṣṇu** (Vishnu) and Śiva in the birth of Ayyappan. In the daily routine of rituals by the Nambūtiris and the strict ascetic life of the Ayyappans, the gods and the humans, the sacred and the mundane, come together in the land that locals call "God's own country".

In Chapter 16 we are introduced to devotional fervour that began in the lives of ***āḻvār***s and subsequently shaped what has later become known as Śrī Vaiṣṇavism. Archana Venkatesan introduces us to this south Indian form of Vaiṣṇavaism through the narrative of Āṇṭāḷ. By focusing on Āṇṭāḷ, she also tells the story of a local female devotee who spent most of her life relating the story of Āṇṭāḷ to the locals. Venkatesan highlights the significance of ecstatic religious experience that characterizes the intense reciprocal relationship between Viṣṇu and his devotees. This intense devotion mediated through the life of Āṇṭāḷ to the contemporary devotees, as exemplified by the life of Tiruvenkatammal enables us to understand how Hindus think of an ideal devotee as an embodiment of the divine. The filial intimacy of philosopher **Rāmānuja** with Āṇṭāḷ again reinforces the interdependent relationship between philosopher and the poet.

In the evolution of Śrī Vaiṣṇavism in the south, Sri Venkateswara temple in Tirupati became one of the major centres of Vaiṣṇavism. However, this temple also has become a symbol of syncretistic religion. In the course of history, both Hindus and Muslims came to associate themselves with the temple. Afsar Mohammad (Chapter 17) demonstrates how in Tirupati, Andhra Pradesh, the Sri Venkateswara temple comes alive as both Hindus and Muslims appropriate it. From the mainstream perspective, it is a Hindu temple dedicated to Sri Venkateswara, who is considered an ***avatāra*** (avatar, or incarnation) of Viṣṇu, and who decided to immigrate to the world of humans and settle and marry a local girl called Padmavati, or, from the Muslim perspective, to marry Bibi Nancharamma. Either way, if visualization is something significant in Hindu religious practice, it is here the devotees can see their most desired god along with his divine consort Śrī bedecked in gold and precious jewels that they have generously given to ease the burden of his debt of bride money. Afsar Mohammad offers an insight into the Hindu religious practice at Sri Venkateswara temple by linking it with the medieval Vaiṣṇava teacher, Rāmānuja, the **Vaikhānasa** ritual tradition with all its unique daily rituals culminating in the annual festival of Brahma. If Kerala was conceived as "God's own country", Tirumala, in the midst of seven hills, becomes the "heaven on earth" for the devotees who throng to this place to give away to their god generously in return for the fulfilment of their vows. This theological notion of reciprocity that marks the Hindu religious practice seems to reverberate here also.

Chapter 18 offers us a different perspective on asceticism in Hinduism. We have already seen earlier how asceticism can be this worldly by intensely combining with devotional attitude. Here we see a different face of asceticism that is both militant and political. Turning the tables around the normative notions of asceticism vis-à-vis various Indian religions, William Harman introduces us to a militant form of asceticism that is expressed not in death defying meditative practices removed from the active society, but rather in "marching barefoot and stark naked into battle against armour-clad military adversaries". These ascetics, however, display the same norms and ideals outlined in the normative accounts of Hinduism and other Indian religions. That is, they "answer to no accepted norms of worldly behaviour". Harman notes their role in the Hindu fundamentalist contexts such as the events associated with the Ayodhya conflict between Hindus and Muslims. However, the significance of this chapter is in Harman's application of this militant ascetic behaviour to the separatist army popularly known as Tami<u>l</u> Tigers in the context of the ethnic conflict between the Tami<u>l</u>s and the local Singala (Simhala) communities in Sri Lanka. The Tami<u>l</u> Tigers saw themselves as the liberation army fighting against the Sri Lankan army to liberate the Tami<u>l</u>s from state oppression. What distinguishes the Tami<u>l</u> Tigers – "a feature they share with the militant ascetic movements of northern India", according to Harman – is "their sense of being able to accomplish remarkable feats in the face of unlikely circumstances, feats believed to be the direct result of their ascetic training, extraordinary discipline, and unwavering concentration and commitment". Harman details their ascetic behaviour modelled on the same ideal of being dead to the world as do the normal Hindu renouncers follow. Making this comparison, he notes that "for both the Indian ascetic and the Tami<u>l</u> Tiger, disciplined devotion to a cause represented by a deity and/or a divinized *guru* affords access to supernatural status. That status offers a path to immortality and to the eventual conquest of death itself."

Hinduism beyond ethnicity and conventional boundaries

Evidently, the chapters included here present a very diverse picture of Hindu practice in contemporary India and abroad. One significant implication of the chapters for the understanding of Hinduism is that the boundaries of what we term as "Hindu" or "Hinduism" are not only very fuzzy, but even the internal distinctions are also not very strict. At the level of practice there seems to be a great deal of pragmatism and inventiveness, and less dogmatism. Especially in the context of diaspora Hindu practice, it is no longer viable to limit the definition of Hindu in ethnic terms. This does not mean that there are no ethnically based Hindu institutions, temples and organizations that profile their ethnic traditions, but they do so with the realization that they are not exclusive. This is evident in Chapter 1. It is for this reason that we have included chapters on Nepali and Sri Lankan Hindus. Although Nepal is geographically and politically separate from India as a nation state (be that because of its ancient connection with Indian culture or its porous geographical relationship with India), it is often a common phenomenon to find that Nepalis, especially in their diasporic context, relate rather closely with Hindus that came from other parts of India. It is one instance of how a Hindu might be defined as beyond the political borders of India. Aside from this nuance, it is because of their affinity to a broader Hindu identity, albeit their unique Nepali cultural identity, that we chose to include their narrative in this book. It is for very similar reasons we have also included Hinduism in Sri Lanka. But here we wanted to emphasize that Hinduism is not just a religious practice, but an instrument for social activism.

Another feature that we notice emerging out of these chapters is the internal conceptual fluidity. We have seen philosophy, religious practice and ascetic life coming together in devotional practice. Not only are the divisions between various sectarian practices such as Vaiṣṇava and **Śaiva** blurred, but often a single religious figure or deity is worshipped by both Hindus and Muslims, as in the case of Sri Venkateswara temple. We have seen caste practice and caste deviation in the case of Vārkarīs of Maharashtra. We have seen in the Swaminarayan practice that liberation of the soul is not exclusive but depends on living in this world with bodily desires. As in the case of Puṣṭi Mārga devotees, we have also seen that devotion to deity is not only individual but also corporate. We have noted that the boundaries between Sikhism and Hinduism are so porous that the Sindhi Hindus are able to identify themselves with both the traditions with ease. The devotional asceticism in Rajasthan is unlike anything we come across in the usual textual representations. If that is not enough, asceticism sits quite well with militancy, and even offered a model for political activism in Sri Lanka.

In the royal festival of Indra in Nepal we witness coalescence of classical and the popular, the religious and the political. In central India religious practice cannot be understood without caste and tribal identities. Tamilnadu might be better known for all its glorious Brāhmanical temples, and if we thought popular goddesses are the domain of illiterate rural folk in India, the educated urban and the rural Tamilnadu is replete with the popular goddess worship in the form of snake goddess. Obviously the various popular goddesses are deeply entrenched in the lives of the diaspora Hindus. The Rāma devotion in the diaspora takes on a more tangible ritualized dimension in the form of hoisting the flag of **Hanumān** and other deities. The combination of diversity on the one hand with the tendency to present a universal outlook in the diaspora demonstrates the fluidity of Hinduism to adapt to various conditions and contexts.

We invite our readers – both students and professors of Hinduism – to witness this colourful contemporary Hinduism. Our focus on Hinduism in contemporary society has enabled us to take into account a vast array of regional narratives of Hinduism. It is our hope that this book will be of significance in reconceptualizing Hinduism and in moving beyond the master narrative of classical texts.

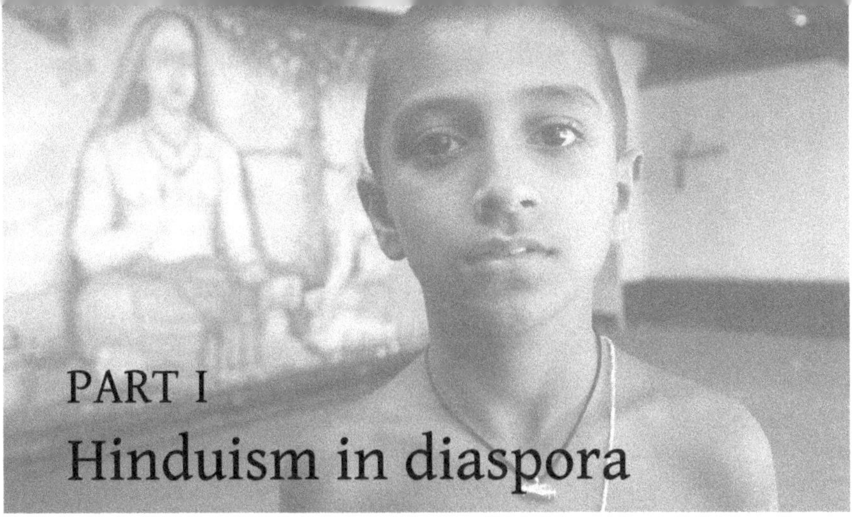

PART I
Hinduism in diaspora

In the last century and a half, and even earlier, millions of south Asians have emigrated to various parts of the world and have made their home in foreign lands, among various cultural and religious groups. While some went to these places due to colonial transfer of labour, others (mostly in the last few decades) went of their own volition in search of better education and careers, mostly in western countries such as North America and Europe. The result of these emigrations of south Asians is the presence of Hinduism in these countries. Hinduism is a flourishing religion today in most Western societies, and is actively practised and studied by Western students as well as south Asians living in these countries. As Hinduism began to take root in these foreign lands, it has adopted new ways of expressing itself in the new environments. To offer some examples of these attempts, we have included two chapters from North America and two from Trinidad. They represent two different traditions of contemporary Hindu expressions. We have also included a chapter on Norway to represent the spread of Hinduism in Europe.

In Chapter 1, Jeffery Long offers an insight into the ability of Hinduism to adapt itself to a new environment as well as into how a localized form of Hinduism, which he identifies as indigenous Hinduism. Here he brings a new connotation to the word indigenous. Deepak Shimkhada, in Chapter 2, offers an insight into how the first-generation Nepali Hindus continued their traditions in California, USA. In his narrative he offers insight into how they adapted to the new environment, their identity issues and the role of women in preserving the traditions. The third chapter in this part, by Paul Younger, offers an insight into the evolution of Hinduism in Trinidad, the changes it underwent, the challenges it faced and the emergence of new ritual forms. The uniqueness of "Trindad Hinduism" is maintained even when the Hindus from Trinidad resettle in other Western countries such as Canada, USA and UK. In Chapter 4 Indrani Rampersad weaves her narrative around the practice of hoisting a flagpole in the domestic and temple grounds, and tells about the role it played in forging the identity unique to the Caribbean Hindus. In Chapter 5 Knut Jacobsen focuses on the establishment of Tamil̲ Śaivism through temples, rituals and festivals, noting distinguishing features of their religious calendar.

1. Diasporic and indigenous Hinduism in North America

Jeffery D. Long

As a number of the articles in this volume illustrate, Hinduism, a tradition (or, perhaps more accurately, a collection of traditions) indigenous to the Indian subcontinent (south Asia) is now an international tradition, practised worldwide in such disparate locations as Europe, Africa, Australia, the Caribbean and North America.

In this chapter, I hope to illustrate both the adaptability of the Hindu diaspora to the relatively new environment in which Hindus find themselves in North America, as well as the emergence of an indigenous North American Hinduism, the membership of which draws not only from the Indian community that has traditionally practised Hinduism, but also from non-Indians, such as myself, who have come to identify ourselves as Hindus.

HARI temple

The Hindu American Religious Institute (HARI) temple is located on a two-lane road that winds through the woods of rural central Pennsylvania. Unlike many Hindu temples in North America, the building does not immediately strike us as distinctively Hindu in its appearance. It looks somewhat like a large, two-storey house, with a parking lot in the front and an American flag flying in the breeze near the entrance. The only clearly Hindu architectural feature is the large gate through which we enter the property, with the holy *mantra Om* (ॐ) written at the top in the Devanagari script of Sanskrit, and the names **Sītā** Rām and Rādha Kṛṣṇa written in the Roman alphabet on the sides.

Entering the temple on a Sunday morning, the first sight to meet our eyes is that of three brightly clothed and highly decorated ***mūrtis***, or images, of three Hindu deities in the central altar of the temple, directly facing the front entrance. At the centre is Rām, or Rāma (as he is known in Sanskrit). Just to his left (the right, from the perspective of the viewer) is his wife, Sītā, and to his right is his brother and "right-hand man" Lakṣman (or Lakṣmana). Unlike many temples, where the central deities often reside behind closed doors, opened only at certain special times for worship, the deities at HARI are out in the open and available for viewing, or **darśana**, at all times.

Before leaving the lobby area and entering the temple proper, we turn to our left and enter a room where shoes are kept on wooden shelves. After removing our shoes – a gesture of respect that is observed not only in temples, but in most Hindu homes as well – we climb a half-staircase and enter the main sanctuary of the temple. Because it is a Sunday morning, the temple is not a quiet place. On the contrary, there is a great deal of activity here. At the far left of the sanctuary, there is a performance stage where cultural events are held. At the moment, a group of elementary school children are sitting cross-legged in a semicircle around a woman playing a harmonium and teaching the children to sing **bhajans**, or devotional songs. All but one or two of the children present are Indian, as is their teacher.

At the far right of the sanctuary, a bearded man – not Indian, but wearing a **kurtā** and **pajāma** – is showing another, smaller group of slightly older children, around middle school age, how to play a sitar. Scattered throughout the sanctuary are smaller groups of adults – mostly, but not exclusively, Indian – engaged in quiet conversation. Seated in front and slightly to the side of the central images of Rām, Sītā and Lakṣman is one of the two priests who serve the HARI temple.

We approach the central images and make a **praṇām**, or a gesture of respect, by bringing the palms of both our hands together, raising them to the level of our face and bowing slightly. Before doing this, we may ring a large brass bell that hangs from a rope suspended from the ceiling. The ringing of the bell does not disturb any of the activity already occurring in the sanctuary. At this point, the priest, unless he is already engaged in conversation with another devotee, will smile at us warmly and say, "*Namaste! Aap kaise hain?*", which in Hindi means "Hello! How are you?". The priest, Śrī Naranji Pandya, who is originally from Ahmedabad, in the Indian state of Gujarat, speaks Hindi, English and Gujarati, but seems most comfortable with Hindi. (He also knows that I am trying to learn it.) The other priest, Śrī Seetharamaswamy, speaks English, Hindi, and Telugu, and is from Hyderabad, in the Indian state of Andhra Pradesh.

After exchanging pleasantries with Śrī Naranji Pandya, known affectionately as "Shastriji", we walk around the central altar in a clockwise direction, keeping the main images to our right side and passing through a small corridor, the walls of which have been decorated with two-dimensional portraits of Hindu deities, as well as various saints from Hindu history. We note that among these sacred figures are included Mahavira, the twenty-fourth *Tirthankara*, or enlightened teacher of the Jain tradition, and Guru Nanak, the founder of Sikhism. And if we are accustomed to thinking of religion as an exclusive, either/or affair, we may be puzzled to find figures associated with these two traditions in a place of honour in a Hindu temple.

After circumambulating the central altar, we hold out our right hand to Shastriji and are given a few drops of water mixed with the oil of the **tulsī** plant – a variety of basil that is sacred to the deity Viṣṇu. After we drink this water from the palm of our hand, we again extend our right hand and are given a mixture of nuts and sugar cubes. This is ***prasād*** – food that has been offered to the deities and is then returned to devotees as a form of divine blessing.

Set in the back wall of the sanctuary, extending to either side of the central altar, are smaller altars that house the images of other Hindu deities. From left to right, moving towards the central altar, we see Sarasvatī, goddess of wisdom; the divine couple, Śiva and Pārvatī; and a large image of Mahavira, who is adorned in keeping with Śvetaṃbara Jain tradition. Continuing from left to right, moving our gaze away from the central altar, we can see another divine couple, Kṛṣṇa and Rādha; **Durgā**, the divine mother, having eight hands and riding a lion; and Balaji, or Sri Venkateswara, a popular southern Indian image of Viṣṇu.

Returning our gaze to the central altar, we see, on the pedestal on which Rāma is standing, a bright red "*Om*", beneath which is a small bronze image of a baby Kṛṣṇa. At Lakshman's feet is a small image of Hanumān, the ape deity who assisted Rāma in his quest to rescue Sītā from the demonic Rāvana in the sacred epic poem, the **Rāmāyaṇa**. A similar-sized image of the elephant-headed Gaṇeṣa is at Sītā's feet. Just to Gaṇeṣa's left is a grey stone abstract symbol of Śiva – the ***liṅgam*** – which is closely guarded by an image of Nandi, the bull – Śiva's animal vehicle, or ***vāhana*** – made from the same type of grey stone as the *liṅgam*. Rāma is the central deity of this temple because its membership is mostly (though, as we shall see, not exclusively) Vaiṣṇava.

The sanctuary as a whole is a large, simple, functional room, with little in the way of adornment, apart from the images themselves – which are brilliantly decorated. On the floor is a dark red carpet, except for a square roughly one metre to a side in the right half of the room, which is bare white marble. Directly above this bare spot is a vent. This space is for the lighting of a small fire (held in a metal container that is placed on bricks) in order that a ***havan***, a ritual offering in the sacred fire accompanied by Vedic chanting, might be performed. The *havan* is held once each month at the temple and on New Year's Day. When we go downstairs, we will find a large communal dining room and kitchen, as well as restrooms, an apartment for the family of one of the priests (the other priest lives with a family of devotees nearby), and a storage space for chairs and tables, which are set up and taken down as needed. The basement also has classrooms. Because it is Sunday morning, these are filled with children learning Indian languages and taking religion classes from volunteers from the community. (I have occasionally served as one of these volunteers, coming in once a month to talk with the older students – middle school and high school age – about yoga and Vedānta philosophy, and to discuss contemporary issues in relation to Hinduism.)

Classes run from about ten in the morning until noon. At noon, all of the children gather in the centre of the sanctuary directly in front of the central images. Their parents and teachers sit to the sides. Almost everyone sits on the carpeted floor, although there is a row of chairs along the back wall for the elderly or anyone who does not feel like sitting on the floor. The head of the Sunday school stands at the front of the room and makes announcements, as well as inviting the children to tell the community something that they learned that day. If any of the children has had a birthday in the past week, the temple community applauds them. Then everyone stands for **ārati**.

Āratī is a ritual that one of the priests performs at the temple daily, at both noon and seven o'clock at night, regardless of whether any devotees are present. Small oil lamps sitting on metal plates are lit and waved in front of the images of the deities to the accompaniment of communal singing. The traditional *āratī* song at HARI temple, as at many North American Hindu temples, is *Om Jaya Jagadisha Hare*, or "Victory to **Hari** (Viṣṇu), Lord of the Universe", as popularized by the Hindi singer, Lata Mangeshkar. After *āratī*, everyone heads downstairs for lunch, which is provided by volunteer families from the temple community.

HARI is a type of temple that is quite common in the Hindu diaspora – a "universal temple"; that is, a non-sectarian temple that does not cater exclusively to any **saṃpradāya** or denomination of Hinduism, but is open to all. The goal of the temple community is to provide a place of worship and cultural experience for

Figure 1.1 Central altar of HARI temple, with priests Śrī Seetharamaswamy (left) and Śrī Naranji Pandya (right) (photo by author).

as wide a cross-section of Hindus as possible. Although the Vaiṣṇava presence is considerable – the central deity is Rām, the song sung at *āratī* is Vaiṣṇava, and one of the priests, Śrī Seetharamaswamy, is a Śrī Vaiṣṇava – the temple is not Vaiṣṇava in any exclusive way. Mahāśivaratri, Durgā Pūjā, Sarasvatī Pūjā, and Gaṇeṣa Caturthī are celebrated with as much fanfare and devotion as Kṛṣṇajanmāṣṭami and Rāmanavamī. And, as we might already have noticed, the HARI community includes Jains, with Mahavir Jayanti being a festival on the temple calendar of no less importance than the celebrations of the various Hindu deities already mentioned.

Some of the festivals just mentioned – and the deities that they celebrate – are more prominent in some parts of India than in others. The ***pūjā***, or rituals of worship, of the goddesses Durgā and Sarasvatī, for example, are celebrated with particular fanfare and devotion in Bengal, while the birthday of the elephant-headed deity, Gaṇeṣa, is special to the Hindus of Maharashtra and Rajasthan. The HARI community, though, is made up of members from all parts of India – plus a handful of non-Indians, like myself, who have been drawn to Hindu traditions either through being married to a Hindu of Indian origin, or because of our personal interest, or both (in my case, it is both). When a festival that is particularly sacred to a given subgroup of this community occurs, families from that sub-community typically take the lead in the cooking for the day, the sponsoring of a cultural programme featuring music or dance from that part of India, and so on. Bengali families therefore sponsor Sarasvatī and Durgā Pūjā events, Marathi families the Gaṇeṣa Caturthī celebration, Jain families the Mahavir Jayanti observance, and so on. The monthly *havan*, or fire ritual, is frequently both performed and sponsored by north Indian families with some affiliation to the aniconic Arya Samaj, a nineteenth-century reform movement that emphasizes the performance of ancient Vedic rites such as the *havan* over the *mūrti* – or image-centred *pūjās* of the dominant Puranic traditions – though I have seen families who perform the *havan* also engaging in *mūrti pūjā*. On Friday evenings, a group of devotees of Kṛṣṇa – mostly members of ISKCON, the International Society for Kṛṣṇa Consciousness – utilize the temple facilities for singing *bhajans* and holding a discourse in English based upon the teachings of their tradition – the Gauḍīya Vaiṣṇava *saṃpradāya* (sect). As mentioned earlier, of the two priests employed by the temple, one is from northern India while the other is from southern India. The distinctive northern and southern styles of *pūjā*, which can be quite different from one another, are therefore both available to the devotees, who are able to hire the priests to perform rituals either in the temple or in their homes.

The HARI community is thus a microcosm of the global Hindu community – many distinct traditions with specific cultural forms and a variety of theological perspectives all sharing a space and the common label "Hindu". Membership does not require that one be affiliated to any specific sect or adhere to any specific view. The temple's website (www.haritemple.org/abouthari.htm) states it simply:

> The mission of the Hindu American Religious Institute is to serve as a centre for Hindu worship, to promote spiritual development, and conduct cultural and educational activities for the benefit of the Hindu community ... The vision of the Hindu American Religious Institute is to bring together people of Hindu faith coming from various parts of the world so as to promote the Hindu way of life and to preserve and protect the rich Hindu cultural heritage in our present and future generations.

The last of these concerns mentioned is particularly central to the HARI temple community – preserving the Hindu cultural heritage for future generations. Passing Hindu thought and practice to their children is a major preoccupation of the families that make up this community. The Sunday school and the activities associated with it are only the most obvious manifestation of this concern. Children are also central to all of the cultural programmes that the temple sponsors and conversations with adults about the purpose of the temple always include some mention of the youth as a primary motivator in participating in temple activities, since temple attendance is not required in most Hindu traditions, and most families perform worship at home. A contrast with India is often made as well. In the words of one community member, "In India, Hinduism is everywhere. It's in the air that you breathe. But in this country you need to work to keep it alive. You need to have a special place for it." For its members, the HARI temple is one such special place.

Washington Kali Temple

In the words of its website (http://kalitemple-washington.org), "Washington Kali Temple is not just another temple. It is a Bengali religious and cultural centre where you will find many opportunities to deepen your spiritual experience and to participate in community events and gatherings." In a clear contrast with the HARI temple, the Washington Kali Temple – just north of suburban Washington DC, between Washington and Baltimore, Maryland – strives to maintain the Hindu traditions of a specific region of India: Bengal. Both its full-time priest and his assistants are Bengali Hindus. The Sanskrit in which the prayers accompanying its rituals are chanted is pronounced with a strong Bengali accent, and the deities and festivals that it celebrates are those most prominent in Bengal. Like HARI, it is not exclusive. We can meet devotees at the Washington Kali Temple from all parts of India, as well as a handful of non-Indians. The atmosphere, like that of HARI, is friendly and welcoming. The goal does not appear to be to create a "Bengali only" setting. Nobody seems unwelcome. But the temple does sustain a distinctively Bengali atmosphere and cultural environment.

The temple, first of all, has a more distinctively Hindu appearance than HARI, but shares with HARI a basically functional nature, consisting primarily of two large rooms – one, like the HARI basement, for communal dining, and a large sanctuary. On entering the sanctuary, our first sight is a large and brightly adorned image of Durgā in her form as Mahishasuramardhini, or "Slayer of the Buffalo Demon". Having ten arms and hands and riding upon a lion, she is impaling the fierce Buffalo Demon while at the same time smiling benevolently at her devotees. She is flanked by images of her children. To her immediate right (to her left, from the vantage point of the viewer) is **Lakṣmī**, goddess of prosperity and good fortune, and just beyond Lakṣmī is the elephant-headed Gaṇeṣa, remover of obstacles. To Durgā's immediate left is Sarasvatī, goddess of wisdom, and Karttikeya, warrior deity and divine general. Each of these deities is accompanied by his or her animal vehicle – Gaṇeṣa by a mouse, Lakṣmī by an owl, Sarasvatī by a swan, and Karttikeya by a peacock. Durgā, of course, is riding her lion. All five of these deities are lined up along an entire wall of the sanctuary and are the main focus of attention during the ten-day festival of Durgā Pūjā.

During the rest of the year, however, most of the ritual activity takes place to the right of the sanctuary entrance. The central deity of the Washington Kali Temple – as we might gather from its name – is Kālī, the Mother Goddess in her fiercest form, as protector of her devotees and destroyer of evil. Of all Hindu deities, Kālī's appearance is probably the most striking – and disturbing – to those not familiar with Hindu traditions. Her bright red tongue is protruding from her mouth, in striking contrast with her black skin. In her upper left hand she holds a fierce-looking, bloody, curved battleaxe. Her lower left hand holds the severed head of a demon by the hair. Her upper right hand, however, is raised in a gesture of benediction – the *abhaya* ***mudrā***, a gesture that literally means "do not be afraid". Her lower right hand is lowered, with the palm outward – a gesture called *dana mudrā*, which symbolizes generosity and divine grace. She is standing upon the body of her husband, Śiva, though this is largely obscured at the Washington Kali Temple by the robes and other finery that have been draped lovingly over the image of the goddess. At the feet of Kālī, to her right (the viewer's left) is a photograph of Śrī Ramakrishna, a saint and sage of nineteenth-century Bengal whose chief disciple, Swami Vivekananda, is often credited with bringing Hinduism to the Western world, particularly through his address at the Parliament of the World's Religions in Chicago in 1893, and later, through initiating Margaret E. Noble – better known as Sister Nivedita – as the first Westerner to join a Hindu ascetic order. On the opposite side, to Kālī's left, is a photograph of Ma Sarada Devi, the wife and spiritual companion of Śrī Ramakrishna, known to devotees as the Holy Mother.

The priest of the Washington Kali Temple, Mr Buddhadeb Bhattacharya, holds Śrī Ramakrishna in great reverence, as do many Bengali Hindus. But the bond between this priest and Śrī Ramakrishna is special, due to the fact that both are priests of Kālī residing on the premises of her temple. In an interview, this priest spoke of aspiring to the level of *bhakti*, or devotion, that is exemplified in the life of Śrī Ramakrishna. In Bengali Hindu tradition, as in other Hindu traditions, it is believed that if the priest in a temple has sufficient devotion, the image of the central deity of the temple will be "awakened", intensifying the power of the spiritual experience of devotees who visit it.

To the left of the image of Kālī is an image of Durgā known as *Jagaddhatri*, the "Protector of the World". This image is smaller than the one on the far wall and has eight, rather than ten, arms, and is not depicted in the act of slaying the Buffalo Demon. To Kālī's right (left, from the perspective of the viewer) is a large Śiva *liṅgam*, above which hangs a two-dimensional painting of Śiva as Yogeshvara, or Lord of Yoga, sitting in a calm posture of meditation (in contrast with his other popular depiction as Nataraja, or Lord of the Cosmic Dance of creation and destruction). A little distance beyond the Śiva *liṅgam*, closer to the wall near which Durgā and her children are housed, is the divine couple, Kṛṣṇa and Rādha, and to their right is a smaller image of Hanumān. Adjacent to and accessible from the main sanctuary is a smaller sanctuary that houses the images of the ***navagraha***, or "nine planets". These do not correspond perfectly with the nine planets of the solar system – or eight, given the recent demotion of Pluto. They are, rather, the planets of Hindu astrology: the Sun, the Moon, Mercury, Venus, Mars, Jupiter, Saturn, and Rahu and Ketu, the latter two being the causes of solar and lunar eclipses. Some Hindus pay devotion to the nine planets in order to maximize the positive benefits – or, especially in the cases of Saturn, Rahu, and Ketu, to neutralize or to ward off the negative effects – of their astrological energies. Just outside the main temple is also a smaller temple to Śiva. The main image in this temple is of a seated Śiva – again, in his form as Yogeshvara – as well as a set of Śiva *liṅgams* modeled upon *liṅgams* located at sacred sites across India. By visiting this smaller temple we can, in effect, undertake an imaginative pilgrimage to all of these various sites and experience some of the spiritual merit of such a journey.

If we visit the Washington Kali Temple on any given day, we will find a fairly small group of devotees present. The numbers are larger if we visit on **Amavāsya**, the day of the New Moon. New Moon nights are especially sacred to Kālī, and a Kālī Pūjā is performed on this day monthly by many devotees. (Devotees of Viṣṇu similarly have a special Satyanarayana Pūjā on **Pūrṇimā**, the Full Moon day.) The *āratī* performed at the Kali Temple is a contrast with that performed at HARI. In both, lit oil lamps are waved in front of the images of the deities as divine blessings are invoked. But rather than a communal singing of *Om Jaya Jagadisha Hare*, Kālī's *āratī* involves the ringing of bells, the clashing of cymbals, and the pounding of drums, all of which are accompanied by the blowing of conch shells and the making of eerie (at least to non-Bengali ears) ululations by the women who are present. The sound can be quite loud, and its intention is to dispel all negative forces from the sacred space at the moment when blessings are invoked. It is also celebratory, and many of the devotees – especially children and young people – clearly have a good deal of fun banging the cymbals and drums.

During the ten-day festival of Durgā Pūjā, however, the Washington Kali Temple becomes heavily crowded. (The same is true of the HARI temple during **Divāli**, the feast of the goddess Lakṣmī and of Rāma's victory over Rāvaṇa.) The very large numbers of people – combined with the drumming, bell ringing, and chanting – make for an intense and exciting atmosphere that strives to recreate the experience of Durgā Pūjā in Bengal.

HARI and the Washington Kali Temple compared and contrasted

The contrast between HARI and the Washington Kali Temple is essentially that between a temple that has been designed to accommodate as wide a swath of the North American Hindu community as possible and a temple that has been designed to replicate, as closely as possible, the experience of being completely immersed in one specific Hindu culture (or sub-culture). Though a superficial examination might suggest that the two institutions are at cross-purposes, closer analysis shows that this is not necessarily the case. The two temples being only about an hour and a half apart from one another by car, many Bengali Hindu families in the region are members of both, and participate in the services of both. Bengali Hindus in the Harrisburg area of Pennsylvania will thus typically be members of the HARI temple and participate in its regular events – having their children attend Sunday school, for example, and going for activities such as Satyanarayana Pūjā and the festivals of the various deities. They will also put a great deal of time and energy into celebrating those festivals that are special to their sub-community – such as the aforementioned Durgā and Sarasvatī Pūjās – at HARI, so the entire community can participate. If time permits, however, they also participate in the longer and more elaborate celebrations of the Kali Temple. (The HARI Durgā Pūjā is typically held on one of the ten days of the festival, while the Kali Temple has events on all of the ten days. HARI also tends to hold many of its festival observances on Sunday mornings, whereas the Kali Temple tends to observe its events on Saturday evenings, making participation in both possible.) In interviews on this specific issue, Harrisburg area Bengali Hindus, when speaking of their participation in HARI events, spoke mainly in terms of "loyalty" to their local temple, as well as the convenience of having a Hindu temple nearby. As one person said, "This is where our children go to Sunday school." On the other hand, when speaking about the Washington Kali Temple, there were frequent references to a desire – both for themselves and for their children – to experience a "real" or "authentic" Bengali Durgā Pūjā. Nostalgia for India in general, but for Bengal in particular, seemed to be a prominent emotion connected to the Kali Temple, whereas HARI was connected more with a broader sense of commitment to Hinduism as a whole, and to passing Hindu traditions on to the next generation. Children were mentioned more frequently in reference to HARI, whereas personal emotions and childhood memories played a greater role in discussion of the Kali Temple.

At the same time, however, there are many respects in which these two temples have far more in common than either does with Hindu temples in India. Both are centres of community activity aimed at preserving traditions, beliefs and practices that are not at all predominant in their larger North American context. In contrast with India, where it can be said that Hinduism is, in the words of one collaborator, "in the air you breathe", in North America a Hindu space is something that must be consciously cultivated, nurtured and preserved. Both place considerable emphasis on education and hold classes in which Hindu children can receive not only religious instruction in a conventional sense, but also instruction in music, dance, and languages (although the focus of language teaching at the Washington Kali Temple is Bengali and Sanskrit, whereas at HARI it includes Gujarati, Tamiḻ, Hindi and other Indian languages as well, as instructors with the necessary skills are willing to share their time and expertise). Both are largely functional spaces, with a minimum of traditional decoration – unlike large North American Hindu temples that try to replicate the more elaborate Indian temple styles. In both cases, interviewees said that this was a matter of both time and financial expense, the more elaborate, traditional styles of temple taking far more time and money to construct than the more basic buildings that these communities have elected to utilize. And in both cases, interviewees said that "it would be nice" at some later point to renovate their buildings in a more traditional style, should the resources become available.

The Vedanta Center of Greater Washington DC

Though not technically a temple, the Vedanta Center of Greater Washington DC, located in Silver Spring, Maryland (and merely a twenty-minute drive from the Washington Kali Temple) is a major Hindu – or Hindu-inspired[1] – institution. With three ***Swamis***, or monks, in residence,[2] the Vedanta Center of Greater Washington DC is a thriving centre, with living quarters for the *Swamis*, a meditation hall, a guesthouse, and plans to build a full-fledged temple.

Entering the meditation hall on any given morning, we are immediately struck by the fact that it is structured not so much like a Hindu temple as like a Christian church, with rows of seats that are facing a main altar or shrine at the front of the building. The beautifully carved wooden shrine holds, at its centre, a large photograph of Ramakrishna. To his left (the viewer's right) is a photograph of Ma Sarada Devi, and to his right (the viewer's left) is a photograph of Swami Vivekananda. We cannot help but notice that the structure of this placement is similar to that of the three main deities of HARI temple, with the central male deity in the middle, his female companion – his *shakti*, or power – to his left, and his male helper, or "right-hand man", to his right.

Along the walls of the meditation hall, roughly where the Stations of the Cross would be located were this space a Catholic church, are photographs of the other fifteen of Ramakrishna's original male disciples who, along with Vivekananda, established the Ramakrishna Order of monks after Ramakrishna left his body in 1886. Along a ledge that runs beneath these photographs are smaller images of Hindu deities – Rāma, Kṛṣṇa, Gaṇeṣa, Lakṣmī and a small Śiva *liṅgam* – as well as Jesus and the Buddha. One of the *Swamis* (this duty rotates among the three) performs a daily *pūjā*, which involves – as *pūjās* typically do – an offering of fruits and flowers to the deities. The *Swami* quietly chants prayers in Sanskrit that honour each of the deities represented in the altar, starting with Śrī Ramakrishna and the Holy Mother.

After the *āratī*, which is accompanied by the *Swami* continuously ringing a small bell, there is a period of silent meditation. Devotees can sit and meditate for as long as they like, quietly getting up to leave as they please.

The composition of the devotees who attend the events sponsored by the Vedanta Center of Greater Washington DC – *pūjās*, talks, meditation retreats, and so on – is a mix of Bengali and non-Bengali Indians and non-Indians ("white", African-American, Hispanic and east Asian, by ethnicity). Like the sacred space of the meditation hall, the Vedanta Center has a greater appearance than either the HARI temple or the Kali Temple of being a "hybrid" organization, with elements of both Indian and North American culture mixed together. Both HARI and the Kali Temple have adapted from North American Christian practice elements such as the Sunday school, the communal meal after religious services, and the general "community centre" feel of a church or synagogue – youth groups, events for senior citizens, charitable activities, fund raisers, and so on. Both also utilize spaces that are of a more sparse and functional, and less elaborate and decorative, nature than the traditional temple spaces of India. The meditation hall of the Vedanta Center, however – like that of many other Vedānta centres in North America – looks like a church, with rows of seats and an altar at the front (albeit one housing photographs of Ramakrishna, Sarada Devi, Vivekananda, and various Hindu deities, rather than a cross or crucifix).[3]

Participation of non-Indian devotees is also far more pronounced in the Vedanta Center, with non-Indians making up a significant portion (though not a majority, at least whenever observed by this author) of the congregation. Indeed, two of the three *Swamis* who are currently in residence at the Vedanta Center of Greater Washington DC – Swami Atmajñanananda and Swami Mahayogananda – are "white" (i.e. European) Americans, while one – Swami Brahmarupananda – is Indian. The observed non-Indian participation is lower at both HARI and the Kali Temple – often as few as one or two people in a crowd of over a hundred. At the same time, there is absolutely no policy of exclusion in any of these institutions, and indeed a good deal of overlap of membership. (My wife and I, for example, are members of all of them, and attended the Durgā Pūjā functions sponsored by all three organizations this year.)

But each institution clearly has a specific appeal to a different (although, again, overlapping) set of clientele, with the HARI temple appealing mostly to Hindus of Indian descent – albeit of all sub-communities from India – the Washington Kali Temple appealing specifically to Bengali Hindus, and the Vedanta Center – although having as its primary clientele Indian Hindus (with a considerable portion being Bengali) – having the greatest appeal of all the three institutions to non-Indians raised in a North American, primarily Protestant Christian, religious milieu.

The question of non-Indian Hindus

The question is sometimes raised whether the non-Indian members of organizations and movements such as the Vedanta Society, the Self-Realization Fellowship, Transcendental Meditation and Siddha Yoga can properly be designated as "Hindu". If it is true that one must be born a Hindu, then all Hindus must, by default, be Indian or of Indian descent. It would be oxymoronic, on this understanding, to speak of "non-Indian Hindus". From this point of view, it is not technically correct for a discussion of the Vedanta Center of Greater Washington DC to be included in an article exploring Hindu institutions in North America.

Although she does not insist, in an essentialist manner, on defining Hindus in any particular way, Lola Williamson (2010) makes a distinction between those who were raised in an ethnically Indian Hindu tradition and those who have taken up a Hindu or Hindu-inspired spiritual practice, pointing out that there is "a qualitative difference between people who have been raised in a tradition in which the rituals, the foods, the prayers, and the ethics are second nature, and people who have incorporated only parts of a tradition into their religious style" (Williamson 2010: 4). While Williamson's observations about the differences between the somewhat chaotic atmosphere of a Hindu temple – such as HARI and the Washington Kali Temple – and the highly serene atmosphere of a Hindu-inspired meditation hall – such as that of the Vedanta Center of Greater Washington DC – do justify making some kind of distinction between the types of practitioner gravitating to these spaces, might variations on Hindu thought and practice that incorporate elements of the broader North American cultural environment – like having quiet halls with rows of seats facing a central altar – end up being, in the long run, just another way of being Hindu? For surely the differences between traditional Hinduism and Hindu-inspired meditation movements are no more or less stark than those between a Roman Catholic Latin mass that is said in the Vatican and an evangelical revival meeting in Appalachia? Yet most observers would not hesitate to designate the latter two events as instances of a single phenomenon called "Christianity". As more second- and third-generation Indian American Hindus grow up practising their traditions in the North American cultural environment, with its predominantly Protestant Christian ethos, I suspect that the distinction between "ethnic" Hinduism and "Hindu-inspired" movements is likely to grow increasingly tenuous.

This issue has been somewhat contentious, particularly among those non-Indian practitioners whose "Hinduness" is in question. On the one hand, many practitioners do not wish to identify themselves as Hindu because they do not identify their practice with the totality of Hindu practice – which includes elements such as caste and patriarchy that may be foreign, or indeed objectionable, to a contemporary North American sensibility. At the same time, it could be replied that there are many Hindus – born Hindus – who also do not practice Hinduism in its totality. Indeed, Hinduism is such a vast tradition, with such a great variety of systems of belief and practice that it is hard to conceive of anyone in a single lifetime practising it "in its totality". Some scholars would even object that there is not even an "it" there to practise, the term "Hinduism" creating a false sense of unity in a highly varied collection of traditions.[4]

But there is also a tendency among practitioners of Hindu or Hindu-based paths to see their practices not as religious – and therefore localized in a faith community – but as "scientific" and universal. This tendency has been facilitated by the founding figures of these paths. For example, Swami Vivekananda, on numerous occasions, claimed that the Vedānta that he taught was not a religion, but the philosophy underlying all religions – including, but not limited exclusively to, Hinduism. Hinduism, for Vivekananda, was something particular to India and to the people of India. Vedānta, though, was universal, prompting Sarvepalli Radhakrishnan to write that Vedānta "is not a religion, but religion itself in its most universal and deepest significance" (Radhakrishnan 1927: 18). According to this understanding, one could be a Hindu Vedantist, or a Christian Vedantist, or a secular Vedantist. It is therefore not uncommon, even today, to encounter practitioners of Vedānta who identify themselves with either no religious label at all, or with the label with which they grew up (if their Vedānta has not led to a break with their original tradition). This author has met self-identified Catholic Vedantists, Presbyterian Vedantists, and Jewish Vedantists – as well as, of course, Hindu Vedantists. Similarly, both Maharishi Mahesh Yogi and Swami Muktananda presented Transcendental Meditation and Siddha Yoga, respectively, not as Hindu or Hindu-based spiritual paths, but as universal practices, available in principle to anyone. In the words of Jean MacPhail, a former nun of the Ramakrishna Order (formerly known as Pravrājika Gāyatrīprāṇa):

> Vedānta is my belief system and what I am trying to live in practice. Does it make me a Hindu? In my own mind, the answer is no. I think of myself as a Vedantist, in the sense in which Swami Vivekananda used the word. The word does not imply any specific forms of religious observance. Swami Vivekananda himself felt that Vedānta is of universal significance, because it is a map, as it were, of the whole range of spiritual possibilities, covering the dualist through non-dualist positions, including all levels of consciousness which humanity has as yet manifested, and open to all possible forms of depth inquiry, including contemporary science. (MacPhail 2008: 55)

On the other hand, there are non-Indian practitioners of Vedānta and other Hindu-inspired systems of thought and practice who *do* identify themselves as Hindu, pointing to the Hindu provenance of their practices and worldviews, and suspecting unconscious racism and other holdovers from a colonial mentality of operating in the strong insistence of some non-Indian practitioners that they not be thought of or referred to as Hindu. The fact that some of those non-Indian practitioners who do choose to identify themselves as Hindu have been accepted as such by substantial numbers of born Hindus suggests that it would be arbitrary to insist that these persons are not Hindu because they were not born as such – just as it would be similarly arbitrary to insist that those practitioners of Hindu-inspired paths who choose *not* to identify themselves as Hindu *must* do so. For a scholar, the question is not "Who is really a Hindu?" or "Who is not really a Hindu?" Rather, the category of *Hindu* is a scholarly tool. The fact that some people, not of Indian descent, do choose to identify with this term, while others, who are engaged in the same practices and even inhabit the same organizations, make the opposite choice, is neither more nor less than an interesting fact. It is a fact that further heightens our awareness that the term *Hindu* is itself a slippery and imperfect category for describing a highly complex set of phenomena, and one that is not neatly separable from discourses of race, ethnicity, nationality, class and gender.

Conclusion

What can be learned from juxtaposing our participant observations of these three Hindu institutions (or two Hindu and one Hindu-inspired institution, depending upon how one defines these things, deferring always to the chosen self-identification of the individuals who participate in the life of these institutions)? What do these three organizations tell us about Hinduism in North America?

The HARI temple points toward the adaptability of Hinduism to a (relatively) new cultural environment. In India, temples are traditionally oriented toward the practices of a particular sect, or *saṃpradāya*, with a single central deity who presides over that temple and its community. So there are Vaiṣṇava temples, Śaiva temples and Shakta temples. Though "universal" temples, housing many deities central to a variety of denominations, are not unknown in India – and are emerging with ever greater frequency in the modern period, as a more singular "Hindu" identity, as opposed to numerous sectarian identities, has begun to coalesce – historically, they have not been the norm. This does not mean that sectarian affiliations have not been quite fluid in practice – that the same person or family might, at one point, observe rituals in a temple to Viṣṇu, and at yet another point do the same in a temple to Śiva, or even shift between Jain or Buddhist institutions and Hindu ones. But the institutions themselves have tended to remain fairly distinct.

In central Pennsylvania, however, Hindus are not – or not yet – present in sufficient numbers to warrant the expense to particular families that would be involved in building separate temples for each Hindu sub-community. Even Jains, who are traditionally even more distinct from Hindus, as practitioners of a non-Vedic path, than the various groups of Hindus are from each other, have easily assimilated to being part of the HARI temple community. A combination of necessity – due to being a relatively tiny minority in a sea of Christianity

– and an emerging ideology that presumes a more unified "Hindu" identity than has been the case historically, have created the conditions for a temple community that draws from all the facets of Hindu tradition and houses them, quite literally, under a single roof.

At the same time, though, the Washington Kali Temple points us in the opposite direction, indicating that when numbers and resources allow for it, many Hindus prefer to replicate the situation of India and develop temple institutions that more directly reflect their family and community affiliations: a specifically *Bengali* Hindu temple, rather than a universal – or, to use a less flattering term, generic – Hindu temple. And yet the Bengalis of HARI temple, who live in sufficient proximity to the Kali Temple to participate in its activities – and indeed do so – have not abandoned HARI. The coexistence of these two would seem to suggest that, ideally, at least some Hindus would like to have it both ways: to affirm solidarity with a larger Hindu community as well as having a space for their own, distinctive expressions of Hindu devotion and practice, since Hinduism in practice is about plurality, rather than homogeneity.

Finally, the Vedanta Center of Greater Washington DC points to a Hindu tradition that is reaching beyond the boundaries of the culture from which it emerged, including both persons and cultural styles not of Indian origin, but drawn from the North American environment itself. The degree to which the non-Indian practitioners in institutions like the Vedanta Center embrace the idea that such practice makes them Hindu, we have seen, varies. But it does not prevent their coexistence within an institution with practitioners, Indian and non-Indian, who *do* identify themselves as Hindu, and who even practice at the Kali Temple and at HARI, as well as in the Vedanta Center's sponsored events.

All three of these examples taken together illustrate a tradition that is adaptable, internally complex, and without fixed boundaries: in a word, Hinduism!

Acknowledgements

I would like to offer a special word of thanks to Antoinette DeNapoli for reading and giving very helpful commentary on an early draft of this chapter. She was of great assistance in helping a scholar trained mainly in philosophy to find the voice of his inner anthropologist!

Notes

1. This distinction will be explored – and critiqued – below.
2. Most Vedānta centres in the USA have only one or two *Swamis*. Having three is unusual and is a mark of this centre having a particularly large and active membership.
3. For more information on the adaptation of the Ramakrishna Vedānta tradition, particularly to North American cultural norms and practices, see French (1974) and Jackson (1994).
4. See Kulke and Sontheimer (2001) and Llewellyn (2005) for good overviews of the complex issues and scholarly debates involved with the definition of Hinduism.

2. Nepali Hindus in southern California

Deepak Shimkhada

The setting: here comes the bride

A marriage ceremony is in progress. A ***purohit*** (*Brāhmin* priest) conducts the marriage ceremony according to the Vedic tradition. Seated cross-legged in a lotus position, he instructs the parents of the bride to place a flower garland on a copper pot filled with water. Several green magnolia leaves are layered around the mouth of the water pot.[1] A coconut sits firmly on the wide mouth of the water pot, which, in turn, sits on the bed of rice spread in a large metal tray. Vermillion paste, a sacred thread, a piece of red cloth and flower petals adorn the coconut. The tray contains various accoutrements, such as betel nuts, coins and sacred threads. Light glows from the oil lamp and aromatic smoke wafts from the incense sticks standing nearby. Chanting Sanskrit *mantras* from the *Yajur Veda*, the *purohit* rings a ***ghaṇṭi*** (small bell) as he offers flower petals to a small statue of Gaṇeṣa, the elephant-headed God of Beginning. The priest pours a little water to the deity from an *achmani* (small spoon-like utensil) and performs a ritual called *pūjā*, asking the deity to remove obstacles during the ceremony of holy matrimony. Gaṇeṣa also is the remover of obstacles, and hence his blessings are considered redemptive for during a long wedding many things can go wrong.

While we could easily be in a south Asian city such as Varanasi, Delhi or Kathmandu, the location of this wedding is the backyard of a private home in Southern California that has been converted to a makeshift holy ground. A large canopy is pitched for the occasion. From the edges of the canopy, colourful streamers, flower garlands and electric Christmas lights dangle. Invited guests are seated on the carpeted floor as well as in the chairs lined up around the canopy. Everyone intently watches the ceremony in progress, including the author of this chapter.

After spending a considerable amount of time on the wedding ***maṇḍapa*** (sanctified ground), the *purohit* finally instructs the parents to invite the ***dūlaiharu*** (brides) to the *maṇḍapa* (Figure 2.1). That's right: there are indeed two brides! Two beautiful girls – dressed in red, highly made up, covered with gold jewellery – walk through the door escorted by another girl, the brides' relative, to the *maṇḍapa*. The girl brides are seven and nine years old – both sisters. The first question that comes to mind: is it polygamy, where a man takes more than one wife? Second, is it a child marriage? Both, of course, are illegal today in the USA and most other parts of the modern world, including India and Nepal, where Hinduism is mostly practised. The answer to both these questions is obviously *no*. Then, what is going on? This will be put on hold for the time being while we shift our attention to the groom.

The grooms had been sitting there all this time, but no one noticed them because they were not human beings, but a pair of bel (*Aegle marmelos*) exotic fruit.[2] Before we proceed any further with the wedding, the reader is no doubt left puzzled or even confused. Naturally, it is difficult for an outsider to understand the culture when it is presented to her or him at face value, because it seems illogical for a woman to take a fruit as her husband. Finally, what is that fruit called *bel*, and what is so special about it? Everything will be explained shortly.

What is presently taking place in this house is an old Hindu custom called ***yihi*** (also spelled *ihi*) practised primarily by the Newars[3] of Nepal. Information about the origins of *yihi* is scanty because very few studies have been done. Yet it is believed that it was instituted a long time ago in response to widowhood. Given the high expense of the *yihi* wedding incurred by the parents, such weddings are usually performed in large groups consisting of as many as 100 girls.

Figure 2.1 Newar girls participating in a *yihi* ceremony in southern California (photo by author).

Such a large wedding consisting of young girls ranging from four to nine years old was witnessed by an American researcher in Kathmandu very recently.[4]

Yihi: a response to widowhood

Widowhood in Hindu India has been thought to be something sinister where a woman, upon the death of her husband, was forced to follow him to his funeral pyre to be burned alive herself. Yet that she was forced was not true. It was often purely voluntary on the part of the widow.[5] Such an act of burning one-self with the dead husband was called ***satī*** – infamously termed as *suttee* by the colonial British in India, and eventually outlawed in 1829 (Thompson 1928; see also Sharma 1988).

According to **Manusmṛti**, the book of Hindu codes of law, a widow is not to take a second husband, nor is she to live a sensual life. She is advised to live with the sad memories of her departed husband by observing chastity, fasting and restricting activities that might put her in direct contact with situations that are likely to deter her from living a simple life (Doniger 1991: 156–60, 165–6). So losing a husband in ancient India meant two things: either one chose to become a *satī*, or one lived a spiritual life. Either way, the life of a widow was not pleasant. So the Hindu Newars of Nepal came up with an ingenious way of dealing with what was considered life's thorny issue by marrying pre-pubescent girls to a *bel* that stood for the Hindu God Viṣṇu (**Nārāyaṇa**; Coon 2010: 4).[6] Because God never dies, even though the mortal husband with whom the girl eventually winds up marrying might die while she is alive, she does not become a widow – theoretically, that is. So by marrying a *bel* she may remarry if she chooses, and she would not carry the same stigma of a widow as is often encountered in India.

Because there have been no studies on the origins of *yihi*, much of what is written is based on supposition. However, what is presented here is culled from various interviews conducted over the years and information gathered from a smattering of written documents. One author has termed it a puberty rite like the *bratabandha* for boys (Coon 2010: 4). But clearly, as the evidence presented here shows, it addresses the thorny issues of widowhood, not a puberty rite as proposed.

Religion frozen in time: the Nepali diaspora

The tradition of *yihi* made sense when widowhood carried a stigma. But today people have moved on with a new outlook of culture, and widowhood is not taken as seriously as it was a century ago. Then why do the Newars of Nepal still practice the ritual of *yihi*, even in the USA? For the people in the diaspora, culture and religion seem to be frozen in time. People who moved to the USA from Nepal, for example, in the 1970s, do things exactly as they did when they left the old country. Those transplanting an old culture in a new land would make sure the roots took. Hence, the elements of culture that the Newars brought to the USA stayed with them with little or no change.

While the culture in the country of its birth has changed, it has remained frozen in time for the Nepali diaspora in the USA. The people in the diaspora tend to hark back to a time when they lived in their homelands, because that is what they remember most. Their romance with the culture of their motherland continues until the new generations begin to modify their culture/religion based on the climate of their birthplace. For the people of the first generation, the USA is their new adopted home and there is a tendency for them to feel nostalgic about the land in which they were born and raised. A culture tends to dilute only after a generation has passed. In the case of the Nepali diaspora, the first generation of immigrants has not yet passed, so they are still very much in control over their "undiluted" traditions.

Home away from home

The first person to take notice of the Nepali diaspora in southern California is Karen Leonard, who, in her book *The South Asian Americans*, studied the Joshi family. The Joshis, according to Leonard, immigrated to the USA in the late 1960s (Leonard 1997: 97). I myself came to southern California in 1972, not as an immigrant, but as a graduate student. However, I stayed on to become a US citizen. While I was a graduate student at the University of Southern California, it took me almost a year to discover the Joshis, and through them I was introduced to another Nepali immigrant living in San Fernando Valley.

The first Nepali to apply for an immigrant visa did so in 1952. There was a second in 1956, and three more in 1957.[7] Dhungel, a Nepali scholar, in his paper published in a research journal, cites several reasons for the presence of such a miniscule number of Nepalis in the USA in the 1950s and 1960s (Dhungel 1999: 120–21). Even after another decade, the number of Nepali immigrants in the USA did not increase significantly. This was the state of the Nepali immigrant population in the 1970s; one could literally count the number of Nepali immigrants on one's fingertips.[8] Now, however, it is a different story. There are believed to be more than 100,000 Nepalis living throughout all fifty states of the USA. The influx of Nepalis began to be felt in a noticeable fashion in the late 1990s when Congress, under the terms of Section 203(c) of the Immigration Act of 1990, amended INA 203 to make available 50,000 new immigrant visas for the citizens of the countries who were under-represented in the USA. This is also called the Green Card Lottery.[9] Because Nepal is deemed an under-represented country, a constant flow of Nepalis have been coming into the USA since the 1990s.

A second contributing factor to the influx of Nepalis in the USA is the resettlement of Nepali refugees of Bhutanese origin that began in 2008. Although they were born in Bhutan, they were born of the Nepali parents whose parents immigrated to Bhutan centuries ago, but had been kicked out of the country upon passage of a politically motivated law that made life unbearable for people of non-Bhutanese descent. More than 100,000 people of Nepali descent returned to Nepal as refugees. To alleviate the economic pressures on Nepal, the USA decided to accept 60,000 Bhutanese-Nepalis living in various refugee camps of Nepal. As of the end of June 2010, more than 27,000 people of Nepali origin had been resettled in most states of the USA, bringing a new culture as well as some linguistic, cultural and religious challenges.[10]

Some of these refugees are being sponsored by Catholic Social Services (CSS).[11] Some were converted to Christianity in Nepal, and others are being converted after they arrive in the USA. To give an example, when family members of refugees first arrive in the USA, they are received by the CSS, which provides them with medical care and other needs – such as religious and social support. The first thing that the CSS volunteers do is ask the refugees whether a pastor at the centre may pray for them. The answer is usually yes because refugees – most of whom are illiterate – are afraid of being impolite to the hosts. So the process of proselytization is set in motion. Then they are invited to attend church services and, within a year or so, some, according to the data collected during a recent study by myself, become Christian converts.[12] Those who remain staunch Hindus keep practising their religion at their own homes because a home can be a temple.[13]

Like any other Hindu immigrants from south Asia – from India in particular – Nepali immigrants who identify themselves as Hindus dedicate a small corner of their home for worshipping. This corner is called ***pūjā koṭhā***, or *pūjā* closet. Hence, in every apartment or home, a small statue or a picture of their favourite deity – Kṛṣṇa, Śiva, Viṣṇu, Gaṇeṣa or Durgā – may be seen where the head of the household, usually the mother, takes a few minutes of her time to worship the deity on a daily basis. My own home has a small shrine constructed in a room where my wife sits to perform daily worship (***nitya pūjā***) by lighting an oil lamp, using an incense stick, and offering some freshly plucked flowers. When I hear the bell ring, I know she is in the *pūjā koṭhā* conducting her daily morning and evening *pūjās*.

Adaptation: new land, old religion

New land also affords many opportunities for change and innovation, resulting in new tradition and eventually the creation of new myths. Hence the new immigrants are also creators of new Hinduism in the diaspora. What they have brought transforms over the years. For example, a Hindu ritual that demands outdoor cremation on a funeral pyre cannot be practised in the USA because it goes against the Judaeo-Christian practice of burial. So the Hindus are expected to conform to the prevailing tradition, including local codes and laws. Hence the cremation of the dead is done within an enclosed space provided by a funeral home or mortuary.

Similarly, in traditional Hinduism, demarcation between the sacred and profane is strictly observed, especially when it comes to latrines. As a result, one does not see latrines near a Hindu temple in India or Nepal. In the USA, however, a temple is considered a house of worship that brings a large number of people to one place. People have biological functions that must be met, even at a public space. Hence, building a latrine is required by city codes even in a temple. Although this may go against Hindu tradition, Hindus in the diaspora have made an exception to this rule as they have with many other aspects of their religion.

Hindus are likely to bend the rules if they are inconvenient or conflict with their daily lives, or if they require a rite that legally or practically cannot be observed. For example, on the day of a solar or a lunar eclipse, a traditional Hindu is supposed to purify himself by taking a ritual bath in a river or at home when the eclipse is over. It is impractical for a devout Hindu to observe this rite in a foreign land because s/he may be at work or on the road. Similarly, it is also impractical for a Hindu not to socialize with people of lower caste because in the USA people have no caste.[14] The decision to move to a new land signals that the person has already divorced from Hinduism's rigid traditions to which he was married to some degree. Conservative folks who are unwilling to divorce themselves from age-old traditions would not usually leave their homelands. Immigration to a new land, the USA in this case, is for those who are liberal in their thinking and are willing to adapt to a new land by sacrificing some of their age-old traditions. So changing or modifying a few rules to fit their lifestyle is readily accepted by the Hindus of all *saṃpradāyas* (persuasions, theological groups).

I recall a time when one of my close relatives died in Nepal. According to strict Hindu tradition, the surviving relatives must observe funeral rites for thirteen days by withdrawing salt and meat from their diet and abstaining from sex. However, I was told by a senior member of the Hindu community that the funeral pollution did not apply to me because I was living beyond a large body of water (Pacific Ocean in this case), and ritual pollution cannot cross the ocean. Hence, withdrawing salt and meat from my diet only for a day, in the form of a token, was sufficient. This is a remarkable characteristic of Hinduism: it allows various modifications depending on time, situation and location, as supported by the Manusmṛti.[15]

However, when a number of people migrate on a large scale, as has happened in recent years with the Nepali–Bhutanese refugees, the demography and religious landscape change because they bring new dynamics. It has been determined that almost all of the Nepali–Bhutanese refugees served as labourers in Bhutan. Hence they have limited formal education. Only their children who were born in the refugee camps have had some high school education. However, this chapter deals, in part, with their parents who are devout Hindus, observing most of the traditional rituals of Hinduism and practising in the diaspora of southern California.

Before the influx of the refugees, few Hindu festivals were observed in southern California. However, in recent years, the Nepalis have banded together to observe many Hindu festivals, including those that were not observed before, namely the ***tīj***. *Tīj* is celebrated in both India and Nepal, mostly by married women wishing for good health and the long lives of their husbands. However, in Nepal it takes on a special meaning because on that day all women (except widows) dress in red and go to the Pashupatinath temple to pray to God Śiva. Some unmarried girls also participate in the festival with the hope that they might get good husbands as the Goddess *Parvati* did when she prayed to Śiva.

The festival is celebrated for three days, starting with ***dar khāne***, when the ladies get together in a group and eat lots of delicious delicacies. They do this because on the second day they fast, withdrawing from food altogether. The third day is *rishi panchami*. On that day they break their fast by performing a *pūjā*. While they are fasting on the second day, they go to the temple of Pashupatinath to offer *pūjā* to the deity. On the way they sing and dance to pass the day. On the *risi panchami*, which is the third day of the *tīj* festival, the women also go through a purificatory rite by cleansing their *yoni* (female genital) with a *datiwan*, a green branch from a sacred tree. This purificatory rite is kept secret from men because of the intimate nature of the ritual.

Old wine in a new bottle

Now that the population of the Nepali diaspora is growing, Hindu women of southern California have been organizing a *tīj* festival annually. Indeed, this takes place not only in southern California, but also in other parts of the USA where there is a large concentration of Nepalis. But there are substantial changes in the way the *tīj* festival is practised in the USA as opposed to how it is done in Nepal. The women do practice *dar khāne* and fasting, but without the purificatory rite simply because the *datiwan* tree is not found here. However, it has been reported that some older women still do it symbolically without the use of the *datiwan*.

The *tīj* is now seen as a celebration, a women's day with lots of fun and entertainment. In Nepal, it is strictly a religious festival of women for women. However, in the USA it has come to be a festival for women, men and their children as well. As a social gathering, it is an excuse to have a party with lots of sumptuous food and entertainment. In the last *tīj* party, I had an opportunity to participate as an observer, and I came away with the following conclusion.

First, the programme was organized on Sunday, a week earlier than the actual date of *tīj*. This was done for two reasons: first, for the practical reason that most women in the USA work during the week, and second, it coincided with the arrival of a travelling group of musicians from Nepal. The women were dressed up in their finest as though they were actually participating in the ritual of *tīj* (Figure 2.2). This goes to show that the Nepali community had taken religious

Figure 2.2 Women going to celebrate a *Tīj* party in southern California (photo by author).

matters into its own hands. In Nepal, the celebration of *tīj* could not have been celebrated a day before or after the actual date, at any cost. To be able to negotiate is the unique aspect of Hinduism seen not only in the land it was born but also (and in particular) overseas. In the USA it is a matter of convenience, and this comes first before proper adherence.

In the past, when the population of Nepali immigrants in the USA was small, everyone seemed to know one another. There was a strong bond between them, each one lending support to the other in time of need. They tried to be more resourceful than they are today. For example, I remember a time when I officiated at the weddings of three Nepali girls in the 1980s when there were hardly any *purohits* (Hindu priests) available in the area. I agreed to serve as a *purohit* just because I happened to be a *Brāhmin*. But I did not know how to conduct a Hindu wedding – I only had a vague knowledge of the ritual. When asked by the Joshis to officiate at their daughter's wedding, I was flattered and nervous at the same time. So I had to design a wedding plan by gathering information from the university library where I was a graduate student. The wedding was accepted on the ground that I used all the necessary steps, though much of what I did was improvised and shortened. I could only cover the essentials, but my performance was completely accepted by the bride, groom, the parents of the newlyweds and the guests who came to attend the ceremony. By virtue of the presence of sacred fire, the statues of deity, and the Sanskrit verses I recited from the *Ajur Veda*, the ceremony took the form of a sacramental ritual. The marriage was consecrated not because of my perfect adherence, but because of the religious nature of the ritual based on Vedic principles in the minds of the participants. I tried to emulate the tradition to the best of my knowledge as prescribed in the ritual texts.[16]

Seeking Nepali identity

The process of seeking his or her own ethnic identity begins with the awakening that s/he is different. With the realization that s/he is different from the rest of the population in a new land, the new immigrant desires to come together with other immigrants of her or his own kind for sharing not only the native food but also other aspects of life that they hold dear. So they stick together as a group to share food, exchange views of politics at home and discuss issues that affect them in a new country. Slowly as the number of immigrants swell, they feel a need for forming a new social organization. And so, a new organization with ethnic identity is born.

While some form their own organizations that cater to the needs of their communities, others who cannot do so join facilities founded by other ethnic groups with whom they find close affinity. For example, Nepalis share certain cultural and cuisinal similarities with north India and Bangladesh, Nepal's immediate neighbours. When the population of Nepalis in southern California (and perhaps in other regions) was very small, they would have patronized the businesses and religious centres owned and operated by them. I remember driving seventy-five miles to buy groceries at an Indian or Bangladeshi store. Similarly, all Nepalis at one time or another have visited Hindu temples founded by Indians. While some Nepalis have owned a few restaurants and grocery stores, they still have not managed to found a temple of their own in southern California. Hence, Nepali Hindus still use Hindu temples built by Indians. However, with the influx of Nepalis in recent years, this will change.

With such a large group of different people comes unity as well as dissension. The Nepalis, once a cohesive and fairly homogenous group albeit not in ethnicity but in national identity, are now breaking up into communal groups resulting in several organizations based on ethnicity and ideology. In southern California alone there are now approximately six organizations, some more loosely formed than others. They are the America–Nepal Society of California, Friends of Nepal, Yekta Samāj, Śrī Pashupatinath Foundation, Gurung Association, and Thakali Association. The America–Nepal Society of California is the oldest, founded in 1973. The others were formed within the last five years.

Although each of these organizations claims to be autonomous and are often seen as competing in terms of organizing programmes, there is some cross-fertilization between them. Often some members of one organization are seen participating in a programme organized by another group. When it comes to having fun, most Nepalis like to take advantage of it. Nepal's national holidays are Dasai, Tihar and New Year, which are celebrated in the USA along with many American holidays such as the Fourth of July. Nepal's national holidays are happy occasions that call for celebration. Food, language, dance, music and religious components are elements that help inculcate culture in the hearts and minds of the young generations.

Each organization aims to fulfil the needs of its members by organizing programmes in the local community. While all of the organizations are of a social nature, the Śrī Pashupatinath Foundation was formed to meet the religious and spiritual needs of Nepalis living in Southern California. Pashupatinath is a temple dedicated to the Hindu God Śiva in Kathmandu, the patron deity of Nepal. As a religious site, it also is well known in south Asia. Many Hindu pilgrims from both India and Nepal come to the temple on the day of *Maha Sivaratri* to pay homage to Lord Śiva, represented in the form of *liṅgam* (Śiva's creative aspect symbolized by his phallus). Because the Pashupatinath temple is located in Kathmandu, the capital of Nepal, it has become a national identity of Nepal. Hence, Nepalis living in southern California came together to create a foundation for the purpose of building a temple named after Pashupatinath and a community centre that caters to the needs of all the Nepalis living in southern California.

A trust to build the temple and a community centre was created in 2009, and efforts are under way to raise $5 million to build and equip the structures. The committee has been headed by young and active Nepalis who have made efforts to tap the wisdom of older members of the community. Within the span of one year, the foundation has been able to raise more than $100,000 and it soon hopes to raise the needed funds to purchase the land on which to build the temple and a community centre.[17] The building of the Pashupatinath temple is a concerted effort on the part of Nepalis to establish their identity as a unified group.

Mainstay of Hinduism

Perhaps it is presumptuous to state that Nepalis are more interested in religion than spirituality. However, based on samples gathered during a span of five years, I have come to the conclusion that most Nepalis living in southern California are not interested in intellectual spirituality as transmitted through *vedantic* discourse. A few *vedantic gurus* from Nepal, who visited southern California with the purpose of transmitting *vedic* knowledge of *advaitic* type, returned to Nepal disappointed. Because only a few people showed up at the discourses, the traveling *gurus* were of the opinion that the Nepali diaspora of southern California was either not ready for or uninterested in intellectual Hinduism. This assumption is based solely on the fact that when religious programmes are blended with food, ritual and singing of *bhajans*, a large number of people do turn up. It is evident from these contrasting events that the Nepali Hindus of southern California are more interested in celebratory religion than purely knowledge-based spirituality as provided by discourses or lectures.

Conclusion

Invariably all people who immigrate to America have a desire to be accepted by its citizens. There is a deep desire to blend into the new land by behaving like an American. This is especially the case with first generation immigrants. The community with which I am dealing in this chapter is primarily first generation Nepalis, and hence my remarks have been limited to them. In other words, the new immigrant wants to become like a white Christian American. Some even take a new, anglicized name. Some parents give their newborn children Christian names in the hope that they will be readily accepted in the new land. The traditional Nepali names can be difficult for most Americans to pronounce. Most new immigrants are very sensitive to this issue when the time comes for selecting a name for their newborn baby.

By the same token, conversion to Christianity is also, in part, an effort to blend into American society as much as it is to seek financial benefits from Christian community. However, in spite of these efforts, the ethnicity of the person who is trying to change does eventually get in the way. Soon s/he realizes that his/her roots are not in the new land but in the land s/he left behind. They may change their names and convert to a new religion, but they cannot change the colour of their skin. Their inherent ethnicity eventually plays a role. The person comes to realize later in his/her life that his/her roots are in Nepal and s/he must embrace it rather than discard it, as some did long ago by converting to Christianity.

Acknowledgements

I express my gratitude to LaChelle Schilling and Adam Pave, two PhD candidates in the School of Religion at Claremont Graduate University, for providing constructive comments on the draft of this chapter.

Notes

1. *Bel* leaves are desirable whenever and wherever they are available. In the event they are not available, any leaves resembling *bel* are interchangeable on account of Hindu liberalism. As will be seen later, improvisation is common when a specific item cannot be found or a rule cannot be followed due to unavoidable circumstances. Hindus find it convenient to change, alter or even do without as time, place and situation dictates. This adaptable quality of Hinduism has been the key to its continued survival.
2. *Bel* is native to south and southeast Asia, so it had to be flown in from Nepal just for this purpose.
3. Newars are the original inhabitants of Kathmandu, a valley of about 19.6 square miles consisting of two sister cities – Patan and Bhaktapur – now with a population of approximately one million people of all races. The Newars speak a distinct language called Newari or Nepal Bhasa (Newa Bhaye) belonging to the Tibeto-Burman family. Today the Newars comprise of only 3 per cent of Kathmandu's population. The valley is situated at an altitude of 4,600 feet above sea level.

4. Ellen Coon was a Fulbright scholar who went to Nepal in 2004 to study Newar ritual practices.
5. I am reminded of a story shared by an American woman who met an Indian man in 1954 when she was attending Ohio State University. They fell in love and the man proposed marriage to her. She rejected the offer after giving it serious thought because she did not want to follow him to his funeral pyre should he die first. The woman was utterly misinformed about the *satī* practice because it was outlawed in 1829. Moreover, it was never a mandatory tradition; it was sporadically practised even in ancient India. On a side note, she now regrets passing up what would have been a good offer, because the man was a member of an aristocratic family in India. This woman took my course in 2010 and shared her personal story in class when the topic of *satī* came up, admitting her ignorance.
6. Although *bel* is traditionally associated with Vishnu in the form of Nārāyaṇa, it also is associated with the god Śiva. This ambivalence makes this fruit doubly important because Vishnu and Śiva are immortal gods with the qualities of omniscience, omnipotence and omnipresence. So why the *bel* is a preferred fruit is, for this purpose, self-evident.
7. According to the chart provided by Ramesh K. Dhungel (1999: 123).
8. A view shared by another Nepali as reported by Leonard (1997: 97).
9. The Diversity Immigrant Visa programme is a US congressionally mandated lottery programme for receiving a United States Permanent Resident Card. It is also known as the Green Card Lottery. The lottery is administered on an annual basis by the Department of State and conducted under the terms of Section 203(c) of the Immigration and Naturalization Act (INA). Section 131 of the Immigration Act of 1990 (Pub. L. 101–649) amended INA 203 to provide for a new class of immigrants known as "diversity immigrants" (DV immigrants). The Act makes available 50,000 permanent resident visas annually to persons from countries with low rates of immigration to the USA.
10. According to Bhutanese Refugees (2010): "Since 1991 over one sixth of Bhutan's people have sought asylum in Nepal, India and other countries around the world. The vast majority of the refugees are Lhotshampas [the heterogeneous ethnic Nepalese population of Bhutan] ... who were forced to leave Bhutan in the early 1990s. There is ample evidence, as documented by Amnesty International and other human rights organizations, that the expulsion of large numbers of Lhotshampas was planned and executed with meticulous attention to detail. Over 105,000 Bhutanese have spent more than 15 years living in refugee camps established in Nepal by the United Nations High Commission for Refugees. Thousands more are living outside the camps in Nepal and India, and some in North America, Europe and Australia. Since 2008 a resettlement process has seen many thousands of Bhutanese refugees from the camps in Nepal being resettled primarily in the USA but also in Canada, Australia, Denmark, New Zealand, the Netherlands and Norway."
11. Exact statistics are not available to cite here because the immigrants are still being resettled and it will take another decade to arrive at quotable data.
12. I have been conducting research since 2008 by meeting with local refugees and interviewing others by telephone that live in more than twelve states. There are enough data to suggest that conversion of the Nepali-Bhutanese refugees took place several years ago in the refugee camps of Nepal by Christian missionaries that provided humanitarian help. Only a small number have been converted in the USA. The number, however, is growing and, as a result, there are Nepali churches in states where the population of Nepali-Bhutanese is heavily concentrated, such as Tennessee and Kentucky, and they are run by pastors of Nepali origin that mostly cater to the Nepali-Bhutanese congregants.

13. The data collected for this paper come from the Nepali immigrants who have settled in the USA since the later part of 1960 as well as newly arrived refugees who are practicing Hindus.
14. In fact, even in the urban settings of India, the belief in caste pollution through intermingling with a member of a lower caste has been abandoned as people travel on public transport such as buses and trains. It is unthinkable for a Hindu – whether devout or non-devout – to follow this observance in the USA. The belief in caste pollution is only seen in some pockets of rural India and Nepal, albeit in decreasing degree.
15. The Manusmṛti – the law codes of Hindus – is full of these exceptions and modifications to rules. For example, it states a specific rule and punishment for breaking a rule. However, in the next rule it also states that the rule will not apply in case of emergency or in unavoidable circumstance (e.g. see Manusmṛti chapter 11 on restoration).
16. The steps I used for the ritual came from the *Gommatsara Karma-Kanda* by Nemichandra Siddhanta Chakravarti (1927–37). Although this was a sacred book of the Jains, there are certain similarities between the Hindu and Jain weddings; hence I used the book as a guide. This flexibility alone is evident of the eclectic nature of Hindu tradition in that it is not closed to other traditions. The reason for using this book as a guide was in part that I could not find any other book in the university library that dealt with Hindu marriage ceremony.
17. On 4 July 2011 a religious programme called Shreemad *Bhāgavata Purāṇa* was held for seven days by the Shree Pashupatinath Foundation in southern California with the intent of raising funds. During the seven-day period, more than a million dollars was collected toward building a temple.

3. Trinidad Hinduism

Paul Younger

Indian labourers began to arrive in Trinidad in 1845. The contracts or indentures under which they came involved them being assigned to a sugarcane plantation for five years. If they signed up for a second five years they would have their passage paid back to India, or, if they chose, they could have land of their own instead of a passage back. With the incentives to stay laid out in this way, most chose to stay, and a community of Indian villages developed on the previously unused land of the island. Although Indians eventually constituted over forty per cent of the population on the island, for a number of generations they remained a primarily rural and somewhat marginalized segment of the population.

The Indian labourers who came to work in Trinidad came on ships that left from Calcutta or Madras, with the majority being from the Hindi-speaking north Indian plains via Calcutta and the minority being from Tamiḻ and Telugu-speaking districts fairly close to Madras. The north Indians were recruited from a wide range of castes and included some higher castes such as Brāhmans and ***Kṣatriya***s, a significant number of Muslims, and a much larger number of ***Chamārs***, who were once leather-workers but had become general agricultural labourers. The south Indians came from a more rigidly structured caste system and were all from agricultural labouring groups (Brereton). The different caste groups from north India had rituals they tried to keep up in the new environment. Brāhmans who could recite the story of Rāma from the popular Hindi version of Tulsīdāss called the ***Rāmcharitmānas*** were given a lot of respect, and their recitations were often attended by the whole village in Trinidad. Lower castes from north India continued their tradition of holding pig sacrifices. In south India the agricultural labourers tended to worship different goddesses in different regions, but in Trinidad all focused on the most widely known goddess, Māriyamman, and the subsidiary deities they worshipped along with her. Her worship included the sacrifice of chickens and goats, and was know for the possession states the worshippers went into as they asked for healing and the exorcism of evil spirits (Younger 2010).

The villages

During the first couple of generations in Trinidad, Indian villages were formed on the land allotted to the indentured workers, and most Indians continued to work on sugarcane plantations and to sell the sugarcane that they produced on their own land to the mills on the nearby plantations. They spoke a creole-style English in the work environment, but primarily Hindi in the village environment (Laurence). They observed from a cultural distance the already established society around them. They probably hardly knew that the island was once ruled by Spain and that many of the plantations had been started by French plantation owners, because after the British colonial authorities took over the island in 1802, most of the plantations were taken over by the British and they dominated the white ruling class by the middle of the nineteenth century, when the Indians arrived. The British-led society was organized into a rigid racial hierarchy with Whites at the top, middle management in government and plantation reserved for those with mixed European/African heritage, and blacks as the labourers (Khan 2004). Indians, oddly, were never drawn into this racial hierarchy and were thought of as living in their own cultural enclave off to the side. Unlike the situation in Guyana, where blacks and Indians worked together on the plantations and lived together in the settlements at the end of each plantation, Afro-Trinidadians and Indo-Trinidadians lived largely separate cultural lives from the mid-nineteenth to the mid-twentieth centuries.

During these early generations, life within the Indian village had its own distinctive rhythm. Religious life initially seems to have largely centred around three spectacular festival celebrations. The three festivals later remembered nostalgically were Phagwa or **Holī**, Fire Pass, and Hosay or Mohurram (Jha 1985). One assumes that all three festivals were enjoyed by the whole population of the Indian village, but that these three were chosen in accord with an informal agreement that one should be north Indian, one south Indian and one Muslim. Phagwa is still a bacchanalian-style celebration from north India, where women, girls and people of lower status throw coloured powders on those they would hesitate to approach at other times of the year. Fire Pass is an arduous ritual of walking in a semi-trance state on burning embers. It is associated with goddess worship in south India, and is still popular in places such as South Africa where a majority of the labourers were from south India. Hosay commemorates the beating and death of Hasan and his brother Husain who would have become the leaders of the Shi'a branch of Islam. Even though most Indian Muslims are not Shi'a, this story and its celebration were prominent at the time the indentured workers left India, and it became such a big celebration in Trinidad that in 1884 it was the occasion of a major riot (Singh 1988).

Festival religion does not require any special priestly leadership, but the recitation of the *Rāmcharitmānas* gave a prominent role to the small number of Brāhmans within the villages, and they gradually also took on priest-like roles. The most important of these roles was the performance of ***saṁskāras*** or ritual celebrations of some of the life cycle ceremonies. Families that could afford to have a Brāhman perform the ceremony associated with the naming or the marriage of a child gained status in the village, and the Brāhmans gradually became people of status themselves and their presence reinforced the status distinctions of the villages. When the anthropologist Morton Klass studied a village in the 1950s he described it as divided into four classes that had some of the features of a caste system in that the wealthiest maintained their status by being noticeably vegetarian, the next wealthiest ate meat, the largest number participated in the pig sacrifices and ate pork, and the homeless lived at the edge of the village and caught crabs for food (Klass 1961).

Agents of change

The most important agent of change in the second generation of these Indian villages was the opening of the Canadian Presbyterian mission schools starting in 1868. John Morton was a very strong-minded person and he took the unusual step of developing a school system for Indians only, and he made it an elite school system with only a secondary interest in the potential it might have for conversion. By the end of the century there were schools and some colleges (including an important one for women) all over the island, and an elite of second generation Indians was returning to teach in these schools and to interest the still rural Indians in the political and economic issues of the country. The first Indian appointed to the legislative council was the Reverend C. D. Lalla. He had become known for challenging the mission's control of the school system, and, even though he was the first moderator of the Canadian Presbyterian Church of Trinidad, he could not persuade the missionaries to turn the school system over to local Indian leadership. Another Christian leader, Sarran Teelucksingh, realized the leadership imbalance being created by the monopoly the Mission had in the field of education, and in 1932 started the **Sanātana Dharma Mahāsabha** of Couva in the hope that it could start some Hindu schools. At the time the government offered to subsidize Hindu or Muslim schools in the same way they did the Presbyterian ones if there were religious organizations to manage them, but at the time that was a problem and the colonial government was happy to leave education in the competent, even if religiously biased, hands of the missionaries (Campbell 1985).

A second agent of change that eventually found it impossible to squeeze into the structures of Trinidad Indian society was the Hindu missionary movement known as the Arya Samaj. The Ārya Samāj had been started in the 1870s in India by Dayananda Saraswati who felt that Hindus were being unfairly criticized for things like image worship when they also had even older traditions of worship at a Vedic fire altar. He decided to copy the missionary style of the Christians and design a specific Vedic fire-altar ritual, encourage education and develop a ceremony to parallel Christian baptism that would make it possible for Muslim and Christian Indians to return to the newly organized Ārya Samāj version of Hinduism. In 1905 a follower of the Ārya Samāj visiting Gandhi in South Africa realized how eager the Indian indentured workers living in a variety of different places around the globe were to form new Hindu communities. At his suggestion, the Ārya Samāj missionary, **Bhai** Paramanand, offered a series of lectures on the Ārya Samāj ideas in these various places. As a result of these lectures, Ārya Samāj organizations were formed in Mauritius, South Africa, Fiji, East Africa, Guyana and Trinidad, and over the following decades missionaries from India made visits to each of these places and established Ārya Samāj organizations there. In Guyana and Trinidad these missionaries were vigorously opposed by the Brāhman leadership already established in the Indian communities. In Guyana, the Brāhmans had long-established ***mandirs*** or temples in every settlement, where on Sunday morning they competed with the services of the Afro-Guyanese churches. In this situation the Ārya Samāj leadership had little choice but to open their own temples nearby. In Trinidad, the controversies had more to do with education. While the Ārya Samāj could effectively criticize the local Brāhman ***pandits*** for not knowing the traditional priestly language of Sanskrit, they were challenged from the other side by the well-educated elite trained in Presbyterian schools who could argue that the Ārya Samāj missionaries did not understand the political and economic issues Trinidad Indians were facing. In the end the Ārya Samāj played a marginal role in the fortunes of Trinidad Hindus, but the controversies it provoked reminded the local Hindus that they needed a more aggressive institutional voice if they were to play their part in society as the colonial era unravelled.

The third agent of change in the lives of the Hindus of Trinidad came from the broader questioning that had begun by the 1930s as to what kind of society would eventually replace the colonial power. The educated Indian leadership involved in these discussions realized that the whole society of this small island would be one social and political unit in the future, and the three best-known Indian leaders, Sarran Teelucksingh, Timothy Roodal, the mayor of the second-largest city of San Fernando, and F. E. M. Hosein, the leading lawyer in the country, all entered the Legislative Council in 1928 when its members were first chosen by election. At much the same time an aggressive labour movement was being started by Arthur Cipriani, and he was joined in 1934 by a Brāhman student who had gone to England to study and became involved in radical political movements there. While in England he had changed his name from "Kṛṣṇa Deonarine" to Adrian Cola Rienzi so that he would not be thought of as an ethnic Indian leader, and upon his return to Trinidad he started a paper called *The People* and quickly became the main organizer of the labour unions among the oil workers and the sugar workers. In 1937, T. U. B. Butler opened up the political situation still further when he had the British Empire Workers and Citizens Home Rule Party based in Grenada call a general strike throughout the Caribbean. When most of the older labour leaders were put in jail, Rienzi entered the Legislative Council in 1938 and convinced the Moyne Commission, which was looking into the unrest, to call for a socialist state with health and welfare benefits and a universal franchise. When some of the black leadership became envious of the prominence of this young Indian leader, he decided that he did not have a mass base of support and withdrew from day to day politics when he took a position in the executive council or the advisory body of the colonial government in 1944. It would be fifty-one years before an Indian would become prime minister of the country, but the 1930s ensured that Indians would soon leave the village setting where they had stayed for so long and become an effective part of a post-colonial Trinidad society (Samaroo 1985).

The post-war Hindu renaissance

Surprisingly, the Second World War turned out to have a decisive influence in Trinidad's history. The USA used the island as a major military base, oil and other industries replaced the agricultural base of the economy, and the British decided to end their colonial rule in this part of the world. With these changes under way, the Indian community finally left its rural identity and joined the new economy. And in this context it decided to rethink every aspect of its religious and cultural heritage and present itself as a modern ethnic community with a unified and clear cultural identity.

The person who led the community at this decisive stage in its history was Bhadase Sagan Maraj, who had made a fortune when he took the contract for dismantling all the US military bases. He was a Brāhman, but he acted more as a businessman than a religious leader when he decided that what Trinidad Hindus needed was a modern institutional form to represent them. In 1952 he founded the **Sanatana Dharma Maha Sabha**, and it immediately set out to build a parallel set of Hindu schools to match the long-established Presbyterian school system. He relied on the poorly educated village Brāhmans to help with this plan in the various regions, and in many ways this system of parochial schools never became as academically distinguished as the Presbyterian system had long been. At the same time, the Maha Sabha did serve as a kind of administrative centre of Hindu religion and spoke out for the interests of Hindus in a way that was unknown in India and not really found in other places where Hindus had settled (Vertovec 1992).

Recognizing that Britain was serious about its plan to give Trinidad and Tobago its independence, Bhadase Maraj also started a parochial political party for Indians that he called the People's Democratic Party (PDP), and in 1952 most Indians supported that ethnic party just as the major political choices were being set out in Trinidad politics. By 1958, the election was for the first parliament of the experimental Federation of the British West Indies. Bhadase Maraj recognized how Indian interests in Guyana and Trinidad might get swamped in what would be a black majority in the region as a whole, and he reformed his party into the Democratic Labour Party (DLP) to fight the idea of federation, and won six of the ten Trinidad seats. The federation dream was given up, but, as independence for Trinidad and Tobago arrived in 1962, the renowned historian of slavery Eric Williams mocked Bhadase Maraj for mixing up religion and politics, and it was Williams's People's National Movement (PNM) that came to power and ruled right through to 1986.

What Bhadase Maraj's post-war leadership had done for Trinidad Hindus was to form a kind of ethnic enclave in which they could redesign their religious practices outside of the village setting and determine how best to participate in the political life of their newly democratic nation. Modernist-looking temples sprang up all over the island, specifically Hindu festivals began to be celebrated, and the Maha Sabha issued a number of Hindu creeds that attempted to give form to the Hindu identity. On the other hand, this ethnic enclave made it hard for Hindus to participate in the intellectual questions of the day, to figure out what political parties to support, and to join wholeheartedly in the musical and artistic trends in their society. In time the sense of need for a protective enclave would fade, and Hindus, as the largest single community within the society, would begin to assert their more natural role, but Bhadase Maraj had taught them to cling to their heritage and that made them hesitate about embracing the modern world.

The intellectual challenge

In 1950, just as Bhadase Maraj was thinking about forming a Hindu school system, an eighteen-year-old Brāhman youth named V. S. Naipaul went to England to study, and four years later he became a renowned writer who explored some of the most difficult intellectual questions of his day. As one might expect, his early focus was on diaspora consciousness and the challenge communities such as Trinidad Hindus have in finding their feet in the marginalized setting their colonial masters and their fading motherland memories have left them with. In the brilliant novel *A House for Mr Biswas* (1961), Naipaul explores his father's desperate effort to set aside the *pandit* role his parents had groomed him for and the clawing second-hand domestic Hindu customs his wife's family imposed on him, so that he might find a "house" or a place in the world as a journalist. Naipaul did not agree with Bhadase Maraj that a distant Hindu heritage was a strong enough base to build a coherent modern identity on, and he even did a pilgrimage to his ancestors' village in north India to demonstrate in *An Area of Darkness* (1964) that it was also impossible to recover such a foundation by working backward. In his own day he chose to take what strength he could from the closing chapter of the colonial story, even as he looked out from the Britain he despised onto the diasporas developing around.

In what seems almost at times like a sequel to *Mr Biswas*, Rabindranath Maharaj in 2006 wrote a story about his father called *A Perfect Pledge*. Once again the father stumbles around trying to build some kind of monument on his old sugarcane land, but now the scene has moved on. In this story it is the colonial power and the indenture era that is fading, and a new generation is slowly figuring out how much credence they want to give to their father's "pledge" before they go on to find a foundation for their own futures. In this case the author writes from a diaspora setting that has been extended to include Canada, and the "homelessness" that Naipaul had described so powerfully and turned into a metaphor for the universal human condition is no longer so much a threat as a kind of new murky homeland in which tentative foundations can be established by the next generation.

Cultural and political developments

In Guyana the cut-off of colonialism was not clean, and the Afro-Guyanese and Indo-Guyanese pursued different political agendas for a time as the dictatorial regime of Forbes Burnham tore the political framework apart for a whole generation. Fortunately, in that case the strength of the local settlement pattern, where the Indo-Guyanese and Afro-Guyanese continued to live in harmony, prevailed, and a new political arrangement was developed in the 1990s. In Trinidad, even though Indian aspirations were muted at the time of independence by Bhadase Maraj's conservative ethnicity, a more stable political arrangement was put in place at the beginning by the capable management of Eric Williams. By the 1970s, however, the "black consciousness" movement was insisting that Indians decide if they were going to be part of a shared Trinidad culture. Intense conversations began within the Indian community between the older generation that wanted to cling to the Indian heritage and the younger generations who were inclined to join in the local culture by active participation in the shared university, by introducing the old Indian *tan*-singing and *chutney*-dancing into the carnival celebrations, and by making an effort to form political parties that were not ethnic enclaves (Manuel 2000).

The first effort to form a new style of political party was the National Alliance for Reconstruction (NAR), which swept to power in 1987. That party had been assembled hastily, and by the early 1990s the more experienced PNM was back in power. The Indians had in the meantime matured politically, and the United National Congress (UNC) they backed in 1995 was clearly a secular party that had moved beyond Bhadase's ethnic vision, but at the same time it relied heavily on the fact that Indians were the largest single group in society and they should be able to play a leadership role in national politics. Unfortunately, Basdeo Pandey, the first Indian prime minister of Trinidad and Tobago, was not above suspicion, and when he could not fully explain his bank account in London, the PNM once again came back to power. By 2010 the popular female lawyer Kamla Persad-Bissessar had taken over the leadership of the UNC, and the widely respected economist Winston Dookeran had started the multi-ethnic Congress of the People (COP), and they together were swept to power, with

Persad-Bissessar as the first female Prime Minister. She was born in the sugar-cane heartland of Siparia, but from a beginning in a Hindu school, a high school education in a Presbyterian school and more education in England she came to represent not only the dream of her Hindu ancestors but also the hope of her modern and culturally united nation.

New ritual forms

When the indentured workers first arrived in Trinidad in 1845, their dream had not been to transplant Hinduism as a full religious system to their new homeland. Even in Siparia, the town the new prime minister now represents in parliament, they discovered a black Madonna in an old Spanish church, and crying out "***Kālī kī Mātā***" or "Mother Kālī" they had rushed to worship her. Even 160 years later they were still celebrating her power in a festival that overwhelms the priests of the church who acknowledge that they understand very little of the power of that worship (personal visit 1995).

Among those who still insist they understand the Kālī kī Mātā best are those whose ancesters came from south India and were accustomed to being possessed by the goddess they normally called "Māriyamman", but were quite prepared to call by the name "Kālī", which was known all over India. Because the south Indians were a distinct minority in Trinidad, they did not maintain a regular worship tradition for Māriyamman, but after Independence they heard that the tradition was better preserved in nearby Guyana and many began going there for healing or the exorcism of evil spirits. In the early 1970s, Bharat Moonaswamy, whose family had taught him ecstatic possession rituals as a boy, went to Guyana to learn the detailed rituals from Jamsie Naidoo, the most renowned ***pūjāri*** of the south Indian tradition (personal visit with Naidoo in 1995).

In Guyana the south Indian traditions had been well preserved because in 1917, when the Indians moved from the slave housing in the middle of each of the many plantations along the coastal plain, both south Indian and north Indian temples sprang up in the settlement at the end of each plantation. The south Indian temple in Albion, to the east of New Amsterdam, became famous, and a Canadian overseer of labour on that plantation named Leslie Phillips wrote a little booklet about his visit to its popular festival in 1923. The standard arrangement for these temples was that a large compound was fenced off and a large image of the main deity, Māriyamman, was placed in her own small temple facing east. Just outside her doorway was her protector deity, usually called Madurai Viran, who guarded her doorway by sitting to the south of it facing north. Straight across the compound from her was a sacred spot called a Nakura that was without an image and later served as a place where Muslims were invited to worship. Just to Māriyamman's left was the housing for a black image, usually called Cankani Karuppu but also Dih Baba or Lord of the Land, and he carries a whipping rope and Indian workers as well as former slaves

Figure 3.1 The priest making offerings to the goddess (photo by author).

of African background are often eager to worship him. Opposite Cankani is an image of the white deity Munisvaran, to whom people go with psychological ailments. All these deities accept meat offerings, but in an area to the north of the compound that is roped off vegetarian deities are found, including images of Gaṇeṣa, Kṛṣṇa, Rāma and Śiva, and these must be worshipped first.

When Jamsie Naidoo became one of the priests or *pūjāris* of the Albion temple compound in the 1950s his possession-induced dances were considered spiritually powerful and huge crowds of north Indian and African background began to arrive in addition to the regular worshippers. He "creolized" the worship when he taught some of these people the ritual details and they too went into possession states. Many of these assistant *pūjāris* were female and had earlier worshipped lesser-known goddesses such as Koterie or Ganga or even Orisha spirits from the African heritage. He allowed these forms of worship and gave them place within the compound, and allowed the everyday Creole, rather than the old Tamiḻ still used by the older *pūjāris*, to be the ritual language of those possessed. People flocked to his temple from all over the Caribbean and it became known as the Kālī-Mai cult (personal visit 1995).

After Bharat Moonaswamy had worked with Naidoo as an assistant *pūjāri* in the 1970s, Jamsie Naidoo went with him to St Augustine in Trinidad, where they developed a very similar temple compound, and began to hold weekly services and great annual festivals much like those in Guyana. Because the island is smaller and the south Indian segment of society is no longer publicly recognizable, the Kālī-Mai cult in Trinidad is less closely linked with the south Indian heritage, and has evolved into a modern Trinidad phenomenon. Temple compounds copying that of Bharat Moonaswamy have sprung up in a number of places, and they are now led by *pūjāris* of different ethnic backgrounds and the crowds that pack themselves in for healing and the exorcism of evil spirits are from every spectrum of Trinidad society.

Among those of north Indian background, the ritual changes were more varied as people left the village setting after the Second World War. The ritual patterns Bhadase Maraj's Sanatana Dharma Maha Sabha attempted to teach the Hindu community were a narrow set of Brāhman-led rituals designed exclusively for the home and temple. The home-based ritual had older village roots in the performance of *saṁskāras* and the singing of *bhajans*, and with urbanization and the rise of pockets of wealth individual families could consolidate their status by celebrating these older traditions in a big way, and erecting a bamboo pole with a flag or *jhandi* in their yard. In this context musical groups that had won recognition by entering some of the music and dance competitions characteristic of Trinidad society found their way into the celebration of these domestic rituals as well. In the village setting, some of the best known *Tan*-singers and dramatists were Muslims such as Bel Bagai, who was really an Imam named Ghulam Mustafa, and Fakeer Mohammed, but the religious distinctions were not considered central at that time and all entertainment was thought of as "Indian". In the post-Independence period, as a "*callaloo*" (or mixed nation) rapidly developed, all these artistic traditions were put to new uses, and ambitious families sometime celebrated cultural and religious events together.

In the case of the new urban temples, the Sanatana Dharma Maha Sabha initially tried to establish a standard Brāhmanized ritual and even suggested the idea of a creed of central beliefs that would make the Hindu identity clear to

Figure 3.2 Calm temple setting with a few worshippers entering (photo by author).

all concerned. Unlike Guyana, however, where one or more semi-public *mandirs* would be found in every settlement and recognized as such by the government and the Afro-Guyanese neighbours, in the Trinidad Indian village there was little need to make a statement about Hindu identity. Most of the *mandirs* in the villages had been established by Brāhman families, and in the urban setting as well the ornate temples that began to spring up were largely projects set in place by Brāhmans with the help of wealthy friends. Most of these temples honoured a wide range of Hindu deities and included as a minimum Rāma, Sītā, Hanumān, Kṛṣṇa, Viṣṇu, Lakṣmī, Śiva, and Gaṇeṣa on the altar. The temples were usually known by the Brāhman who had founded it, and the founder or his replacement sat on the altar and often gave a long ***kathā*** or sermon.

In many cases the new ritual form of these urban temples was the way they celebrated the festivals. The three major festivals of the village had a religious character in a general sense, but they were meant for the whole village and involved celebratory excesses and provided the Indians with a Carnival atmosphere of their own. The Sanatana Dharma Maha Sabha encouraged the celebration of more specifically Hindu holidays such as Divāli, Rām Leela and Śivarātri. Now that people with an Indian heritage are recognized as the largest single group in society these festivals are given national recognition and often celebrated very publicly in the parking lot of large malls. The Disney-inspired Divāli Nagar near Chaguanas is a kind of theme park based on the Rāma story, and its theatres are often used for major dramas and music performances of a religious nature.

One of the temple complexes most willing to identify with local Trinidad culture was the Hindu Prachar Kendra started by Ravindranath Maharaj ("Ravi Ji") in 1983. In order to meet the blossoming calyposo and soca music traditions halfway he developed the *pichakaree* as a local Indian music tradition, and even introduced the typical performance competitions in that style as part of the celebration of Phagwa or Holī. He also assisted in the restoration of the colourful Sea Temple, originally built by Siewdass Sadhu (who died in the 1970s) in the mudflats of low tide in such a way that it appears to float on the sea. And he ordained a number of women to be Hindu priests before he retired and turned over the running of the Kendra to Pundit Gita Ramsingh in 2009.

Conclusion

Trinidad Hinduism is now one of the most distinctive of the growing number of diaspora Hindu communities that have taken root in various parts of the world. Because the ancestors of this community were transported half way around the globe in the middle of the nineteenth century, they have had very little contact with India over the years and four or five generations of them have grown up in this island environment.

During the early years there would appear to have been little interest in the specifically Hindu part of their identity, because it was relatively easy for everyone in the Indian villages to share their cultural heritage with those around them whether they were Hindu, Muslim or Christian, or were gathering ideas from those of African background living nearby. By the 1930s the Presbyterian school system had made everyone in the Indian community aware of the changing cultural and political environment, even though Indians did not yet have much say in how things might turn out. By 1952 the coming changes in society were no longer unclear, and Bhadase Maraj tried to impose a very specific Hindu identity on the people when he started the Sanatana Dharma Maha Sabha and a Hindu school system. While that organization continues to play a central role, the wide-ranging set of popular religious practices that one might call Trinidad Hinduism today began to flourish late in the twentieth century when people found that they could give public form to their family memories in any way they chose.

Today, one could almost say that "Trinidad Hinduism" has spread beyond the island setting where it was nourished. Many in Trinidad's Indian population have gone off the island for education and employment, and often associate with their fellow citizens or other Caribbean Indians in Britain, Canada or the USA. In those settings they meet more Hindus who have come directly from India than they normally would in Trinidad itself, but even after making those contacts they tend to seek out Caribbean-based worship centres for their regular worship. As these new Caribbean-style temples have developed, a new comparison has emerged within the community itself as people frequently travel back and forth between the island and their new setting, and find themselves comparing the worship patterns of the two locations. For those of us who would study these ever-newer forms of Hinduism, this latest trend is an especially interesting one because Trinidad's Hindus themselves have come to recognize these newest changes and are more than willing to talk with us about them or write about them more creatively in their novels and short stories.

4. Hinduism in the Caribbean

Indrani Rampersad

They are called *jhandis* – these colourful flags flying atop bamboo poles in the front yards[1] of Hindu-Caribbean homes. They are not adornments, but are ritually raised and planted on the Earth as a symbol of victory to a deity that was worshipped in *pūjā*; they personify the deity and are therefore equivalent to a *mūrti* or sacred object of worship; they also constitute the axis mundi that connects individuals to three worlds.[2] These *jhandis* are annually renewed and cannot be uprooted or relocated. In the Caribbean or West Indies, these *jhandis* are some 15–20 feet tall and located in the northeastern corner of the yard. In urbanized spaces, including American space, they may alternatively be located inside apartments or outside on small terraces (2–3 feet tall) and if placed in yards they are shorter (3–5 feet tall); they all look like dwarf replicas of their Caribbean antecedents.

While the word "*jhandi*" (the feminine of the taller *jhanda*) is associated with pennants, streamers, newspaper banner headlines, flags on poles and so on, for Caribbean Hindus, a *jhandi* only refers to a ritually consecrated bamboo pole flying a colour-coded flag that is raised and planted on consecrated earth after ritual worship called a *pūjā*.[3] All other flags on poles (e.g. national flags) are simply called flags. A *jhnadi's* colour denotes the divinity that was worshipped. For example, a red flag says that Hanumān or Durgā was worshipped.

The Caribbean *jhandi* is a cognate of the Dhwaj (flag associated with Indra and Śiva; Woodward 2006: 95), which is still common in the north Indian landscape – tall bamboo poles flying red flags (dedicated to Hanumān) and located at crossroads and *mandirs*, and sometimes in front of homes. Caribbean Hindus associate the *jhandi*, also, with the famous image of the red flag (with its picture of Hanumān) flying on Kṛṣṇa's chariot in the battlefield of Kurukshetra in the **Mahābhārata**. The *jhandi* is also a cognate of the ancient Vedic Yupa or sacrificial pole.

There have been cases in Trinidad and the USA where the right to display a *jhandi* has been challenged. Veteran journalist Lennox Grant comments on the actions of one prime minister to remove the *jhandi* raised and planted in the prime minister's official residence by his predecessor, and replace it with a permanent chapel. Grant comments that it appears "*jhandis* are flags of an alien power whose invasion must be resisted" (Grant 2009). Journalist Artie Jankie writes about a politician leading a march against a school principal who reportedly asked Hindu children to remove their *jhandis*, which they had planted on school grounds after their worship for success in exams (Jankie 2011). In Trinidad and Tobago, there is no strict separation of the sacred and secular as in America. Here state institutions and the people celebrate their identities in state-owned space, generally without rancour.

In December 2006, the Rivermill Homeowners Association of Florida ordered the Persauds, an American Hindu family (that had migrated from Guyana), to remove *jhandis* from their front yard, saying there were complaints that the *jhandi* looked like "a torn, tattered towel in a tree". The Association advised that the *jhandis* be put in the front yard during a holiday period, but the Persauds refused to uproot their *jhandis*, only conceding to lower them and hide them behind some small trees (Tranum 2010). Since the *jhandi* sacralizes space, is the major axis mundi of Caribbean Hindus and is renewed annually, it is usually never uprooted or relocated. It is not a seasonal religious symbol.

The descendants of the indentured Indians are found across the Caribbean region, in varying numerical strength. In islands like Jamaica, St Lucia, St Vincent, Barbados, Grenada, St Lucia, Martinique and Guadeloupe they are in small numbers, but in Trinidad, Guyana and Suriname they are numerically and culturally visible. *Jhandis* flourish in the rural areas of Trinidad, Guyana and Suriname and they are a very visible and strong symbol of Hindu–**Vaiṣṇava** identity in Caribbean diasporic space. Indian–Caribbean peoples and their culture are visible in the USA in areas like New York and Florida and in other parts of the world such as Canada, Britain and Europe.

The *jhandi* in Caribbean Hindu diasporic space

Between 1838 and 1917, British, Dutch and French colonial powers brought workers from India to work on Caribbean sugarcane, cocoa, coffee and coconut plantations under an oppressive system of indentureship. The *jhandi* is a legacy of the north Indians who formed the majority of the workers.

The first recorded street procession of indentured Indians in Trinidad was that of the Hosay in December 1846 (recorded in the Trinidad Spectator of 20 February 1847) indicating community spirit, organizational skills and an early move to claim cultural space. The first *jhandis* could very well have been raised and planted in Trinidad as early as the first year of arrival because Brāhmans[4] were present and as "religious man" (Eliade 1959) is wont to do, the indentured Indians would have wanted to consecrate their new space as soon as possible.

In eastern Uttar Pradesh and Bihar (the two main catchment areas for recruiting indentured workers), Hanumān Pūjā is very popular especially with bachelors. The male–female ratio in indentureship recruitment shows a heavy

Figure 4.1 Several *jhandis* outside a Hindu home (photo by author).

bias towards males. The males were therefore, in the main, forced to live bachelor lives, which might explain the popularity of the Hanumān *jhandi* from the inception of the Indian presence in Trinidad.

The sanctification of space through *pūjās* and *jhandis* is an annual ritual that dates back to north Indian Hindu folk culture. These initial *jhandis* would symbolize the rootedness of the Hindu-Caribbean people and their culture in Caribbean physical and cultural landscape.

Jhandis would spring up in greater numbers around 1871 as Indians acquired new land, built homes, nurtured families and became more economically stable, and as they increasingly converted Trinidad into their Mother Earth (**Dharti Mātā**).

The first flags flown on *jhandis* would have been in red and white colours corresponding to the popular *pūjās* of the indentured Indians, namely Hanumān, Satyanarayan (Satnarine) and Suruj Narayan (Surujnarine). The deity Hanumān is the devotee par excellence of the *Rāmcharitmānas*, and Hanumān Pūjā is the most popular *pūjā* that adherents of *Rāmcharitmānas* perform to overcome adversities in life. A red *jhandi* is raised after this *pūjā*. The Satyanarayan Vrat Kathā consists of a fast (*vrat*) and *pūjā* and lasts from 2–3 hours. A *kathā* is a traditional, engaging style of telling sacred stories to transmit cultural values. This ritual has been popular since indentured times, especially among women. It is performed on special occasions and at full moon time every month. A white *jhandi* is raised after this *kathā*/*pūjā*. Surujnarine or Surya Dev Pūjā is dedicated to the sun. Here the sun is addressed as Suruj Narayan Swami and *kathās* focus on the theme of "light removing darkness". A white *jhandi* is raised and planted after this *kathā/pūjā*. Kālī devotees raise and plant *jhandis* with a square flag of three horizontal bands in the colours red, yellow and white.

The diverse colours in *jhandis* emerged in the post-Second World War period which was a period of creativity and consolidation with new landowners and small business owners. The *pandits* (leaders in ritual life who, in the Caribbean, combine functions like performing rites and rituals, singing devotional songs, making and interpreting astrological charts, delivering learned discourses, being a *guru*, etc.) had more access to sacred texts coming from India and they read from these to the people, describing in greater detail the various deities, their physical characteristics, their dress, favourite foods and so on. Since the *jhandi* is a physical manifestation of the deity in whose honour it is raised and planted, new colours evolved to personify qualities and characteristics of the different deities worshipped.

In the Kabīrpanth (sect of devotees in the lineage of Sadguru Kabīr Saheb) the *jhanda* is raised at the time of **Guru Pūrṇimā** (full moon in month of Ashadh or June–July) or in the new moon phase of a month. This *jhanda* represents their founder and *guru*, Sadguru Kabīr Saheb. The entire bamboo pole is clothed in white and flies a white flag, with white symbolizing the purity of the *guru*.

Driving through especially the rural areas of Trinidad, Guyana and Suriname, I could not help but marvel at the sight of multi-coloured *jhandis* in all stages of existence – some of freshly cut bamboo poles showing green sprigs atop and with brightly coloured cotton cloth flags, not yet worn out by nature; some whose poles had turned brown, flying flags with fading pictures or drawings; some with bending bamboo poles and worn flags on their way down to join Mother Earth (it is considered inauspicious to destroy *jhandis*, and they are left to disintegrate and rejoin nature on their own).

In Guyana, the term "*jhandi*" is used interchangeably with "*wuk*" (i.e. "work" meaning a ritual duty). It is not unusual to hear, "we are having a *jhandi*" or "we're having a *wuk*", meaning that they are having a *pandit* come over to their home to perform a *pūjā*. This reinforces the centrality of the *jhandi* in *pūjā*. Trinidadians interchangeably use "*pūjā*" with "prayers" and differentiate between *jhandi* and *pūjā*.

In Trinidad, one is also likely to see very large square flags with horizontal bands of white, green, yellow and brown cloth, flying on poles, but these are from the African traditional religion of Orisha. The flag pole here is named Opa and these flags are located at their worship centres. They, like *jhandis*, represent divinities, but unlike *jhandis* they are not raised and planted after a ceremony like a *pūjā*.

In Uttar Pradesh and Bihar, India, after a *pandit* performs *pūjā* at a home, *jhandis* are raised and planted in the front yard of the house and preserved for one year, after which the ritual is renewed annually. In Trinidad, Hindu families have at least one annual *pūjā* – a tradition that goes back to indentured times – when they raise and plant new *jhandis*. They may have other *pūjās* during the year for special occasions, but there is this special one for renewing

Table 4.1 Colours associated with jhandis raised in honour of deities worshipped in *pūjās* in Trinidad (created from diverse sources, notably Mayawatti Vahini, Pandit Ramsoondar Parasram and Ravi-Ji of Trinidad, and Pandit Radharaman Upadhyaya of New York).

Male and female deities (*devatas/devis*)	Colour of flag on *jhandi*	Day of worship
Dih	Red	Any time
Ganeṣa	Golden yellow	Wednesday, or any other day
Hanumān	Red	Tuesday, Saturday
Lakṣmī	Pink	Any day
Durgā	Red; yellow (used in the Nawratam period of the Indian Spring)	Monday or Friday
Surujnarayan	White	Sunday
Satyanarayan	White	Any day
Śiva	Blue (some use black and white instead); in Guyana and USA devotees use white (for purity and the snowy abode of Śiva), saffron (Śiva as yogi) and blue (vast nature of God)	Monday or special day for worshipping Śiva (e.g. thirteenth day of the lunar fortnight)
Saraswatti	White	Any day
Viṣṇu (as Rām/Kṛṣṇa avatāra)	Yellow	Any day
Geeta Recitation (Geeta Patha) where Kṛṣṇa is worshipped)	Yellow	Any day
Ganga	Yellow	Monday and Friday
Kālī	Red, black (sometimes a square flag of three horizontal bands in red, yellow and white is used)	Any day (some choose Monday and Friday)
Sadguru Kabīrsaheb (of the Kabīrpanth)	White flag with entire length of the bamboo pole clothed in white cloth	At Guru Pūrṇimā time, or in new moon phase

*jhandi*s related to worship of the deity of the home or the deity of the head of the household.

While, in India *jhandi*s are found at crossroads, *mandirs* and in the yards of some homes, they are not as ubiquitous and as colourful as we find in the Caribbean. Here, the *jhandi* has evolved into a unique Caribbean symbol and signifier of Hindu identity – social and spiritual.

Ritual of the *jhandi*

The *jhandi* ritual is traditionally performed by the householder to annually renew the *jhandi* and the family's relationship with the devi or devata that they worship, as well as their relationship with the cosmos. Family members may also perform this ritual for special individual needs like demonstrating thanks or praying for success. The performer or patron of a *pūjā* is called a Yajman.

Nowadays, the items for a *pūjā* are mass produced and one can purchase a *pūjā* packet beforehand, reducing and even eliminating the traditional ***sādhanā*** in preparation for the ritual. *Sādhanā* refers to the spiritual frame of mind and the spirit of sacrifice with which a devotee approaches the performance of a ritual. For example, the personal collection of flowers and other materials for a *pūjā* is considered an important step in the process of preparing for *pūjā*. Devotees normally pick flowers with a prayer seeking permission from the Creator for doing so. The indentured Indians (who were mainly vegetarians) would spiritually prepare themselves by "fasting" (abstaining from salt, onions, garlic, spicy foods, alcohol, cigarettes, etc.). Nowadays, "fasting" means just staying away from intoxicants and non-vegetarian foods. Traditionally, on the day of *pūjā*, all members of the family would rise long before dawn to begin preparations. The men go out to cut the bamboo and make a new vedi for the *pūjā*. The women clean the home, prepare the *pūjā* vedi, pluck fresh flowers, and cook different kinds of vegetarian foods and sweets. Long ago, they fasted until the *pūjā* was completed which could be around noon. Nowadays, the *pandit* allows the yajman to eat before *pūjā* unless it is a special *pūjā* that requires fasting.

One can purchase a *pūjā* packet specific to a deity from specialist *pūjā* shops in the Caribbean and North America (where the Indian Caribbean diaspora is located). This will contain all the ingredients except, for example, fresh flowers and the bamboo pole which must be freshly cut, at least in the Caribbean. In the USA, where bamboo poles might be difficult to locate, then Hindus use poles of metal or wood. The important characteristic of the pole is that it should be straight and near perfection. One has a choice of style in cotton flags. There are flags with a picture or line drawing of the divinity to be worshipped; there are those with auspicious yantra-like[5] markings and decorative fringes on the edges; and there are those which, by their colour alone, indicate the deity to be worshipped. Some families still make their own flags as part of their *sādhanā*.

To get the right bamboo poles, the men in the family would go to those forested areas known for good bamboo. This is done on the evening before or early in the morning of the *pūjā*. The men look for well shaped, tall bamboos and are careful not to cut off any sprigs at the top of the bamboo. The idea is to have as perfect a bamboo pole as possible, tall and straight, with more than five knots or nodes on it. The bamboo cutters will first "say a prayer" asking permission of the Creator to cut the bamboo. After cutting the "right" bamboo, they load it on to the truck, transport it to the home and place it in *jhandi–vedi* area where it will be raised and planted after the *pūjā*.

Before the bamboo pole is used in the *pūjā*, a young male or the male yajman[6] prepares it by washing it with water. Toward the end of the *pūjā*, he will bring it to be consecrated by the *pandit* next to the *pūjā vedi* where the *pūjā* is being performed. A vedi in the Caribbean setting refers to a raised piece of earth on which *pūjā* is performed. Most Hindu families have a portable one made of a wooden square box that averages 36 inches long by 36 inches wide and 6 inches high. Earth is packed into the box and is freshly "lepayed" before a *pūjā*. Lepaying is the process of using the hands to apply coats of a mixture of cow dung, clay and water, in a semi-circular fashion, to refresh and smooth an earthen surface; it is like applying a new coat of paint. This *vedi* represents the earth during *pūjā* and has evolved to what it is today because *pūjās* are now conducted inside homes and *mandirs* where the floors are of wood, tiles and other materials.

For the consecration of the *jhandi*, the *pandit* will purify the pole with the sprinkling of holy water, then the yajman will anoint the bamboo pole with three tilaks[7] – one of sindoor (a sacred red or orange powder used in rituals and by married Hindu women in the parting of the hair on their heads, one of *haldi* (turmeric powder) and one of *chandan* (sandalwood) – and then secure the cotton flag to the top of the pole, as the *pandit* chants sacred *mantras*. The *pandit* then accompanies the *yajman* to the *jhandi–vedi* for raising and planting the *jhandi*. Here another short ritual takes place. The hole for planting the *jhandi* would have been dug before by a male family member.[8] Now, the *pandit* consecrates the hole with milk, coins and flowers, and to the victorious sound of "Jai", the name of the deity is called (Jai Hanumān, Hanumān Baba ki Jai, Jai Durge, etc.). The bamboo pole is then raised, ideally by five pairs of male hands, and planted in the hole made for its purpose and in victory to the deity worshipped. The tradition of having five males raise and plant the *jhandi* has changed since the Second World War, when *pandits* started allowing women to participate in this process.

The *jhandi* is raised and planted in the earth in the northeast corner of the boundary of the yard, or sometimes the east. This area is simply referred to as "by the *jhandis*"; it is the spot where a portable *vedi* is sometimes located after use in *pūjā*. Sacred trees, plants and flowers adorn this area. A *deeya*[9] is located here, along with *mūrtis* and a Śiva *liṅgam*,[10] in most cases. This area is usually open to the skies. A small household *mandir* may evolve, over time, in this space. This spot of the *jhandis*, therefore, may be called the "*jhandi* Vedi" – it is the sacred space in which the major Caribbean Hindu axis mundi of the *jhandi* is located.

The *jhandi* as axis mundi

The *jhandi* pole is the major axis mundi of most Hindus in the Caribbean. It anchors religious man (Eliade 1959: 12) at the navel of the universe, making it the centre of his cosmos. It tangibly sacralizes the physical space of indentured Indians and their descendants who see the world through the Rām–Vaiṣṇava lens.

For Caribbean Hindus, the *jhandi* carries deep emotional and sacred meaning. It is not a religious symbol that is moved around at whim or displayed seasonally. Once raised and planted in sanctified earth, it must be allowed to degenerate naturally. Newer *jhandis* may be raised and planted around the older ones, but the latter are never uprooted to make way for newer ones.

The *jhandi* is the axis mundi that symbolizes Mount Meru, the mythical centre of the Earth, and connects the Earth's upper regions and lower regions. It locates the individual in his earthly space within the cosmos. It is the central point where earthly time and eternity meet, where all compass directions meet, and it becomes a mysterious channel that connects humans with the higher and lower realms in creation. The *jhandi* locates the home as the centre of everything. In one prayer for installing it at the main door of a new home, the performer of the ritual prays: "Here, in this space on Mother Earth, I construct this building which is like the centre of the globe and which is the spring of prosperity and river of wealth" (Shastri 2002: par. 3.4.4).

The *jhandi*'s function as an axis mundi is reinforced by the *sankalpa* (intention) or ritual vow at the start of a *pūjā* which establishes the *yajman*'s identity and intent in time and space, using detailed cosmic and ritual time, genealogical data,[11] and geographical details[12] like Mother Earth, region, name of country and village, almost like the virtual experience of a Google Earth search precisely zeroing in on some geographical location.

Another kind of axis mundi associated with the *jhandi* is the *raksha* (or *rakhi* as it is commonly called in Trinidad). This is a red, yellow or saffron-coloured cotton thread that is wrapped three times (with the ends of the thread tied in three knots) around the right wrist of men and the left wrist of women at the start of any *hawan*[13] or *pūjā*. This *raksha* symbolizes a protective bond between the individual, divinity and the *guru*; the circle of thread suggests an umbilical relationship between individual and divinity (like that between mother and child). This *rakhi* is a renewal, reconnection or rebirth in original spirituality (i.e. original union with supreme divinity). The *rakhi* has the protective function of a *yantra* when the *pandit* blesses it and ties it on the wrist of the *yajman*. Another type of *rakhi* is tied around the bamboo pole of the *jhandi*, endowing it with the protective power of healing and harmony between self and higher self, and protection from the threefold sufferings: *adhyatmic* (suffering that affects the body and mind), *adhibhautic* (suffering caused by other living beings) and *adhidaivic* (suffering caused by tangible and intangible forces in nature).

In order to appreciate the centrality of the *jhandi* as a Caribbean Hindu axis mundi, it would be useful to understand the culture of this group.

Caribbean Rām–Vaiṣṇava tradition

In the Caribbean, Hindus are likely to describe themselves according to two major categories: Vedic and Sanatani. The former includes those like the Ārya

Samāj that accord canonical status only to Veda or Sruti, and the latter includes groups like the Sanatan Dharma Maha Sabha, Kabīrpanth, Siewnarine Dharam Sabha and Kali Temple that extend the canonical status of Veda to include a variety of sacred *Smriti* texts including the *Puranas*, or follow in the lineage of a *guru*.

The Sanatani stream dominates Hindu–Caribbean traditions, and this in turn is dominated by the Rām–Vaiṣṇava lens of Tulsīdās through the *Rāmcharitmānas*. Tulsīdās is termed the "father of Caribbean Hindu Dharma" because his *Rāmcharitmānas* has supreme canonical status among the majority of Caribbean Hindus. This was the dominant culture of the indentured Indians. It was a traditional culture passed on from one generation to the next through the oral tradition. It was embodied knowledge.

The eclectic nature of Tulsīdās's brand of Rām–Vaiṣṇava philosophy seamlessly weaves diverse religious expressions into one acceptable fabric known as the *Rāmcharitmānas*. While promoting an all-inclusive approach to spirituality, it allowed people to retain their specific identities, such as being worshippers of Rām or Kṛṣṇa or Devi, for example, even as it promoted the supremacy of Rām.

Trinidad Hindu folk worship is *bhakti*-oriented, and fuses Vaiṣṇava, Śaiva and Shakta worship which are all aspects of the one absolute reality. Devotees have an ***iṣṭadevatā*** (a specially chosen form of god assigned to them by their *guru*s when they take initiation). The major deities worshipped in Caribbean Hindu *dharma* are: Gaṇeṣa, Viṣṇu, Śiva, Surya, and Devi (in her various forms). In recent years, global media, movement of *gurus*, and travel between India and the Caribbean have led to more deities like Skanda and Dakshinamūrti in the spiritual landscape of the diaspora.

Varna and Jati are no longer functional in Caribbean Hindu culture, except for entry into the priesthood of a few Pauranic organizations that insist on Brāhmin-by-birth status. There is clearly a more equalitarian trend today even if pockets of resistance remain. And this extends to gender as well, as more and more women are taking up formal positions of authority in religious organizations with some even breaking the ceiling of the priesthood.

Conclusion

Caribbean Hindu *dharma* is rich in folk traditions that are transmitted via the oral tradition, and this is reflected in the *jhandi*. The *jhandi* dominates the Hindu Caribbean landscape standing as a unique indentured diasporic symbol and signifying a unique Caribbean experience and identity with people struggling to "be themselves" amid rapid creolization.[14] It is the pole that connects individuals to the three worlds. This symbol of the *jhandi* is likely to be dwarfed or absent in urban, elite spaces where Caribbean Hindus live. It remains a colourful symbol that is annually renewed to reaffirm a social and spiritual identity.

Notes

1. A yard is the common space shared by more than one family who live in near proximity, or it may refer to the open space in front of or behind a house.
2. Three worlds refer to the upper region or celestial world, the middle region or the earth, and the lower region or naraka or hell.
3. A *pujā* is ritual worship to a deity in a tangible form and is very popular in *bhakti* worship. There are daily *pujās* and *pujās* for special occasions. Some are performed individually; some collectively; some are done in homes and mandirs; some in public spaces like the seaside; and, in the case of **Rāmlīla**, in community space. In Trinidad the earliest type of *pūjā* seems to have been to Hanuman-ji and a red flag on a *jhanda* was raised in his honour at the end of the *pūjā*.
4. Brāhmins were the traditional carriers and transmitters of Hindu Culture. They daily recited the Hindu sacred texts and performed their daily rituals. Thus, it is highly likely that the early Brāhmins, few though they were, would have been able to replicate many aspects of Hindu culture here in Trinidad.
5. Examples of *yantras* are geometric designs that map cosmic realities and have special spiritual powers; protective amulets; and the langote on the *jhandi*.
6. Females are now the main *yajman* or performer of the ritual. However, males usually perform the task of preparing the bamboo pole.
7. Tilak or *tika* is a religious mark on the forehead or other parts of the body.
8. Females can also perform this task if they wish, but it is usually left up to the males.
9. A *deeya* is a small clay or brass lamp. A cotton wick is placed in the *deeya* filled with oil or *ghī* (ghee) and then lit on ritual occasions.
10. Śiva *liṅgam* refers to the symbol of Shiva that demonstrates the male principle in creation.
11. The lineage of the *yajmān* is mentioned during *pūjā*, linking him/her to the ancestors, *rishis*, and, for Rāmāyana devotees, to the lineage of Rām or the Surya (sun) dynasty.
12. In Trinidad, some aspects of the sacred geography of India have been replaced with Trinidad places (e.g. while Hindus continue to recognize the Ganga as a sacred river, in their *pūjās* they use the local Caroni river in the place of Ganga).
13. Hawan is also known as Homa. It is a ritual where the main offerings are made to the holy Fire.
14. Creolization is a dominant Caribbean ideology that promotes creole culture as the source of Caribbean identity. Prem Misir (2006) challenges this as ethnic dominance. Creolization sees the true West Indian/Caribbean person situated in hybridized "creole" space along a continuum with the pure European on one end and the pure African on the other.

5. Tamil̲ Śaivism in Norway

Knut A. Jacobsen

The heat from *āratī* lamps in the temple, the smoke and smell from camphor flames, the fresh colourful flowers, coconuts and bananas, priests and male devotees naked above the waist dressed for the warm climate of Sri Lanka, and the bright colours of the saris contrasted dramatically with the colourless and bitterly cold Norwegian winter outside. The sounds of bells and the joyful greeting of the gods by the congregation as they moved around the inside of the temple for the evening *pūjā*, following behind the priests who removed the curtain at one shrine after the other, bore witness of a Tamil̲ Hindu religious world – a Tamil̲ Hindu diasporic home away from home.

Introduction

A distinctive feature of Hinduism in Norway is the eagerness with which the Hindu population has established a large number of temples and temple organizations. In the last twenty years, eight Hindu temples with busy ritual calendars have been established in the largest cities of Norway, and in 2012 there were thirteen official Hindu religious organizations (Jacobsen 2011a). Most of them serve the around 12,000 Tamil̲ Hindus from Tamil̲ Īl̲am (the Tamil̲ areas of Sri Lanka) living in Norway. The largest temple, Sivasubramaniyar Alayam in Oslo, was opened in 1998. The main purpose of these temples is to offer devotees the opportunity to participate in ritual traditions according to their needs on a daily, weekly, monthly, occasional or annual basis. However, the temples function not only as places of worship, but also as centres of Tamil̲ culture and as Tamil̲ "comfort zones" (Ebaugh & Chafetz 2000), with everyone speaking the Tamil̲ language, wearing Tamil̲ dress and eating Tamil̲ food, and with Tamil̲ music, Tamil̲ rituals and so on. However, the temples are not the only Tamil̲ organizations. The Tamil̲s from Sri Lanka have established a large number of secular Tamil̲ organizations in Norway such as Tamil̲ language schools, Saturday schools, health organizations and so on, and these organizations share many of the functions with the temples.[1] The most important function of the

Hindu temples (and, for the Tamiḻ Roman Catholics in Norway, the churches) is to offer religion. The Hindu temple is first and foremost a place of worship and for the Hindus, the temples are the homes of the gods and a place of religion.

It is mainly only during the sacred time of the festivals that the temples are very crowded and bring together large parts of the Tamiḻ Hindu populations, and it is on these festival days that the temples come alive as centres of Tamiḻ culture with large groups of devotees coming together. The management committee and priests of the largest Hindu temple, the Sivasubramaniyar Alayam, have attempted to make the visitors able to be one hundred per cent Tamiḻ Hindus for the period of time they spend in the temple. One aim of religious festivals in the diaspora is to recreate the atmosphere and sentiments of the country of origin. This strengthens identity and the solidarity of the group and for the individual it is often an important source of well-being. From a religious point of view, the way the gods and goddesses were worshipped in the country of origin becomes a source of orthopraxis in the establishment of the religious traditions in the new place. In the Tamiḻ Hindu temples in Norway, it is primarily the ritual world of the temples of the country of origin that is attempted to be recreated. Such recreation makes religion seem authentic and the foreign place seems like home. But the diaspora situation often leads to an increased focus on the temple as a place for the preservation and generational transfer of culture, and as a place to confirm identity, and the temple often becomes the single most important cultural institution of the group. This increased importance of the temple might motivate the diaspora group to invest more time and effort in the ritual activity of the temple.

Hindu religious life in diaspora depends not only on the establishment of Hindu temples for the rituals, but also on the establishment of the Hindu liturgical calendar for the sacred time for the performance of rituals. It is exactly this interaction of sacred space and sacred time that constitutes the Hindu temples. An increase in ritual activity is noticeable in the liturgical calendar of the temples. Tamiḻs from Sri Lanka have brought the sacred time of Hindu Sri Lanka to Norway and this sacred time has become manifest in the temples. Sacred time marks the high point of temple life, both the daily periods of ***abhiṣeka*** and *pūjā*, and the annual festival calendar.

The cycle of rituals of the Sivasubramaniyar Alayam in Oslo includes daily *āratī* and *pūjā* (Tamil: *pūcai*) rituals, a weekly programme of *abhiṣeka* (Tamil: *apiṣekam*) on Fridays, and an annual cycle of festivals, some of which last several days (see Figure 5.1).[2] Murukaṉ is the main god of the temple Sivasubramaniyar Alayam. The temple is devoted to Murukaṉ (Subrahmaṇya, Skanda, Kārttikeya), a god that is popular today primarily in south India and Sri Lanka. He is the son of Śiva, and belongs, therefore, to the Śaiva tradition. The Tamiḻs of Sri Lanka are mostly Śaivaites and their dominant theological system is the Śaiva Siddhānta. Murukaṉ is one of the most popular gods among the Tamiḻs of Sri Lanka: "The shrines dedicated to the worship of Murukan are numerous and one could hardly come across a village or town inhabited by Saivite Tamils

Figure 5.1 Priests and worshippers during evening *āratī* in Sivasubramaniyar Alayam, Oslo (photo by author).

where temples dedicated for his worship are not to be found" (Pathamanathan 1990: 89).

The main festivals of the Sivasubramaniyar Alayam celebrate Murukaṉ. Murukaṉ is the eternal youth and a warrior God, but he also symbolizes the time cycle and he personifies the year. He is associated with time and the changing of the seasons. Murukaṉ is born on the new moon day and his birth is equated to the rising of the sun (Clothey 1982: 158). The repeatability of the annual festivals underlines the cyclical nature of ritual time.

Annual Mahotsavam festival

The most important festival of the temples is the annual **Mahotsavam** festival. The annual festival period of the temple is marked by the hoisting of the flag with the cock, the symbol of Murukaṉ. This flag hoisting has marked the beginning of the main festival of the temple, since the temple celebrated its opening more than ten years ago in 1998. At Sivasubramaniyar Alayam the annual festival period lasts for twelve days.[3] The Mahotsavam centres on processions (see Jacobsen 2008a). In the processions of the festival, movable *mūrtis* of the gods (***utsavamūrtis***: Tamiḻ: *utsavamūrttis*) are taken out of the temple on the streets, often using a different *vāhana* or vehicle for each festival day. Often one or two days of the festival are the most important, while the single most important event is usually the festival of chariot (***tēr, ratha***). It is also the case with Sivasubramaniyar Alayam (see Figure 5.2).

Usually the big annual festival in Hinduism in Sri Lanka is celebrated to mark the star-day of the temple-image, or to commemorate when the temple was consecrated (Smith 1982). In Sri Lanka, all temples have a festival period which may last from two to three weeks, and the date of the festival varies from temple to temple, but "each temple holds its own festival annually at a fixed time" (Cartman 1957: 100). Cartman also notes that "on the day before the festival ends, there is the very special car procession when the images of the gods are placed upon huge jaggernaught cars. These huge vehicles are rope drawn round the temple by the devotees" (Cartman 1957: 100). Some of these festivals are more famous than others. There is a competition between the temples to have the best temple festival. This competition is about the length of the festival, rituals, music and the size and beauty of the vehicles. In the Sri Lankan Tami<u>l</u> diaspora, this competitive feature of the chariot festival has become a global phenomenon. The ambition of the temple committee of the Sivasubramaniyar Alayam has been to have the greatest and best temple festival outside of Sri Lanka.

Three chariots, which were specially made in Sri Lanka for the temple and shipped to Norway, are at the centre of the festival. On this day the *utsavamūrtis*, statues of the gods and goddesses made of metal, are transported on the festival carts around the streets. With 4,000 and 6,000 men and women usually participating, this day has become the major festival day for the Tami<u>l</u> community in Oslo and Norway. In Sivasubramaniyar Alayam three chariots are moved around the temple with thousands of people participating either in the procession or as

Figure 5.2 Rathotsavam, Sivasubramaniyar Alayam, Oslo (photo by author).

audience. Each chariot is pulled by two ropes. A large number of people divided into two rows pull the ropes in front of the chariots when they move upwards, and in the back of the chariots when they move downwards. Downwards is more difficult and risky and they are careful to pull the ropes to hold back the chariots so the heavy vehicles move at a very slow speed with frequent full stops downhill on the streets of the temple. To pull them upwards again on the uphill road on the other side of the temple concluding the circumambulation is also heavy work, but the devotees who pull the chariots seem to enjoy being part of this ritual. The chariots come often to a complete stop, which is also necessary for making the procession last for several hours. Women pull the ropes on one side and the males pull on the other side. The males are dressed in white *dhotis* and are naked above the waist and barefoot to indicate their devotedness, as it is considered the best way to dress in the temple and when performing rituals. Women are dressed in *saris*. Even though many of the women in their daily life will dress in jeans and shirts, the *sari* is considered the appropriate dress for women for ritual and festive occasions.

The ritual starts early in the morning with elaborate rituals inside the temple, which already at that time is crowded with devotees, and from around 9 a.m. the festival statues of the gods Murukaṉ, Piḷḷaiyār (Vināyakar, Gaṇeśa) and Amman (Tamil: Ammaṉ) start to be taken out in procession inside the temple, and then slowly and solemnly they are moved outside and finally placed in their separate chariots. These are elaborate rituals. By this time thousands of devotees have arrived. The breaking of the coconuts in front of the chariots as an offering to the gods is an important ritual to mark that the chariots are ready to move. The chariots are large and heavy and the streets around the temple are steep. The manoeuvring of the chariots is difficult, especially the steep downhill. Groups of devotees have to use all their powers to pull the ropes behind the chariots to make sure the chariots do not rush forward which could be very dangerous for the bystanders. A large number of people follow behind the chariots. Foremost are the ***kāvaḍi*** dancers and women with pots on their heads. The majority stand along the road and watch the procession of chariots and start walking after the procession when it has passed. The festival music played by the Tamiḻ musicians is an important part of the sacredness created by the procession ritual. The same musicians come from Sri Lanka every year. They tour the Tamiḻ temples of Europe to play at the different festival processions.

It was only a few years ago that *kāvaḍi* dancers with hooks and spears pierced on their body were introduced in the procession. Before that a few, mostly children *kāvaḍi* dancers had been part of the procession, but after the introduction of hooks and spears, the adult *kāvaḍi* dancers became the prominent feature of the procession. Since then the music of the procession has focused on their dance instead of the gods in the chariots, and since it is to a large degree the music that makes processional sacred space, the *kāvaḍi* dancers have become the central actors of the procession (Jacobsen 2008a). The procession stops for longer periods for the *kāvaḍi* dance. It is the musicians that give speed and rhythm to the *kāvaḍi* dancers, and thus also decide the speed of the movement of the chariots.

As is the case in all the Tamil̲ Hindu temple festivals, the bathing festival takes place on the last day at the Sivasubramaniyar Alayam in Norway. For temples with tanks, this means bathing of a festival image in the tank. Many devotees take advantage of the sacred water to bathe in it. Sivasubramaniyar Alayam of Oslo does not have a tank, as is usually the case with the diaspora temples. Instead, *mūrtis* are taken in procession to a lake some distance from the temple where a ***tīrtha*** had been established (Jacobsen 2004). Murukan̲'s ***vēl*** (his sacred weapon) is given a sacred bath. In some texts it is written that the faithful who bathe at the same time as the image is immersed in the sacred water will have their moral impurity washed away (Smith 1982). This annual ritual attracts many people and is a festive but also a solemn event as ***śrāddha*** (ancestor rituals – rituals to honour the recently dead) are performed after the bathing of Murukan̲'s *vēl*. But the festival is mainly a happy occasion. Some, especially those in the temple management responsible for the festival, are happy that the twelve-day festival has been a success and now comes to a close. Another source of happiness is the bathing in the sacred lake and the playfulness of the ritual. Some of those who jump into the water after the bathing of the *vēl* has been completed are squirting water on the group of people standing on the beach watching the rituals. The warm weather, the holiday mood, the Tamil̲ food and drinks, the priests, the statues of the gods adorned for the festival occasion, the procession umbrellas for the gods and goddesses, all the persons present (with a few exceptions) being Tamil̲s from the same community, speaking Tamil̲, dressing Tamil̲, and sharing a common history – all these factors contribute to make the festival day a Tamil̲ event.

Mythological narratives and festivals

The Sivasubramaniyar Alayam is a Murukan̲ temple, and therefore Murukan̲'s killing of Sūran Asura is a major celebration, celebrated in the six-day *Sūran Pōr* (fight of Sūran) or Skanda *ṣaṣṭi*-festival. The festival celebrates a story of the victory over good over evil, and with the tragic civil war in Sri Lanka which lasted from 1983 to 2009, the theme is important for the community. Sūran Asura had gained extraordinary power as his reward for austerities. He then used his powers to do evil against humans and gods. To stop him, Murukan̲ descended to Earth, and there was a battle between the two. Sūran first assumed the form of the elephant-headed Tārakan̲. Murukan̲ cut off his head, but he then assumed the form of the lion-headed Siṅgham. Murukan̲ cut off the lion head. But because of his previous merits he then assumed his own form as the Asura king. Murukan̲ again cut off his head. The Asura took the form of a huge tree and Murukan̲ then destroyed the tree. The Asura appeared as a cock and then as a peacock. Murukan̲ conquered both. Sūran then surrendered. The cock became the sign of Murukan̲ and the peacock his *vāhana*, his vehicle. During the *Sūran Pōr* festival the battle between Murukaṉ and Sūran Pōr is re-enacted. The image of Sūran has a detachable head, and each of the three heads is placed on the image and are subsequently knocked off. The re-enactment of the battle therefore takes place inside the temple. In Sri Lanka this fight is part of a procession that proceeds around the outside of the temple. The *Sūran Pōr* festival, however, takes place in the middle of November, and this time in Norway is very cold and dark.

Another important festival celebrated in the temple is the main festival of lights of the Tamiḻs, *Tirukārttikai* or *Kārttikai Dīpam* in the month of *Kārrtik*. The most famous place of this festival is the Mount Kailāsa of south India, the Arunachal Mountain in Thiruvannamalai. Here the festival celebrates Śiva's manifestation as *jyotirliṅga*. In this sacred narrative Śiva appeared as the pillar of light from the ocean, and Viṣṇu and Brahmā both thinking of themselves as the supreme god, wondered what it could be. Brahmā became a bird and flew up to see if the pillar had a limit upward, Viṣṇu swam down in the form of a boar to see if it had a limit downward. But the pillar had no limit, neither upwards nor downwards. Śiva then manifested himself in his anthropomorphic form from the pillar. In many places in Sri Lanka this festival is celebrated with huge bonfires made by placing coconut leaves pointing upwards and placing light inside to imitate the *jyotirliṅga*. The *Tirukārttikai* or *Kārttik Dīpam* (*Kārttikai Villakkidu*) is celebrated differently in Sivasubramaniyar Alayam in Norway from the way it is done in Sri Lanka. In Norway it is celebrated only with small lights inside the temple.

The Navarātri and Vijayadaśamī are also major festival events. The first three days during the festivals celebrate Durgā, the following three Lakṣmī, and the last three Sarasvatī. As part of Sarasvatī *pūjā* the tools of work are blessed, as is the tradition among the Tamiḻs (in Āyudha *pūjā*; Tamiḻ: *āyuta pūcai*). A number of other special days are also celebrated. Every year Śiva is celebrated during six days. Twelve days every year are sacred days of Piḷḷaiyār or Vināyakar (Gaṇeśa), these are the fourth day of the new moon, *caturthī viratam*, and these were also celebrated. Each month also has a special *nakṣatra* that is celebrated. Tuesdays in July–August are sacred to Umā, and special *pūjās* are made to her, while Mondays in March and October are sacred to Śiva and Umā, and are celebrated by worship of them.

Sivasubramaniyar Alayam is a Śaiva temple, but it celebrates also Vaiṣṇava festivals. Because for several years it was the only Tamiḻ Hindu temple in Oslo, it had also to celebrate auspicious (*tithi*) days associated with other gods. Two days a year are sacred to Kṛṣṇa, the *ekādaśī* of the eleventh *tithi* of each rotation (see below), and Dīpāvali.

Unique for Sivasubramaniyar Alayam, according to the temple management, has been that the last Friday in the month was devoted to *bhajan*-singing. This tradition was started by an earlier priest of the temple, who also wrote *bhajan*-songs himself. The purpose of the *bhajan*-singing was to cure old people who were sick. The perception was that most problems had to do with health, and therefore to pray for good health is in fact to pray for a divine power to solve all problems.

Several festivals of Hinduism in Sri Lanka are agricultural festivals, and two traditional agricultural festival days were celebrated. On 5 February is *Thaippūcam*, the harvest festival that marks the first bringing home of harvested crops – that is, the bringing home of some rice to hang in the house – and 16 July is the beginning of the dark half of the year. This is traditionally considered a period of little food and a special simple soup is eaten that day.

Some of these annual festivals have been more important than others in terms of number of people participating and the amount of work invested. The ritual event of highest importance, as mentioned above, is the annual twelve-day temple festival (*Mahotsavam*). No other ritual could compare in terms of amount of work invested, ritual expertise employed, and number of people participating. But also the annual ritual *Skanda Ṣaṣṭi* and its concluding ritual the *Sūran Pōr* are major events of this temple. Likewise the *Kārttikai Dīpam* and the *Śivarātri* draw many people to the temple.

Narratives of South Asian immigration

The Hindus participating in the rituals of the Sivasubramaniyar Alayam in Oslo are part of a steadily growing Hindu population. Awareness of the history of Hinduism in Norway is part of what it means to be a Hindu living in this country. The Hindus are aware that Hinduism in Norway has been growing since the late 1960s when an immigration of Hindus from Sri Lanka and India started in continental Europe including Norway, but also that Hinduism in Norway did not start with their immigration. When the first Hindu immigrants arrived in Norway from India and Sri Lanka in the late 1960s they were surprised to discover that Hinduism was not a new religion in this country. Hinduism had been established in Norway already in 1914 by the first Hindu to settle here, Swami Śrī Ānanda Ācārya (Surendra Nath Baral 1881–1945), a *guru* from Bengal, who established an ***āśram*** in the mountainous area of Alvdal (in 1917) in eastern Norway, where he lived until he had passed away in 1945. This Hindu *guru* had settled in England in 1912, but moved to Norway with his two female British disciples to protest against British nationalism, which was growing because of the onset of the First World War. Ācārya came to Norway to spread the message of ***advaita*** *Vedānta*, and he meant Norway would benefit from his Hindu philosophy (Jacobsen 2011a). He published a large number of books, attracted Norwegian devotees and worked with the famous Norwegian author Arne Garborg to translate parts of the *Rāmāyaṇa* into Norwegian. One Norwegian disciple, Einar Beer (1887–1982), lived in the *āśram* from its beginning and in 1975 established Swami Śrī Ānanda Ācārya Foundation to promote the ideas of Ānanda Ācārya, and especially the idea of a peace university at Mount Tron (Mt Tron University of Peace Foundation was founded in 1993; see www.tronuni.org/nb). A memorial monument has been built on Mount Tron, next to where a group of devotees hope one day to establish the peace university.

Ācārya's *āśram*, although still active, did not lead to immigration of Indians, but many of the Hindu Indian immigrants that arrived from the late 1960s and early 1970s have made a pilgrimage to Ānanda Ācārya's *āśram* in Alvdal. That Hinduism was at home in Norway many years before the main Hindu immigration started gave meaning and comfort to some of the early immigrants.

The story of Ānanda Ācārya illustrates that early immigrants are often unusual individuals with heroic stories. They are the pioneers who open up the new country for immigration from their homeland. The immigration from South Asia to Norway contains many such stories (for heroic stories of early Indian Sikh immigrants to Norway, see Jacobsen 2011b). The immigration from Sri Lanka also started with a heroic story: the story of Anthony Rajendram, who many Tamiḻs in Norway remember with affection. Although a Roman Catholic, he was an important figure in the history of the establishment of Hinduism in Norway because he initiated a migration of Tamiḻs from Sri Lanka to Norway of which the large majority were Hindus (for the Tamiḻ Roman Catholics in Norway, see Jacobsen 2008b and 2009b). Rajendram left Jaffna in Sri Lanka on a motorcycle in June 1955 and reached London in September the same year. His purpose for travelling to Europe was to be able to develop skills so he could help improving the conditions of the fishermen in the Jaffna area. In England he soon met two Norwegian students who told him that if he was interested in learning about fisheries he should go to Norway. He arrived in the city of Bergen, Norway in 1956. He was schooled in fishery training in the city of Vardø; he attended the Technical College of Fisheries in Aukra; he attended the Boat Builders' School in Saltdal and the Technical College of Canning in Stavanger. He established cooperation with Norwegians interested in his development project, and returned several times to Sri Lanka, where he established projects, the most important being Cey-Nor. Cey-Nor became important in the early phase of Tamiḻ immigration to Norway. The first fifty Tamiḻs arriving in Norway were all friends and relatives of Rajendram (Jacobsen 2008b). Migration increased during the 1970s, and after the civil war in Sri Lanka broke out in 1983 the number of persons arriving increased. Many of the early arrivals were Roman Catholics, but the great majority of Sri Lankan Tamiḻs in Norway are Hindus. Rajendram became a hero for many Tamiḻs in Norway since he had opened up the country for Tamiḻ migration. It was as if he had had a premonition of the suffering the Tamiḻs in Sri Lanka would have to endure later because of the war. The majority of the Tamiḻs entered Norway by means of educational institutions, the fishing industry and as refugees in the 1980s and 1990s.

In 2012 between fifteen and twenty thousand Hindus lived in Norway. Similar to many other countries in continental Europe such as Germany, Denmark and Switzerland, the majority of Hindus are Tamiḻs from Sri Lanka, with a minority of Hindus coming from north India. In many European countries the majority of persons of Indian origin are Sikhs and belong to the religion of Sikhism (Jacobsen & Myrvold 2011, Jacobsen & Myrvold 2012). There are therefore two main Hindu populations in Norway: Tamiḻ Hindus from Sri Lanka (around 70 per cent of the Hindu population) and Indian Hindus from north India (around 30 per cent). They organize separate temples and maintain quite different ritual and aesthetic traditions, as well as a different liturgical calendar. There are also a few hundred Hindus from Nepal and Malaysia in Norway, but they have not established separate Hindu organizations or temples, probably because of size, pattern of settlement and immigration history.

Regional identities

The Hindus visiting the Sivasubramaniyar Alayam are aware that they are part of a larger tradition, but that their tradition is a regional one and different from the practices of the north Indian Hindus. Hinduism is a mosaic of regional traditions. Hindu religious practices are often local and connected to place and are often associated with specific divinities and sacred narratives. As witnessed in Norway, the term Hinduism does not refer to a homogeneous religious tradition but is the name of a plurality of activities and related but heterogeneous traditions. Hinduism is polycentric and decentering (Jacobsen 2013a). Two regional Hindu traditions dominate Hinduism in Norway – the Tami<u>l</u> Hindu traditions of Sri Lanka and the north Indian Hindu traditions of the Greater Punjab. Some Gujaratis also arrived from East Africa in early 1970s. The many differences of these traditions, in temple styles, rituals, language and history, and the close connection between religion and ethnicity, mean that Tami<u>l</u> Hindus do not in general attend the north Indian temples in Norway, and the north Indian Hindus do not in general attend Tami<u>l</u> Hindu temples. Most aspects of the Tami<u>l</u> temples appear foreign to the north Indians and vice versa. Also, the Sri Lankan Tami<u>l</u>s are Śaivaites, mostly following the Śaiva Siddhānta theology and temple rituals. Most of the north Indian Hindus in Norway are Vaiṣṇavas, worshippers of Kṛṣṇa/Rādhā and Rāma/Sītā. The goddess Durgā (Tami<u>l</u>: Thurkai Amma<u>n</u>) and the god Gaṇeśa (Tami<u>l</u>: Piḷḷaiyār, Vināyakar) are important for both groups, but the iconography as well as the worship rituals differ. In addition, it should be noted that even though a temple usually has a main god, a plurality of gods are worshipped in separate shrines in each of the main Hindu temples in Norway, and therefore usually one does not need to go to other temples for the worship of a specific god or goddess. In the diaspora the temple also functions as a place to be reminded of the home culture, and to confirm ethnic and linguistic identity. The temple attracts those who identify with the regional tradition of the temple. The result of all this in the Hindu diaspora in Norway is that there are two clearly segregated forms of Hinduism, the Sri Lankan Tami<u>l</u> Hinduism and the north Indian Hinduism. There is hardly any interaction between the two Hindu regional traditions. In this essay we mainly discuss the Sri Lankan Tami<u>l</u> Hindu tradition.

Establishing sacred time and liturgical calendar

It has been observed among the Hindus living outside of South Asia that the diaspora situation often leads to an increased focus on the temple as a cultural centre and as a place to confirm identity in a minority situation. Nevertheless, what distinguishes a temple from a cultural centre is religion, and the main function of the temple is performance of rituals. The increased importance of the temple (for some) often motivates the diaspora group to invest much time and effort in the ritual activity of the temple and this often results in a busy liturgical calendar. Space has received much attention in the study of religion in diaspora, as diaspora as a concept is about space. However, implied in the reference to space in the diaspora is also a reference to the concept of "time". Diaspora is about the past and the present. It is about moving away from the past and creating a future, and at the same time it is about preserving the traditions of the past. It is about memory, nostalgia and things frozen in time. In the context of religion, it is also about establishing a sacred time in which the religious culture is preserved, transferred or recreated. In the concept of diaspora, therefore, space and time are closely related. Sacred space and sacred time are to a large degree interdependent: to establish a sacred place, sacred time has to be incorporated. Rituals create, and depend on, sacred time. Establishment of religion in the diaspora includes creation of sacred time and it is the system of sacred time of the country of origin that is attempted to be recreated in the diaspora.

Sacred time does not create itself; it is produced by the hard work of the community. To produce sacred time for a diaspora community, many elements are needed: buildings, rituals, ritual artefacts, ritual experts, devotees, ornaments, sacred sounds (music), etc. All these things were absent to the first Hindus in Norway. They did not even know the dates of the main festivals. Some of them attended Roman Catholic churches just to have an experience of sacred time and space. Sacred time became institutionalized among the Hindus in Norway when wives and children arrived from India and Sri Lanka, first in homes and rented buildings, but during the 1990s and the following decade the Hindus of Norway invested money, know-how and work to institutionalize sacred time in permanent buildings, and priests from India and Sri Lanka were hired to serve the gods and goddesses in the temples. The memory of the sacred time in the country of origin put a demand on the organizers of the new temples to recreate the atmosphere of the old places. The devotees expect religious traditions to remind them of the past.

The sacred time of the diaspora group sets the group apart. In the minority situation, the liturgical calendar confirms a separate religious identity. In Norway, as in many other nations, there are several annual ritual cycles overlapping. For the Hindu diaspora groups, the Hindu liturgical calendars come in addition to the ritual cycles of the host society in which they usually participate to some degree, especially if they have children in school age. In Norway, as in most pluralistic societies, there is an annual cycle of ritualizing events of the nation, such as the national Independence Day, the writing of the constitution, or days associated with war. There is also the annual cycle of the rituals of Lutheranism, the religion allied with the state. The annual cycle of public holidays and the weekly cycle of Sunday holidays, are determined by national history and the religion of Christianity. In addition, the Hindu communities have their own religious calendars. Their sacred days are not public holidays, and events are sometimes celebrated twice, once in the temple at the same time that it is celebrated in the country of origin, with only a few participants in the temple, and once during the weekend. In addition, a number of Hindus settled in Norway continue to celebrate a few days of the annual national ritual cycle of India and Tamiḻ Īlam.

Before the opening of the Sivasubramaniyar Alayam in Oslo, ritual activity in the form of festivals took place in school buildings rented specifically for each festival, but the establishment of the temple represented an opportunity for growth in the number of festivals included in the ritual calendar and in the number of ritual elements included in each festival. The growth in ritual activity was a function both of the ambitions of the leadership of the temple and the expectations and desires of the devotees. The liturgical calendar of the temple Sivasubramaniyar Alayam is found in a document written in Tamiḻ and is available in the temple. The Tamiḻs have from their earliest period in Norway organized language schools for children and youth to preserve their language, and Tamiḻ and Sanskrit are the languages most used in the temple. The festival calendar is constructed on the basis of the ***pañcāṅga*** (see below). The temple committee selects from the *pañcāṅga* the festivals, which they want to celebrate and identifies the dates on which to celebrate them. In Sri Lanka most temples are devoted to one god or goddess. They therefore often limit their festival celebrations mainly to that one god. In Norway, Sivasubramaniyar Alayam was the first Tamiḻ Hindu temple and therefore included all the major gods. The temple therefore has to celebrate the festivals of a large number of gods and goddesses. It is of course impossible to celebrate every festival and a selection has had to be made. Nevertheless, the perception of the temple committee has been that the temple has a busier ritual calendar than any temple in Sri Lanka and that there is more work involved with this temple than with any temple in Sri Lanka. The manager of the temple has compared the busy ritual schedule of the temple to the ritual schedule of the famous Naṭarāja temple in Cidambaram.[4] In addition to the celebrations of the gods, the devotees also expect there to be celebrations in the temple at some of the major Norwegian festival days such as the New Year.

The *pañcāṅga* is based on a rather complicated system of division of time. Its name means "five parts". These five parts are, first, the days of the week (*vāra*); second, stages of the moon's waxing and waning (*tithi*); third, a further division of the stages of the moon's waxing and waning (*karaṇa*; a *karaṇa* is half a *tithi*); fourth, regions in the sky through which the moon passes during its orbit (*nakṣatra*); and fifth, a division of the year in which the joint longitude motion of the sun and moon is 13.2 degrees (*yoga*; there are 27 yogas in the year). *Vāra*, *tithi* and *nakṣatra* are most important for the temple calendar. The *pañcāṅga* calendar is based on the movements of the sun and the moon. The movement of the sun produces a daily cycle of sacred hours, a weekly calendar and a yearly cycle. The movement of the moon produces *tithis*, stages of the moon's waxing and waning and *nakṣatras*, regions in the sky through which the moon passes during its orbit. In the ritual calendar, the agricultural cycle also plays a role. Sivasubramaniyar Alayam has made pragmatic use of the *pañcāṅga*. The management and the priests have taken from the *pañcāṅga* what they thought was necessary and what they believed the congregation needed and would enjoy. They discarded that which was too impractical. This is also common in Sri Lanka, where there is no uniform pattern of worship: "The mode of worship conducted at the temples of Murukan and the rituals and practices associated with worship are by no means of a uniform pattern and they exhibit great variety" (Cartman 1957: 90).

In the Murukan̠ temples in India, there is a daily schedule of sacred hours, called ***tirukkālam***. In south India most Śaiva temples schedule according to some version of *tirukkālam*. A few temples perform nine *pūjās* every day, most temples observe six *pūjās*: dawn, early morning, mid-morning, noon, early evening, and late night, but in small temples only four are performed (Clothey 1982). According to *tirukkālam* dawn is very important, especially between 4am and 6am, and likewise the middle period of the day, the zenith, "which represents the culmination of the ritual performance of the daytime" (Clothey 1982: 159). Diaspora often means that the population is spread around a large area. Few people lived in the vicinity of the temple. The demands of job and school have made it almost impossible to visit the temple in the morning or at midday. The opening hours of the Sivasubramaniyar Alayam have been adapted to the work schedule. The temple has been open for visitors on a daily basis in the evening (5.30pm to 8pm), convenient for a visit after work. The daily cycle has also been determined by the weekly cycle. On Tuesdays and Fridays it is open also from 12pm to 2pm. On Fridays it closes at 9.30pm instead of 8pm as this is the main *pūjā* day of the week, as is the pattern in Sri Lanka (introduced by the influential Aramuka Navalar; see Jacobsen 2013b). Tuesday is the day especially associated with Murukan̠. It is the day of the planet Mars. The association of Murukan̠ with the planet Mars rests on two factors: both are associated with the colour red and with military force. In some other countries in the Western Hemisphere, Tamil̠ temples have Sunday as their main ritual day (Younger 2002), but Sivasubramaniyar Alayam in Oslo has kept the tradition of Sri Lanka.

The moon cycle is also central in the worship of Murukan̠. Murukan̠ was born on Amavāsya, the new moon day. He is connected to the *kārrtika nakṣatra*. This is due to Murukan̠s association with the six Kṛttika maidens who suckled the infant god Murukan̠. There are twelve *kārttika nakṣatras* in a year and these days are sacred to him. There are therefore twelve special *abhiṣeka* for Murukan̠. These come in addition to *the skanda ṣaṣṭi*. *Skanda ṣaṣṭi* is observed every month on the day there is a conjunction of the moon with the *kārttika nakṣatra*.

Conclusion

The recreation of Sri Lankan Tamil̲ Hindu sacred space and time characterizes the ritual traditions of Hinduism in Norway. The temples function primarily as places of worship but they also function as centres of Tamil̲ culture. They are "little Jaffnas", with everyone speaking the Tamil̲ language, wearing Tamil̲ dress, eating Tamil̲ food, and with Tamil̲ music, Tamil̲ rituals, and illustrate the close relationship between religion and culture. How to distinguish, or even whether it is possible to distinguish, between the culture of Tamil̲ Sri Lanka and the religion of Hinduism has become an important challenge for the new generations of Tamil̲ Sri Lankan Hindus who have been born in Norway.

Notes

1. Researchers writing about Hindu temples in the diaspora often exaggerate the significance of the temples for the community by not mentioning that the Hindus often have a number of other organizations. The researchers seem to suggest that the temples are the only organizations that provide opportunities for Hindu community building. However, in the case of Norway, and I assume in many other countries as well, the Tamil̲s have founded many organizations in addition to temples to preserve their culture and traditions, and to support the Tamil̲ population. There is therefore a need, in the scholarship on Hinduism in the diaspora, for a balanced view of the role of temples and for the inclusion of secular organizations in the analysis of the Hindu communities. There are a large number of Tamil̲ organizations in Norway and only a few are religious. In fact, while most of the organizations founded by Tamil̲s in Norway are not religious, they fulfil many of the functions of fostering, integrating, and solidifying a sense of community usually ascribed to religion. These secular organizations offer a number of social services, such as Tamil̲ language instruction for children, Norwegian language for the parents, help with school homework, football tournaments and other sports activities such as yoga and karate, classes in physical and mental health, counselling services for parents and children, cultural events offering people the opportunity to perform in front of a large audience, music and dance, activities for elders such as trips, birthday parties for members, and information about health issues, youth clubs and so on (see Jacobsen 2010).
2. The cycle of rituals is not static, and new rituals are added when needed.
3. In Sri Lanka some temple festivals last 20 days or more, and the temple management may expand the period of the festival.
4. Interview with author, 2010.

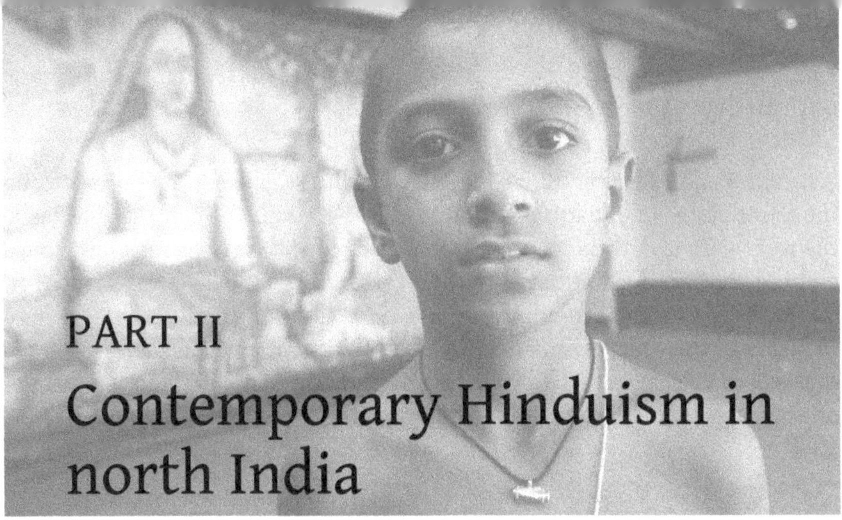

PART II
Contemporary Hinduism in north India

North India is geographically vast and culturally very diverse. Although Nepal is politically not part of India, culturally it shares abundantly with the north Indian milieu. We therefore chose to include Nepal as part of our north Indian illustration of Hinduism. Nepal, Rajasthan, Sindh, Gujarat, Maharashtra, central India and Orissa – all represent very different aspects of Hinduism. Popular festivals of Indra in Nepal, devotional asceticism in Rajasthan, Hindu–Sikh syncretism in Sindh, and devotional expressions that are intrinsically tied to ethnicity and caste from the west to the east of India – the Hindu expressions are as vibrant and colourful as they offer deeper insight into the daily lives of Hindus in these regions.

In Chapter 6, on Hinduism in Nepal, Michael Baltutis develops the narrative around the Indrajatra festival and as he takes us through the celebration, along the way he introduces us to the popular religion in Nepal, the political connections with the festival and the central role it played in the perpetuation of royalty in Nepal. In Chapter 7, Antoinette E. DeNapoli takes us through Rajasthan, where she immerses us in a unique female ascetic tradition that is so different from the conventionally familiar male dominant ascetic tradition of Brāhmanical Hinduism. In the following chapter Steven W. Ramey introduces us to Sindhi Hindus. In his depiction of Sindhi Hinduism, he shows how the expression of their form of Hinduism is intrinsically connected to Sikhism and Sufism, and their unique affinity to Jhule Lal, who remains the central focus of their devotion. In Chapter 9, Hanna H. Kim narrates the significance of the temple, the community and the role of spiritual leadership in the Swaminarayan community in Gujarat. Revolving around the story of a college freshman, she narrates the significance of daily rituals for this community. Staying in western India, in Chapter 10 we are introduced to the devotional community of **Vallabhācārya** tradition in Gujarat. Here ***sevā*** as service to God acquires a unique meaning for the community in the form of formal ritual.

Moving to west-central India, we are introduced by Jon Keune (Chapter 11) to the **Vārkarīs** in Maharashtra state. He takes us through the pilgrimage to their sacred place called Viṭṭhal temple in the town of Pandharpur. Moving into central India, in Chapter 12 we are introduced to the Hindu practices among the lower castes in Chhattisgarh and Madhya Pradesh. The centrality of caste, the role of Rāma devotional traditions associated with various regional groups and the continued significance of older forms of tribal beliefs, all shape Hinduism in this region. From here we move to west Bengal, in the east, where Abhishek Ghosh (Chapter 13) introduces us to Vaiṣṇavism in Bengal, also known as Gauḍīya Vaiṣṇavism. The expression of devotion particularly in the form of offering and receiving food offered to Kṛṣṇa is emphasized in his narrative.

6. The Indrajatra festival of Kathmandu, Nepal

Michael Baltutis

Getting to the forest was more difficult than we had imagined. Prevented from riding on the military truck with the royal army, we boarded one rickety government bus that took us to the city of Bhaktapur and a second that dropped us off at the village of Nala, about twelve miles east of Kathmandu. We travelled the final uphill mile by foot, on the unpaved roads of the Kathmandu Valley's steep eastern hills that the September monsoon rains had turned to mud. Our destination was the temple of the forest's protective goddess, Ban Devi, where we were greeted with a traditional Nepalese meal of potatoes, lentils, beaten rice, and cold boiled meat. The festival of Indra officially began early this morning at the royal palace in Kathmandu, and the festival's forest rituals were set to begin in a matter of hours. The focus of these rituals is a single tree that we are to cut down, transform into a ritual pole, and pull twenty miles by hand to the city of Kathmandu for the celebration of the nearly two-week long Indrajatra festival.[1]

Hindu texts have described the details and goals of the Indra festival for some two thousand years, but this chapter is concerned only with the festival's contemporary performance in and around the city of Kathmandu, the capital city of modern Nepal, and the only place where the rites of the classical festival are still performed. These classical rites also had as their focus the pole that is brought from the forest. One of these texts, the Sanskrit epic Mahābhārata, contains the festival's myth of origin that depicts the relationship between Indra, the ancient Hindu king of the gods, and Vasu, the king of the city of Chedi. In this story, Vasu desires to renounce the world and his responsibilities as king and to live in a monastery. Indra gives the pole to Vasu as a reminder that his primary duties as a king are to protect his people, generate wealth, and uphold dharma. Indra further states that glory, wealth, and victory come to any kingdom where the festival is celebrated. This royal meaning of the festival was also important in contemporary Nepal – often referred to as "the only Hindu kingdom in the world" – at least until recently, when a popular nationwide movement (in 2006) and a special assembly of parliament (in 2008) put an end to the Nepalese monarchy. Despite the end of the Nepalese monarchy, the Indrajatra continues to be performed as one of the most important festivals in Kathmandu. This continued performance reflects the festival's flexibility and points to the fact that the festival is about more than just the classical rites surrounding kingship and power. The festival in Kathmandu today contains many ritual and narrative elements that had no place in the classical texts but that now provide some of the festival's most memorable moments. The festival's thematic emphasis on the remembrance and worship of the city's ancestors in a festival previously known for its focus on the victorious king provides a clear example of a Hindu festival that has adapted its classical and textual meanings to a local concern. Due to its long history and the attention it has received in both orthodox Hindu texts and popular practice, the Indrajatra provides a unique perspective on the history of Hinduism in south Asia.

The plan of this chapter is as follows. In the first section, I will provide a larger Hindu context for the ritual diversity that underlies the Nepalese Indrajatra; I will refer to this diversity, common to both annual festivals and daily worship, as "popular religion". In the second section, I will categorize the festival's many myths, rituals, and deities according to the three movements of Indra's pole through the Kathmandu Valley. Finally, I will conclude with a brief analysis of the underlying unity and themes contained within the contemporary Nepalese festival.

Popular religion in Nepal

Religion in Nepal's Kathmandu Valley is largely free from an emphasis on doctrine or orthodoxy. Thus, despite the celebration of the Indra festival by Nepal's kings according to ancient ritual texts from India, the people celebrating on the streets of Kathmandu today operate according to a more flexible standard. This flexibility includes the participation of Buddhist priests in an otherwise Hindu festival, the daily presence of goddesses dancing in public squares throughout the city, and nightly ritual battles between masked demons and local drunken youths. Though the Indian texts do not allow for Buddhist priests, dancing goddesses, or fighting demons, it is this local dimension of the festival that has the greatest impact on participants and scholars alike.

Kathmandu's Indra festival is not just one of the many festivals celebrated throughout the year, but it is said to be the "root festival" of the city of Kathmandu.[2] As the city's most important festival, it incorporates a wide variety of rituals, places, and people; these religious elements are made to serve a larger goal: the festival's twin emphases on the unifying presence of royalty within the boundaries of an urban kingdom and the living presence of the city's ancestors among their urban descendants. The festival reinforces these two themes through its repeated emphasis on three specific ritual and symbolic elements, common in many other Hindu religious performances: public street processions, the presence of many gods and goddesses, and the use of aniconic images of these deities, objects that have no distinct human form.

Among the many different styles of ritual practised within the Indra festival (temple worship, veneration of images, chanting of Sanskrit *mantras*, etc.), the most visible of these types is the public street procession. The street procession reverses standard and daily modes of worship; rather than worshippers leaving their homes and visiting a temple on their way to school or work, the procession brings a god or goddess out of their temple and into the public space of the city. As deities are publicly paraded through the streets of the city, they attract the attention of people from a cross-section of society, regardless of age, gender, caste, or ethnicity, bringing people together in communities that they might not experience in everyday life.

The Indra festival contains a number of such processions. In the three processions of Indra's pole, we will see how the festival's central object marks out the different parts of the city as well as the beginning, high point, and end of the festival. In the chariot procession of the goddess Kumārī, we see a single goddess, preceded by her two divine brothers (Gaṇeṣa and Bhairav) and followed by hundreds of people on foot. In the **upākū** procession on the festival's first evening, however, we most clearly see the festival's local emphasis on rites to the ancestors.[3] In the *upākū*, families of the recently deceased walk the borders of Kathmandu in a three-hour long funeral procession that visits the shrines of the eight Mother Goddesses, who in the form of aniconic stones protect the city's borders. Though the procession of Kumārī begins and ends at the royal palace in the centre of the city, the *upākū* focuses on the homes of the families of the deceased. This difference in ritual geography – palace versus home – reminds us of the festival's two primary points of emphasis on the king and the city's ancestors.

Though the festival is named after Indra, he is by no means the only deity worshipped during the festival. Indra is referred to as "king of the gods" in the oldest Sanskrit texts, and he is worshipped for the rain he provides to farmers and for the victories he provides to kings. But this festival is now one of the few times that Indra is ever worshipped; the majority of the festival's rituals actually focus on other gods and goddesses. Due to the festival's status as Kathmandu's root festival, the Indrajatra puts on display all of the city's most important deities, bringing together these gods and goddesses and their temples and shrines during the festival's many urban processions.

Three deities feature prominently in Indra's festival. Kumārī, a goddess worshipped by both Hindus and Buddhists, lives year-round in a building immediately outside the palace. Her status as the "living goddess" refers to her unique appearance; rather than taking the form of a statue or aniconic image, she takes the form of a four- to eight-year old girl. During the Indrajatra, this royal Kumārī – there are approximately a dozen other Kumārī throughout the Kathmandu Valley – is placed on a large wooden chariot and taken on three processions through the upper, middle and lower parts of the city. Her chariot procession through the city's lower section occurs on the festival's third day, a day that marks the festival's high ritual moment when villagers from all over the Kathmandu Valley come into the city to take *darśana* of Kumārī and, until recently, of the King of Nepal, who makes his only festival appearance on this day.

The fierce god Bhairav is the divine king of the local Newar people, and his several large images are situated throughout the old city. A standing image of Black Bhairav nearly twelve feet tall is located one hundred feet north of the main gate of the palace; it is to this somewhat frightening image of Bhairav that people who are engaged in legal battles have traditionally made offerings. An eight-foot-tall golden-coloured mask of White Bhairav is affixed to the north wall of the palace about one hundred feet west of the main gate; this mask, invisible behind a heavy wooden screen for most of the year, is fully exposed only during the Indrajatra when the pipe placed in his mouth dispenses beer to the boisterous crowd that nightly gathers in front of him. And the temple of Blue Bhairav in the neighbourhood of Indra Chowk undergoes a transformation every year during the festival. A local myth explains the prominence of Bhairav during Indra's festival. One night, Bhairav came to a farmer in a dream and told him to go down to the confluence of the region's two rivers. Here on the riverbank, the farmer would find the head of Bhairav, who was recently killed in battle; the farmer was to carry this head from the river back to his own neighbourhood, where he was to ritually install and display this head every September. Thus, early in the morning on the festival's second day, priests from the temple of Blue Bhairav move his large mask from the temple's second story to a newly constructed street-level shrine. The construction of this new shrine, in addition to recalling the farmer's dream, functions like the street processions of Kumārī, providing people with the opportunity to view and access this important deity more directly.

Finally, the eight Mother Goddesses appear in different locations during the festival. In addition to the visits mourners make to their shrines on the city's borders during the *upākū* procession, eight short poles, cut from two additional trees obtained in the forest, are installed around Indra's large central pole. The texts refer to this installation as a ***maṇḍala***, a geometric array of powerful and aniconic objects that offers protection against social, political, and religious disorder. As these goddesses' border shrines protect against the potential danger of ancestors who have not safely reached heaven, their aniconic poles protect Indra and the king from equally dangerous external threats. These two sets of Mother Goddesses operate together in Kathmandu's root festival, protecting the city from external and internal threats, safeguarding both the kingdom and its living inhabitants.

The three movements of Indra's pole

Returning to the forest on the eastern ridge of the Valley, we see little more than a small village and an open-air shrine to Ban Devi. The forest's most important contents, of course, are the very trees that allow us to consider this plot of land a "forest" or, as it is referred to in Nepali language, a "jungle". For centuries, this royal forest has supplied the trees that have been cut down and used as ritual objects, installed throughout the neighbourhoods and royal squares of the cities of the Kathmandu Valley.

The rural location of this site is not coincidental, as forests have served as important locations in Hindu myths and rituals for millennia. Forests and jungles have been key sites for establishing the authority of Hindu kings. Both Sanskrit language epics (the Mahābhārata and the Rāmāyaṇa) tell the stories of kings who temporarily lose their right to rule and who are exiled to the wild forests outside of their urban kingdoms. In these forests, the kings battle dangerous demons and receive instruction from wise sages as they gradually regain the power necessary to reconquer their kingdoms and rule in eternal *dharma*. The Indrajatra is an annual festival whose purpose is similar to that of these epics; acquiring the pole from the jungle, transporting it to the city, and installing it outside the palace, the modern ritualists reinforce the victory of Nepal's king over the dangerous elements of his kingdom, a victory symbolized by the presence of this natural object in Kathmandu's urban landscape.

After our meal inside Ban Devi's shrine, we walked the short distance back to the tree, where a small crowd was slowly gathering to witness the Cutting of the Tree, the second of the festival's six official events.[4] Due to the late hour, this cutting was more ritual than real; rather than felling the entire tree, a few Sanskrit *mantras* were chanted, a few quick chops were made with an axe brought from a nearby village, and a goat brought from Kathmandu was sacrificed and its blood sprayed against the base of the tree. The function of this sacrifice, according to the texts, is to evict the ghosts and demons living in the tree; it is only once these demonic obstacles are removed that the tree can become an object fit for a king. Just as the goat's throat was cut and its head removed, the monsoon rains returned in full force; attending members of the military fired two shots marking the end of the rite, and the ritualists quickly packed up their belongings, returned to the military vehicle that brought them from the city, and left us alone standing on a muddy downhill path in the pouring rain.

After a forty-minute trudge through rice fields and village streams lit by nothing more than the small candles a few of us brought (my flashlight was powered by local knock-off batteries and was, therefore, useless), we arrived at the farmhouse of Mr Kumar, whose family provided us with another full meal of potatoes, lentils, beaten rice and cold boiled meat ... and home-brewed rice beer! Exhausted, we slept on the floor in our damp clothes, and I fought off insects flying through the open wooden windows for most of the night. The next morning, we returned to the forest riding in the back of a tractor and arrived as the work of felling the trees had just begun.

The first movement

One of the most time-consuming parts of the entire festival, this first movement requires nearly twenty-four working hours stretched out over three days, and the brute labour of nearly one hundred men of the oil-pressing *Manandhar* caste. The *Manandhars* are responsible for nearly all of the work in the forest, work that begins with chopping down the three trees, one for Indra and two for the eight Mother Goddesses. This work took no more than an hour, with all of the hard labour still to come. Once they cleared the branches off of Indra's tree, the workers cut a ridge around the circumference of the tip of the pole and secured two heavy ropes – ropes that would be used in all three of the pole's movements – inside this ridge. The next few hours of work would be the most difficult of the entire festival: with the pole laying on its side and the ropes attached, two teams of men working in short bursts strained to pull the pole across nearly one hundred yards of the forest's very uneven ground. Once they finally reached the outer limits of the village and of the forest, their next goal was simply to make it as far as possible down the Valley's hills before sundown, when they would drop the pole and return home for the night. Work began again the following morning and continued for nearly fifteen straight hours, concluding when they finally reached the eastern border of Kathmandu, almost three full days after the festival's opening rites began.

This first movement highlights workmanlike efficiency over the performance of devotional rituals: no images of gods were present, no Sanskrit *mantras* were chanted, and no acts of *pūjā* were performed. This lack of explicit Hindu ritual allowed, however, for behaviour not expected in a religious festival, behaviour that explicitly violated and transgressed standard south Asian norms of public decency. Simply put, there were many occasions during our three days on the road when workers engaged in behaviour that we – and they – would describe as violent and obscene. The difficulties of pulling a forty-foot pole down the centre of one of the nation's busiest highways in rush-hour traffic posed problems not only for the workers, but also for the many drivers who simply wanted to go home after a hard day's work. These difficulties frequently bubbled over into verbal sparring and occasionally into fistfights between workers and drivers, as the fish-tailing pole obstructed buses, rammed into cars, and knocked over motorcycles. In addition to the violence wrought by the pole – it caused fights, broke the limbs of several workers, and was run into by a motorcyclist at full speed – it was also the source of much obscenity.

Workers used call and response work chants to keep the men on the two ropes pulling in time with one another. The first, most general, and most-used work chant consisted of a call of "*Hos ṭe*", called either by one of the supervisors or by the team on the first rope, with the men on the second rope responding, "*Haiṅ se*", the Nepali equivalent of "Heave ho!". This chant is used in various other festivals as well, especially those that involve the difficult pulling of large heavy objects, often old chariots with large wooden wheels carrying images of the gods and their human caretakers. While pulling the pole through midday traffic on the Arniko Highway, the call and response changed to various but related Nepali-language complaints regarding the task at hand: "*hāmī lāī gāhro*" ("This is really difficult for us!"), and "*tānne gāhro*" ("The pulling is really difficult!").

As the afternoon wore on, the chants became a bit more playful and bawdy, a tone not inappropriate for a festival to Indra. There are many stories of Indra's affairs with women, and one of the Nepalese words for Indra's pole is *lingo*, a word that often refers to the sexual member of the male god Śiva. Several times during the day, in response to the usual call of "*Hos ṭe*", the response changed to the slighly naughty "*lyāse*" ("young girl"), evoking the smirks of many onlookers. More memorable, however, was the call of "*Indra ko lāḍo*" and its response, "*Kathmandu chiryo*". These chants assert, in an extraordinarily obscene way, that Indra is on his way to sexually and violently penetrate the city of Kathmandu.

Though somewhat shocking, this use of obscenity in a Hindu ritual is not uncommon. Though not used in polite company or during auspicious rituals, it is frequently used in rituals involving death and the ancestors. The funeral celebration of someone who has lived a full life, for example, might be met with similar transgressive behaviour, where young male mourners will perform sexually explicit dances "in a burlesque of female sexuality".[5] The use of sexuality in the Indra festival suggests a similar focus on death and the ancestors, again challenging the festival's classical focus on kingship and power.

The second movement

The work of pulling the pole from the jungle to the city ended in the early hours of the following morning, the third day. After arriving at the eastern border of Kathmandu, the weary workers dropped the pole near the curb of the street that leads through the old city's busiest markets, two gunshots marking the end of their work. The pole's second movement, much more like a religious procession than the first, will begin in a few days, when the pole is taken up by another group of *Manandhar* men, who will pull it to the palace, a half-mile to the southwest. A flute- and drum-playing marching band from the palace had arrived, people began to gather in the market around the pole, and the motorcycles that had been parked against the pole were cleared away, all in anticipation of the Entrance into the City, the festival's third official event (see Figure 6.1). Once the ropes that were used for the first movement were reattached, people came forward to perform *pūjā* to the pole, making offerings of rice, coins, fruit, and incense; these offerings replicated the daily *pūjās* that officials from the palace had performed.

The workers pulled the pole on a line through the city's oldest markets, passing by three of the most popular temples in the city – including that of Blue Bhairav – and finally to the palace where it would be raised four days later. The

Figure 6.1 A man performs *pūjā* to Indra's pole before it is pulled to the palace (photo by author).

workers stopped only when they got tired (they were apparently unaware of the three day journey the previous workers had endured!), working in short bursts that allowed people to offer *pūjā* and to take *prasād* in the form of the flowers and red powder ***kuṃkuṃ*** that palace officials had earlier placed on the pole.

Upon entering the royal square, the workers pulled the pole straight up to the hole in which it would be raised. Once the pole was laid down, many of the people who had gathered came forward to touch their heads to it, make offerings of coins, and take *kuṃkuṃ* from the base and tip in order to place a red ***ṭīkā*** on their foreheads. Finally, mirroring the four gunshots fired at the start of the day's pulling, four more shots were fired, signalling the end of the day's work and the end of the festival's preparations. The pole would lie there for four days; then, amid a throng of people, the pole would be raised and, according to most people, the festival would officially begin.

The following four days would see a number of additional rituals that would prepare the city for the festival's central eight days. Whereas *Manandhars* performed all of the rituals involving the pole, it is *Jyapus* (farmers) who perform most of these other rituals. Over the next few days, *Jyapus* in the central city neighbourhood of Kilagal perform the Devi Pyakha, the "Dance of the Goddess". This dance, which will be performed during each of Kumārī's three chariot

Figure 6.2 Captive image of Indra inside the courtyard of Kathmandu's royal palace (photo by author).

processions as well, depicts the battle between divine good and demonic evil. In this dance, the *daitya* (demon) challenges a succession of masked gods and goddesses; it is only with the presence of Kumārī – here in the form of a masked goddess and not a young girl – that the *daitya* is finally vanquished. Interestingly, among the many deities who are called upon to challenge the demon, Indra is not present.

Indra's presence is felt, however, with five of his images that will be placed on tall platforms throughout the city – one in each of five local neighbourhoods – with a sixth placed on a low table inside the palace. Despite the diversity of the ways that Hindu and Buddhist deities are depicted – their postures, the objects they carry, and the colours used to decorate them – the form that these images of Indra take is quite unique. Indra sits in a *yogic* lotus position with his arms fully extended at his sides (Figure 6.2). No other deities are ever depicted in this posture, and this image appears to have no connection to the classical Indian festival. Most Nepalese people connect this image to the festival's primary local myth, a myth connected to the agriculture of the Valley, to crime and punishment, and to the ritual remembrance of the dead.

Despite Indra's traditional identity as a royal god, this myth portrays Indra slightly differently. One version of the story is as follows.

> Indra's mother, residing with her son in heaven, wanted to perform a religious ritual that required a flower from the parijat tree, a tree that does not grow in heaven. To assist his mother and to obtain the flower, Indra travelled on his elephant down to earth. He arrived at Kilagal Tol and wandered around the city before arriving at Maru Tol, the centre of Kathmandu and the site of the city's largest garden. In Maru Tol, Indra approached a *Jyapu* gardener who was tending the garden. Without telling the gardener of his identity or of the purpose of his visit, Indra requested a single parijat flower for his mother's ritual, and the gardener freely gave it to him. The gardener's *Jyapu* neighbours, however, did not recognize this "outsider" and seized the "thief", bound him with strong ropes, and placed him in a cage high above the ground. While Indra sat bound and arrested, his elephant continued wandering around Kilagal, becoming increasingly worried about his master's disappearance. Indra's mother, also worried, descended to Kathmandu in the guise of a white-faced demoness along with a group of fierce Bhairavs. The Bhairavs engaged in combat with Indra's captors, liberated Indra from his prison, and raised wooden poles as a symbol of their victory. In return for her son's freedom, Indra's mother promised to furnish the valley with the fog and dew necessary for productive agriculture and to take those captors of Indra who were killed in battle to heaven with her when she departed.

This story provides both an explanation of the unique form of Indra's captive images, as well as the logic behind Indra's Newar title of *khun dyah* (thief god).

More significantly, however, this story also provides connections to, and explanations of, many of the festival's rituals. Three such examples follow. Immediately following Kumārī's first procession on the festival's third day, a *Jyapu* man wearing the white mask of Indra's mother will lead a procession of white-clad mourners through the streets of the city. This group is a subset of those mourners who walked the *upākū* procession to the shrines of the Mother Goddesses on the festival's first day. Later that night, an even smaller portion of this group will go on a much longer procession to Indra's Lake near a temple outside the Valley's western hills; it is from this place that Indra's mother will depart to heaven with the souls of the deceased. The story's reference to Indra's elephant refers to a second example, that of Pulu Kisi ("the Death Mat Elephant"). Throughout the evenings of the festival, two young boys from Kilagal will play the role of Indra's wandering elephant by manipulating a six-foot-long white-masked elephant. Dancing through the city streets with a group of torch-wielding and instrument-playing neighbours, they will extract donations of money, snacks and rice beer from local residents and shop owners. The name of Indra's elephant not only tells us what the elephant is physically made of – the woven mats that individuals are placed on immediately before their death

– but it also connects the story and the movements of the elephant to the festival's underlying theme of death and the ancestors. Finally, the raising of victory poles by the victorious Bhairavs points not only to the festival presence of the city's multiple Bhairavs and to Indra's pole dragged by hand from the forest but also to the many poles that individual families will raise in their own neighbourhoods in honour of their ancestors.

Though small and typically local crowds had gathered for many of the earlier rituals, the raising of the pole drew one of the festival's largest crowds; it would be surpassed in attendance only by Kumārī's first procession two days later. Thousands of people gathered in the palace square, on the steps of its many temples, and on the balconies of nearby buildings to watch the event. Consistent with the absence of modern technology in dragging Indra's pole by hand from the forest to the city, *Manandhars* used only pairs of variously sized bamboo poles tied together to raise Indra's pole into place. With these V-shaped tools, with ropes that guided the pole into place, and with the accompaniment of multiple brass and drum corps, they completed this difficult and dangerous work in about twenty minutes. Once the military bands announced the successful raising, hundreds of people walked clockwise around the pole, and many peeled off a small piece of the pole, shredded from its long forest journey, as a powerful memento.

The work of installing the complete *maṇḍala* is far from over, however, though few people stay to watch. The eight small mother goddess poles trucked in from the jungle are now raised by hand around the central pole, the bamboo poles that were used to raise Indra's pole into place are attached horizontally in order to make a cage, and a small image of Indra seated atop his elephant is placed in a metal cage at the base of the pole. The *maṇḍala* garners relatively little attention; at best, individuals strolling by will throw a coin towards it, touch their hands to their heads and hearts in a respectful gesture, or simply admire the size of this annual forty-foot intrusion into the landscape of the palace square. During the festival, the city's attention is drawn to other and more mobile objects and people, especially to Kumārī's three urban processions. The *maṇḍala*'s ultimate significance is that it provides a miniature replica of the city of Kathmandu. With one single male surrounded by eight protective females, this *maṇḍala* draws our attention back to the *upākū* funeral procession at the festival's beginning: the earlier worship of the eight Mother Goddesses – the protectors of the city's borders, of its king, of his palace, and of the royal god Bhairav – recurs immediately outside the palace, bringing the Hindu king together with the city's ancestors.

The third movement

The pole remains in place for eight days. Most of the festivities occur during the festival's first four days and draw to a close on the fourth day, the full moon day of September. On the festival's final day, Kumārī makes a final chariot journey through the city's centre, her chariot resting for a long time at the *Jyapu* neighbourhood of Kilagal Tol. Once she returns to the palace square, she is visited by Nepal's head of state, whom she blesses. Later that night, a group of *Manandhars* returns to the square to loudly and violently destroy the *maṇḍala*, signaling the end of the festival. The mother goddess poles are uprooted and brazenly tossed to the side, the boards that were used to wedge the main pole in place are removed and similarly thrown aside, and in the dim light of the evening, the Indra pole is shoved from behind and comes crashing to the ground. The scene quickly devolves into a mock ritual battle where the main weapons are the bunches of straw used as the pole's landing pad. During the monsoon rains, these bunches become soaked clumps that pack quite a punch, and many participants come prepared for the fight wearing motorcycle helmets.

The third movement of the pole begins once the battle wears itself out. The ropes are reattached to the head of the pole, and the difficult job of manoeuvring the pole out from between the two adjacent temples begins. Once the workers negotiate the pole onto the square's main paved road, the work goes rather quickly. The pole, accompanied by armed guards from various branches of the military, has as its destination the northern bank of the Bagmati River on Kathmandu's southern border.

This final event is referred to by the Sanskrit term ***visarjan***, the pole's disposal. The most famous example of a *visarjan* is in the Durgā festival, where images of the goddess Durgā are brought into homes throughout India, and are tossed into the sea at the end of the festival. Made of unfired clay, these images will rapidly dissolve and provide the material for next year's images. Similarly, as a ritual object that has served its purpose and is no longer needed, the Indra pole will be brought to the Bagmati River at the end of the festival. Rather than being fully submerged as the images of Durgā are, it is merely abandoned on the marshy bank of the river where it can be reused.

Several different stories tell of what happens to the pole after its *visarjan*, and all of these stories contain elements that associate the pole's disposal with a funeral rite. In one story, members of the low sweeper (Pode) caste take the pole and sell it to the *Manandhars* who use the wood in their oil-presses. In another story, Pode purchase the wood from the *Manandhars* and use it for their building projects. In yet another story, the pole is cut into pieces and used to feed the cremation fire at the Bhairav temple near the cremation grounds on the riverbank, the same place to which the farmer was mythically directed to find Bhairav's severed head. In the two stories regarding the sweepers, we see members of a low caste repeating their ritual role as beggars at Hindu funerals, where they take up the cast-off clothing and goods of the deceased. By allowing themselves to receive the "deceased" pole, they reassert their inferior social position in relation to the *Manandhars*, to the king, and to the city of Kathmandu. And in the final story, we see the wood of the pole used in the service of Bhairav, a royal deity whose riverside temple is closely associated with the cremation of the deceased.

Conclusion

In the Indian ritual texts that describe the festival, the king is commanded *not* to attend the *visarjan*. Were he to see the disposal of the pole, an object that annually represents both king and kingdom, he would die within six months. In contemporary Nepal, this is no longer a problem. Even before Nepal's parliament acted to formally end the nation's nearly 240-year-old monarchy in 2008, they had voted into law several bills that stripped the king of his real and ceremonial powers. The cumulative effect of these bills on the Indra festival was the king's absence at the 2007 festival, where the royal Kumārī gave her blessing not to the king but to the secular prime minister, who had recently been appointed the head of state. In 2008, the Communist Party of Nepal–Maoist (CPN-M) was elected by the Nepalese people as the ruling party, with the head of the CPN-M becoming the nation's new prime minister. Though explicitly atheist, the Maoist prime minister or a member of his cabinet has replaced the Hindu king as the ceremonial leader of the Indra festival; in this office, he will both bestow blessings on his people as well as receive blessings from the royal Kumārī. This radical change in leadership, together with the continued performance of the festival, speaks to the festival's flexibility. The Indra festival of Kathmandu continues to support the classical rites of Indian royalty directed to an ancient deity and his representative of dharma on earth, while at the same time focusing on a robust and local set of funerary rites that annually celebrates the presence of the city's ancestors. Even though the nation of Nepal is now without a monarchy and a king to celebrate, the residents of Kathmandu will continue to celebrate the Indrajatra, a festival directed as much to the local divine king Bhairav, the royal Kumārī, and the city's ancestors as it is to the ancient Hindu god Indra and the political leader of Nepal.

Acknowledgements

This chapter was supported by a Fulbright grant (2005–6). Thanks to my Hindu Tradition class at the University of Wisconsin, Oshkosh, for their productive and critical comments that made this chapter so much better. Throughout the chapter, the "we" that I refer to denotes myself and my research assistant, Manoj Srestha.

Notes

1. Most Nepalis say that the festival lasts eight days, from the time the pole is raised until the time it is taken down. Nepal's court astrologer is responsible for determining the times (Nepali *sāīt*) of the festival's six main events, and these events occur over the course of eighteen days, beginning ten days before the pole is raised and ending with its lowering eight days later.
2. "Root festival" is the translation of the Nepali *mūl jātrā*.
3. The Newar word *upākū* means "boundary" and is the short form of the procession's formal name, *upākū vanīgu*, "to walk the boundary".

4. The first of these events, the Forest Journey, took place earlier in the morning immediately outside the royal palace in Kathmandu, as court officials began their travels to the forest.
5. Cf. Parry (1994: 155, 179). Axel Michaels (2008: 116) describes the Nepalese Trishuljatra, in which children play the role of corpses by being ritually "impaled" on spears that emerge from portable goddess shrines. He writes of the bearers of these shrines: "they start to shout loudly, in the direction of Kathmandu. The words they utter at this point are so vulgar and pornographic that we must limit ourselves here to the mere hint that they are aimed principally at Kathmandu's girls."

7. Vernacular Hinduism in Rajasthan

Antoinette E. DeNapoli

This world is like a carnival. Love brings us here. If there is love, we will meet again. (Ganga Giri Maharaj, 28 March 2005)

It is difficult to meet [God].
How will I meet my beloved?

We cannot climb the land
Where it is impossible to climb.

The many alleyways leading to the bathing pools are wet.
We cannot stand where it is slippery.

It is difficult to meet God.
How will I meet my beloved?

I am stepping carefully on the ground.
I cannot stand still, lest I fall down.

The path to God is narrow,
Like sand that you cannot grasp.

It is difficult to meet God.
How will I meet my beloved?

I met my real guru who showed me the path to God.
So, make a guru.

Lord Kabīr has said that God, the giver of liberation, will embrace you.

It is difficult to meet God.
How will I meet my beloved?[1] (Kabīr, *c.*15th century)

This chapter introduces the reader to a female expression of vernacular asceticism as it is lived, interpreted, practised and performed by the ascetics (*sādhus*) of Rajasthan with whom I worked. Ganga Giri, whose words I quoted in the epigraph to this chapter, sang this devotional song (*bhajan*) in a religious group (***satsang***) consisting of Hindu householders (women and men of various ages and socio-economic backgrounds), me (an American anthropologist) and my unmarried adult "sister" Shamta of the Brāhmin family with whom I lived between 2004 and 2006 in the north Indian state of Rajasthan. Shamta Didi[2] often accompanied me on my visits to Ganga Giri's hermitage, which was located a kilometre from our colony. At the time of this *bhajan satsang* (2005), Ganga Giri was ninety years old and full of energy. She told me that singing *bhajans*, along with telling the stories of legendary saints and reciting the ***Bhagavad Gītā***, a classical Hindu sacred text, gives her "power [*shakti*]" and connects her to God.

Ganga Giri is a female Hindu ascetic who has left behind or renounced normative societal roles, rituals, institutions and expectations, such as marriage, family, domesticity and householding, in order to devote herself permanently to the worship of God (***bhagvān***). Female ascetics like Ganga Giri, and the other *sādhus*' whose lives and practices I describe and analyse in this chapter, are unusual women in India. They are viewed in their society and communities with a mixture of reverence and suspicion, for the reason that their lives illustrate a radically different life alternative to the more dominant roles of wife and mother. Of the different terms commonly used to describe Indian ascetics I have chosen the word "*sādhu*", which is a generic and a grammatically gendered masculine term for ascetics, because the female *sādhus* referred to themselves as *sādhus* ("we are *sādhus*" was a common statement in their discourses), and did not use the word *sadhvi*, the grammatically feminine equivalent of *sādhu*, in their individual self-descriptions. Apart from their use of the term *sādhu*, the female *sādhus* referred to other female ascetics like themselves by characterizing them as "***mātā**-ram*", "***mātājī***", and/or "*mai-ram*" (literally "mother of God"). The use of these terms enabled the *sādhus* to make explicit an ascetic's feminine gender, which they also made clear to me and others by saying "lady *sādhu*".

I conducted two years of ethnographic field research with Hindu female *sādhus* in the region of Mewar, in southwest Rajasthan. I limited my fieldwork in Mewar to the districts of Udaipur, Rajsamand and Jaisamand. Most of the *sādhus* resided in Udaipur, either in the city or in the surrounding rural villages. These *sādhus* have taken formal initiation as ascetics into the Dashanami (literally "ten names") or the Natha traditions, which represent two Śaiva forms of asceticism, meaning that ascetics in these pan-Indian traditions perceive the god Śiva as their patron deity and exemplar for their way of life. Śaiva *sādhus* distinguish themselves in their styles of dress from other (non-Śaiva) ascetics by wearing the distinctive colours of ***bhagwā*** (literally "God's colour"), namely ochre, orange or salmon. Clothing for females tends to consist of a blouse and long piece of fabric wrapped around the waist that typically falls below the ankles. Those with whom I worked frequently wore oversized blouses and shapeless

Figure 7.1 Female Hindu ascetics in Rajasthan. Ganga Giri is standing in the middle of the group (photo by author).

skirts that cloak overt signs of female form from (male) view. Other distinguishing symbols are the three horizontal white (or ash-coloured) lines drawn on the forehead with a huge, red dot in the middle, and the dark brown beads made from the seed of a **rudraksha** tree that *sādhus* use for their daily religious practices (prayer, meditation, chanting), and which they wear as a bracelet or necklace.

Ascetics in India, including Śaiva *sādhus*, comprise a socially and religiously heterogeneous group of people, priorities, and practices. Because Hindu asceticism has no central (or single) authority or spiritual head, system of belief, or institutional (decision-making) body, it historically has been a religious-cultural phenomenon that displays a wide range of diversity in its constituency, conceptualization and practice.[3] And yet, as represented in Sanskrit textual sources (**Samnyāsa Upaniṣads**, Laws of Manu, Bhagavad Gītā), and academic and popular discourse, asceticism also illustrates an underlying constant that undercuts such diversity. Specifically, it is often represented as a radical and negative way of life.[4] Its predominant values are detachment, individualism, isolation, wandering and severe penance (***tapas***). Asceticism in its outlook and practices typically involves severing oneself emotionally, psychologically, ritually and/or physically from the world (*sansar* in Hindi; the Sanskrit term is ***saṃsāra***) and its everyday concerns. Classical texts exhort ascetics, presumed to be men, to escape from the world, a purported place of chaos and suffering, to the wilderness – a forest, jungle or the mountains, a place of solitude and peace. Similarly, renunciant rhetoric is filled with vivid images that portray the world as an abode of illusion, ignorance and impermanence. In this orthodox framework, the world symbolizes an endless cycle of birth, death and rebirth. Ascetics therefore intentionally seek to break away from such a world completely, because they desire total liberation (*moksh*; the Sanskrit equivalent is ***mokṣa***) from both existence and rebirth. A traditional saying among Śaiva ascetics is that liberated beings never return to the world. In many of their classical texts and official renunciant discourse *moksh*, the ultimate ascetic goal, is more than becoming liberated from a suffering world; it is also experiencing oneself as God, and *vice versa*.

The *sādhus* I met, however, experience and express asceticism differently from the ways that it is predominantly imagined, constructed and interpreted in the classical Sanskrit texts and academic scholarship. The kind of asceticism that these *sādhus* articulate in their practices identifies a phenomenon that is communal and positive, rather than individualistic and negative. While the *sādhus* speak about the importance of detachment and solitude for their asceticism ("there is no asceticism without detachment" is a common statement in their discourses), their practices underscore other equally significant (ascetic) values to those that are found in the classical texts. In the vernacular expression illustrated here, the *sādhus* "perform" what asceticism means to them by means of their singing, storytelling and textual practices.[5] These practices characterize what I have termed a "rhetoric of renunciation" and offer a powerful cultural resource with which the *sādhus* performatively construct a model of devotional asceticism as an alternative to the more dominant text-based (male) model of asceticism discussed earlier.

The *sādhus'* asceticism model emphasizes in particular the interrelated values of relationship, devotion (*bhakti*), and love, which are seen as supreme ascetic goals and collectively articulated at the level of everyday renunciant performance in Rajasthan through the motif of "meeting God". Moreover, the values the *sādhus* highlight in their performances, in fellowship contexts they characterized as *satsang*, serve as the basis for their experiences of asceticism in other social–religious contexts, so that their devotional asceticism is created and expressed in their everyday relationships with each other, their devotees, and the divine beyond *satsang*. Furthermore, those (spiritual) relationships created beyond *satsang* promote the *sādhus'* idea of asceticism as a relational path of devotion and love as it is performed in their everyday *satsangs* with householders and other *sādhus*. We look once again to the *bhajan* above, which Ganga Giri performed, in order to understand how these *sādhus* live their devotional asceticism.

A carnival of love: performing devotional asceticism in everyday *satsangs*

By virtue of its radical nature, asceticism is a difficult path to God. Recall Ganga Giri's *bhajan* at the beginning of this chapter: significantly, it emphasizes the experience of God as "difficult". In a repertoire that includes over 350 *bhajans*, this song is one of Ganga Giri's favourites. She sings it for me and the householders, and other *sādhus* who regularly visit her at her hermitage in Udaipur city. As the signature line in the text suggests, this *bhajan* is attributed to the legendary poet-saint Kabīr (probably around the fifteenth century), who, as several scholars have explained, was born a Muslim into a community of (low-caste) weavers. Kabīr's poetry, and its predominant motifs, metaphors and messages, have come to identify more globally the immensely popular *bhakti* or devotional movements of medieval north India. The *bhakti* poetry of this period commonly challenged the religious boundaries of Hinduism and Islam (Kabīr's poems in particular often question the validity of these categories and their perceived fixed boundaries) and the hierarchical social classification of the Indian caste system. More importantly, though, it was composed in the vernacular (north) Indian tongues, such as Hindi, Rajasthani, Gujarati, and Bhojpuri. Not surprisingly, north Indian *bhakti* poetry depicts in its content idioms and symbols that are characteristic of certain linguistic–cultural contexts and milieus. By composing their poetry in a vernacular medium rather than the more official text-based Sanskrit language for example, *bhakti* poets like Kabīr made their religious teachings available to everyone, regardless of one's gender, religion, caste, class or education. As Ganga Giri often says, "anyone can sing *bhajans*", because, as her statement indicates, they are seen to express the everyday language of the people, instead of the educated elite, and thus communicate a language not of the head but of the heart.

The language of the Kabīr *bhajan* that Ganga Giri sang at the March 2005 *bhajan satsang* consists of a mixed Rajasthani-Hindi vernacular. The devotional language this *bhajan* uses to describe the experience of God is significant for understanding the ways the Rajasthani *sādhus* experience, understand, interpret, and practice devotional asceticism. For instance, in its message that "it is difficult to meet God", a theme highlighted both in its refrain as well as its vivid poetic imagery, the *bhajan* emphasizes the idea of "meeting God" as illustrative of a devotional experience of the divine. Meeting God constitutes the ultimate religious experience, the highest goal, for the devotee (***bhakt***), who in theory could be anyone, *sādhu* or householder, man or woman, adult or child, Indian or American. Whenever Ganga Giri sings this *bhajan* and others that express a similar message, she adds that "as long as there is love in the heart, anyone can meet God". Ganga Giri's statement accordingly indexes her egalitarian view of *bhajans* as the *lingua franca* of the commoner.

Like Ganga Giri, most of the *sādhus* consider the devotional experience of "meeting God" as the goal of *sādhus*' ascetic practices. To meet God is to know God, and to know God is to experience supreme peace of mind. The *sādhus* frequently employ the language of *moksh* in their individual descriptions of this experience. Their view provides an alternative understanding to the more dominant (text-based) notion of *moksh* as an experience of becoming God. The language of becoming God in particular implies that no distinction of identity, of self and other, exists between devotee and deity; the self of the devotee recognizes the divine other as one's own God-Self. This experience characterizes the idea of non-duality (***advait***). The (devotional) language of meeting God, however, suggests that the separate identities of devotee and deity, of self and other, remain during such an encounter.

Meeting God, therefore, for these *sādhus* describes an experience of duality (***dvait***) that not only enables but also fuels devotees' devotion to God. The concept of *bhakti* itself connotes duality, because devotion requires an object of love and worship. It does not happen alone. In fact, *bhakti* is derived from a verbal root that means "to share", "to love", "to worship", and/or "to adore" another. The Indian *bhakti* poet-saints of ancient south India (around the sixth to ninth centuries), and the medieval poets of Bengal (around the fifteenth to seventeenth centuries) often described *bhakti* as an experience or feeling in which the devotee "savors" (*ras*) the flavour of God. Without a sense of God as separate and distinct from oneself, the experience of being in a relationship with the divine, and the concomitant feelings of love, respect and devotion that emerge on the basis of such a relationship, would not occur. Notice too that our *bhajan* imagines God in the most intimate of ways, as a devotee's lover (*piya*). Ganga Giri begins her discourses on the nature of God by saying, "Who is God? God is our beloved". In connection with the *bhajan satsang* that occurred at her hermitage

Figure 7.2 Female *Sadhus* holding *satsang* with devotees in a village. Ganga Giri is on the far left (photo by M. Singh by permission).

on 28 March 2005, after making her statement on God as one's beloved, Ganga Giri sang the Kabīr *bhajan* to explain further her understanding of God as relational, which she has also described in other contexts as love. In her words, "love is what God is". In imagining God as one's lover the *bhajan* constructs the idea of meeting God as relational. Also, by singing this *bhajan*, Ganga Giri performs her experience of meeting God as a relationship of love.

In their discourses, the *sādhus* invoke the image of a carnival as a metaphor for the relationships of love that humans create in the world of existence. The Hindi word they use is ***melā***, a noun that is derived from the verb ***milnā***, which means "to meet".[6] In popular discourse *melā* functions as a polyvalent term; it has various significations depending on the conversational contexts in which it is used. It can signify a secular event (a festival in celebration of India's independence; a wedding ceremony; the opening of a new business) and/or a religious event, such as, in the case of Indian ascetics, the Kumbh Melā (literally "the festival of the water-pot"). This carnival, which occurs every three years in a rotating twelve-year cycle at a site that is astrologically determined to be auspicious, constitutes the largest gathering of *sādhus* on Earth. Here, *sādhus* from all over India and beyond meet one another and the householders who seek their blessings, and publicly display their knowledge, bodies, skills, constituencies and so forth, for a month, the duration of the festival (Hausner 2007). The *melā* provides *sādhus* not only a powerful social experience but also a transcendent experience of "meeting God" in the world (*ibid.*: 127–47). Meeting God is symbolically performed by the different *sādhu* organizations (*akharas*) through the ritual act of bathing in the confluence of three sacred rivers: the Ganga, Jamuna and (mythical) Saraswati. The meanings that individual *sādhus* attribute to this prestigious bathing experience will depend on the individual *sādhu* having the experience. No single description captures what the experience of meeting God means to all *sādhus* at the Kumbh Melā. While not all *melā* are of the size, nature, duration, or expense of the Kumbh, they enable *sādhus* to constitute relationships with each other and with the divine.

When Ganga Giri speaks about a *melā* she explains that "we all took birth in this world to participate in the carnival of life. We came to make a *melā*." An implicit tension underlies this metaphor. Whether in the religious or secular sense of the term, a carnival involves meeting others as well as parting from them. At a carnival people come together, albeit temporarily, and then part ways. A carnival, then, consists of people's comings (hellos) and goings (goodbyes) in the cycle of life. The Hindu idea of reincarnation (*sansar*) suggested by the concept of the cycle of life (*sansar*) further supports the applicability of the carnival metaphor: birth provides a passageway to meet in the world of existence – meetings which, regardless of one's form as human, animal or other, result from one's actions or *karm* (Sanskrit: ***karma***) from previous births – and death offers a way out of that existence. Until it experiences *moksh*, liberation from the cycle of rebirth and material existence, the soul will continue to come and go from this carnival of life *and* death.

In the official discourse of most classical texts on asceticism *sansar* is synonymous with death; birth is synonymous with death. What makes *moksh* so desirable among ascetics, according to the dominant textual model, is that it constitutes a veritable escape from death. Not only that, both textual discourse and religious studies scholarship on asceticism frequently represent the ritual of initiation into asceticism, which signifies perhaps one of the most symbolically formative events in an ascetic's life, as a type of (ritual–social) death: the *sādhu* "dies" to his or her previous social identity, as well as to the world, forever (Bharati [1961] 2006). In this framework, the parting dimension of the carnival metaphor carries the most currency for *sādhus*.

The female *sādhus* recognize this inherent tension in their use of the idea of a carnival as a metaphor for human relationships of love in the world. They understand that human bonds of love are ultimately impermanent. A *bhajan* Ganga Giri sings in *satsang* articulates this idea:

> Take the name of God [*alakh*] daily;
> Take the name of the Master [*sahib*] daily.
>
> Chant God's name and remember its qualities.
>
> Let's go together to God's country,
> To the Master's country,
> To the country of someone well-known.
>
> Take the name of God [*alakh*] daily;
> Take the name of the Master [*sahib*] daily.
>
> Hey brother, those who chant God's name
> They neither die nor are they reborn
> Nor do they get old.
> Put on the ochre robes and renounce the world!
>
> Hey brother, those who chant God's name
> They neither die nor are they reborn
> Nor do they get old.
>
> The mind is like a wild horse;
> Tie a saddle on it and control that unruly horse
> With a great desire in your heart.
>
> Put on the ochre robes and renounce the world!
>
> And let's go together to God's country,
> To the Master's country,
> To the country of someone well known. (Traditional)

On the day Ganga Giri sang this *bhajan* she added as commentary, "this [world] is not our country at all. We belong with God. Remember God and you will reach God's country. We come from there only; that's our home. Everyone's home is the same. We all return to the same home." Like Ganga Giri, many of the *sādhus* with whom I worked would agree that the *melā* of life, and the bonds constituted therein, do not last forever. Because those ties are of this world rather than God's they are by their very nature transitory. At the same time, these *sādhus* would also agree that while worldly relationships may be impermanent, they are not, however, illusory; their inherently transitory nature does not diminish their value and transformative potential. The love people experience by virtue of the relationships they create with human, non-human, and divine others in their everyday social and religious lives are, indeed, real, meaningful, and powerful. "Meeting is good, but parting is painful", Ganga Giri teaches householders and other *sādhus* in her discourses. Her words echo a poignant message found in the Rajasthani oral epic about the "reluctant" renouncer-king Gopi Chand (Gold 1989).[7] In a moving scene from the text, Gopi Chand, who has renounced the world, begs for alms at his sister's palace, Queen Champa De. She refuses to recognize that the simple *sādhu* begging at her door is her brother, the once illustrious king, Gopi Chand. Her maidservant convinces the queen of the *sādhu*'s identity, and says: "Meeting is good and parting is bad and the snare of illusion's net is always very bad. It is a carnival of parting" (*ibid.*: 783).

In her analysis of the epic, anthropologist of religion Ann Grodzins Gold uses Gopi Chand's example to make transparent the often opaque emotional worlds of *sādhus* who leave everything behind (*ibid.*). Her analysis offers thoughtful and compelling insights into the ways vernacular asceticism is lived "on the ground". Every moment of parting from his loved ones (mother, wife, son, and sister) causes Gopi Chand enormous emotional pain and regret.[8] His reactions illustrate the difficulties of the ascetic life, for *sādhus* as well as for their families. While Ganga Giri did not discuss this epic in the context of her statement (she has, however, narrated parts of the story to me in other contexts), its impact on her interpretation of asceticism is evident. It hurts to separate from loved ones, regardless of the circumstances, good or bad. And the pain of separation is no less palpable or real for *sādhus* than it is for householders.

Although, as Ganga Giri says, we have to remember that everyone must eventually leave the *melā* of life and return "home" to God, the human emotions of love and loss are real; the friendships and connections we create together in this world are precious. Life is precious. Consider the words of another female *sādhu*, Tulsi Giri: "There are only two truths in this world: we are born and we die. Everything that we do in between [those moments] matters. God put us on this earth to love. That is why God sent me here. Otherwise what else are we to do?"

In everyday *satsangs*, *sādhus* like Ganga Giri and Tulsi Giri, and others I met, create relationships of love and devotion with each other, their devotees, and the divine through their performances of asceticism. By emphasizing the motif of meeting God and the corollary values of relationship and love, these *sādhus* construct asceticism not as a death (to the world or to those living in it), but rather as a celebration of life in the world, of meeting and loving others in the *melā* of existence. To this extent, *satsang* becomes a *bhakti* context for the construction of community, a celebration of meeting others "with love". The term *melā* in fact connotes the idea of a celebration. The *satsangs* in which the *sādhus* perform their songs and stories with householders and other *sādhus* constitute in their practices celebrations of remembering and loving God together, and in doing that, loving one another as individual manifestations of God. To love others is to love God; to love God is to meet God. In her *satsangs* Ganga Giri reminds her audience that "we are all sitting together. This is a *melā*. We are different from each other only by bodies. We have come here to make a *melā*, because there is love. As long as there is love we will meet. I'm looking at you and you're looking at me; this is heaven [***vaikuṇṭha***]".

"Meeting is good": living devotional asceticism in everyday relationships

What is the relationship between the ways the *sādhus* perform asceticism in and outside of *satsang*? How do the values they speak about in *satsang* relate or not to their other everyday social practices? In this section I will show the continuities between the *sādhus*' lived asceticism in *satsang* and elsewhere. Their performances and the values they underscore by these means become the basis for their experiences of asceticism in other social contexts, such as in the bazaar; in bus or car rides to the city and/or village; in householder homes; in other *sādhus*' hermitages; and so forth. Also, the ways the *sādhus* live their path in such contexts in turn promote and shape the meanings of asceticism that they construct in their *satsang* performances.

The *sādhus* construct their ascetic worlds together, in *satsang* and elsewhere. The relationships and/or friendships that emerge from their daily meetings with each other frame their experiences of asceticism as a relational *bhakti* path. They learn from one another through their conversations and practices what constitutes asceticism, how to be an ascetic, and how to live their way of life. As with other ways of being and acting in the world, asceticism, too, involves daily processes of socialization. Ascetic relationships, therefore, play a significant role in defining the *sādhus*' perspectives, priorities, and identities. To this extent, *sādhu–sādhu* relationships offer an important, yet underexplored interpretive lens with which to think about female ascetics' everyday lives beyond *satsang*, and that such seemingly ordinary moments enable them to meet God in the world by meeting each other "with love".[9] Perhaps no better example illustrates the continuities between the *sādhus*' experiences of devotional asceticism in and outside of *satsang* than the (unfortunate) news of a *sādhu*'s failing health. When news that a *sādhu* is ill reaches someone in this *sādhu* community (*samāj*), regardless of the distance that separates them, the *sādhus* come together to help one another through their life circumstances.

An ordinary day in the extraordinary life of Rajasthani female *sādhus*

"If she would only sing the name of God [Rām-Rām] intensely", said Ganga Giri, "Jnan Nath would become healthy [again]. She need only take God's name with love, you have to take it with love, and within three minutes she would improve." Ganga Giri, Tulsi Giri, Manvendra (a householder devotee) and I were sitting in Ganga Giri's hermitage when she commented on the declining health of her friend. An orange fan placed near Ganga Giri's cot was running; it barely cooled the small, hot, crowded space on that June afternoon. Jnan Nath, a then eighty-eight-year-old female *sādhu* who lived a kilometre or so from Ganga Giri's hermitage, had been ill for some time. She visited Ganga Giri at her hermitage three weeks ago complaining of fatigue, nausea and sharp stomach pains, and had not returned since. Ganga Giri and Tulsi Giri both went to see Jnan Nath a week before, but there had not been any improvement in her condition.

"She's forgotten [God]. That's the problem. She doesn't sing anymore. Within three minutes, just three minutes, she would improve, but she's forgotten. What to do?" Ganga Giri repeated. "She won't improve if she doesn't sing", Ganga Giri emphasized again. She seemed frustrated, possibly by Jnan Nath's persistent stomach illness and/or by the fact that she had stopped singing *bhajans*. "What power does this body have? My power comes from my *bhajans*", Ganga Giri explained, trying to make sense of her world and the diseases that impinged on it.

Ganga Giri and the other (male and female) *sādhus* who lived near her hermitage in Udaipur city received frequent updates on Jnan Nath, because Jnan Nath's eldest daughter came regularly now to Ganga Giri's place and spoke about her mother's illness, which the doctors did not diagnose in any specific way. Most of the *sādhus* in the area knew that Jnan Nath was ill and that her condition was worsening with each passing day. Six female *sādhus* lived within a few kilometres of each other near the beautiful Lake Fateh Sagar in Udaipur city. Tulsi Giri lived the furthest distance away from the city. Because of Jnan Nath's declining health, she came daily to Udaipur by means of cheap public transportation, stopping first at Ganga Giri's and then continuing her journey to Jnan Nath's. Like Tulsi Giri, many of the female *sādhus* began frequenting Ganga Giri's hermitage to inquire about Jnan Nath and/or to share the news that they had about her condition. Ganga Giri and Jnan Nath were especially close. Only two years separated them in age. In the personal life narratives that she has told me, Ganga Giri mentioned several times that she and Jnan Nath became ascetics at approximately the same time. On one occasion she narrated one of these stories in Jnan Nath's presence. After Ganga Giri finished her narrative, Jnan Nath added, "She asked me, 'hey, you want to become a *sādhu* and live with me?' I said sure, why not? I had nothing else to do." Both *sādhus* and I laughed heartifuly at her statement. Today, though, Ganga Giri remembered her friend with growing concern. "She won't sing! That's the problem", Ganga Giri reiterated. She was noticeably worried. So, when Manvendra offered to drive our small group to Jnan Nath's place we all packed into his black hatchback Hyundai Santro and headed to the other side of the lake where she lived.

Outside of the joint family compound where Jnan Nath stayed with her daughter, her son-in-law, their children and grandchildren, we could hear her moaning in pain. She was surrounded by family, mostly women and children, and some women from the neighbourhood. Jnan Nath's family resided in a neighbourhood consisting primarily of people from a brick-laying caste. Jnan Nath, too, came from this caste. Five generations of her family lived in that compound, a detail Jnan Nath proudly announced in our first meeting four years earlier in 2001. In her visits to Ganga Giri's place, Jnan Nath occasionally brought along her five-year-old great-grandson, Manu.

The relationship that Jnan Nath has maintained with her family since the time that she took initiation into asceticism almost half a century ago is not unusual for these *sādhus*. Many of the ones I met have continued to maintain strong bonds with their families. Whether their kin visits them at their *āśrams* or temples, or whether the *sādhus* visit their householding kin in the cities and villages throughout Rajasthan, the connections that tie them to their families, and vice versa, remain intact. What has changed, however, is the ways these relationships are conceptualized. Most of the *sādhus* described these kinds of bonds in terms of a *guru* and disciple (***chelā***) relationship. They saw family members as their disciples; and their families (at least those who had accepted the *sādhu's* decision to renounce) regarded them as accomplished religious teachers, and served them with devotion and love. One *sādhu's* son left his job in Bombay to help his mother manage her *āśram* in Udaipur. When I asked him why he left everything for his mother, the son responded: "she is no longer my mother; she is my guru. I am serving my guru." Today he, his wife and their three young children permanently reside with their *guru* at her *āśram*. Here, the son and his wife serve as the chief priest and priestess of the *āśram*-temple in their *guru*'s absence. Like most of the *sādhus*, Jnan Nath, too, meets her family. These days, though, her illness has forced her to live in the immediate family compound. Otherwise Jnan Nath normally resides in the small Bholenath (Śiva) temple that she had built forty or so years ago on an empty plot of land situated directly across from the family compound.

As we made our way through the steel gates that led into the compound's front courtyard Ganga Giri called out "O Jnan Nath!" several times. The crowd greeted the *sādhus*, Manvendra, and me respectfully. None of them looked surprised by our unannounced visit. Immediately, Ganga Giri turned to me and said, "Take out your tape recorder." Tulsi Giri repeated her words. With my recorder in her hands, Ganga Giri walked over to Jnan Nath, who was lying on several blankets on the concrete floor, and placed it carefully near her mouth. "Sing", said Ganga Giri. "Take the name of God. Come on. Take the name of God [Rāmnām]." Ganga Giri began to chant Rāmnām, the same divine name that both of the *bhajans* discussed earlier say to chant. Slowly Jnan Nath, too, started to chant Rāmnām, and within minutes everyone there, including the children and me, was chanting it. Despite her obvious physical pain, Jnan Nath kept on chanting God's name, encouraged (or perhaps intimidated) by Ganga Giri, who now held the recorder high in the air like a baton as if she were conducting an orchestra, with God as her audience. "Rām-rām, rām-rām, rām-rām." No one dared to break the steady chant, and possibly the healing that our recitation seemed to facilitate. As people continued to chant, Ganga Giri turned to me and said, "It's time to leave now." She, Tulsi Giri, Manvendra and I packed back into the Hyundai and headed once again to Ganga Giri's hermitage on the other side of the lake. As Manvendra drove away from Jnan Nath's family compound, and as Jnan Nath's daughter and several grandchildren came out to say goodbye, Ganga Giri seemed at peace and remarked, "Now she will remember."

About two months later, I was traveling in a public bus to Udaipur from Gogunda village, a small principality nearby, and the location where Maya Nath, another *sādhu* with whom I worked, lived. As the bus made its way toward my stop, which was a few blocks from my Brāhmin family's home in Shyalpura colony, I noticed an elderly *sādhu* dressed in faded orange clothes sitting in a tea stall in a bazaar that was on the busy main street. It was Jnan Nath. The bus was moving too quickly for me to get out and greet her properly. Nonetheless, because I was seated beside a window I was able to lean my head out and yell, "*Om Namo Narayan*", a typical Dashanami *sādhu* greeting. Just then, Jnan Nath lifted her right hand in a blessing gesture and responded vigorously, "*Om Namo Narayan*". I do not think she knew it was me who called out to her from the bus that day. But I do think that Ganga Giri's and Tulsi Giri's visit to Jnan Nath's compound on that hot June afternoon when she appeared to be lying at death's door, and the relationships of love that these *sādhus* have created over the years by singing *bhajans* together "with love" in *satsang* and elsewhere, had something to do with her seemingly miraculous recovery.

Reflections: vernacular asceticism in Rajasthan and the study of religion

This chapter has sought to provide a more complex and nuanced portrait of Hindu asceticism as Rajasthani female *sādhus* like Ganga Giri, Tulsi Giri, Jnan Nath and others live, understand, interpret, practise and perform it in and outside of *satsang*. When we turn our attention to the vernacular or everyday, local and/or regional expressions of asceticism – to asceticism as lived in India today – the multiplicity and diversity as well as hybridity of the lived realities of the individual practitioners become clearer, challenging some of our own academic assumptions and/or models about what asceticism is all about.[10] Contemporary lived practices may, indeed, tell us something important about how the ascetics of ancient, classical and pre-modern India conceptualized, experienced, and interpreted their lives. Moreover, lived practices can provide significant interpretive frameworks with which we may further reflect on whether, and to what extent, the models and representations of asceticism featured in the classical texts define, shape, and impact ascetics' lives on the ground. The *sādhus'* practices suggest the formative role of regional/local epic and song traditions in their conceptualizations, experiences and interpretations of asceticism. These texts offer cultural resources and (alternative) models of asceticism that are equally as relevant and significant as the more dominant ones prescribed in the classical texts. Ganga Giri, for instance, draws upon the traditions of Gopi Chand and the *bhakti*-poet saints as well as the Bhagavad Gītā in her construction of devotional asceticism. In my own work I try to discover the continuities and discontinuities between textual and vernacular asceticisms, the conceptual spaces where these discourses meet as well as part.

Sociologist of religion Meredith McGuire has said that

> When we focus on religion-as-lived, we discover that religion – rather than being a single entity – is made up of diverse, complex, and ever-changing mixtures of belief and practices, as well as relationships, experiences, and commitments ... religions are the products of considerable human creativity, cultural improvisation, and construction from diverse elements, only some of which were inherited from the same tradition. (McGuire 2008: 187)

The (female) expression of vernacular asceticism described and analysed in this chapter represents one discourse of how asceticism is lived in a postmodern, postcolonial, and globalizing India. But there are others. The recent work of Kalyani Devaki Menon (2009), Ramdas Lamb (2008), Sondra Hausner (2007), Maya Warrier (2005), Meena Khandelwal (2004), Anne Vallely (2002) and Wendy Sinclair-Brull (1997), for example, thoughtfully demonstrates the multiple discourses, persons, priorities, practices, and performances that constitute the rich, lived traditions of asceticisms in India. These ethnographies illuminate in different ways, and from different theoretical vantage points, the lives and practices of female and/or male *sādhus* in north and south India. No single practice or perspective describes the religious–social lives of the *sādhus* with whom these scholars lived and worked. Rather, consistency exists in – and because of – the multiplicities. Here lies the creativity, innovation, and transformative potentiality of asceticism, because it represents the locus of lived practice, an emergent space of individual agency and performativity. I quote the words of historian of religion Robert Orsi: "The religious person is the one acting on his or her world in the inherited, improvised, found, constructed idioms of his or her religious culture" (Orsi 2003: 173, as quoted in McGuire 2008). In the everyday lived practices of *sādhus*, asceticism shows not only multiple discourses but also discourses that coexist, complement, contradict, and/or compete with one another. My work with female Hindu ascetics in Rajasthan contributes another perspective to this engaging scholarly conversation.

Let us return once more to the practices through which the Rajasthani *sādhus* create and communicate their tradition of devotional asceticism. What have we learned about these *sādhus*' lives and worlds? They construct asceticism in *satsang* contexts of fellowship through means of their song, story and sacred text performances, in which, in connection with the *bhajans* that I have documented in this chapter, the *sādhus* emphasize the motif of "meeting God" and by extension the *bhakti* values of relationships and love. In the views of the *sādhus*, meeting God describes the ultimate ascetic goal, the *summum bonum* religious experience (*moksh*), where the individual identities of devotee and deity remain and, on the basis of such duality, each is able to savour the flavour of the other in that intimate encounter. Devotee meets deity as a lover meets her or his beloved. Theirs is a passionate embrace. In this model of asceticism, liberation happens not by becoming God (where duality dissolves), but rather by experiencing oneself in relationship with God. Liberation, therefore, constitutes a relational-devotional experience of love between devotee and deity. In the language of the second *bhajan* discussed earlier, when the devotee reaches God's country, the country of someone "well known", the embrace never ends. S/he remains in God's presence permanently. "This", to use Ganga Giri's words, "is heaven".

For the *sādhus*, though, heaven exists in this world. While asceticism involves both a ritual and a symbolic separation from the world of existence for ascetics (and hence from the everyday social relationships through which they once constituted their lives), these *sādhus* meet others in the world as a way to meet God. According to Ganga Giri, the world symbolizes a carnival of relationships of love: "we have come into this world to make a *melā*. We have met today because there was love [in the last birth]. As long as there is love, we will meet again." In these *sādhus*' practices the (spiritual) relationships they create with other *sādhus* and their disciples/devotees enable them to experience God in their everyday religious–social lives. Even the familial relationships that the *sādhus* ritually renounced at the time of their initiations into asceticism have become a powerful means for them to experience God in the world. These bonds, however, take on a new valence of *guru* and disciple. Mothers and sons (or daughters), sisters and brothers, daughters (or daughters-in-law) and parents, see one another as teacher and student, respectively. Relationships by blood (or marriage) are performatively, symbolically and discursively reconstituted in spiritual terms and idioms. In the beginning the transition from householder to *sādhu* is difficult, not only for the *sādhus* but also for the family members who often have trouble accepting the *sādhu*'s decision. Nonetheless, in my fieldwork experience family members eventually come around and construct themselves in their relationships with the *sādhus* as devotees and/or disciples. Indeed, for some families, having a *sādhu* in the family lineage represents an honour. Interestingly, in most cases, none of the *sādhus* talked about their husbands, many of whom had died by the time the women became *sādhus*, as disciples at all.[11]

Thus, devotional asceticism is performed/lived in the context of these relationships of love and devotion, in the commitments the *sādhus* and their devotees make together, in *satsang* and elsewhere. At the same time, relationships are bittersweet. The *sādhus* emphasize this idea in their practices. In the world of existence meeting implies parting and, as Ganga Giri poignantly reminds us, parting is painful. Relationships are impermanent. For this reason, the *sādhus* speak often and eloquently about the importance of detachment as an ascetic value, because they understand the nature of existence to be ultimately transitory. "Don't get attached to this world or to this body, because they don't last", Ganga Giri explains. Even so, the *sādhus* also understand that relationships teach us how to love and treat one another as manifestations of God. In Tulsi Giri's words: "God is right here, in the love we have for each other."

The relational values of love and devotion that the *sādhus* underscore in their performances of asceticism are not simply philosophical platitudes. On the contrary, their performances define and shape their experiences of this radical life path beyond *satsang*. The case of Jnan Nath's illness (and recovery) illustrates the continuities between *satsang* and other social–religious contexts in connection with asceticism as lived by these Rajasthani *sādhus*. This example shows, too, that the boundaries between such contexts are neither as fixed nor as static as they might appear to the analyst. *Satsang* can happen anywhere: in *āśram*, in a Hyundai hatchback, in the bazaar, in a joint family compound; and with anyone – householders, other *sādhus*, children or an American anthropologist. The transformative potential of these contexts, including *satsang*, has to do in part with the relationships and commitments that the *sādhus* and their devotees create together, everyday. In practice, the kind of asceticism that these *sādhus* perform in *satsang* and elsewhere distinguishes itself from the more dominant Sanskritic and academic representations. Their experiences, too, are what asceticism is all about in India.[12]

Notes

1. The Indian terms used in this chapter (e.g. *moksh*, *karm*, *sansar*) represent the Hindi (rather than Sanskritic) pronunciation of these terms. The *sādhus* used Hindi pronunciation for all these terms.
2. *Didi* is a generic Hindi kinship term and means elder "sister". My Brahman host family often called me Anita Didi, and some of the *sādhus* with whom I worked also referred to me in this intimate way (the majority of the *sādhus* called me "*bai*" or sister).
3. Meena Khandelwal (2004) emphasizes this point in her ethnography of female asceticism in north India.
4. In using the adjective "negative" here, I am referring to the predominant (textual) idea of asceticism as a path of negation (of the world) as described in the *Samnyasa Upaniṣads* and *Upaniṣads*.
5. "Performance" is a term used by scholars from many different disciplines in a variety of ways. In this chapter my use of the term "performance" follows the usage established by performance and folklore studies scholars as a "heightened" speech act (singing, storytelling, personal narrative performance, and textual recitation, for example) that serves as an interpretive frame with which to understand the implicit and/or explicit meanings of such speech acts. Not only that, each performance event not only creates and communicates meaning but also creates and shapes the ways participants experience and construct their everyday social-religious worlds.

6. *Melā* is originally a Sanskrit term, derived from the verbal root *mil*, and was later adopted in Hindi. Thanks to Ramdas Lamb for pointing this out. Personal communication 6 June 2010.
7. See also Gold's (1992) translation of the epic as it was performed by the bard Madhu Nath in the district of Ghatiyali, Rajasthan.
8. Gold (1989) explains that "Gopi Chand's renunciation is gradual and difficult, not sudden and total. Rather than disjunction, his tale poses continuities between ruling and ascetic states; rather than epitomizing resolution, he repeatedly succumbs to regret and grief." Gold adds that the scenes in which Gopi Chand separated from his family brought about emotional responses from the audience. These parts of the narrative were the most painful for the audience to watch.
9. Several scholars have discussed the spiritual relationships that *sādhus* create together in their day-to-day lives. These relationships are often conceived in terms of kinship relationships and hierarchies. See Hausner (2007: 127–47) and Gross (1992).
10. My observations about religion-as-lived have been influenced by the work of Meredith McGuire (2008), Joyce Burkhalter Flueckiger (2006), Robert Orsi (2005, 2003) and Leonard Primiano (1995).
11. All of the female *sādhus* with whom I worked are celibate practitioners. Most (but not all) ascetic traditions, including Śaiva forms, require the renunciation of sexual activity as a defining part of a *sādhu*'s spiritual discipline. Celibacy constitutes a bodily "performance" of ascetic identity and situates *sādhus* across religions and sects within a broader cultural discourse of power and sexuality (Flood 2004; Khandelwal 2004; O'Flaherty 1973). While most of the *sādhus* I met had been married, all of them considered celibacy as constitutive of their practice of asceticism.
12. I regret to inform my readers that Ganga Giri passed away on 26 July 2008. She was 93 years old. Her daughter has established Ganga Giri's resting place (***samādhi*** shrine) at the joint family compound in Kirit, a Brahman village located on the border between Rajasthan and Gujarat.

8. Sindhi Hindus

Steven W. Ramey

In a temple in Lucknow, India, hundreds of Sindhi Hindus brought silk cloths, some with gold brocade, others adorned with silver, to present as an offering to a book ceremonially being recited under a canopy. The offering of cloths was the climax of a week of special expressions of devotion celebrating the birthday of Guru Nanak (1469–1539), whose compositions form a significant portion of the text under the canopy, known as the **Ādi Granth** or Guru Granth Sāhib. This temple maintained the Guru Granth Sāhib as the central object of devotion, while a copy of the Bhagavad Gītā sat beside it, and various statues of deities like Gaṇeṣa, Durgā and Kṛṣṇa resided in shrines along the sides of the main worship area.

These expressions of devotion challenge understandings of these religions that are common both within and outside India. While the worshippers in this temple generally identified themselves as Hindus, the dominant understandings of religions in India recognize the Guru Granth Sāhib and Guru Nanak as central to Sikhism, and many people who identify as either Hindu or Sikh emphasize how Sikhism is a separate religion from Hinduism, which common understandings associate with devotion to the Bhagavad Gītā and deities like those images worshipped in this temple. According to typical narratives describing the formation of Sikhism, retold by many who identify as Sikh and non-Sikh, Nanak was born in a family that identified with Hindu practices. Nanak, though, began emphasizing devotion to the Supreme Being who is beyond any form or image. This teaching diverged from the common devotional practices of Nanak's time (and of many of the groups described in this volume) that involved expressing devotion (*bhakti*) with statues (*mūrtis*) of various deities who are described as having a physical form. Nanak, during his lifetime, had a range of followers, some born into families that identified as Hindu and some as Muslim, primarily from the region known as Punjab (now divided between India and Pakistan). Nanak's lineage continued after his death in a succession of *gurus*, each selected by the preceding *guru*. The fifth *guru* in this lineage, Arjan Dev (1563–1609), collected poems of Nanak, the other *gurus* in the lineage, and other figures identified specifically as Muslim and Hindu, to create what became identified as the central text of Sikhism, the Ādi Granth. The succession of human *gurus* continued until the tenth *guru*, Gobind Singh (1666–1708), declared that his successor was the Ādi Granth, which then also came to be known as the Guru Granth Sāhib. Therefore, ceremonially opening and closing the Guru Granth Sāhib each day, offering food to it before others eat, and offering gifts such as the brocaded silk cloths that Sindhi Hindus presented during Nanak's birth celebrations are practices that many in India and outside India associate with Sikhism.

So, why do Sindhi Hindus place the Guru Granth Sāhib in the centre of their temple and express such ardent devotion to the text and Nanak?

Sindhi Hindu understandings of the Guru Granth Sāhib

Many Sindhi Hindus, not only in Lucknow but also in New Delhi, Singapore, London and Atlanta, express significant devotion to the Guru Granth Sāhib, but do not identify themselves as Sikhs. In contrast to the predominant understanding that Nanak and the Guru Granth Sāhib relate to Sikhism, a common Sindhi understanding argues that Nanak and the sacred book are both Hindu. This assertion begins with Nanak's birth as a Hindu. Rather than intending to initiate a new religion, Nanak was teaching reforms within Hinduism, like a range of other figures who are still commonly recognized as Hindu. Therefore, this common Sindhi understanding asserts that the Guru Granth Sāhib is a part of a tolerant, reformist Hindu tradition, as it contains the teachings of Nanak, his successors, and a number of other Hindu poets, along with some Muslims. These assertions recognize these Sindhi practices as clearly a part of Hinduism, rather than a combination of Hinduism and Sikhism.

This Sindhi understanding has some historical basis. Before the early twentieth century, the relationship between Sikh practices and Hinduism was commonly debated. A political/religious movement developed in the late nineteenth century, in the context of British colonial control in the region, that argued that the Sikh lineage of *gurus* and the Guru Granth Sāhib belong to a distinct religion, not a subgroup under Hinduism. As this movement became successful, including receiving legal recognition and control of Sikh houses of worship (***gurdwāras***) in the Punjab, the conception of Sikhism as a separate religion became dominant (Oberoi 1994).

Do Sindhi Hindus have other practices that challenge common assumptions of separate religions?

Sindhi Hindu Sūfis

Beyond incorporating elements commonly recognized as Sikh, some Sindhi Hindus also emphasize the importance of Sufism. Commonly defined as mystical Islam, Sufism generally emphasizes an individual experience of the divine,

Figure 8.1 Guru Granth Sahib under a canopy in a Singapore temple (photo by author).

often using analogies of the intensity of romantic love, which leads to union with the divine. Sūfi masters (*pīr*, *qalandar*, **fakir**, dervish) use their depth of spiritual experience to assist their followers in reaching the divine. In Sindh, the shrines (***dargahs***) of deceased Sūfi masters were important sacred sites for people who identified with a range of religions, including Hinduism and Islam. Some Sindhi Hindus recall visiting both Hindu temples and Sūfi *dargahs* with their grandparents when they were children in Sindh. Accounts of a Muslim Sūfi in Sindh, known as Qutb Ali Shah, emphasize his acceptance of Hindu followers, providing separate lodging arrangements for them so that they could maintain their Hindu identification. Qutb Ali Shah also combined yoga and other disciplines that are generally recognized as Hindu with traditional components of Islam (Gajwani 2000: 39–45). One of his Hindu followers, Rochal Das, continued to use Islamic terminology for aspects of his practices while also teaching from the Bhagavad Gītā. Many Sindhi Hindus specifically recognize Rochal Das as a Hindu Sūfi, and several other Sindhi Hindu *gurus* advise their followers to be Sūfis.

Sindhi Hindus frequently present a different understanding of Sufism than is commonly accepted. While they recognize Sufism as having an Islamic heritage, they generally do not limit Sufism to Islam. Sufism for many Sindhi Hindus is an extreme expression of devotion to the divine that is not exclusively associated with one religion. A person can be a Christian Sūfi, a Buddhist Sūfi or a Hindu Sūfi. The only requirement is that the person express a heightened level of devotion to the divine, whatever name they may use to identify the divine.

Who are the Sindhis? Are all Sindhis Hindu? How did they and their ritual formations develop?

Background of the Sindhis

Sindhi Hindus trace their heritage to the region of Sindh, which has existed on the periphery of Hindu-dominated areas for centuries and now forms the southeastern province of Pakistan. Sindhis have adapted cultural aspects from the neighbouring regions of Persia and Punjab that non-Sindhis commonly identify with Sūfi Islam and Sikhism, respectively. Sindh was the first region of south Asia to be entered by armies from west Asia during the expansion of the early Islamic empire in the eighth century. Since that initial invasion, the region has frequently been under the control of rulers who identified with Islam. By the time of the annexation of Sindh into the areas under British control in 1843, about three-quarters of the population of Sindh identified as Muslim. Despite being a minority under a Muslim government, many Sindhi Hindus thrived in business. Others served as administrators in the government of the Muslim rulers, sometimes holding significant power. The Muslim rulers appreciated the services of these Hindu administrators and rewarded them appropriately. So, assertions of the oppression of Sindhi Hindus as a minority within Sindh do not match the historical record. In fact, by the time that India and Pakistan gained independence from Great Britain in 1947, Hindus, though a minority, controlled much of the wealth of Sindh, including a portion of the land.

With independence came Partition. Following the assumption that different religious communities would oppress each other, the British divided British India into two countries. Generally, Hindu majority areas became India, and Muslim majority areas became Pakistan, placing Sindh entirely within Pakistan. In response to Partition, millions of people migrated, as some Muslims in Hindu areas went to Pakistan and some Hindus in Pakistan migrated to India, and violent clashes erupted between the opposing groups. The government of Pakistan directed many Indian Muslim refugees to settle in Karachi, the major port of Sindh. This influx of refugees destabilized Karachi, as some refugees particularly resented the Hindus who remained in Karachi because the Hindus occupied resources (homes and jobs) that the Muslims had to leave behind in India. These tensions created concerns among Hindus about their safety and long-term prospects as a minority in Pakistan. In the years following Partition, most of the Hindus of Sindh migrated to India, with some eventually migrating around the world through a network of Sindhi businesses (Markovits 2000).

Various components of this general history have contributed to the formation of Sindhi Hindu practices. With its proximity to Persia (directly west of Sindh) and the long presence of Islamic rulers in the region, religious and cultural influences from Persia and Islam were significant. Elements of dress, such as the traditional Sindhi hat, and culinary traditions, including the frequently non-vegetarian diet of Sindhi Hindus, have greater connections to Persia than to Hindu cultural traditions. The migration of various Sūfi masters from west Asia into Sindh centuries ago developed a strong cultural influence as both Sindhi Hindus and Muslims frequently recognized Sūfi masters as sources of sacred power and wisdom.

Even though they adopted some of the Sūfi practices, the ancestors of the contemporary Sindhi Hindus chose not to convert, and based on their growing influence and prosperity in Sindh, the Islamic majority in Sindh generally respected their decision to remain Hindu. Many Sindhi Hindus have described Sindh as an idealized place of communal harmony and contrasted it to the terrors of Partition and their departure from Sindh. Because of the various contemporary examples of Hindu–Muslim tensions, including Partition, many Sindhi Hindus differentiated the Muslims of Sindh from other Muslims. One element that various Sindhi Hindus explicitly emphasized was the distinction between Sindhi Muslims who followed a Sūfi approach and other Muslims, whom some Sindhi Hindus stereotyped as fanatics who tend towards violence. In these descriptions, the Sindhi Muslims were like brothers to the Sindhi Hindus, which encouraged Sindhi Hindus to recognize their commonalities with Sindhi Muslims.

Beyond the influence of Persia, Sindhi Hindus had various connections to Punjab, which borders Sindh to the north. Punjab and Sindh historically are shifting categories that maintain a large area of overlap. Some Sindhis have claimed that Greater Sindh (which has not existed as a political realm) included much of Punjab, while some Punjabis claim parts of Sindh within the borders of Punjab. Beyond this vision of overlapping regions, some scholars have asserted that historically various Punjabis have migrated south into present-day Sindh where they were absorbed into the broader Sindhi community. Traditional Sindhi Hindu accounts describe Nanak traveling through Sindh, bringing his teachings directly into the region, and other sources relate how the **Nirmalas**, now recognized as heterodox Sikhs, spread Nanak's teachings through Sindh (Oberoi 1994: 128). These regional interconnections present one way of understanding the practices among Sindhi Hindus.

Do Sindhi Hindus have other unique elements?

Jhule Lal, the god of the Sindhis

In addition to their devotion towards the Guru Granth Sāhib and Sindhi Sūfis, many Sindhi Hindus also emphasize Jhule Lal, a specifically Sindhi Hindu god. A typical image of Jhule Lal shows an old man with a full white beard riding on a fish in the river. While the image has various elements commonly seen in images of Hindu deities, including an animal vehicle, a lotus flower and symbols of royal status such as a crown, several elements distinguish him from other Hindu deities. Two notably unique elements are the colourful tunic he wears, in contrast to the typically bare-chested male deities, and the open book that he holds. While many deities hold various elements in their hands, often offerings or weapons, holding a book is uncommon. Moreover, when a deity holds a book, it is often understood to be the Vedas, and is depicted as a narrow palm leaf manuscript, rather than a larger bound volume like a modern book. Despite these unusual elements, or perhaps because of them, some Sindhi Hindus have emphasized connections to other Hindu gods to reinforce Jhule Lal's Hindu identification. Some assert that he is one of the ten appearances on earth (*avatāra*) of Viṣṇu, like Kṛṣṇa and Rāma, while others associate him with Varuṇa, the god of water in the Vedas, because of Jhule Lal's connection to the Sindhu (Indus) River, from which the region of Sindh takes its name.

According to various Sindhi Hindu accounts, in the tenth century CE, Mirkhshah, a Muslim ruler in Sindh, declared that all Hindus must convert to Islam or be killed. Contemplating their options, many Hindus gathered along the banks of the Sindhu River to pray for deliverance. A voice came from the river, declaring that a god would take form as a child to deliver them from this evil. Soon afterward, the deity Jhule Lal was born in Sindh. His powers, including the ability to transform himself from an infant to a grown man and

Figure 8.2 Image of Jhule Lal in a shrine in Lucknow temple (photo by author).

to ride upstream on a fish, amazed Mirkhshah's minister, leading Mirkhshah to summon Jhule Lal to the palace.

When Jhule Lal arrived, he impressed Mirkhshah with his understanding of Islam, telling Mirkhshah that the **Qur'an** forbade forced conversions and that **Allah** and the god of the Hindus were the same. Mirkhshah's advisers, however, convinced Mirkhshah to disregard Jhule Lal's teachings and to arrest him. When Mirkhshah's guards approached Jhule Lal, simultaneously an inferno and a flood engulfed the palace. In desperation, Mirkhshah relented. He then begged Jhule Lal to save his court, and Jhule Lal graciously caused the waters to recede and the flames to be extinguished. Greatly relieved, Mirkhshah and many other Muslims began to worship Jhule Lal, alongside the Hindus. Even today, a shrine to Jhule Lal in Sindh attracts both Hindu and Muslim devotees (Ramey 2008: 107–11).

While the initial conflict with Mirkhshah (the historicity of which is debated) suggests tensions between the Hindus and the Muslim rulers, the resolution of the conflict (as the Muslims honour Jhule Lal, while remaining Muslim) reflects the sense of religious harmony that many Sindhi Hindus associate with their heritage. Some have even used this story to suggest that Jhule Lal taught Sindhi Muslims the proper way to be, confirming the uniqueness of Sindhi Muslims as Sūfis, in contrast to the stereotyped Muslims more generally.

Prior to Partition, however, Jhule Lal was popular among only a segment of Sindhi Hindus. With the migration from Sindh and the despair that followed the losses of Partition, one Sindhi leader, Ram Panjwani, chose to emphasize Jhule Lal and the celebration of his birthday, **Cheti Chand**, to provide a point of unification and encouragement for the community and to aid their retention of their regional identity. He wanted to both bring Sindhi Hindus together and provide hope and pride in those difficult times (Ramey 2008: 107). Panjwani's emphasis took root in many Sindhi Hindu communities, as seen in the addition of Jhule Lal by Sindhis to institutions in India, Singapore, and the USA, among other places, and celebrations around the world for Cheti Chand, including many cities across India as well as Atlanta (Georgia), New York City, London and Gibraltar, among others. Interestingly, the effort to provide a rallying point for Sindhi Hindu identity has worked, as measured by increased participation in Sindhi online groups during Cheti Chand.

While Sindhi Hindus use the story of Jhule Lal to support their description of the harmony of Sindh, Muslims usually do not characterize the figure that they venerate, even in shrines shared with Hindus, as someone who saved Hindus from tyrannical Muslims or as an appearance of Viṣṇu. A common Sindhi Muslim account identifies Jhule Lal as a *Sūfi pīr* related to Sindh, and one specific story describes Jhule Lal saving a Muslim maiden from a debauched Hindu ruler. One of the names for Jhule Lal, Zinda Pīr, which literally means the eternal *pīr*, reinforces the sense of Jhule Lal as a Sūfi. Therefore, the implication that Muslims began to worship a Hindu deity does not reflect the understanding that Sindhi Muslims maintain.

More specifically, most Muslim accounts associate Jhule Lal with an enigmatic figure in the Qur'an, commonly identified as Khwaja Khizr, who is associated with the water of life (the equivalent of the fountain of youth) and appears in each age to teach people to connect to the divine. While the exact nature of Khizr is contested among Muslims, both Khizr's knowledge, which differs from Islamic law, and his mission to teach people to relate to the divine resemble aspects of many understandings of Sufism. Elements in stories about Khizr resemble elements associated with Jhule Lal. Khizr, like Jhule Lal, saves the devout when they pray at the river and does so by showing mastery over the river, in this case changing its course rather than causing the river to inundate Mirkhshah's palace. The connection between the figures is also apparent in their visual images, as both wear a tunic and ride on a fish in the river. The differences in the characters and plot nevertheless illustrate the similar role that they play in the understanding of these two communities. For both communities, Jhule Lal illustrated their superiority over problematic members of the opposing community. This stark difference reflected the tensions and differentiation between Hindus and Muslims that existed alongside the examples of Sindh's harmony and the concern of each community to define Jhule Lal as a figure who clearly fits into their traditions.

On a different note, contemporary devotional practices among Sindhi Hindus illustrate another connection to Sufism. The most common devotional song (*bhajan*) associated with Jhule Lal is the Sindhi song "Dama Dam Mast Qalandar", the refrain of which repeats the phrase "Jhule Lal, Jhule Lal, Jhule Lal". As the reference to Qalandar in the title of the song suggests, it was originally associated with a thirteenth-century Sūfi *pīr*, Lal Shahbaz Qalandar, and some Sūfis still use it to honour him. Although many Sindhi Hindus are not aware of the Sūfi origin of this devotional song, some have suggested that the song was created to honour both figures. Rather than confirming Sindhi Hindu assertions that Muslims began to worship Jhule Lal as a Hindu deity, the use of "Dama Dam Mast Qalandar" for Jhule Lal suggests that Hindus adopted and reinterpreted Sūfi practices in Sindh. Debates concerning which elements developed first or influenced the others, however, remain much less important than the ways the stories and practices help each community to make sense of their experiences and their own identifications.

Do Sindhi Hindus follow additional practices that other Hindus follow? How does devotion to the Guru Granth Sāhib, Jhule Lal, and Sūfi masters relate to those practices?

Sindhi Hindu practices generally

Temples such as the Sindhi Hindu temple described in the beginning of this chapter are found in a number of cities around the world with significant Sindhi Hindu populations. Along with a prominent canopy containing the Guru

Granth Sāhib, many of these temples have a number of shrines with statues of various gods and goddesses (Thapan 2002; Ramey 2008: 66–70). The same is true of many Sindhi Hindu homes, where they have images of gods and goddesses along with Nanak and, in some cases, a ritually installed Guru Granth Sāhib. Because the rituals for a properly installed Guru Granth Sāhib require daily attention and the ability to read its **Gurmukhi** script, many Sindhi Hindus who express significant devotion to it have chosen not to install it in their homes. As many Sindhi Hindus have family extended around the world, those who are financially able often travel for extended periods of time, making the care for a Guru Granth Sāhib in their home especially difficult.

The figures enshrined in temples and in home shrines reflect a range of traditions. Along with Jhule Lal and other deities who were popular in Sindh, like Viṣṇu and his *avatāra*, Śiva, and Durgā, many Sindhi Hindus have added gods and goddesses popular in the area where they settled after Partition. For the Sindhi Hindus in Lucknow, Hanumān became particularly prominent in their temple, while Sindhi Hindus in parts of south India are more likely to have added Murukaṉ or Venkateswara to their regular devotions. Beyond the addition of different deities, some Sindhi Hindus include images of particular *gurus* in their temples or home shrines. These particular *gurus* may be selected because of the family's long-term connection to that *guru* lineage or because of a new connection, often to a Sindhi Hindu *guru* who is active in the area where the family has settled.

Among these *gurus*, several specifically emphasize their Sindhi heritage. After Partition, the Hindu Sūfi Rochal Das (described above) established his main centre outside Mumbai (Bombay) in an area where many Sindhi Hindus resettled. He and his descendants have continued to emphasize the importance of Sindhi understandings of Sufism and Hinduism in that context, and thus have attracted primarily Sindhi Hindu followers. T. L. Vaswani, who migrated to Pune, India, following Partition, and his successor have established an international network of centres that emphasize their Sindhi Hindu heritage and Sindhi language while incorporating discussions of Nanak and Sūfis within that description of Hinduism. Along with large pictures of the *gurus*, these centres often have small images of a few deities such as Kṛṣṇa, and sometimes an image of Nanak. The followers of another Sindhi Hindu *guru*, Shahenshah, have established a centre in Chennai (Madras), India that exhibits the expansive nature of Sindhi Hindu understandings, enshrining elements commonly associated with various religions, including a Guru Granth Sāhib and images of Durgā, Venkateswara, Jesus, Mary, Nanak and Dastagir, among others. Dastagir is a Baghdadi Sūfi whose image receives special ritualized attention at a specified time each afternoon. In contrast to these examples, other *gurus* who have a Sindhi heritage, such as Asharam, have attracted a wide range of followers and no longer emphasize their Sindhi heritage explicitly.

Beyond Sindhi Hindu temples, home shrines and *gurus*, some Sindhi Hindus participate in a range of practices outside of the Sindhi community. Even in cities where Sindhis have created specifically Sindhi Hindu temples and *guru* centres, some Sindhi Hindus continue to visit non-Sindhi temples and *gurdwāras* (religious centres of Sikhs that have installed a Guru Granth Sāhib but no images of Hindu deities) along with the specifically Sindhi temples. While sometimes they may choose to visit these sites because they are more convenient to their home than a Sindhi temple, some also choose to visit these non-Sindhi sites because they find them especially meaningful. When travelling, some Sindhi Hindus also visit notable shrines associated with various religions.

What other practices are important for Sindhi Hindus in relation to their family relationships and festivals?

Other common Sindhi Hindu practices

Although caste hierarchies have often been identified as a major aspect of Hinduism, accounts of Sindhi Hindu society prior to Partition emphasize that caste identifications were not particularly important among most Sindhi Hindus. Interdining was common, perhaps because solidarity was important for the minority Hindus and/or Nanak's requirement to eat together influenced the culture significantly (Thakur 1959: 25). The majority of Sindhi Hindus have been described as **Lohana**, an all-encompassing caste classification that, however, does not function as a strictly bounded group. The Lohana generally absorbed smaller groups, such as when Punjabis migrated into Sindh. While primarily made up of merchants (known as **Bhaiband** among Sindhis), some Lohana took professional posts, primarily in government, and then were designated as **Amil**. The Amil/Bhaiband distinction is the closest element to a division that produces stereotypes of the other's inferiority. Amils generally feel superior due to their emphasis on education, while some Bhaiband identify their acumen for business as a core attribute of Sindhi Hindu culture. However, Amil and Bhaiband categories are more fluid than traditional understandings of castes and subcastes, as Bhaibands who moved into professional or bureaucratic occupations are often absorbed into the Amil community, and some accounts recognize that some Bhaibands are not Lohana but fall within other subcastes. Beyond the Bhaiband and Amil divide, small groups of various priest (Brāhmin) subcastes, including the Thakurs, led some rituals in Sindh, but their status and numbers were limited (Thakur 1959: 25). Through these examples, the Sindhi Hindu community illustrates that caste does not comprise a single stratified system across India.

Some Sindhi Hindus perform the sacred thread ceremony (***upanayana***), in which boys and young men receive their sacred thread as a sign of their status as an adult uppercaste male. Some Sindhi *guru* movements even provide mass rituals for those who cannot afford the expense. How widely they performed this ceremony before migration to India is unclear. Some Sindhi Hindus have described performing this ceremony in relation to a wedding, because they had not performed it earlier and understood it as a requirement for marriage, and it also reinforces their status as upper caste within the larger Hindu society.

Marriage provides an intriguing example of some of these dynamics in the period after their migration from Sindh. With the dispersal of Sindhi Hindus across India and around the world, Sindhi arranged marriages have not followed a strictly caste-based limitation for locating a life partner. Some parents have emphasized finding a spouse for their adult child who shares the Sindhi heritage, rather than an emphasis on a specific subcaste. This emphasis on Sindhi cultural heritage over caste reflects a practical issue of the relative size of the global community, as well as reflecting a lack of emphasis on caste among Sindhi Hindus more generally. For others, marriage to another Amil or another Bhaiband is preferred.

However marriage partners were determined, including some non-arranged or love marriages, the rituals of the wedding illustrate the variety of emphases among Sindhi Hindus. Within the communities, two main ritual formats exist. Many emphasize a Vedic based ritual during which the bride and groom walk around a fire into which particular herbs have been placed. Others follow a ritual that fits with a distinctive Sikh identity. In this format, the marriage is consecrated in a Sikh *gurdwāra* in front of the Guru Granth Sāhib, and the couple walks around the text instead of a fire. The selection of which ritual format to use reflects a variety of considerations. The devotional emphasis in the extended family and the larger community is one factor. The tensions that Sindhi Hindus have experienced over their Hindu identification, in light of their varied practices, encourage some to emphasize their Hindu identification through their marriage rituals. In some families, they perform both marriage rituals, while other families include a visit to a *gurdwāra* or a *guru*'s centre after completing the ritual around the fire.

In addition to Nanak's birthday, Sindhi Hindus celebrate a range of festivals. Wherever they have migrated in India, they often celebrate regional Hindu festivals, as well as those that have become popular across much of India, such as Gaṇeṣa Caturthī, Divāli and Holī. While celebrating these pan-Indian or non-Sindhi festivals, Sindhi Hindus often distinguish themselves with foods specific to their regional heritage, such as a particular spinach dal and a different style of an Indian sweet known as ***jalebis***. Two festivals that are particularly unique to Sindh Hindus are Cheti Chand and **Tijri**. Cheti Chand commemorates the birthday of Jhule Lal and the Sindhi Hindu New Year. These commemorations typically include a procession to the river with a special tray of offerings that they immerse in the river. Through this ritual, Sindhi Hindus, wherever they live, emphasize a connection to the Sindhu River. Another distinctive festival for Sindhi Hindus is Tijri, a festival during which wives fast for the well-being of their husbands. Tijri, therefore, is similar to the Hindu festival of **Karva Chauth**, which also involves wives fasting, but it occurs at a slightly different time.

Conclusion

Through the examples of Sindhi Hindu practices, the contested nature of the category "Hindu" becomes apparent. While Sindhi Hindus assert their own understanding and justification for the various practices that diverge from traditional definitions of Hinduism, those traditional definitions strongly influence the experiences of Sindhi Hindus. Sikhs and other Hindus have questioned the assertions that Sindhi Hindus are Hindu, which has also created defensiveness among Sindhi Hindus (Ramey 2008: 185–93). Tensions between Sikhs and Hindus in the 1980s have further complicated Sindhi Hindu practices, pushing some Sindhi Hindus away from *gurdwāras* (Williams 1988: 82). Their emphasis on taking the sacred thread, connecting Jhule Lal to Viṣṇu or Varuṇa, and incorporating regional deities into their practices also cannot be separated from the context in which they must prove their true Hindu identification.

9. Devotional expressions in the Swaminarayan community

Hanna H. Kim

If you go to the village of Bochasan today, a village in Kheda district, in the western Indian state of Gujarat, you can visit the very first temple constructed by the Bochasanwasi Shri Akshar Purushottam Swaminarayan Sanstha Hindu community. This stone temple, with its tall carved pinnacles, each adorned with a red and white striped flag, is the daily site of pilgrimage and of intense devotional activity. It is also the physical beginning point of a remarkable history. On 5 June 1907, when the Bochasan Swaminarayan temple was inaugurated, there were few amenities for visitors, and no landscaping or leafy trees under which to seek some shade. There was only an unfinished temple that housed, in its central and therefore most important shrine (**garbha griha**), the precious icons, or *mūrtis*, of **Akshar** and Purushottam. Side by side, with Akshar standing to the left of Purushottam, this positioning of the two *mūrtis* would distinguish the Bochasan Swaminarayan temple from other existing and older Swaminarayan temples. The ritual awakening of these *mūrtis* (Figure 9.1) and

Figure 9.1 *Mūrtis* of Akshar (right) and Purushottam (left) (photo courtesy of BAPS Swaminarayan Sanstha).

the corresponding consecration of the Bochasan temple signalled, in a public way, the inauguration of not just a place of worship but a new devotional community.

The community that grew out of the Bochasan temple debut becomes known, over time, as Bochasanwasi Shri Akshar Purushottam Swaminarayan Sanstha, or "BAPS". In its formal name, the geographic locus of its beginning, Bochasan, is acknowledged along with the central foci of Swaminarayan devotionalism, the existential and eternal entities, Akshar and Purushottam. Who are Akshar and Purushottam? And how is the dynamic between devotee to Akshar and Purushottam experienced and cultivated by devotees? Or, to put it another way, what does it mean when a devotee happily declares, "I'm Swaminarayan"?

The story of the Bochasan temple is the story of Swaminarayan leaders, the *gurus*, and the devotees, who are known as ***satsangis***. In its practices, rituals and Gujarati language use, BAPS *satsangis* share similarities with much older Swaminarayan and other regional Hindu communities.[1] Yet, it is the ways in which BAPS *satsangis* turn towards Akshar and Purushottam in their practices and rituals that distinguishes BAPS *bhakti*, or mode of offering devotion. For many Hindus, questions about what remains following bodily death and what is reborn into another body are the basis of much reflection and concern. Ideally, for Hindus, it is escape from rebirth that is desired. BAPS *bhakti* from the devotees' perspective provides a reassuringly attainable path towards insuring that the indestructible aspect of one's self, the *ātman*, will not be reborn into another being. In other words, for Swaminarayan devotees, the BAPS tradition succeeds in offering a convincing programme for how to live in the world while simultaneously cultivating one's being, composed of the sentient and non-separable entities of the mind and body, to absorb the knowledge that will lead to the *ātman*'s release from rebirth. This knowledge does not come naturally or easily. To understand the success and appeal of BAPS is thus to see how Swaminarayan devotionalism inspires and resonates within its followers.

The aim of this chapter is to approach the life of the Swaminarayan *satsangi* through two areas of devotional expression: ***nitya pūjā*** and *sevā*. This is a limited focus, but one that can help us to appreciate how being a Swaminarayan devotee rests on understanding the self and body in relation to the entities Akshar and Purushottam.

Nitya pūjā is daily devotional worship that *satsangis* perform each morning. *Sevā* is volunteered work that *satsangis* conduct in order to please Akshar and Purushottam. As we shall see, *nitya pūjā* and *sevā* are crucial components of each individual *satsangi*'s devotional practice. Whether in the personal performance of *nitya pūjā* or the outwardly directed work that *sevā* often entails, both devotional expressions highlight and reinforce the central relationships of *satsangi* to Akshar and Purushottam. Again, we can ask, what makes someone a Swaminarayan Hindu? How do *satsangis* sustain their devotional desires while living in the world? What makes BAPS a successful contemporary *guru*-based Hindu movement? In answering these questions, we will see that it is the concepts of Akshar and Purushottam that permeate, guide, and influence Swaminarayan ways of being.

The BAPS community

More than a hundred years after the Bochasan temple was built, BAPS has expanded from Gujarat to other parts of India, Europe, Asia, Australia and North America. From one temple to over seven hundred, Swaminarayan Hindus are shaping the contours of a global Hinduism that perhaps could not have been imagined in its colonial Indian beginnings.[2] Its temples and the more recent "Akshardham" temple-monument complexes have attracted much interest and have become popular tourist destinations. BAPS counts its membership to be around one million followers, nearly all of whom are of Gujarati heritage. Included in this community, or *satsang*, are the more than eight hundred men who have taken vows of celibacy and dedicate their time and skills fully to BAPS. These men are called *sādhus* (in Hindi) or **santo** (in Gujarati). In addition to cultivating their personal devotional practices, *sādhus* are responsible for supporting the growth of the global BAPS community and insuring that Swaminarayan teachings and practices are properly disseminated. There are currently *sādhus* living in most of the areas of the world where BAPS devotees have settled.

We can think of the broad BAPS *satsang* as consisting of three sections. The smallest section consists of the *sādhus*. The second is the international core of approximately 55,000 followers who are regular volunteers for Swaminarayan projects. The third section is the balance of devotees whose degree of commitment to BAPS events and to Swaminarayan prescriptions for behaviour, diet, and devotional practices varies. The entire *satsang* is centrally administered from Ahmedabad, Gujarat by a board of trustees and the most important BAPS administrative role, the administrative president and religious head who is also known as *guru*.

Swaminarayan *satsangis* meet in a temple (*mandir*) for a weekly get-together that includes hearing and singing devotional songs (*bhajan*) and listening to lessons on the main Swaminarayan texts, the *Vachanamrut* and the *Swamini Vato*. The Gujarati language remains important for participating in BAPS, though publications are available in English, Hindi and several other south Asian languages.[3] Devotees follow rules of behaviour that are prescribed in the *Shikshapatri*, a "code of conduct" consisting of 212 verses. The *Shikshapatri* includes dietary rules on avoiding certain substances such as onion, garlic, and intoxicants, to proscriptions for behaviour in temples, at home, and between males and females. Devotees also regularly read the *Vachanamrut*, a collection of discourses given by Sahajanand Swami from 1819 to 1829.[4] For BAPS, the historical person of Sahajanand Swami is called **Bhagwan** Swaminarayan.

Nitya pūjā: an ethnographic moment

Sector 29 Flats, Gandhinagar, Gujarat, November 1992

In the cold and dark stillness of the morning, the sound of buckets clanging travelled easily through the shuttered windows. Men and women, having arisen well before dawn, were collecting hot water from a large cauldron in the courtyard. The water was brought back to the Sector 29 flats surrounding the courtyard. Next came the sound of cold tap water noisily streaming into empty buckets followed by the addition of hot water to achieve a bearable temperature, one that would cancel out the bather's breaths spiralling into the air. As the sky slowly lightened, the sounds of water splashing onto concrete walls and floors, buckets clanging, and more and more people queuing in the courtyard to collect hot water became layered onto a perceptible quiet in the rooms where those who had completed their bath were now performing *nitya pūjā*, or daily morning acts of devotional worship. Before carefully arrayed laminated cards with printed images, these BAPS devotees were beginning their day with a sequence of meditative and ritual gestures that would bring them into closer relationship with *guru* and Bhagwan. Sitting cross-legged on small cloths placed directly on the cold concrete floor, each devotee was absorbed in her own devotional performance, proceeding at her own pace.

In fact, all throughout the Swaminarayan diaspora, men, women and children, upon arising in the morning and completing their bath, begin their daily *pūjā*, trying to envelop their physically cleansed body with the purifying love and peacefulness that devotion to *guru* and Bhagwan would bring. Within fifteen to twenty minutes, having finished *nitya pūjā*, each devotee carefully repacks the laminated cards and other *pūjā* accessories into a small bag. Then the day officially starts.

I share this moment from my fieldwork with BAPS because, although I have witnessed countless morning *pūjā*, the memory of living with Swaminarayan devotees in Sector 29, all of whom had travelled from the USA to Gujarat, highlights how distance from home, different timing and unfamiliar facilities do not change the requirement of beginning one's day with *nitya pūjā*.[5]

Let us look more closely at how *nitya pūjā* unfolds. What are the components of this devotional ritual? And, what is happening to the devotee who is "doing" *nitya pūjā*?

Nitya pūjā "up close and personal"

Each morning, after awaking, going to the toilet, bathing and dressing in clean clothes, Hiral, a college freshman, does her *nitya pūjā* (daily morning worship). Unlike the many other types of *pūjā*, or devotional worship, that Swaminarayan followers participate in, *nitya pūjā* is deeply personal, is performed daily, and involves only the devotee and her relationship to two central entities, Akshar and Purushottam. *Nitya pūjā* can be performed nearly anywhere though ideally it should be in a quiet place with minimal distractions. Nothing is needed beyond the devotee and a few *pūjā* items that are easily stored in a small bag or case.

Hiral begins by putting a ***āsana***, a mat or small cloth, on the floor.[6] She sits cross-legged on the *āsana* and unpacks her *pūjā* kit, a cloth bag in which her *pūjā* items are stored. She takes out an *āsana* reserved only for her *pūjā* items and spread this before her. On this, to one side, she places the *Shikshapatri* and *Vachanamrut*. It is now time to sit in quiet meditation, with back straight and eyes closed. Hiral is concentrating on trying to quieten her thoughts and focus on Akshar and Purushottam. Akshar, for all BAPS devotees, is the same as the living Guru and Purushottam is Bhagwan Swaminarayan. In the BAPS tradition, the devotee can offer *bhakti*, or loving devotion to Purushottam, only by first becoming ***akshar-rupa***, that is the state of "becoming like Akshar". Thus, in her meditation, Hiral concentrates on the knowledge that she wants to become like Akshar. In order to become *akshar-rupa*, Hiral must recognise that within her physical self is an indestructible and eternal self or soul, her *ātman*. The *ātman* is clothed and embodied in a being that will eventually deteriorate and die. Through *nitya pūjā*, Hiral hopes to cleanse her *ātman* of the complications that arise from its embodiment within her. If she succeeds, then she feels that she can live life without fearing death or pain. Hiral's ontological goal, in other words, is to achieve the contentment that comes from knowing that her *ātman* identifies with Akshar, thereby enabling her to offer devotion to Purushottam while she is alive.

Hiral keeps her breathing even. She silently dwells on the thought "I am *ātman*". Hiral repeats this phrase, "I am *ātman*", while also acknowledging that "*guru* is my *ātman*"and "Bhagwan Swaminarayan resides within my *ātman*". This is a three-part relationship: of devotee to *guru*, of *guru* to Purushottam and of devotee to Purushottam. *Nitya pūjā* is a daily opportunity to remind oneself of the connection of these relationships to the devotee's own devotional growth. It is the *guru* who has the significant role in BAPS *bhakti*. *Guru* embodies the full immanence of Purushottam Bhagwan Swaminarayan and operates in the terrestrial world by helping devotees and seekers to come closer to knowing Purushottam. Hiral focuses on how her *guru* is the model for a continuous devotional stance toward Bhagwan. *Guru* may appear to experience physical discomfort, illness, and even old age. Yet, his unswerving devotion to Bhagwan is reflected in his devotional actions towards the *mūrti* of Bhagwan: in serving Bhagwan, *guru* is also following the commands of his own *guru* to serve BAPS. And all *satsangis* point to *guru*'s state of knowing *ātman*, of being *ātman* personified, and therefore of being beyond rebirth.

By repeating "I am *ātman*", Hiral is following the teachings of Bhagwan Swaminarayan who specified in the *Vachanamrut* that the real self or *ātman* is clothed by the body. In her daily *pūjā*, Hiral mentally disentangles this "real self", the *ātman*, from the self that is intertwined with bodily sensations of desire, attachment and the sense of "ego". Her body is promoting a sense of "ego", and this unfortunately muddles her ability to see that "I am *ātman*". In her meditation on the forms of **Akshar Guru** and Purushottam Bhagwan, Hiral is engaging in an intense introspection, ***antardṛṣṭi***, for the purpose of trying to become like Akshar and therefore to be able to live in-the-world without being derailed by bodily and mundane desires. To become *akshar-rupa* does not nullify Hiral's more worldly and personal goals; neither does it preclude being married and having a family. If Hiral can "become like Akshar", or become like *guru* (for the two are synonymous), then she can, following the death of her physical self, experience the "eternal bliss" of serving Bhagwan Swaminarayan in his "heavenly abode". According to the *Vachanamrut*, Akshar is in fact both the living *guru* and the place where Purushottam resides. Thus, for all devotees, the goal is to be able to serve Bhagwan, much as Akshar does, eternally, and from Akshardham.

Following the *antardṛṣṭi* phase of *nitya pūjā*, Hiral enters the phase of ***mānsī pūjā***, of mentally offering devotion to *guru* and Bhagwan. This form of *bhakti* allows any devotee, irrespective of sex, age, or status, to care for *guru* and Bhagwan in a loving and intimate way. Within her mind, Hiral visualises awakening *guru* and Bhagwan, guiding them through the morning routine, including, for example, helping to brush their teeth. She dresses Bhagwan and *guru* in seasonally appropriate clothing and adorns them with ornaments and flower garlands. *Mānsī pūjā* helps Hiral to develop her devotional commitment to Bhagwan and Guru in that she personally thinks of ways to insure their comfort and to demonstrate her desire to be thoroughly focused in serving them. In *mānsī*, Hiral also recollects the few times that she has actually seen her *guru*. She recalls the excitement of looking at her *guru* from afar, of seeing him settle into his chair on the stage, and of watching his every gesture towards his own *mūrti* of Bhagwan Swaminarayan. She remembers too the excitement of the women around

Figure 9.2 Female *nitya pūjā* (photo courtesy of BAPS Swaminarayan Sanstha).

her as they all craned their necks to look intently at *guru* in an effort to refuel their love towards this embodiment of Akshar, this perfected devotee, always in total devotion to Bhagwan. Hiral recalls thinking how *guru*'s noticeable commitment to Bhagwan has made him impervious to his bodily needs. This is how she wants to be, "like Akshar", a state of both living in-the-world and being dedicated to one's job, and also at the same time, never losing concentration on serving Bhagwan.

For the next part of *nitya pūjā*, Hiral takes out five laminated cards that are imprinted with *mūrtis* or images (Figure 9.2). She carefully arranges these cards in a particular order. In the central place on the *pūjā āsana*, Hiral places a card with the *mūrtis* of Akshar and Purushottam. Akshar in this card is Gunatitanand Swami, the first *guru* of BAPS who lived during the time of Purushottam Bhagwan Swaminarayan's historical presence in early nineteenth-century India. Both *mūrtis* are full-bodied and dressed in nineteenth-century clothes. Gunatitanand Swami is often referred to, in English, as the "ideal" or "god-realized" *sādhu*. For devotees, Gunatitanand Swami represents the first in a lineage of BAPS *gurus* (***guru paraṃparā***). To Hiral's left of this central card, is the *mūrti* of the second *guru*, Bhagatji Maharaj; and to the left of Bhagatji Maharaj is the *mūrti* of Yogiji Maharaj, the fourth *guru* in the BAPS lineage of Akshar Gurus. To the right of the central Akshar–Purushottam *mūrti*, Hiral places the *mūrti* of Shastriji Maharaj, the third *guru* and the one who constructed the Bochasan Swaminarayan temple. Further to the right of Shastriji Maharaj's *mūrti*, Hiral places the *mūrti* for the fifth and current form of Akshar Guru, Pramukh Swami Maharaj. Hiral now focuses her attention on the *mūrtis* and begins her devotion to them by praying and requesting that Bhagwan please be present in her *pūjā*. She gazes at each *mūrti*. This is known as "taking" *darśana*, or offering submission to each *mūrti* while simultaneously receiving the grace of each *mūrti*'s return gaze. Hiral turns the beads of her rosary of 108 beads (***mālā***), relying on this action to help keep the focus of her *darśana*.

Following *darśana*, Hiral arises from her *āsana* and circumambulates the *mūrtis* in a clockwise direction, taking care not to step on the *pūjā āsana*. This movement is called ***pradakṣiṇā*** and is the same that Hindus perform when circling the main shrines or outer perimeters of temples. The *pradakṣiṇā* emphasises the centrality of Akshar and Purushottam and the lineage of BAPS *gurus* in Hiral's life. She does a number of *pradakṣiṇās* of the *mūrtis* while still continuing to turn her *mālā*. Following this, she then sits down again and stretches her body, tipping it forward from her knees and resting on her elbows; with face down, she extends her arms and points her hands with palms together and fingertips stretched towards the *mūrtis*. This act of prostration is one of physical submission to Akshar and Purushottam. Hiral does a number of prostrations before sitting once again on her *āsana*.

Again, Hiral engages in *mānsī pūjā* and the opportunity to offer a plate (***thāḷ***) of foods. She opens her hands, with the palms facing upward as if she were holding a plate of food. She visualises the loving presentation of food items to

Akshar and Purushottam. Following the *thāḷ* offering, Hiral closes her *pūjā* with heartfelt prayers (***prārthnā***). She prays that Bhagwan and Guru will protect and guide her from heeding the temptations and sensations generated by her own mind–body and by living within society. She asks Bhagwan's help for her objective of doing well in college and securing a job that will help to support her immigrant parents. Hiral lightly touches each *mūrti*'s feet with her fingertips and then she touches her closed eyes, a gesture of reverence and adoration.

The *nitya pūjā* is over. However, before packing up her *pūjā* kit, Hiral silently reads five verses from the *Shikshapatri* and a section from the *Vachanamrut*, though this latter reading is not a required part of the daily *pūjā*. She sometimes skips this part of her morning routine due to time constraints but Hiral knows that knowledge of *ātman* (***ātmajñān***) also arises from reading and reflecting on the words of Bhagwan Swaminarayan. BAPS has made the acquisition of knowledge much easier for those who cannot read or understand Gujarati easily. Hiral has chosen to do her *satsang* reading in English. She makes a mental note that she will pay more attention to the discourse (*kathā*) on Swaminarayan texts that is given at each weekly temple gathering. After reading, Hiral touches both books with her fingertips and then touches her eyes.

Carefully, Hiral gathers all her *pūjā* materials and stores them in the *pūjā* bag. She puts the bag away and is ready to begin her day, including having some breakfast. She feels that she has had her personal time with Akshar Guru and Purushottam Bhagwan. For Hiral and all committed BAPS devotees, *nitya pūjā* marks the start of the new day: it is an opportunity to remind oneself of necessary knowledge, and it is a chance to have a personal conversation with Akshar and Purushottam. Hiral shared with me that going to college has been a learning experience in the expected areas of time management and living away from home for the first time. However, Hiral did not expect that doing her daily morning *pūjā* would sometimes be sacrificed due to having stayed awake most of the night and needing to rush off to classes. She soon realized that the tension she felt between trying to maintain her devotional practice and being a good student was greater when she skipped her *pūjā*. Foregoing daily *pūjā* in fact meant that Hiral could not justify eating or drinking anything, the lack of which contributed to her fatigue and problems in concentration. Hiral also discovered that skipping her *pūjā* resulted in the lost chance to have a daily "check-in" and "one-on-one" with Bhagwan and *guru*. She found herself eating prepared foods with onion and garlic, something not permitted for *satsangis*. She also found that she was quickly irritated and more frustrated with fellow students. Without *pūjā*, Hiral described herself as too focused on the "I-ness" and "me-ness" of her situation. When she returned to performing daily *pūjā*, Hiral noted that she knew immediately that Akshar Guru and Purushottam Bhagwan had been waiting for her return. She knew that she was ever more in need of a compassionate teacher, her *guru*, who would guide her, without judgement, to recognize that daily activities and obligations could indeed be better met while satisfying the requirements for eternal fulfilment.

Sevā: an ethnographic moment

Swaminarayan temple kitchen, Neasden, England, February 1993

On a cold winter night in February, I watched as an elderly man stood in a dimly lit and unheated kitchen, and kneaded a large ball of dough. He teased a single strand of dough from the ball until it became as slender as a thread, and as he gently pulled the thread longer and longer, he dribbled ***ghī*** (ghee) into the dough, and he worked it further and further into a growing nest of coiled threads. He made many coils of finely pulled dough and he worked silently. These coils would later be deep fried to a light golden colour, and sprinkled with an aromatic blend of crushed pistachios, almonds and cardamom. I recall this image from 1993, of this "*Rasoi*" *Kaka* (kitchen uncle) making the delicacy ***sūtarfeṇī*** through the night in the BAPS temple kitchen. He had volunteered to do this *sevā*, working mostly alone and, in spite of pains in his legs, standing through the night to make a wide variety of Gujarati sweets too time-consuming for busy women to make at home. Kaka said that this *sevā* was one that he could not miss. Fatigue, cold, and sleepless nights were all worth suffering through because of "*sevā* for my *guru*". Thus, thousands of *sūtarfeṇī* rounds, ***ghārī***, *jalebī* and many varieties of ***nāsto*** (fried snacks) were hand-prepared and then sold. Two years later in 1995, from the labour of "*rasoi kaka*" and thousands of other ***sevaks*** (volunteer workers), of all ages, the Neasden (London) BAPS Swaminarayan temple was completed and the BAPS community, nearly overnight, became a recognisably public face of diaspora Hinduism.

In the years following the opening of the Neasden temple, BAPS has constructed four carved-stone temples in North America. Many thousands of *satsangis* contributed material resources and physical labour to these projects. This is *sevā* – that is, work done for which there is no monetary payment. *Sevā* is work offered as an act of devotion. Given that *sevā* can strain a donor's resources and even physical comfort, why do *satsangis* do *sevā*? What does a devotee hope to gain from doing *sevā*?

Sevā and its consequences

From contemplation to actual work, BAPS devotees do *sevā* for reasons that are explicitly connected to their devotional desires to please Akshar Guru and Purushottam Bhagwan. *Sevā* is thus an important dimension of *satsangis*' daily lives: it is an opportunity to put into practice their understanding of *guru*'s constant devotion to Bhagwan. Of course there are those who will donate large sums of money for a temple project and those who will jockey for more desirable kinds of *sevā* over the more back-breaking options. The committed *satsangi*, however, knows that no matter what *sevā* one is doing, it is the opportunity to try and be like Akshar, or to be like *guru*, that *sevā* allows one to experience.

Thus, at large festivals, *satsangis* may be assigned to collect rubbish from the grounds, to clean the public toilets, and to stir hot cauldrons of food that will be distributed free. And, while *satsangis* may occasionally complain of fatigue and physical discomfort, what one most frequently hears is that *guru* has "inspired all of us to do this", and "*guru* has made this opportunity" for *satsangis* to develop a better knowledge about their mind–body and its obscuring of their *ātman*. *Sevā*, in other words, allows *satsangis* to physically, and in a very visceral way, apply their awareness of "I am *ātman*" to contexts where the discomforts of the mind–body are sure to dominate. In hard labour, financial sacrifices, and donated time, *satsangis* are being reminded by their mind–bodies that *bhakti* is indeed hard work: that giving devotion to Bhagwan full-time when the needs and desires of the physical body are clamouring for attention requires commitment and persistence. *Sevā* thus works as a somatic reminder of the devotee's wish to be free of the body and to experience the self as only *ātman*. As Hansa Masi, a middle-aged married woman, noted, "we need a *guru* in this time of *saṃsāra* ... otherwise there is no way that we can know that we are *ātman*".

For a small percentage of *satsangis*, the desire to be the perfect *sevak* and to please *guru*, and therefore be closer to Bhagwan, has translated into full-time *sevā* for BAPS. This could involve teaching new Swaminarayan devotees how to follow ritual practices, giving discourses on Swaminarayan texts, organizing and coordinating volunteers in BAPS projects, contributing to publications, and working in large Swaminarayan temples. For others, doing *sevā* is living with much less, for example not leasing an expensive model of car and downsizing from a multi-room house to a smaller apartment, with the difference in monies being donated to a BAPS project. For all *sevaks*, it is the awakening of knowledge that, with complete devotion to *guru*, who has inspired the work, the sense of "I-ness" will dissolve. Only then can the *sevak* begin to recognize that *ātman* can indeed be separated from the body.

Many *satsangis* acknowledge that without *guru*'s own non-stop example of full-time devotion to Bhagwan, they would not be willing to dedicate their efforts for a BAPS event or project. *Satsangis* repeatedly point out, "I am only here because of our *guru*, Bapa". They further share that *guru* is "old and ailing, and does not think about himself ever" and "I want to become like him!" *Satsangis* know that if they can mimic the *guru*'s devotional orientation toward Bhagwan, and if they can conquer their bodily desires, then *guru* will help them to become *akshar-rupa*, "to become like Akshar".

Swaminarayan *bhakti* and its ontological objectives

In the *Vachanamrut*, Bhagwan Swaminarayan mentions how the mind is too easily affected by desires. To conquer this state of being, one that will impede the devotee's desire to be released from *saṃsāra* (rebirth), Bhagwan Swaminarayan describes the process of making scented oil whereby sesame seeds are layered "between alternating layers of flowers". Much as the fragrance of the flowers seeps into the seeds which when pressed will yield the scented oil, Bhagwan Swaminarayan notes that "the mind should be similarly saturated with flowers in the form of the constant remembrance of God's [Bhagwan's] divine actions and incidents, coupled with an understanding of His greatness" (Gadhada I-38). This image, one that conveys the potential of the mind–body to be reshaped through discipline and focused action, is what lies at the heart of Swaminarayan ontology: the ideal form of being is the *ātman*, the self that is freed from the sensations, ignorance, and causal leanings of the body. However, as Bhagwan Swaminarayan observed, "a diamond can only be cut by a diamond", and therefore only through the devotee's "profound association" with Akshar Guru can the devotee hope to achieve an eternal *darśana* of Bhagwan (Gadhada I-50).

To be Swaminarayan is thus to accept the immanence of Purushottam Bhagwan in Akshar Guru and to accept Akshar Guru as one's guide. As numerous observers of modern Hinduism have noted, the more popular and expanding Hindu communities are those that are led by charismatic *gurus*. BAPS is indeed led by a *guru*, but as *satsangis* know, he is more than a mortal being with human-like qualities. Purushottam Bhagwan made possible, through his grace, the possibility for *ātman* to be freed from *saṃsāra*; however, this must occur through the guidance of the Akshar Guru. In an essay, "The Infinite Glory of Akshar", Sadhu Anandswarupdas (2004) writes:

> Akshar cleanses the soul of its ignorance, its evil instincts, hatred, jealousy, anger ... Then he [Akshar] presents that pure soul [*ātman*] to God [Purushottam]. Only then does God accept the soul's devotion and services. Only then does he become fit to stay with God and enjoy His bliss perpetually.

We can see that in BAPS, the *guru*'s role is paramount in Swaminarayan ontology. *Satsangis* wish their *ātman* to be released from the bondage of the mind-body and from *saṃsāra*. They see that *guru*'s life of continuous devotion is real and unwavering. Hence, *satsangis* such as Hiral and Rasoi Kaka above know that by offering devotion to *guru*, he will guide them towards eliminating the physical body's grip on the *ātman*.

"I knew he was my *guru*, from the moment he touched my head and looked into my eyes", said a young man from London who admitted that he had favoured "bad company" (***kusaṅg***). The instant attraction to *guru* is not unique to BAPS. However, what is notable about Swaminarayan devotionalism is that it provides a readily accessible means of shaping the devotee's mind–body. Through certain means, such as *nitya pūjā* and *sevā*, devotees can experience a new ontology as well as strengthen their commitment to Swaminarayan *bhakti*. *Nitya pūjā* and *sevā* are but two means by which this is achieved. There are many others such as going to the temple, listening to discourses, and educating oneself through Swaminarayan texts. *Pūjā* and *sevā* are nevertheless two expressions of devotionalism that directly signal a devotee's desire to achieve knowledge of an eternal self that is impermeable to the demands of the physical self. What is remarkable about BAPS is that this modus operandi for personal transformation via intense devotion to Akshar and Purushottam has resulted in the transformation of modern Hinduism itself. The *sevak*'s desire to please *guru* and to serve Bhagwan has resulted in the construction of well over 700 BAPS temples and the growth of a transnational community of devotees, many of whom have never visited the Bochasan temple or even India! Akshar and Purushottam, it could be said, are indeed anywhere and everywhere, always separate and yet always together. Perhaps it should not be surprising that many Gujarati Hindus are finding this fact enormously satisfying, for their present and future lives.

Acknowledgements

The ethnographic data, including quoted conversations, for this chapter come from ongoing fieldwork in the BAPS Swaminarayan diaspora (1991–2010). I thank the BAPS community, its leaders, *sādhus*, and individual devotees, for their always generous engagement with my research.

Notes

1. See Williams (2001) for an English-language introduction to the variety of Swaminarayan groups that connect themselves to the same historical founder, Sahajanand Swami. In BAPS, Sahajanand Swami is Bhagwan Swaminarayan. BAPS shares ritual similarities to the Vallabha Saṃpradāya or Puṣṭi Mārga, a much older Hindu devotional community well-known in western India.
2. Visit www.swaminarayan.org and link to "Global Network" to survey the extent of the Swaminarayan diaspora.
3. Also, assemblies for children and youth are usually conducted in English where English is the dominant national language, such as in North America, the United Kingdom, South Africa and Australia.
4. The *Shikshapatri* and *Vachanamrut* are significant for not just BAPS but the older Swaminarayan communities who predate BAPS and are still extant in Gujarat. There are, however, significant differences in the translation and editing of these texts.
5. This ethnographic material was collected during the "Yogi Shatabdi" event held in Gandhinagar, Gujarat, from 29 October to 2 December 1992 to commemorate the hundredth birthday of Guru Yogiji Maharaj.
6. In describing this sequence of Hiral's *nitya pūjā*, it should be noted that this is a pattern that pertains to an unmarried young woman. Hiral, in this article, is a composite of several young women. In BAPS, there are small variations for males versus females and married versus unmarried females, and acceptable modifications for the elderly, very young and the infirm.

10. Kṛṣṇa devotion in western India

Shandip Saha

The tenth-century Sanskrit text known as the ***Bhāgavata Purāṇa*** has come to occupy an important place in Hinduism as the source of the stories surrounding the exploits of Kṛṣṇa, one of Hinduism's most popular and beloved gods.[1] The *Bhāgavata Purāṇa* recounts how Lord Viṣṇu takes human form to rid the earth of oppression by being born as Kṛṣṇa into the household of the cowherd chieftain Nanda and his wife **Yaśodā** in the region of Braj along the banks of the River Yamuna. The Bhāgavata describes Kṛṣṇa's idyllic childhood, during which time he tends to cows, engages in childhood pranks with his fellow cowherd friends, and performs superhuman feats such as killing demons and lifting a hill named Govardhan on one finger to protect the residents of Braj from a torrential rainstorm. The Bhāgavata also recounts Kṛṣṇa's amorous exploits with the village milkmaids (***gopīs***), and the intense pain and longing they feel for him when he leaves his home permanently to complete his earthly mission. The Bhāgavata, however, makes it clear that Kṛṣṇa is not merely a manifestation (*avatāra*) of Viṣṇu. Kṛṣṇa is the complete and fullest manifestation of the Divine, and it is only through him that one can attain spiritual salvation (*mokṣa*).

There are many devotional communities (***bhakti*** saṃpradāya) in India today that place Kṛṣṇa at the centre of their religious lives and make the *Bhāgavata Purāṇa* the foundation upon which to model their devotional lives. This chapter will focus upon the *bhakti* community named the **Vallabha Saṃpradāya** or, as it is more popularly known, the **Puṣṭi Mārga**. The Puṣṭi Mārga is a vibrant and very active Hindu devotional community whose devotees come largely from the mercantile classes of Gujarat, Rajasthan, and parts of both Madhya Pradesh and Uttar Pradesh. The Puṣṭi Mārga was originally founded in north India by the philosopher Vallabhācārya (1479–1531) and is unusual because its philosophy does not emphasize the rejection of the material world in favour of austere religious practices. The teachings of the Puṣṭi Mārga, instead, emphasize the channelling of one's passions and worldly goods towards the worship of Kṛṣṇa. This community consequently has become known for its lavish rituals and minute attention paid to recreating the divine pastimes (***līlās***) of Kṛṣṇa. This chapter will serve as a general introduction to the practice of worship in the Puṣṭi Mārga known as *sevā*. This chapter will begin by providing a small historical sketch of the Puṣṭi Mārga and will then proceed to provide a very general and simplified outline of some key theological concepts that form the basis for the ritual life of the community. The remainder of this chapter will then focus on the actual performance of rituals in order to understand the devotional experience of Puṣṭi Mārga devotees and why ritual service is considered to be pivotal for relating to Kṛṣṇa in their daily lives.

A brief history of the Puṣṭi Mārga

The Puṣṭi Mārga was founded in the sixteenth century by Vallabhācārya and remained under his leadership until his death in 1531.[2] The leadership of the community was then entrusted to his eldest son **Gopīnāth** (1512–43) and then to Gopīnāth's younger brother **Viṭṭhalnāth** (1515–85), who expanded the community's presence on the north Indian religious scene by seeking the patronage of ruling Mughal emperors and the wealthy Hindu mercantile community in the state of Gujarat in western India. Before his death in 1585, Viṭṭhalnāth established the current method of worship practised in Puṣṭi Mārga temples and he also divided the leadership of the Puṣṭi Mārga equally among his seven sons who inherited the exclusive right to initiate disciples. Viṭṭhalnāth's sons were also given custody over various images of Kṛṣṇa with the principal image named **Śrīnāthjī** being entrusted to Viṭṭhalnāth's eldest son and his descendants.

This distribution of spiritual authority led to the formation of seven divisions within the Puṣṭi Mārga, known as the "Seven Houses", with spiritual leadership of each division based upon the principle of primogeniture. Initiatory rights into the community and leadership of each of the seven divisions could only be in the hands of the male descendants of Vallabha traced through Viṭṭhalnāth who came to be called ***mahārājas*** by their disciples. The *mahārājas* of the first house were given a certain pre-eminence within the Puṣṭi Mārga because it had custody of the Śrīnāthjī image which carried great significance for the community because the image was said to have appeared miraculously to Vallabhācārya while he was travelling in Braj, and depicted how Kṛṣṇa exactly looked when he lifted the Govardhan hill on his hand.

The *mahārājas* of the Puṣṭi Mārga all lived in the Braj area near the Govardhan hill where the Śrīnāthjī image was installed by Vallabha and they continued to live there until 1669, when political instability forced the *mahārājas* to leave Braj and seek protection from Hindu rulers in the state of Rajasthan. The different *mahārājas* came to establish temples across Rajasthan and Gujarat which continue to be very vibrant today with the image of Śrīnāthjī being installed in a large temple in 1672 in the Rajput state of Mewar. The image continues to reside in the temple located in a town named Nathdwara, which continues to this day to be the most important place of pilgrimage for all members of the Puṣṭi Mārga.

Sevā and *bhāva* in the Puṣṭi Mārga

Vallabhācārya preached a form of religious practice that emphasized the importance of living a householder life grounded in the purifying grace *(puṣṭi)* of the Supreme Lord Kṛṣṇa. It is for this reason that Vallabha's community came to be known as the Puṣṭi Mārga or the "Path of Grace". Those who take initiation into the Puṣṭi Mārga are required to express their self-surrender (***ātmanivedana***) to Kṛṣṇa by repeating the *brahmasaṃbandha mantra* that is given by the *mahārājas*. The *mantra* requires devotees to declare that they will rely on no other deity but Kṛṣṇa, and will dedicate their material possessions, their families and indeed their entire selves to his service. Thus individuals are not expected to renounce the world for a life of austerity. The *mahārājas* of the Puṣṭi Mārga themselves are all married and maintain large extended families of their own and devotees are expected to carry on with their worldly duties, but with the understanding that all their future actions and material acquisitions would be offered to Kṛṣṇa before they make use of them themselves. Once devotees have repeated *brahmasaṃbandha mantra*, they are considered to be cleansed of their faults and impurities and are now true servants (*sevaks*) ready to dedicate their lives to the lifelong practice of *sevā* to Kṛṣṇa.

What, however, does *sevā* mean? *Sevā* literally means "service", but in the Puṣṭi Mārga this term takes on the much more specific meaning of performing selfless service to God as an act of love and devotion. According to Puṣṭi Mārga belief, the traditional forms of worship (*pūjā*) performed within Hinduism is done purely for securing specific spiritual or material benefits and thus is motivated out of self-interest. Furthermore, the rules and regulations (***maryādā***) that govern the performance of *pūjā* ultimately inhibit the spontaneous expression of love towards God. *Sevā*, it is stressed within the Puṣṭi Mārga, is not about attempting to secure a specific favour from Kṛṣṇa, be it spiritual or material. The practice of *sevā* is to be understood as the spontaneous expression of the devotee's love for Kṛṣṇa and the desire to put the happiness of God before one's own personal desires (Bennett 1993: 69–75).

Sevā, then, requires members of the Puṣṭi Mārga, to adhere to a strict moral code that places an emphasis on vegetarianism, living a life of constant humility and virtuousness, and maintaining an unswerving faith in Kṛṣṇa even in the worst of circumstances. Being preoccupied with worldly concerns and desires will only serve to render one's devotion to Kṛṣṇa ineffectual and will absolutely not be conducive to the cultivation of ***bhāva***. Bhāva is a devotional state of mind which is adopted by the devotee during performance of *sevā* in order to intensify and deepen his relationship with God. In the Puṣṭi Mārga, *sevā* is done towards images of the child Kṛṣṇa and, consequently, emphasis has been placed upon ***vātsalya bhāva*** or emulating the motherly tenderness and affection that Yaśodā is said to have showered upon her son. This is manifested in the ritual worship of Kṛṣṇa performed in temples and homes in the form of *sevā* performed by one's physical effort (***tanujā sevā***) and through the use of one's wealth (***vittajā sevā***).

However important the adoption of *vātsalya bhāva* and the performance of *tanujā* and *vittajā sevā* may be in the Puṣṭi Mārga, they are not necessarily considered to be the highest spiritual states that a devotee can achieve. The Bhāgavata emphasizes that those who are the ideal devotees of Kṛṣṇa are the milkmaids of Braj because they love Kṛṣṇa with such depth that they cannot bear to be separated from him. Thus their already intense love for Kṛṣṇa not only increases during their union with him, but also in the moments when they are separated from him. This intense yearning for Kṛṣṇa – known as ***mādhurya bhāva*** – is what Vallabha sees as a particularly important fruit (*phala*) of performing *sevā*. According to Vallabha, those who regularly perform their *sevā* will find their devotion maturing into an obsessive devotion (*vyasana*) where one begins to alternate between moments of union and separation from Kṛṣṇa and the devotee's only concern is intensify this love for God. It is at this point that the actual performance of *sevā* becomes unnecessary for the devotee will achieve what is known as ***sarvātmabhāva*** which refers to a mental state of mind in which the individual becomes so absorbed in Kṛṣṇa that he perceives of everything in the world as being nothing but a manifestation of Kṛṣṇa himself. Maintaining this emotional state known as ***mānasī sevā*** can only be achieved if Kṛṣṇa desires to bestow his grace upon the individual, but in the Puṣṭi Mārga it is believed that such spiritually advanced souls are extremely rare to find (Bennett 1993: 74; Narain 2004: 414–34).[3] Thus, *sevā* in the Puṣṭi Mārga finds its most open expression in the performance of *tanujā* and *vittajā sevā* in both homes and temples.

The place of the *havelī* and *svarūpa* in the Puṣṭi Mārga

The objects of *sevā* in the Puṣṭi Mārga are images of Kṛṣṇa typically made of metal, but for devotees the images are far from being lifeless. They are considered to be visible manifestations of Kṛṣṇa and are called ***svarūpas*** because the images themselves are considered to be Kṛṣṇa's own (*sva*) form (*rūpa*). What, however, makes the image of Kṛṣṇa a sentient being is again the *bhāva* or the devotional attitude with which the devotee approaches the image. Given that devotees in the Puṣṭi Mārga relate to Kṛṣṇa by emulating the love of his mother Yaśodā, devotees will perform *sevā* to the image by bathing and feeding the image, dressing it appropriately depending on the weather, and even play games and engage in conversations with the image. Thus, the more the image becomes the object of the devotee's feelings of love and tenderness, the more the image begins to assume its own personality until it finally becomes a full manifestation of Kṛṣṇa himself in the eyes of the devotee (Bennett 1993: 90–93, 97).

The *bhāva* of the devotee is equally important in defining and giving meaning to the sacred space in which *sevā* is performed. Devotees stress a Puṣṭi Mārga temple is not a *mandir*, a word traditionally used when referring to a Hindu temple. The word ***havelī*** is used instead because the temples are housed within the large multi-storeyed residences in which the *mahārājas* and their extended families live. The term *havelī* is also preferred because the large mansion-like structure of the temple is meant to evoke Kṛṣṇa's childhood home in Braj where he was raised by his parents, Yaśodā and Nanda. In other words, the *havelī* is the portal through which one leaves the world of the mundane and is brought into a world which for devotees is the land of Braj and the realm where they can relive and participate in Kṛṣṇa's pastimes and come directly into his presence.

The model for many Puṣṭi Mārga *havelīs* is based on the *havelī* in Nathdwara, which is home to the Śrīnāthjī image.[4] This is a stone image of about roughly five feet in height depicting a seven-year-old Kṛṣṇa with his left arm lifted upwards in the act of lifting Govardhan on his hand. The *havelī* is a large sprawling complex built from brick and stone, and full of balconies, courtyards and rooms used for the preparation of food and the storage of jewellery and clothes, all of which are to be used for Śrīnāthjī's *sevā*.[5] One enters the Nathdwara *havelī* through two wooden doors which are protected by metal plates and walks through a large courtyard *(cauk)* which leads to the inner sanctum (*nijmandir*), which contains the image of Śrīnāthjī. This entrance is known as the **Lāl Darvāzā** to remind devotees that Kṛṣṇa is the darling (*lāl*) of his mother Yaśodā. Just beyond this courtyard is the Govardhan Cauk, a rectangular courtyard which is meant to symbolize the Govardhan hill in Braj that Kṛṣṇa lifted with his one hand. From the Govardhan Cauk one can access the gateway to a courtyard named the **Ḍholīpaṭiya** where florists gather to sell flowers to pilgrims every morning and afternoon. The white marble, with which it is paved, however, is meant to remind devotees of the ocean of milk upon which Viṣṇu is said to recline.

From the Ḍholīpaṭiya, one can access a series of courtyards, which are painted with images to remind devotees of various events in the life of Kṛṣṇa. Of these courtyards, the most important is the Kamal Cauk. This is a large courtyard that has a floor design of a lotus *(kamal)* with twenty-four petals that is contained within a circle. The lotus is meant to represent the river Yamuna and the twenty-four groves surrounding the Braj region while the circular border of the lotus is meant to symbolize the famed ***rāsa līlā***, which refers to the event when Kṛṣṇa performed a circle dance on the banks of the Yamuna with the *gopīs* of Braj. Adjacent to the Kamal Cauk is a court surrounded by triple-arched galleries (***tivārī***) known as the Ḍoltivārī because here the image of Śrīnāthjī is pushed on a swing (*ḍol*) to commemorate the celebration of the spring festival known as Holī. It is in the Ḍoltivārī and the Kamal Cauk where devotees wait anxiously for entrance into the inner sanctum with the women entering from the steps leading to the Ḍoltivārī while the men enter from the Kamal Cauk. Once the doors are thrown open devotees literally run towards the sanctum and cram themselves into the small narrow room that constitutes the *nijmandir* nearly climbing over each other to view the five foot black stone image of Śrīnāthjī. Signs written in Hindi ask individuals to enter the *nijmandir* in an orderly fashion since it will be opened up sufficiently long enough for devotees to see Śrīnāthjī, but the sign is all but ignored. When devotees in not only the Nathdwara *havelī*, but any Puṣṭi Mārga havelī are alerted that the *nijmandir* is to be opened, it is at that moment when devotees feel that they are leaving their mundane (*laukik*) surroundings to enter into the realm of the sacred (*alaukik*) where they are to come into the immediate presence of their beloved lord Kṛṣṇa.

The performance of *nitya sevā* and *utsav sevā* in Puṣṭi Mārga *havelīs*

The transition from the realm of the mundane to the sacred land of Braj is maintained in the *havelīs* through means of the eight viewings (*darśanas*) of Kṛṣṇa. Each of these *darśanas* occur throughout the day at which time devotees will gather in the *nijmandir* to view the *svarūpa* and become active participants in Kṛṣṇa's divine pastimes. Each *darśana*, then, is meticulously planned and has a high degree of realism in order to maintain the *bhāva* of the devotee and to strengthen their emotional connection to the *svarūpa*. The first *darśana* – known as ***maṅgala darśana*** – occurs generally before sunrise when the temple priests in the mode of *vātsalya bhāva* will awake the child Kṛṣṇa in order to offer him a light breakfast of milk and fruits, and is followed an hour later by the second *darśana*, which is known as ***śṛṅgār darśana***, at which time the *svarūpa* is bathed, dressed and given another food offering. The third *darśana* – known as ***gvāl darśana*** – is when Kṛṣṇa is shown to devotees taking his cows to graze in the pastures of Braj. After leaving his cows to graze, Kṛṣṇa is said to return home for his main meal of the day. This *darśana* is called ***rājbhog darśana***, at which point devotees view the *svarūpa* adorned in its most elaborate finery and being offered a large meal of rice, pickles, vegetables, fruits, cakes and desserts, after which the deity is laid down to sleep for his afternoon nap. When Kṛṣṇa is awoken around three o'clock during the ***utthāpan darśana***, the deity is awoken to the gentle strains of vocal and instrumental music and when, an hour later, a snack offered to Kṛṣṇa prior to his departure for the pastures, this *darśana* is called ***bhog darśana***. The early evening *darśana*, known as ***sandhyā āratī***, marks Kṛṣṇa's return home from the pastures; a lamp is then waved in front of him to ward off any evil influences or harm he may have encountered while wandering in the pastures of Braj. The final *darśana* takes place at dusk and is known as ***śayan āratī*** when Kṛṣṇa's bedchamber is readied and he is put to sleep for the evening. The *havelī* then closes and the entire cycle of *darśanas* starts anew the next day.

Each *darśana* is an extremely elaborate affair. Those who are responsible for the *sevā* to the *svarūpa* not only carry the responsibility of maintaining the *bhāva* of devotees, but also the responsibility of caring for the Lord himself in the same way that Yaśodā did.[6] Consequently, great care is taken to ensure that no discomfort will come to Kṛṣṇa over the course of each *darśana*. The doors during the *maṅgala darśana* are kept locked, for example, in order to avoid Kṛṣṇa being startled by the crowds of devotees clamouring to see him or to prevent Kṛṣṇa from running out the door to play with his companions. During the *śṛṅgār darśana*, he is offered a mirror so he may approve the clothes in which he has been dressed, and during the *rājbhog darśana*, Kṛṣṇa's flute, the stick he uses to graze his cows and a little ball for his amusement are kept in front of him before he leaves for the pasture. Throughout the day Kṛṣṇa is constantly provided with water to quench his thirst, small snacks to help keep him healthy, and a mixture of betel leaf and spices known as **pān** to use as a breath freshener and a digestive aid.

The steps are also taken to ensure the *svarūpa*'s comfort during the changing weather. For example, during the summer months, small fountains and ponds are erected in front of the *svarūpa* in order to help cool the child Kṛṣṇa. Small statues of ducks and boats are floated in the ponds; lotuses and jasmine flowers are placed in the fountains; *svarūpas* are brought into courtyards, which are then flooded with water, and are surrounded with various types of flora to help recreate the different groves of Braj where Kṛṣṇa is said to have relaxed while tending to his cows. Sandalwood, famed for its cooling properties, will be applied to Kṛṣṇa's body to keep him protected from the heat and only foods with cooling properties are offered to the child. Both clothing and jewellery are also chosen with great care, for these too have the potential to cause great discomfort to Kṛṣṇa. Only light cotton clothing is offered to Kṛṣṇa during the summer months and, on occasions, his entire clothing will be made from scented flowers for his comfort. Only soft pale colours are used for the pillows, curtains, and coverings in both the *nijmandir* and bedchamber (*śayan mandir*) to offset the harsh glare of the sun and even foods like milk, yogurt, mangos which are known for their cooling properties are tinged with colours of pink, yellow, or light greens to heighten the overall aesthetic experience of the *darśana*.

Since the *sevā* structured around the eight *darśanas* occurs every day, it is termed *nitya sevā* or the daily *sevā*, and is distinguished from the *utsav sevā* or the *sevā* that is offered to Kṛṣṇa during the cycle of festivals (*ustav*) in the Hindu calendar. The practice of *nitya sevā* is not suspended during the celebration of festivals, but it becomes even more elaborate as the *svarūpa* is dressed in special clothing and special forms of worship are performed as an expression of love towards Kṛṣṇa. During the festival of Holī, for example, when Hindus will celebrate the arrival of spring by throwing coloured powder on each other, a *svarūpa* will be dressed in a special white robe and temple *sevaks* will play Holī with the *svarūpa* by applying coloured powders in various designs to the *svarūpa*'s clothes. This is followed the next day by **Ḍolotsava** when the *svarūpa* is placed in a swing (*ḍol*) in the Ḍoltivārī, at which time cardboard cutouts of the milkmaids and cowherds of Braj are arranged alongside a pond surrounded by shrubbery in order to again recreate the groves of Braj in which Kṛṣṇa is said to have spent all his time. One sees something similar during another festival called **Hariyālī Amāvasyā** which occurs during the monsoon months of July and August. Since the countryside becomes lush and green with the coming of the rains, Kṛṣṇa is adorned entirely in green, is rocked in a swing intertwined with sandal leaves and jasmine twigs, and is offered green vegetables and sweets to which green vegetable dye has been added.

The preparation of food is in many ways absolutely central to the performance of *sevā* in the Puṣṭi Mārga. It is stressed within the community that food has the ability to absorb the emotional state of the individual who has prepared it and, while physical cleanliness is extremely important in the preparation of food, so too is the mental purity of the individual who prepares it. A story well known to devotees of the Puṣṭi Mārga about Viṭṭhalnāth details how a dog enters the kitchens of a wealthy devotee and a poor devotee, making both individuals' kitchens ritually impure for the preparation of food offerings (*prasād*) to Kṛṣṇa. Viṭṭhalnāth, however, ultimately rejects the offerings of the rich devotee because he lacked the sincerity and humility of his poorer devotee. In other words, the moral of the story is that the purity of one's *bhāva* overrides all other purity concerns. When food is offered in generous amounts by the individual with true sincerity and devotion, it is considered to be one of the most intimate ways by which the devotee expresses the depth of his devotion for God. It is stressed, however, by devotees that the pleasure of serving the Lord food finds it greatest fulfilment when the devotee is able to partake in the *prasād* after it has been offered to and accepted by Kṛṣṇa. Partaking in the *prasād* has not only the purpose of providing physical sustenance to the individual, but also nourishment to the soul of the individual, since the *prasād* is considered the vehicle by which Kṛṣṇa bestows his grace upon his devotees Thus, it is vital to share the *prasād* with other devotees who are there to participate in the *sevā* to Kṛṣṇa for it will help to continue strengthen one's devotion to God.[7]

This is the message behind the celebration of the **Annakūṭa** festival, which marks the episode in Kṛṣṇa's life when he assumed the form of Mount Govardhan and accepted the food offerings made to him by the residents of Braj who would pile their food offerings to the summit of the mountain. When devotees in the Puṣṭi Mārga today perform *sevā* to Kṛṣṇa on the occasion of Annakūṭa, they make a large likeness of Govardhan out of boiled rice and place it in front of the *svarūpa* along with numerous baskets of food, which is eventually given to all those who are attending the celebration. Celebrating Annakūṭa is extremely expensive and elaborate in nature and generally requires that all devotees to share in the cost of the festival. Thus the celebration is a visible manifestation of the collective devotion that members of the Puṣṭi Mārga hold for Kṛṣṇa and also of their commitment to keep their community spiritually nourished by sharing in the *prasād* infused with Kṛṣṇa's grace. Annakūṭa, however, is most importantly a reminder of how the relationship between God and the devotee in the Puṣṭi Mārga is one of interdependence. Kṛṣṇa may indeed be the Lord of the Universe but the relationship between him and his devotees is a reciprocal one in which both sides subsist upon and are nourished by the boundless love they give to each other.

Conclusion

It may be tempting to say that *sevā* is nothing more than another manifestation of the mechanical ritual formalism that members of the Puṣṭi Mārga associate with mainstream Hindu practice, but that is far from being the case. When the relationship with the Divine is established through the *brahmasaṃbandha mantra* and is maintained through the regular practice of *sevā*, the result is not one of imbalance where the devotee - even if he terms himself a servant of the Lord - feels that he is in a constant state of servitude to the Divine. The adoption of *vātsalya bhāva* as the principal means by which one relates to Kṛṣṇa helps to develop a relationship between Kṛṣṇa and the individual that is shaped by familiarity, intimacy, and most of all interdependence. In this relationship of interdependence, Kṛṣṇa and the devotee are bound irrevocably into a relationship where both subsist on the love that is shared between them. The practice of *sevā* also creates a certain sense of interdependence among devotees by reminding them that as fellow travellers on the Path of Grace, they all have a responsibility to support each other in their relationship with Kṛṣṇa by ensuring that all devotees keep spiritually healthy through the distribution of *prasād* filled with Kṛṣṇa's grace. Thus, while there may be indeed rules and regulations that govern the practice of *sevā* in the Puṣṭi Mārga, these very rules do not result in a slavish attachment to ritual. It, on the contrary, ultimately helps devotees to transcend the mundane nature of everyday life and become active participants in a divine realm where it is first and foremost the spontaneous expression of religious passion and devotion that is at the centre of daily religious life.

Notes

1. For a readable translation of the tenth chapter of the Bhāgavata Purāṇa, which contains the stories for the Kṛṣṇa legends, see Bryant (2003).
2. For general accounts of the institutional history of the Puṣṭi Mārga during the leadership and after the death of Vallabha, see the essays on the Puṣṭi Mārga in Entwistle (1987: 151–4, 160–66, 177–8) and Saha (2004: 99–144).
3. For Vallabha's own words concerning the practice of *sevā*, see his set of short sixteen Sanskrit treatises called **Ṣoḍaśagranthaḥ**. The text has been translated into English by James Redington (2000) under the title of *The Grace of Lord Kṛṣṇa*. For Vallabha's comments on *sevā*, see Redington (2000: 44, 125–6, 160–63, 177–81).
4. Images of Śrīnāthjī can be found at http://www.pushti-marg.net/gal_shriji.htm (accessed June 2013).
5. The basis for this description of the Nathdwara *havelī* is based in part on personal fieldwork at Nathdwara conducted in 1997 and 2004, as well as the descriptions found in Amit Ambalal (1995: 19–20) and in Rajendra Jindel (1976: 80–99).
6. While the eight *darśanas* form the foundation upon which worship is performed in all Puṣṭi Mārga *havelīs*, there are only broad guidelines for how the *svarūpa* is to be adorned and fed during individual *darśanas* and specific periods during the year including the celebration of particular festivals. These guidelines can be found in *sevā* manuals entitled ***sevā praṇālīs*** which are published privately by devotees under the guidance of a particular *mahārāja* or by the *sevaks* of a particular *havelī*. Otherwise, the details are generally left to the discretion of the *mahārājas* and the temple *sevaks*. The description of the *sevā* in this chapter are, consequently, based on a number of different sources and by no means is meant to be an exhaustive description of the

endless *bhāvas* and sacred symbolism associated with the performance of *sevā*. The sources used here are Bennett (1993: 104–22), Ambalal (1995: 21–36), Mahārāj (1937), Ramchandra (1989), Shivji (1931), and Kīrtankār (1994).

7. The story is found in a collection of religious tales called the **Vārtā Sāhitya**, which details the lives of Vallabha and Viṭṭhalnāth's most exemplary devotees. For a general consideration of the Vārtā Sāhitya, see Saha (2006: 225–42). For an analysis of the significance of food offerings within the Puṣṭi Mārga see Saha (2006: 236–8), Bennett (1993: 123–47) and Toomey (1994).

11. Vārkarīs in rural western India

Jon Keune

The monsoon rains had arrived on time this year, so that walking under the blazing sun now was bearable, and the flat, open plains around us had turned vibrantly green. A few farmers were still out in their fields, standing firmly on the crossbeams of their handmade wooden ploughs to push them into the dark soil as their bullocks pulled them along. Most fields were already planted, some with robust cotton seedlings and others with millet and corn that had yet to sprout. A distant clinking of hand cymbals cut through the wind in the trees and the cheerful banter of the pilgrims as we walked. We had just departed from the ancient town of Paithan in the west-central Indian state of Maharashtra. Eighteen days and 150 miles lay ahead of us, due south, before we would reach our destination – the Viṭṭhal temple in the town of Pandharpur. There, the pilgrims would stand before the stone image (*mūrti*) of the god, looking at him as he looked back at them – the basic Hindu act of *darśan.* Pilgrims make this journey from Paithan to Pandharpur every year, as their ancestors have been doing for centuries. New, however, was the tall, pale foreigner who was going along this year to ask questions, take notes and experience the pilgrimage himself.

I had studied, packed and prepared as much as possible, but I still felt more than a little anxiety when I thought about what might lie ahead. How would my feet and sandals endure the journey? Would my stomach cope with their food, or would bacterial intruders wreak their nauseating havoc and stop me from walking further? Where would we all find privacy for the human necessities of toilet and bathing? And most basic of all, how would the pilgrims feel about me simply being there as I tried to learn about them and their traditions? Worries about the last question, at least, were quickly dispelled as ever more pilgrims – complete strangers – would wave, smile and boisterously call out "*Chala!*" ("let's go!"). And so we went.

***

Introduction

Every year in June and July, pilgrims from around west-central India set out walking to a smallish town in southern Maharashtra to meet their god. The deity's name is Viṭṭhal, known more affectionately to his devotees as Viṭhobā (Father Viṭṭhal), and occasionally as Viṭhāī (Mother Viṭṭhal). Following their venerable tradition, pilgrims often call him Pāṇḍurang (the White-Coloured One) as well, although why this name suits him is not clear or remembered. A rough, black stone image of Viṭṭhal, carved in his distinctive posture – standing on two bricks, with hands on hips and elbows out – awaits the pilgrims in his temple in Pandharpur. Although no one knows exactly when the Viṭṭhal image was established there or when pilgrims started visiting regularly, stone inscriptions and old Marathi texts give strong evidence that this tradition is at least 800 years old.[1] Technically, four such pilgrimages in this tradition happen each year, but the one in June/July is by far the largest and most famous. Nowadays, this event draws nearly one million pilgrims, all of them trying to arrive in time to celebrate the tradition's most auspicious time – the eleventh day of the waxing moon in the Hindu month of Āṣāḍh.[2]

Numbers like these make the pilgrimage to Pandharpur the largest and most visible religious tradition in Maharashtra and one of the largest annual pilgrimages in all of India. The name for this pilgrimage in the local Marathi language is ***vārī***, and the pilgrims are Vārkarīs (literally, "people who do *vārī*").[3] As their name implies, this pilgrimage is the defining feature of their Hindu devotional tradition. Although Vārkarīs do have a particular philosophy and religious literature, it is mainly the activity of *vārī* itself that makes them Vārkarīs.[4]

Some pilgrims now travel by car and bus, but most still use the traditional Vārkarī mode of transportation – their own feet – sometimes with sandals or shoes, sometimes without. In this tradition, both the journey and the destination are important, and only those who are physically unable or crucially pressed for time opt for the bus rather than walking. Vārkarīs who live far away from Pandharpur set out forty or even fifty days in advance so that they can traverse hundreds of miles and reach the town on time. A few of the most ardent pilgrims will even turn around and walk back home as well. A very small number continue walking for months and even years on end, travelling among Pandharpur and the towns associated with the Vārkarī saints. Pilgrims who accomplish the whole journey to Pandharpur on foot enjoy great respect in their communities back home, as they are understood to have received Viṭṭhal's blessing for their efforts. For locals who did not go on pilgrimage, reverently touching the feet of a Vārkarī who has returned from Pandharpur is a way to get a bit of that blessing indirectly. The Vārkarīs' commitment and perseverance is widely admired by non-Vārkarīs and non-Hindus in the region as well.

The most common way of making the pilgrimage is to join a procession connected to one of the Vārkarī saints.[5] At the centre of each procession is a palanquin (***pālkhī***) which, depending on the terrain and situation, is either carried by pilgrims on their shoulders or placed on a cart and pulled by bullocks. Centuries ago, *pālkhīs* carried kings and noble people, but in this pilgrimage they bear only the stylized silver replicas of a saint's sandals (***pādukās***). During the rest of the year, the sandals are kept and worshipped in a temple in a town that has a special relationship with the saint – usually the place where the saint was born or left the earthly world.[6] These silver sandals are brought along on the pilgrimage, and people treat them as manifestations of the medieval saints themselves accompanying the pilgrims to Pandharpur. At various stops along the way, priests worship the sandals with rituals and chanting, and local people in the countryside gather to reverently touch the sandals and receive the saint's blessing.

The two largest and most famous processions accompany the *pālkhīs* of the saints Jñāndev and Tukārām, whose temples are located in Āḷandī and Dehu (towns near the city of Pune) on the western side of the state. Amid the hundreds of thousands of Vārkarīs who walk with these two palanquins, nowadays one also often sees television and newspaper reporters, camera crews, and the occasional adventurous foreigner and aspiring film-maker. Consequently, photos and video clips of these two major processions can be found easily on the internet. The size of these processions and their accessibility from the city of Pune has attracted scholars and writers who have published accounts of their experiences.[7] In addition to these two palanquins, hundreds of smaller processions make the journey from around the region where Marathi is spoken, each of them with its own slightly different stories and traditions. These countless small groups, all walking their own separate paths to Pandharpur, are at the heart of the lived Vārkarī tradition.

My research on the sixteenth-century saint Eknāth brought me to the town of Paithan, where he used to live. There I came to know several of Eknāth's descendants, who organize his *pālkhī*'s annual procession to Pandharpur. No scholar or foreigner had ever walked with the Eknāth *pālkhī* before, so in July 2010 I decided to join them. Before we started out, the organizers handed me a chart of the dates and the names of the towns where we would stop to eat along the way and where we would stay for the night. Most of the towns were so small that they didn't even appear on a map; this was *very* rural area. The organizers claimed that they've been taking this route for the last 500 years, so in each town they have reliable contacts that support the Vārkarīs by providing water, snacks, meals, and places for the pilgrims to sleep. Two large trucks (the ubiquitous Indian "goods carriers") also would accompany the procession to haul the pilgrims' luggage and bedding. Throughout the pilgrimage from Paithan to Pandharpur, the pilgrims walked mainly on small footpaths through farmers' fields and hills, while the trucks had to drive longer, indirect routes on the roads to meet up with pilgrims at designated stops. An Indian friend generously lent me his car and found a driver for the trip so that my belongings, camera and laptop could be brought along safely while I was out walking and meeting people. More importantly, the car also carried a supply of bottled water that I could safely drink, and it allowed me quick access to a hospital if I were to fall sick (which, for a couple days, I did).

We were only a couple hundred pilgrims at the beginning, when we set out from Paithan. In addition to the roughly twenty descendants of Eknāth and some townsfolk from Paithan, several small groups came from other nearby towns to travel with the *pālkhī*. All of the pilgrims had unique stories about how they had come to join. This is one of the most fascinating and amazing aspects of this pilgrimage: Vārkarīs organize themselves in local groups across the vast region without any supervising authority or central administration. They have no high priest or institutional hierarchy. There is no formal network or association to which all pilgrims belong or a litmus test of orthodoxy that they must pass in order to join the pilgrimage. Yet there are patterns to how these small groups come together. At the core of each group are usually a few experienced pilgrims who have made the journey before and know what lies ahead. Sometimes there is a locally renowned Vārkarī leader (called a ***maharāj***) who organizes a group as well. These seasoned pilgrims may attract new pilgrims through various ways: family relations, contacts through neighbours, job-related associations, friends of friends, their outstanding reputation in the community, and so on. At the most basic level, the connections of Vārkarīs are intensely local and personal.

The sun was setting on our first day of walking as we rounded a curve in the potholed road and the little village where we would stay for the night came into view. Some pilgrims began to disperse into the town, meeting up with old friends and acquaintances with whom they stayed while on previous pilgrimages. Eknāth's descendants accompanied the palanquin to the *āśram* (shelter/hermitage) of a local holy man and his disciples so that they could pay their respects. This holy man was devoted to a different deity who was not connected to the Vārkarīs, but, as is common in village life, boundaries between religious traditions are rarely strict or rigidly observed. The holy man touched the silver sandals, and his disciples distributed to the pilgrims little plastic cups of potent, sugary tea. After this short pause, during which local villagers came to touch the sandals, four strong men picked up the palanquin again and carried it to the small temple at the centre of town, where it would remain throughout the night. A local priest of the temple started chanting hymns, a couple in Sanskrit but most in Marathi, all of which was blasted over tinny speakers for the whole town to hear, whether they wanted to listen or not. Townspeople crowded together to greet the palanquin, touch the sandals, make small donations, and see the spectacle. A few enterprising small-time merchants laid out their wares on a plastic sheet on the ground – trinkets, sweets and cheap plastic toys. Eventually the priest finished chanting, and a group of musicians began to perform.

Vārkarī music

Vārkarī musical performances are always accompanied by a group of people playing pairs of tuned brass hand cymbals (*ṭāḷ*), which are struck together in various ways to make different sounds in rhythm. At more programmed and elaborate performances, one also finds someone playing a two-headed, tuned drum called a ***pakhvāj***. About three feet long and suspended horizontally by a strap hung around the drummer's neck, a *pakhvāj* is played by hitting and slapping the drum heads with the hands and fingers. In the background is a hollow wooden instrument with one or more strings that are plucked to maintain a tuning pitch for the main singer, although its volume is so soft that the audience rarely hears it. This instrument is called a ***vīṇā*** in colloquial Marathi, although it is so simple as to bear little resemblance to the *vīṇā* of Indian classical music. Nowadays, a loudspeaker system has become practically standard equipment as well, with the emphasis being placed on quantity of sound over quality.

The main singer in the group sets the course for how the songs and performance will proceed, and anywhere from three to twenty *ṭāḷ*-playing men serve as a chorus to back him up, dancing and jumping to the music and leading the audience to sing along at appropriate times. As in most Vārkarī performances, the musicians this night started off with a *bhajan* - a very popular kind of song that requires audience participation. The basic structure of the song is call and response, as the leader sings a phrase and the audience repeats it. The leader sometimes improvises or sings brief solos, but for the most part, the tune and text simply are repeated over and over, growing louder and faster as the musicians and audience become entranced by the sound. Vārkarīs also sing more serene versions of these *bhajans* on the road as they walk, so these songs are very well-known to the pilgrims. This night, after singing several *bhajans*, the lead musician moved on to a more instructional kind of performance called a ***kīrtan***. Following the typical Vārkarī *kīrtan* form, he began by singing a poem composed by Eknāth and then narrated some episodes from the Vārkarī saints' lives to illustrate the poem's spiritual message. Most of the saints were accomplished and popular poets - a fact demonstrated by the most common Marathi term for them: "saint-poets" (***sant-kavi***).[8] The Marathi compositions of the *sant-kavi* function as a scriptural base for this tradition. The singer performed the *kīrtan*, regularly mixing in additional *bhajans* to keep the townspeople and pilgrims in the audience engaged during his three-hour performance. The sun had gone down and aside from the glow of a few fluorescent tube lights, darkness covered the village. Having walked all day, the pilgrims began looking for open spaces to lie down, pull a light blanket over themselves to keep away mosquitoes, and many of them soon fell asleep, oblivious to the loud music around them.

Being a guest

While the musicians were performing, I joined Eknāth's descendants and some other pilgrims to go to the home of a town elder to eat. At every stop along the way in the pilgrimage, Eknāth's descendants were treated with great respect; it was obviously an honour for local people to host them (and to be seen doing so). In this particular town, the elder happened to be a wealthy doctor who had practised in a nearby city for a time but returned home to build a hospital and take care of his family's business affairs. In one large room of his stately stone house, servants had set out rows of thin, disposable plastic placemats on the floor for eating. On each mat was an ingeniously designed plate made of large tree leaves that had been stitched together and pressed into a mould to form three separate sections for holding different kinds of food. The pilgrims washed their hands and feet and then filed into the room quietly and sat down on the floor in front of the place settings – men in rows on one side of the room and women on the other (as is common in most Vārkarī events, with men and women being seated separately).

In the process of washing up before the meal, most of the men had also removed their shirts, revealing white sacred threads (*jānave*, in Marathi) tied around their upper bodies – over the left shoulder, diagonally across the chest and under the right arm. These threads visibly identified the men as Brāhmans, as Eknāth himself was and his descendants are.[9] Men who served the food, many of whom were shirtless Brāhmans as well, walked between the rows of mats and doled out mounds of steaming rice, bite-sized chunks of aubergine in a spicy sauce, soft wheat flatbread, a dollop of sour, pickled green mango and cups of yellow lentil soup. Despite walking all afternoon and now having hot food placed before them, and with the enticing aroma of spices filling the room, the pilgrims waited. Off to the side, one of the Brāhman pilgrims was conducting a small ritual to bless the host for his generosity. The ritual soon finished, and servers returned with pots of liquid clarified butter (*ghī*) and dropped a spoonful of it onto the rice on each plate. The serving of the *ghī* marked for the Brāhmans the permission to start eating, and everyone was clearly happy to begin. Servers continued circulating among the rows for the next twenty minutes, attentively watching and offering the pilgrims second and third helpings. At the end of the meal, the pilgrims stood up, several of them belched openly in satisfaction, and they all set out to find places where they would sleep. Other pilgrims who had eaten elsewhere were already sleeping in the warm night under the stars. For Eknāth's descendants and their troupe, the doctor had cleared out some rooms in his old hospital building to make space where they could roll out their thin travelling mattresses and slumber away without fear of being rained on. Outside, the loud, over-amplified *kīrtan* continued on into the early morning, but none of the pilgrims seemed to mind.

The meal was a rich experience, and not only because of the delectable food. Nowadays in long-running religious traditions like the Vārkarīs, the influence of caste in social life is often still present but in subtle and changing ways. The meal had been served in a very Brāhman style, and most of the attendees there were clearly Brāhmans. Strictly according to orthodox Hindu laws of ritual purity, Brāhmans should not eat with non-Brāhmans, especially at a religious function. Yet I (a Christian) was there, and next to me was the driver of my friend's car, Imran, whose name instantly revealed him as a Muslim. We were obviously not Brāhmans. Also, some of the pilgrims in the room had not taken off their under-shirts. When I spoke with them later, they mentioned that they were not Brāhmans either but belonged to communities that were considered ***shūdras***, the lowest of the four castes. No one for a moment showed any qualms about us eating there; we were obviously welcome. Yet the meal's strongly Brāhman character and the awareness that years ago these events would have strictly excluded us non-Brāhmans, made for some mixed feelings. Later, the *shūdra* pilgrims pointed out how one of the older Brāhman pilgrims kept finding convenient excuses not to join them for meals. He never explicitly refused to eat with them, but the pattern was noticeable. We were all also very aware that millions of *dalits* (former "untouchables") now in Maharashtra no longer take any interest in this pilgrimage, having instead followed the example of Bhimrao Ambedkar and converted to Buddhism in the hope of securing greater social and political equality. Caste nowadays may not function as it did one thousand or even fifty years ago, but its effects are still felt in many ways.[10]

Vārkarī saints

In terms of caste background, the Vārkarī saints are a remarkably diverse group. Of the four most popular saint-poets, Nāmdev and Tukārām were both *shūdras* while Jñāndev and Eknāth were Brāhmans (albeit unorthodox ones). The wider constellation of saint-poets revered by the Vārkarīs includes untouchables, *shūdras*, women of various castes, and a Muslim as well. Traditional stories about the Vārkarī saints often depict them getting into trouble with the orthodox Brāhman authorities for not following social and religious norms. For example, Eknāth incurred his Brāhman neighbours' wrath by feeding a group of untouchables the food that he had originally prepared for the Brāhmans on a religious festival day.[11] Brāhmans in Tukārām's town allegedly snatched the book of Marathi poems he was writing and threw it into a river because they felt that religious poetry should not be composed in an everyday language like Marathi and especially not by a *shūdra*.[12] The writings of the saint-poets regularly insist that Viṭṭhal welcomes and accepts the devotion and love of everyone, regardless of caste, and that everyone is equally qualified to walk this spiritual path. This sentiment has led some people to envision the Vārkarī saint-poets as premodern social reformers.[13] Yet the saint-poets never explicitly condemned the caste system nor argued for its total abolition. And skirmishes and disagreements still arise occasionally between Vārkarī groups of different castes over who is entitled to walk near the palanquin throughout the pilgrimage. As with many contemporary Hindu traditions, the role of caste among the Vārkarīs is neither rigid nor always clear, and opinions about it differ widely depending on the person one is talking with.

Bhārūḍ performance

One afternoon, after walking under the sun for three hours, we came across another group of pilgrims who were seated on the ground in front of a farmer's house on the side of the road. We joined them, grateful for the shade of mango and *neem* trees, and we watched as two women sang a poem by Eknāth. This was one of the main ways the Vārkarīs pass the time, entertain themselves and rehearse the teachings of the saint-poets who composed the words. Usually, the performers are Vārkarī men dressed traditionally in simple, long white cotton shirts (*kurtās*) and white cotton trousers, who play the hand-cymbals and sing. Occasionally now one finds women in these roles as well. In this case, two middle-aged women wearing simple, neat saris played the *ṭāḷ* and danced modestly as they sang a poem that seemed out of place for a socially conservative rural audience: "*Phāṭakeca lugaḍe, tuṭakisī coḷī. Shivāyā dorā nāhī. Malā dādlā nako ga bāī* ..." ("My sari is old and torn, my blouse is tattered, but there's not even a thread to stitch them. I don't want this husband ..."). Eknāth writes this poem from the perspective of a poor woman lamenting how everything around her is old and falling apart, yet her inept husband cannot do anything to improve it. So, with startling frankness, the woman decries his uselessness. As the two pilgrim women performed this popular song, the audience smiled and paid close attention, clearly appreciating the imagined poor woman's legitimate complaints. In the final verse, however, the message of Eknāth's poem takes a very sharp turn that puts all that came before into a very different perspective – something that Eknāth was especially good at doing. Stepping back from the character and speaking for himself, Eknāth concludes: "*Ekā Janārdanī samaras jhāle, paṇ to ras yethe nāhī*" (Eknāth merged with the essence of God, but that essence isn't here).[14] In other words, ultimate peace should not be sought in fragile, temporary, earthly things. This short piece is one of the hundreds of **bhārūḍs** (allegorical drama-poems) for which Eknāth is renowned among Marathi speakers. Like most of his *bhārūḍs*, the one sung by the Vārkarī women here has two simultaneous meanings: in this case, a woman complaining about her husband, as well as the true Self lamenting its existence in a body that breaks down, decays and ultimately fails to bring contentment.

This kind of writing is very common among the Vārkarī saint-poets, who sought to reach an audience whose education has come more through work and life than through school and books. The saint-poets accommodated their audience skilfully by using everyday objects and experiences as pedagogical metaphors to teach more abstract theological messages. The Vārkarī saint-poets also intentionally and proudly composed in everyday Marathi language rather than in the elite language of classical Hindu literature – Sanskrit – which was accessible to only a small minority of the people. A few outstanding and very important Vārkarī writings in Marathi are based on classic Sanskrit Hindu texts: Jñāndev's rendering of the *Bhagavad Gītā* and Eknāth's commentaries on the *Bhāgavata Purāṇa* and the *Rāmāyaṇa*. These have become central to the Vārkarī literary

Figure 11.1 Two Vārkarī women perform a bhārūḍ for fellow pilgrims (photo by author).

tradition and to the development of Marathi literature in general through the centuries.[15] For average Vārkarīs who tend not to come from the elite levels of society or have high levels of education, however, the saint-poets' shorter compositions are more popular and regularly sung while on pilgrimage. Saint-poets and *kīrtan* performers have a good feel for their audiences, and they know how to entertain them while teaching.

Eknāth procession

Through forests and valleys, over rocky hills and on muddy paths between farmers' fields, we continued on our way to Pandharpur. Occasionally we walked on roads marked by signs that the state government had posted, declaring that this was the "official" path of the Eknāth procession. Further to the west of our route, two much larger Vārkarī processions (devoted to the saints Jñāndev and Tukārām) walk along other roads to Pandharpur and are organized much more strictly to accommodate the hundreds of thousands of pilgrims that join them. Pilgrims pay a fee to join a group (***diṇḍī***) within the processions that takes care of fixing their meals, carries their luggage and arranges tents to sleep in at night along the pilgrimage road. These large processions are often described as moving cities, since along with all the trucks and pilgrims go shopkeepers, book vendors, tea makers, doctors and water tankers to provide whatever the pilgrims need. In contrast, smaller processions such as the Eknāth *pālkhī* depend on the hospitality of local people along the way for support. Over the course of the pilgrimage I encountered Vārkarīs who had made the pilgrimage with both kinds of groups. Some liked the bustle and buzz of the big crowds of the Jñāndev and Tukārām processions, and they complained about the lack of organization in the Eknāth procession. Others complained about the traffic and pollution in the two large processions, and they praised the tranquillity of the Eknāth procession's route through the picturesque countryside.

As we walked through the rural landscape, farmers and their families regularly came out to offer the Vārkarīs water, tea, snacks, a meal or just a place to rest in the shade. It was hard to decline these offers, both because we often needed that extra shot of sugary tea for energy, and because the potential hosts were very insistent and disappointed if we turned them down.[16] One afternoon, two pilgrims and I happened to be walking past a small colony of farmers' huts, when an elderly woman waved at us and called us to come and have tea. It was getting late and we still had several kilometres to go before reaching the next town, so I was inclined to keep walking. However, the others insisted that we actually had a *duty* to accept her invitation. So we followed her.

In front of her small hut with walls built of mud and straw, she had spread out two tattered cotton blankets on the ground, which had been smeared with cowdung that was now dry (a common and auspicious practice). Goats and chickens wandered through the yard, nibbling and pecking at whatever they found. A bullock, tied to a wooden post not far away, munched on his grass and watched us as we sat down. The old woman hobbled into her hut just as her daughter-in-law came out with three plates of *pohe* - a Maharashtrian snack made of soaked rice flakes lightly fried with onion, turmeric, onion seeds, chopped chilli,

Figure 11.2 Vārkarīs accompany the Eknāth pālkhī on its way to Pandharpur (photo by author).

peanuts and shredded coconut. The old woman soon reappeared with three old, chipped ceramic cups full of steaming tea. As we ate, the old woman sat down nearby and we talked about her farm, her son who was working in the field, the weather, the pilgrimage, and whatever else came to mind. Fifteen minutes later, as we thanked them and rose to return to the road, they quickly motioned for us to stop. The women approached each of us pilgrims, put their hands together in front of their chests in the traditional Indian sign of respect, and then bent down to touch our feet. Just as the Vārkarīs believe they will meet God in Pandharpur, many local people along the way consider the pilgrims who walk by to be God as well. So by assisting the Vārkarīs, many of these local hosts felt that they were serving Viṭṭhal himself.

Reaching Pandharpur

When we initially set out from Paithan, the paths we walked were fairly empty. As we neared Pandharpur, the crowds of pilgrims swelled, flowing from all directions like rivulets joining streams, which would all merge into great rivers of Vārkarīs entering Pandharpur to see Viṭṭhal. With the larger crowds also came a different sense of courtesy, as pilgrims began addressing each other as ***māulī*** ("mother") and *mahārāj* ("great one"), reflecting their understanding that the saint-poets were very much among them.[17] On the final day of the pilgrimage as we entered Pandharpur, the number of pilgrims was overwhelming and the streets entering the town were packed. Yet despite the extremely crowded conditions, the pilgrims were in a joyful mood as they sang, danced, played traditional games and revelled in having reached their destination.

With over a million other pilgrims around, actually walking into Viṭṭhal's temple and seeing him in person presents a significant logistical challenge. Immediately outside the temple stands a building with several floors filled with gates and fences to facilitate a queue of pilgrims that can stretch nearly two miles. At the peak times of pilgrimage, pilgrims can wait two whole days for the chance to stand before the stone image of Viṭṭhal and see him. Not surprisingly, many pilgrims take comfort in a practical alternative understanding of "seeing Viṭṭhal" – catching a glimpse of the peak of the temple's tower – to feel that their pilgrimage has been fruitfully completed. Moreover, the town's facilities (such as sanitation) cannot accommodate the massive influx of pilgrims, and the hygienic conditions in Pandharpur deteriorate rapidly when all of the pilgrims arrive. So despite the great anticipation of arriving in Pandharpur that pilgrims feel during the pilgrimage, the ecstasy of celebrating the arrival of a million other pilgrims gradually fades. Slowly, a bittersweet feeling sets in: the pilgrimage is now over, goodbyes need to be said, and everyone must return to the ordinary lives they were leading before. But Viṭṭhal beckons every year, and the Vārkarīs eagerly set out again and again, walking their many paths to Pandharpur.

Reflections of a scholar

Readers should understand two things in order to put this chapter on the Vārkarīs into perspective. First, the descriptions and observations in this chapter are based on my experiences with the Eknāth procession. This group of pilgrims, as with all groups in the Vārkarī pilgrimage, has its own peculiar characteristics which are not necessarily representative of all Vārkarīs. For example, because of Eknāth's Brāhman descendants and the peculiar history of Paithan, more Brāhmans walk with the Eknāth procession than is the case with most other processions and groups. Another notable difference is that the processions of Jñāndev and Tukārām are much larger and more tightly organized than the Eknāth procession. The daily routine of pilgrims in those processions is quite different than I have described. Scholarship published on the Vārkarīs in English until now has always observed those two processions as the standard for Vārkarīs in general, sometimes to the extent of reinforcing the misperception that *vārī* equals the particular route from Āḷandī, through Pune, to Pandharpur. My chapter acknowledges that while those two major processions are indeed important, they are actually only two of many processions. Hundreds of thousands of pilgrims still walk in much smaller groups and take other routes to Pandharpur.

Readers should also be aware of how my approach in this chapter differs from that of other publications on the Vārkarīs. Other scholars have written helpful introductions to the tradition by focusing on their history, philosophy and literature, and I have coauthored one such publication myself.[18] In writing this chapter, however, I have focused on lived practice as the lens through which readers may encounter the Vārkarīs for the first time. This methodological decision is the result of some basic questions. How should we understand a tradition, such as the Vārkarīs, that clearly makes the practice of the pilgrimage its highest priority? What if, in the pilgrims' understandings, the activity of walking to Pandharpur is of such great importance to them that beliefs, texts, and doctrines play more of a supportive role? In recent decades, scholars of religion have increasingly found this focus on religious practice to be useful for illuminating the social roles of living religious traditions. In some cases, at least, it is clear that ritual and practice actually inform doctrine and belief, so that the doctrine and belief don't so much prescribe what devotees should do but rather attempt to explain what devotees were doing already (although this sequence of events is often quickly forgotten). Of course, belief and practice are never two completely separate categories, and in many ways they are interdependent. Philosophy, beliefs and literature are still relevant or important to the Vārkarīs. I would suggest, however, that if we are trying to understand the tradition as it is lived today, the first thing that we should observe is the pilgrimage activity itself.

Notes

1. The most extensive examination of Viṭṭhal's background in history and literature is Dhere (2011).
2. This date is fixed now according to the Indian lunisolar calendar, which corresponds to a different date in June or July each year in the Gregorian calendar.
3. *Vārī* is pronounced "*wah*-ree", in which the *ah* sounds as it does in *father*. *Vārkarī* is pronounced "*wahr*-kuh-ree". Due to the use of different transliteration schemes to render Marathi into English, one finds the word also spelled Varkari, Wārkarī, Warkari, and Warakari. All these English spellings are the same single word in Marathi.
4. For a recent overview of the Vārkarī tradition, see Keune and Novetzke (2011).
5. We should understand the English word "saint" in its general sense here as an extremely good person or a model for how to live and not in the specific sense of someone who has been recognized and beatified by religious authorities. The original Marathi word for this person is *sant*, which literally means "one who is good or true".
6. Out of reverence, theological understanding and tradition, people usually do not say bluntly that these saints died. Rather, they are remembered to have taken on a high state of spiritual consciousness in which they no longer cared for their bodily needs. This state of consciousness is called *samādhi*, and temples or shrines are commonly built where the saints did this activity which ended their earthly lives. These sites now draw pilgrims who seek to experience a particular saint's power and blessing. Of course these practices are not unique to the Vārkarīs; many Hindu groups have similar traditions.
7. Interested readers should seek out two important but now dated descriptions that capture the emotion and general environment of the Jñāndev procession in the 1950s: Karve (1988) and Mokashi (1987).
8. In Marathi literature, *sant-kavi* (saint-poets) are conventionally distinguished from the *paṇḍit-kavi* (scholar-poets), who composed poetry for the sake of poetry itself and to show off their creative skills to wealthy patrons rather than for more popular and religious audiences.
9. Traditionally, the three highest castes are entitled to wear such a thread. In contemporary Maharashtra, usually only the Brāhmans continue to wear it.
10. A great deal of scholarship in the last few decades has demonstrated how "the caste system" is not as neat and clear-cut as it first appears. For an accessible introduction to some of these issues see Mines (2009).
11. For additional stories about Eknāth, see the translation of part of an important eighteenth-century Marathi hagiographical text on the Marathi saints by Mahipati and Abbott ([1927] 1997). For more background on Eknāth see Keune (2011, 2012).
12. For additional stories about Tukārām, see Mahipati and Abbott ([1930] 1980).
13. One often hears this connection between the Vārkarī saints and social reform among Maharashtrians. Public school textbooks in Maharashtra have presented the saints in this way since the 1970s.
14. This is a loose but faithful translation. Technically, Eknāth says he became the same essence as his guru Janārdana, whom Eknāth revered as God.
15. For a more thorough examination of how the saint-poets' writings fit within the broader picture of Marathi literature, see Tulpule (1979).
16. Many Vārkarīs used these breaks as chances to recharge their mobile phones. Due to the informality of the Eknāth procession, with some groups walking ahead, others lagging behind, and everyone stopping along the way for tea and rest, the pilgrims relied on their phones to keep track of each other (whenever reception was available).
17. *Māulī* is an old Marathi word that is applied especially to the saint-poet Jñāndev, who is considered the "mother" of the Vārkarī tradition. So by calling fellow Vārkarīs

"*māulī*" they are actually referring to each other as incarnations of Jñāndev. The word *maharāj*, although technically the name for addressing a king, is now the standard title of the trained spiritual leaders who perform *kīrtans*, give talks on Vārkarī sacred texts and organize some of the local Vārkarī groups. In practice, *maharāj* is used as an address of great respect among Vārkarīs.

18. Cf. Philip Engblom's and Eleanor Zelliot's introductory essays in D. B. Mokashi's *Palkhi* (1987). For a consideration on the political side of one group of Vārkarīs, cf. Youngblood (2003: 287–300). See also Keune and Novetzke (2011).

12. Low-caste Hinduism in central India

Ramdas Lamb

Central India (referred to hereafter as "the region") is one of the most culturally diverse sections of the country. Its recorded history dates back to the time of the Buddha more than twenty-five hundred years ago. Centrally located, the region is bordered by most of the country's larger states and provinces. Over the millennia, various dynasties, tribal groups, bands of refugees, and wanderers have come from these bordering lands, as well as from distant places, and settled into the region. Due to this, one can find there pockets of nearly all the major Indian ethnic and linguistic groups, as well as the religious traditions and movements they brought with them. Not only has the distinctive character of each group exchanged influences with the existing religious cultures, at the same time they have all been affected by the calm and relaxed nature that tends to pervade the region. With time, there has come to exist a richly interwoven fabric of diverse religious beliefs and practices.

Currently, the region is made up of two states: Chhattisgarh and Madhya Pradesh. During much of the British rule, the two were politically united, and this continued after Indian Independence until 1 November 2000, when they were separated. Nevertheless, the religious traditions in both states have much in common. Because of the vast number of immigrant ethnic and religious groups in the region, more than thirty languages and a hundred dialects are spoken there. This linguistic spread is found mostly in the more urban areas, which tend to be dominated socially and culturally by various immigrant groups. Rural areas, on the other hand, are still the domain of the more indigenous groups and dialects, both tribal and non-tribal. Central India, then, is a mixture of indigenous and immigrant, rural and urban, tribal and non-tribal. Yet, most have found a way to live together more harmoniously than has been the case in some of the surrounding provinces. This has much to do with the approach to life of the more indigenous peoples of the region, who are known to be easy-going, straightforward and hospitable.

The variability between urban and rural influences can be easily seen in the general religious approaches in each area. In the cities and larger towns, a form of the popular Hinduism found throughout most of the country is blended rather seamlessly with the immigrant traditions that have become integrated in the life of most urban residents, irrespective of caste. In the village areas, where three fourths of the population resides, popular Hinduism takes on some unique rural forms as it more easily mixes with indigenous beliefs and practices. Here, several movements that use religious identity to promote social upliftment of the lowest caste groups can be found, as well as a wide variety of tribal religious forms that vary greatly from area to area within the region.

Caste in central India

The role the caste system plays in the life of the people of central India is extremely nuanced and complex. Its influence is felt more in rural areas than in cities, and an overall understanding of it would require a much deeper analysis and discourse than is possible in the context and purpose of this chapter. Reference to caste, therefore, will primarily be limited to the role it plays in religious adherence and distinction among the various groups. The definition of caste terminology and the information on caste dynamics provided below is meant to give the reader some basic parameters of the contemporary situation.

In rural central India, the vast majority of non-tribal residents are officially designated as either "Other Backward Caste" (OBC) or "Scheduled Caste" (SC). The bulk of the former were traditionally known as ***shūdra***, which is the lowest of the "touchable" caste categories of the Hindu social hierarchy. The latter appellation is the government designation for those who were once labelled "untouchable". Herein, the two groups will collectively be referred to as "low caste". In the region, those SC who are Hindu are also referred to collectively as **Harijan**, the dominant sub-group of which is Satnāmi. The various tribal communities are officially labelled as "Scheduled Tribe" ("ST"). How these three are situated hierarchically is complex. In non-tribal villages, OBC are generally the dominant community in terms of land holding, economy, and socio-political power, while SC are situated below them in the social hierarchy. SC only possess a level of dominance in those villages where they make up an overwhelming majority of residents. Although the overall number of ST in the region is actually highest of the three groups, they are primarily concentrated in tribal areas away from the towns and villages where most OBC and SC reside. However, those who do live in villages with a non-tribal population are generally viewed on a similar social level as OBC, and most adhere to the existing OBC practice of prejudice against SC.

Dynastic rule and central Indian Hinduism

During the last two and a half millennia, numerous dynasties have exerted political control over various portions of central India, and each brought with it and left remnants of its own religious beliefs and practices. The first empire in known history to rule the entire region was that of the Maurya, which introduced both Buddhism and Jainism during its stay. King Ashoka (third century BCE) converted to Buddhism and left inscriptions in the region on rock pillars. They express the Buddhist ideals the king is said to have sought to live by and promote, and these have influenced the practice of Hinduism there. The Shunga dynasty, which followed Mauryan rule in the region, introduced a more orthodox form of Hinduism. This was reinforced by the subsequent Gupta Empire (fourth century CE), including a strong adherence to the caste system, believing it would foster a more stable society. In the late ninth century, the kingdom of Chedi started its own dynasty in the region, known as the Haihaya. It helped to promote a more pan-Indian form of Hinduism with a strong focus on the worship of and devotion to Lord Rām. The Haihayas essentially controlled the area until the sixteenth century. Since that time, the region has been under various rulers, including the Maratha Empire from western India, Muslim rulers, the British, and finally the current state and central governments of India.

Contemporary religion: urban

The contemporary religious ethos of central India remains diverse and multifaceted, especially in the urban areas. However, most Hindus in the region do not seem bound by these differences as they participate with one another during commonly celebrated holidays and practices. Participation in most common religious events typically transcends both sectarian and caste boundaries, and involves people from a variety of religious traditions and movements. Thus, in the cities, there is relatively little difference between the religious beliefs and practices of the various caste groups. Some of the more popular and significant aspects of this current urban religious environment are discussed below, beginning with the one aspect of Hinduism that clearly dominates throughout the region, in both cities and villages, and acts as a strong religious unifier for most people. This centres on devotion to the Divine as Lord Rām.

Rām bhakti – devotion (*bhakti*) to Lord Rām (pronounced "rom") – predominates as the major religious sentiment in central India, especially for the low caste. It is integral to most religious rites and celebrations; "Rām Rām" is the common phrase used when greeting someone or on departure, and the chanting of devotional prayers to Rām are regularly heard throughout the region in temples, homes, and at almost any festive Hindu occasion. Here and throughout most of northern India as well, the sixteenth century writing of the Rām story in the Avadhi dialect of Hindi by Tulsīdās is the most prevalent sacred text. Officially named the *Rāmcharitmānas,* it is usually referred to as either the "***Ramayan***" or the "***Mānas***". Because Avadhi is somewhat similar to several of the major spoken dialects in the region, it is relatively easy for people there to understand significant portions of the text without the need for a translation.

Verses from the *Mānas* punctuate many a conversation, segments of it are chanted during various rituals, and ritualized and communal nine-day readings of the entire scripture occur several times of the year in most towns and villages. Religious booksellers stock more copies of the *Mānas* than any other text, and its style has been copied in a variety of subsequent religious texts that are of use in the region as well.

One of the more important aspects of the religious ethos of the region connected with Rām *bhakti* is devotion to Hanumān, who is often called "the monkey God" in English. He is an important figure in the Rām story as the faithful servant of Lord Rām. He is believed by most followers to be both an incarnation of Lord Śiva and of devotion, and is by far the most popular deity there. More temples and roadside shrines are dedicated to him than all other deities combined. On almost any road connecting two cities or towns in the region, Hanumān appears regularly, in a temple, in a small shrine, as a solitary image or orange-coloured stone under a tree, or as a carving or painting on a wall of a home or shop. Belief in the presence and power of evil spirits is strong in the region, and Hanumān is said to be the remover of obstacles and protector against such evil powers. Thus, he figures in many ritual prayers for protection or to ward off evil. Even the shaman-like ritualists in the region, known as *Baigās* (see below), typically include prayers to Hanumān in their rituals.

Festivals and holidays

Holy festivals (*melā*) are important religious activities for Hindus all over India. They are generally periodic, with their occurrence based on the lunar calendar. Typically, *melā* celebrations take place in both city and village with the urban manifestations being larger and more elaborate. As previously mentioned, attendees at the various festivals come from diverse religious and cultural backgrounds, and it is not uncommon to find Hindus, Buddhists, Jains, and Sikhs at the *melās*. Among the most important and popular festivals celebrated in the region are Gaṇeṣa Caturthī, Navarātri, Rām Navami, Divāli and Holī.

Gaṇeṣa Caturthī, which is celebrated in late summer, honours the birth of Lord Gaṇeṣa, the son of Śiva and Parvati.[1] He is typically worshipped in a human-like form with an elephant head. He is said to bestow wisdom, good fortune, and prosperity on all those who pray to him. An image of him can be found in nearly every store front or business owned by a Hindu, and many of the more elaborate Hindu religious events begin with prayers to him. Although Gaṇeṣa Caturthī is believed to be ancient, it was not a part of the region's traditions until it was brought by the Maratha Empire in the eighteenth century. Then, at the beginning of the twentieth, thanks to the efforts of the Indian freedom fighter, Lokmanya Tilak, the celebration was transformed from a regional Maharasthrian festival into a popular national event. In most central Indian cities, Maharastrian businessmen sponsor an eight day *melā* that grows each year and is currently the most expensive communal festival for businesses and individuals in all of central India. Many business owners believe that praying to and honouring Gaṇeṣa will assure a prosperous and profitable year, while villagers pray to him for a plentiful fall harvest.

Navarātri is a nine-day event that is celebrated twice a year, during the spring month of Chaitra and the autumn month of Kunwar. The Chaitra festival takes place during the first nine days of the Hindu New Year and celebrates the nine forms of the goddess Durgā, one on each day. In addition, the ninth day is Rām Navami (see below). During the autumn Navarātri, the nine forms of Durgā are again worshipped, while the tenth day, known both as Dassehra and Vijay Dasami, recalls Lord Rām's vanquishing of the demon Rāvan, and the freeing of his wife Sītā from the demon's captivity. Thus, both festivals blend devotion to Rām with worship of Durgā.

Rām Navami, a spring festival that occurs on the ninth day of the Hindu new-year, celebrates the human incarnation of Lord Rām. It is seen as highly auspicious and is usually observed with prayers at homes or in temples. In addition, nine-day (Navarātri) readings of the *Mānas*, culminating on the holiday itself, are undertaken throughout the region, while troupes (*līlā maṇḍalis*) of young male performers enacting portions of the Rām story on makeshift stages can be found at various venues in both urban and rural areas. The holiday is considered by Chhattisgarhis to be the most auspicious day for marriages as well. At those sites within the region that are most connected to the Rām story, such as Chitrakut, festivities are the greatest. However, in comparison to Gaṇeṣa Caturthī, it is a day of more introspective celebrating, and does not have the glitz that is the hallmark of the Gaṇeṣa holiday.

Deepavali, known as the festival of lights, is an autumn holiday celebrated by Hindus, Buddhists, Jains and Sikhs in the region, all for different reasons. Nevertheless, festivities overlap, and participants will easily move from one religious performance and ritual to another. Hindu forms of celebration are the most prevalent and focus both on Lakṣmī, the Goddess of wealth, and on Lord Rām and Sītā, the latter of whom is believed to be an incarnation of Lakṣmī. In the Rām story, Rām's father, the king of Ayodhya, is tricked into exiling his son to the forest for fourteen years. He is accompanied there by Sītā and his brother Lakṣman. Deepavali commemorates their return to Ayodhya at the end of the exile. Hindus in the region typically prepare for the day by thoroughly cleaning their homes. New bedding may be bought and new clothing worn, while rows of lighted oil lamps or candles decorate homes, rooftops, or courtyards to welcome back Rām and Sītā. In the case of the latter, she is revered both as Rām's wife and also as Lakṣmī. Boxes of sweets are given to family, friends, and neighbours.

Holī is the main day of devotion to Lord Kṛṣṇa in central India, but, like Deepavali, it is celebrated for several reasons. It takes place in the spring during the last month of the Hindu year. On the night before the main festival day, bonfires are lit in honour of the child devotee of Viṣṇu named Prahlād who was miraculously saved from a fire in which he had been taken by the demoness Holikā. On the day itself, people put colours on each others' face recalling the love between Kṛṣṇa and his consort, Rādha. In contemporary times, many city youth fill water guns with coloured water and spray it on people as they go by. On that day, caste barriers are typically forgotten, and it is common to see people from various castes commingling, hugging each other, and so on. In the evening, people put on new or clean clothes and visit friends and relatives.

Contemporary religion: rural

In India overall, a large majority of OBC, nearly 80 per cent of SC, and more than 90 per cent of ST live in village areas. When discussing religion in the rural areas, then, the presence and influence of these groups are most strongly felt. As previously mentioned, OBC dominate in most villages, where they tend to practise a more pan-Indian form of Hinduism blended with local elements. All of the above-mentioned religious celebrations are included, except at a much smaller scale. While SC adhere to many of these same beliefs and practices as well as some popular immigrant traditions, they are a pivotal force in keeping alive most local practices also. In addition, many also belong to one of several regional religious movements in which their caste community predominate. Moreover, an important feature of the rural religious environment is the multiple organizations and socio-religious movements that have become established in central India during the last several centuries and that have a rejection of caste and religious orthodoxy a primary focus of their teachings. Founded by and essentially for low castes, three of the groups continue to exist in contemporary times and still exert an influence on people and religious traditions of the region. They are the Kabīrpanth, the Satnāmi Samāj and the Rāmnāmi Samāj.

Kabīrpanth

The teachings of the medieval poet/mystic Kabīr and others in the north Indian Sant tradition have had great impact on the popularization of the practice of *nirgun bhakti* (devotion to the Divine without form) in north and central India. This approach has been especially attractive to the lowest castes, whose entrance into temples was often forbidden. The Chhattisgarh branch of the Kabīrpanth was founded in the fifteenth century and is named after Dharamdās, one of Kabīr's primary disciples. It is arguably the largest branch of the followers of Kabīr. Although there are Kabīrpanthi members in Madhya Pradesh, the bulk of the central Indian following is found in Chhattisgarh.

Until the early twentieth century, the two main branches of the Kabīrpanth were the original in Uttar Pradesh (UP) and the Chhattisgarhi (Dharamdās) branch. Unlike the UP branch, in which caste hierarchy has become an important factor in what occurs there, the Dharamdās branch has more closely adhered to Kabīr's rejection of caste and gender bias, and is thus far more accepting of low castes and women. Sect members in central India are referred to as "Kabīrpanthi" or "**Panthi**" in Hindi, but are also known as "**Kabīrha**" in the local dialect. In Banaras, women play a minimal role in the functioning of the order, but in Chhattisgarh, they can and do take a more active role, and there are several female Panthi teachers in the region. The branch is primarily made up of OBC and SC. More recently, ST membership has been on the rise.

The sacred texts of the central Indian branch include the ***Bījak*** and the ***Anurāg Sāgar***. Both are revered by Kabīrpanthis throughout India, and some show reverence to the physical text of the Bījak in much the way the *Guru Granth Sāhib* is looked upon by the Sikhs. In gatherings, devotees sing verses from both texts or recite chants in praise of Kabīr. Although both are said to have been written by and contain the teachings of Kabīr, followers in central India believe the *Anurāg Sāgar* was actually authored by Dharamdās. The text is written in the form of a dialogue between Kabīr and Dharamdās and is regarded on the same level as the *Bījak* by Chhattisgarhi devotees.

Both male and female Panthis in the region traditionally wear all white, especially when they get together for ritual purposes. The Chhattisgarh branch has a centre in Banaras as well, and even though Kabīr rejected image worship, the main temples of both branches there have an image of him as the object of worship. There, the same rituals are performed as those done in Hindu temples. In Chhattisgarh itself, however, Kabīr's concept of formless devotion remains in place, although he himself is treated by many as an incarnation of the Divine.

Despite the degree of change in the direction toward mainstream Hinduism that the central Indian Kabīrpanth has undergone, it still stands in the region as one of the symbols of the rejection of caste prejudice and orthodox values and authority. Because of the participation by many different castes, SC followers view the sect as providing a vehicle for religious involvement that crosses the immense chasm that can exist between caste Hindus and themselves. Significantly, it was the first successful Hindu religious movement in the region to openly court the latter and offer them the possibility of a religious life with Hindu devotional trappings but without intense orthodox restrictions.

Then, in the nineteenth century, an SC by the name of Ghāsidās founded another movement that he envisioned would bring spiritual encouragement and upliftment specifically to his own caste brethren at the bottom of society.

Satnāmi Samāj

Ghāsidās (1756–1850) was born to a poor *Chamār* (leather-worker) family in the village of Girod. His sub-caste was and still is the predominant group of SC in the region. Little is known of his life although his hagiography has been growing over the last few decades. What is commonly agreed upon is that as

Figure 12.1 Satnāmi devotees performing a ritual trek to the Girodpuri temple (photo by author).

an adolescent, his awareness of and disdain for the caste system and the way it functioned to keep members of his community at the bottom of the prevalent social hierarchy had grown to the point that he began to speak out angrily against it. He became frustrated at the rigidity of the system and sought a way to confront it. Then, when he was about eighteen years of age, he had a vision that led him to renounce his budding social activism, village and family life, and to retreat into the jungle not far from his home in search of a renunciant life. He spent several years living mostly in solitude and contemplation. Gradually, he began to visit nearby hamlets and give talks based on his inner experiences and growing wisdom. The number of villagers attracted to Ghāsidās gradually grew, and many began to visit him in the forest regularly to hear his teachings. What made him unique was that he aimed his teachings directly at those in his own community although he also encouraged all caste members to join together and follow the teachings.

First and foremost among these teachings were an emphasis on the worship of one true god through the focus on and chanting of "*satnām*" (literally, "true name"), the rejection of caste, and the abolition of any form of image worship. Others teachings included strict prohibitions against consuming flesh, alcohol and tobacco products, working with leather, and using cows for ploughing. Many of these rules also resonate with the teachings attributed to Kabīr and other promoters of formless devotion before him. Like Kabīr, he rejected not only image worship but also rituals in general. He stood firm against the injustice and discrimination that permeated the lives of the Untouchables of his day, but he also argued that the attitudes and lifestyles of the low castes provided excuses for the continuing prejudice against them. Guru Ghāsidās, as he came to be called, encouraged his followers to change not only their lives but their surnames as well and to use "Satnāmi" for both sub-caste and religious identity. Other than the abovementioned dicta, little record actually exists of Ghāsidās's teachings. Although he wrote nothing, nor did he apparently delve into philosophical controversies and most classical religious questions, more recently developed hagiographic accounts now include such teachings. However, one practice that has long been attributed to him was the reading and memorization of verses from the *Mānas.* Although many Satnāmis continue to read and use the *Mānas*, it is not an official practice of the sect, likely because of the fact that it has become such a dominant text for the Rāmnāmis (see below), another religious movement in the region that draws its following from the ranks of Satnāmis.

By the beginning of the twentieth century, the Satnāmis had become an influential religious movement in the region. One of the group's leaders in the early twentieth century became an ardent supporter of and closely affiliated with the Indian National Congress and the Quit India Movement. This eventually led to the ability of the *samāj*'s heads to have the name of their subcaste officially changed to "Satnāmi", separating their caste community from the pejorative connotation of the name "*Chamār*".

As Guru Ghāsidās's following developed in the early days of the movement, several of his devotees set up a wooden pole topped with a white flag near his forest hut to help newcomers find him more easily in the jungle. The pole (referred to as a ***jai stambh***) and a white flag have collectively become the main symbols of the sect, and can be seen along the roads and next to village residences throughout much of the state. They are set up to mark a holy spot or the place of a Satnāmi festival, gathering, or home. In place of temples, Satnāmis gather in homes or around a *jai stambh* to chant or for their gatherings. Satnāmis and Kabīrpanthis share a similar style that is largely reflective of the local style done by mainstream Hindus.

By the time Chhattisgarh became its own state in 2000, the Satnāmi religious movement had the following and support of the majority of its caste members as participants, on one level or another. Understanding this, the new state government began to develop the area around Guru Ghāsidās's home village and the place where he lived in the jungle. Expansion and improvement of various sacred sites in the state as pilgrimage/tourist attractions was seen as a valuable tourist draw and thus source of income. Thus, developing Girodpuri (the new name given to Ghāsidās's home village) was in line with the larger plan, but it was also done with the goal of gaining the political support of the Satnāmis. At the site, the state government has built a new temple and other infrastructure, including several hostels, parking areas, and pads where makeshift shops and stalls can set up during the annual festival in honour of the *guru*. In addition, during the last decade the government has invested millions of dollars on roads leading to the area, as well as a great deal of money advertising the site as a primary pilgrimage centre in the state.

The results have exceeded their expectations: in less than a decade, the annual gathering at the temple has grown from approximately 20,000 attendees in the year 2001 to over half a million in 2008. This has given new impetus to Satnāmi members to feel pride in themselves and in their movement, and it is bringing in a great deal of money into the area around Girodpuri in the process. However, it is also causing tension within the movement over issues such as religious identity, political alignment, and so on. In some ways, it is a replay of what happened in the latter part of the nineteenth century. At that time, the membership was growing due to the popularity of Guru Ghāsidās's teachings among the low caste. As the *samāj* got larger, there was an increase of political infighting and struggles for leadership power. Because of the intensity of the internal conflict and the way it was affecting the membership, some of the more devotionally oriented individuals began to seek a new religious avenue that utilized elements of Ghāsidās's teachings but avoided politics. They were also looking to bring a closer focus on devotion to Rām in their lives. The result came in the form of the Rāmnāmi Samāj.

Rāmnāmi Samāj

Founded by a villager named Parasurām in the 1890s, the Rāmnāmi Samāj is clearly the most unique low caste religious movement in all of central India. Very little is known about the life of the founder. Tradition says that he was born in the mid-nineteenth century to a poor *Chamār* family in the Chhattisgarh area of central India. His father was a follower of the teachings of Guru Ghāsidās, but he was also devoted to the various stories and tales in the *Mānas* and to chanting the name of Lord Rām, a practice known as Rāmnām. Parasurām had a similar attraction to Rām *bhakti*, and attempted to follow in his father's footsteps in his approach to life and spirituality. In his village, he came to be known as an ardent Rām devotee.

In his mid-thirties, Parasurām contracted a disease that friends and family suspected to be leprosy. He decided to leave his village so as not to infect anyone else and retire to the jungle to live whatever life he had left. However, just as he was about to depart, he had a chance encounter with a renunciant monk (*sādhu*) of the Ramanandi order, the largest monastic order in India. The *sādhu* is said to have given him a blessing that resulted in a miraculous healing and also the appearance of the name of Rām tattooed on his chest. As word of the double miracle spread throughout the area, villagers from miles around came to see Parasurām and hear his story. Attracted by his personality, intelligence and devotion, a following gradually developed around him. This led to the eventual establishment of the Rāmnāmi Samāj in 1893. From the outset,

Parasurām sought to avoid the mantle of *guru* and would instead encourage those who sought guidance from him to recite Rāmnām regularly and try to understand and follow the teachings of the *Mānas*. He also encouraged them to take part in group chanting in their own homes with their families. In honour of the miracles that happened to Parasurām, several of his original followers had the name "Rām" tattooed on their foreheads. Tattooing "Rām" on the forehead soon became an important identity marker for members of the group.

Parasurām and others would gather in the evenings to sing and chant Rāmnām and to listen to his telling of the various events and teachings in the Rām story. Often, these sessions would last until sunrise the following day. Those assembled would usually wrap themselves in cotton shawls to keep out the chill of the night. At one point, some Rāmnāmis began to write the name "Rām" on their shawls, and this practice became another mark of identity. In addition, Parasurām liked to stick a peacock feather in his turban, so his followers began to do likewise. These practices eventually led to the distinct-style peacock-feather hats and Rāmnām-covered shawls worn today by the members of the *samāj*. Early on, Parasurām gave many of the same teachings as Guru Ghāsidās, especially the rejection of caste, alcohol consumption and meat-eating. He also told his followers to give up image and spirit worship, and see Lord Rām in everyone and everything instead.

Figure 12.2 Rāmnāmi in ritual dress (photo by author).

By the time of Parasurām's death in the early 1920s, the movement had nearly 20,000 tattooed Rāmnāmis. Unlike the traditions attached to the previous founders of low-caste religious movements in the region, Parasurām chose no successor. Instead, he told his followers that whatever instructions and guidance they need in their lives are contained in the chanting of Rāmnām and in the *Mānas.* Honouring his words and his refusal to initiate a single successor but desiring someone to be able to turn to for teachings and guidance, members of the *samāj* turned to elder Rāmnāmis for help. This led to the appointment of a council of elders that would be responsible for inspiring new practitioners and encouraging all Rāmnāmis, both new and old, to make a sincere effort to live a life of humility and devotion. Parasurām made very few rules, and the *samāj* has continued this approach. Over the decades, among the only requirements that have persisted for members to follow closely is a vow to chant Rāmnām, abstain from alcohol and meat, and get at least one "Rām" tattoo somewhere on the body.

The *samāj* continued to grow and attract Satnāmis and members of other low castes from all over Chhattisgarh. In the mid-1930s, one female member's body became entirely covered in Rām tattoos (some say they miraculously appeared on her, others say she had them done). Nevertheless, this led to a sharp increase in the practice of tattooing. By the early 1970s, the number of initiated and significantly tattooed Rāmnāmis was over 40,000, while the number of uninitiated devotees of the *samāj*, often having at least one "Rām" tattoo somewhere on their bodies, approached 200,000. The latter would show their faith and support by chanting Rāmnām in their homes and by attending the various festivals and events held throughout the year whenever possible. The vast majority also adhere to a vegetarian diet. Many are members of an initiate's family, and they make up the majority of those who attend Rāmnāmi events.

The *samāj* continued to grow until the oil embargo of 1973, which caused rapidly increasing fuel and energy costs, which raised the prices of staples for most Indians. At the same time, Chhattisgarh experienced an extreme drought, which forced countless poorer villagers to travel outside their area, and even outside their state, in search of work and food. The Rāmnāmi governing council decided as a consequence to drop the mandatory rule, prevalent at that time, of forehead tattooing. This was done so that future members who would have to work outside the region would not be subjected to the ridicule that many tattooed members faced within the region. However, this single change has been, on reflection, a significant catalyst for the subsequent decline in the *samāj* membership. Since the Rāmnāmis and their forehead tattoos had become synonymous in the minds of so many Chhattisgarhis, only those with such tattoos were viewed, by many outside the order as well as some within, as "real" Rāmnāmis. Additionally, many of the younger members of their caste community did not want to get tattoos that would signal to everyone that they were low caste. As a consequence, the tradition of tattooing began to diminish, and the number of new members and individuals getting easily visible tattoos has dropped precipitously since the late 1970s. Due to an ageing membership, the core of the *samāj* has dwindled in size to the point that there are currently fewer than 1,000 members who have a significant number of tattoos and are actively participating in Rāmnāmi functions. Nevertheless, the movement remains a symbol of the creativity and independent thinking of Harijan Hindus in the region, of their devotion, and of their ability to have their own religious existence outside the boundaries of caste and hierarchy. Also, unlike with the case of Kabīr and Ghāsidās, Parasurām is not the object of devotion and worship by members of the *samāj* he founded. There is not even a formal written account of his life, although there have been some attempts to construct one. The view held by many is similar to the one expressed by an elder Rāmnāmi who reflected, "Parasurām was a poor Chhattisgarhi villager, similar in many ways to us; therefore, we all have the capability and opportunity to become as great a Rāmnām devotee as he was."

Tribal (*ādivāsi*) religion

Together, Madhya Pradesh and Chhattisgarh have the highest concentration of ***ādivāsi*** groups in India, with nearly fifty recognized tribes and many more subtribes. The largest of these is the Gond, which itself has nearly sixty subgroups. The other dominant tribal groups include Bhil, Oraon, Kanwār and *Baigā*. While some tribes have existed in the region since ancient times, others have migrated in over the centuries or millennia, mostly from the north and east. In the more distant past, the various *ādivāsi* all had their distinctive beliefs and practices that shared relatively little with the pan-Indian aspects of Hinduism known to and practised by most Indians today. However, elements of popular Hinduism have gradually been included over time, and most tribal religions have become a blend of local, regional and pan-Indian beliefs and practices. The last century and a half have also brought increased connection with outsiders in the form of Christian missionaries, government officials and workers (first British, then Indian), and businessmen and traders. Together, all of these have affected the lives of many *ādivāsi*. Catholic missionaries early on saw in tribal lands a rich potential source of new converts, and they started the process of infiltration into the various tribal areas throughout India. However, it was not until the twentieth century that missionaries began to have significant influence. About the same time, the British government had initiated development of the region's infrastructure, which helped give missionaries access. The post-Independence government has continued the process. The result has been an increasing number of government programmes directed at tribal lands and peoples to stimulate education and economic development. However, many of these outside influences have gradually eaten away at traditional beliefs and practices of those tribes targeted by such programmes. Nevertheless, because of the remoteness of many of their homelands, there are still tribal groups whose ways of life have maintained much of their traditional religious styles.

As previously mentioned, beliefs and practices among the tribes tend to blend animistic and more mainstream Hindu elements. Nearly all believe in a dominant male deity, who may be referred to by a variety of local or Sanskritic names, such as Bara Deo and Thakur Deo, or Bhagwan. Many of the primary deities, once viewed as strictly tribal, are now seen to be manifestations of more popular Hindu deities. One of the more common deities worshipped by *ādivāsi* in the region is Hanumān, and images of him can be found in most tribal areas. The Bonda, in southern Chhattisgarh, is one of the few tribes whose primary deity is female. The tribe's main homeland is in Orissa, but many members have moved into Chhattisgarh as well. Sītā Mā, the wife/consort of Lord Rām, is their dominant deity. She is seen to be mostly benevolent, but fearsome if aggravated and disobeyed, and she is the focus of nearly all their ritual worship. Interestingly, Lord Rām has little or no part in their religious system of worship.

Although the dominant tribal deities are almost all believed to be formless, drawings or carvings on wood may be used to represent them for certain ritual purposes. The majority of daily worship for most tribals is generally not directed toward the dominant deity but instead toward various animistic deities who personify natural forces such as the earth, rivers, mountains, rain, and so on. Most *ādivāsi* worship an Earth goddess, known by many different names, and she is one of the most important deities in their pantheons. Some *ādivāsi*, such as the *Baigā*, will not use a plough, since they believe that it hurts Mother Earth. Instead, they will plant by making a hole in the ground with a staff, in which they will place their seeds. Others will use hand ploughs, but not those attached to an animal. In more recent years, government programmes and incentives have influenced many to begin to adopt ploughing and planting methods used by the non-tribal peoples in the areas where they live.

Similar to many animistic religious belief systems, there can be found a variety of deities who are benevolent and beneficial, as well as those who are frightening and detrimental. Thus, worship of them may be either to ask for favours or to supplicate them so they do not cause harm. There tends to be a great fear of the latter type as they are believed to cause misfortune, disease and even death to those who transgress tribal law or custom, or in some other way offend them. Depending on the degree of wrongdoing, the misfortune may carry over into subsequent generations unless it is expiated through specific rituals and offerings. Animal sacrifice is one of the ritual forms used in such cases by various tribes. Moreover, the prevalence of animal sacrifice among tribals seems to be the main reason for its presence in the region.

Baigā, tonhī *and the world of spirits*

Rural people throughout many areas of the world tend to have strong beliefs in spirits, both good and bad, and the power of curses and evil beings. This is especially the case in tribal areas in eastern and central India. Because of the high percentage of tribal people in Chhattisgarh, and the state's proximity to Bihar, Bengal and Orissa, such beliefs are more pronounced there than in Madhya Pradesh. In both states, however, rituals are regularly performed to ward off illnesses and other calamities and problems. The ritual officiants in such instances are referred to in a variety of ways, the most common in the region being *Baigā*. This is not to be confused with members of the *Baigā* tribe, but is a more generic term for someone who does healings, spirit communication and other shamanic types of work. It is this latter sense that will be discussed here.

Baigās can be of any caste and can be either male or female, although in the region they are almost always male. They are called upon to discern the cause of a disease or another problem, which they almost always interpret to be an evil spirit or curse, and they are expected to be able to cure the problem or problems through prayers and rituals. As such, they may be asked to do anything from ridding a village of demonic spirits to stopping a child from crying. The methods they use involve rituals, incantations, prayers, and offerings to various spirits. The rituals of some *Baigā* are said to be very effective for ridding the body of illnesses, even the effects of a snake bite.

There is also a widespread belief among many *ādivāsi* in the presence of ***tonhī***, females who are said to have powers through which they can cast spells, make people or animals sick, and sometimes even kill. Although there are ***tonhā*** (males) as well, they are very rare and are not believed to have the same level of demonic power. The more powerful *tonhī* are said to be able to raise a child who has recently died and then use the child as her assistant. The belief in *tonhī* is generally restricted to tribal areas among the more uneducated villagers, but it can also be found in non-tribal villages as well. Because of the fear that *tonhī* can inspire, there have been, from time to time, violent attacks against women suspected of witchcraft. The stories that are told remind one of the fear of witches that existed in seventeenth-century Salem, Massachusetts. As a consequence, several states in India, including Chhattisgarh, have passed laws to try to prevent such attacks, but they are seldom enforced or enforceable, especially in the rural and tribal areas where the problems exist.

Conclusion

Throughout its history, the Hinduism of central India has been added to, modified, elaborated upon and attacked by various people, philosophies and ideologies. Consequently, the low caste of the region have had a relative ease of access to a wide variety of religious forms of expression and practice. Arguably, however, one of the biggest challenges that religion has faced, both in the region as well as in India as a whole, comes in contemporary times in the form of the concepts of secularism, materialism and individuality as they are being adopted from the West. All three have currents that run counter to religious belief, tradition and culture, and all three are increasingly becoming the focus of the urban life and the youth of central India. While these threaten to undermine much of the existing traditions, at the same time, all three provide elements of change that are welcomed by many of those who have long been at the fringes of society. Here, the divide is not so much between urban and rural or high and low caste as between those who hold fast to tradition and those who are antagonistic to it and seek change. As the situation plays itself out, the richness and diversity of the religion in central India continues to provide an important dimension to the overall fabric of the Hindu tradition.

Acknowledgements

I would like to thank the Hindu American Foundation for providing me with a grant that aided my research for the present chapter.

Note

1. In Hinduism, even though deities are believed to be eternal, most are also believed to have taken birth in one form or another on Earth. Thus, the main holiday for many of them is the day that recalls this "birth".

13. Vaiṣṇavism in Bengal

Abhishek Ghosh

> Perhaps in no other religion have human emotional potentials been so considered, categorized and sacralized than in the codification accomplished by the Bengal Vaiṣṇavas. (Brooks 1990)

Imagine a religious tradition that presents God as a handsome teenage boy, whose favourite activity is singing and dancing with his girlfriends in a moonlit forest at the dead of the night, after they escape from their homes without their families' consent. How would it be if the central ritual of this tradition demanded nothing but celebrating through congregational singing of certain *mantras* (chants) and dancing, without the slightest care whether the context was a private home or the busiest city thoroughfare? And if the sacred texts of the tradition, despite its philosophical sophistication and wrangling scholastic arguments, ultimately concluded that this method of singing, dancing and celebrating was not only the best kind of spiritual meditation, but also the easiest way to ultimate salvation? What if it claimed that salvation was not so much about redemption from sin or release from worldly bonds, but rather the experience of love of God that most resembled the thrilling emotions of a first teenage romance?

In very general terms, the above description summarizes the devotional movement of Gauḍīya Vaiṣṇavism inaugurated by Chaitanya Mahaprabhu (1486–1533) in Bengal. During his time, it was seen as a unique innovation by his contemporaries, but like many other strands of the varieties of Hinduisms,[1] this one got absorbed in the mainstream. In this exploratory chapter, we will look at the contexts, texts, tenets and practices of this devotional tradition called Gauḍīya or Chaitanya-Vaiṣṇavism, and attempt to seek the rationale behind the singular theology and practices of this tradition. But before we explore the details of this tradition, it is necessary to situate it in its socio-historical and intellectual contexts.

Background

From the eleventh century onwards, major areas of northern parts of the Indian subcontinent came under Muslim domination. It was during these phases of Turkish and Mughal rule that a mystical brand of Islam known as Sufism began to take root in this region. A similar kind of mysticism called *bhakti* (loving devotion) simultaneously developed within Hindu traditions, and though the conception and practice of *bhakti* could be traced back to some of the earliest developments within Hinduism, on a popular level it never happened on the same scale as in the fifteenth and sixteenth centuries. One of the basic commonalities between both the Sūfi and *bhakti* movements was the rejection of religious orthodoxy or ritualism that existed in the mainstream Hindu and Islamic traditions, and the stress on the more individualistic revival of the personal loving relation one had with God. Music and dancing to the names of God became an important mode of worship/meditation, and the individual teachers, prophets and mystagogues sprang up within both Sūfi and *bhakti* traditions, and started to take an important role in spreading these new versions of their religion. Along with this came a lot of syncretistic processes between both the movements on many different levels.

The origins of the kind of emotional *bhakti* Chaitanya inherited had its roots in eighth to tenth centuries in southern India. It very quickly swept across northern India during the fifteenth and sixteenth centuries century under the auspices of several prominent *bhakti* movement leaders, such as Vallabha, Mīra, Kabīr, Sūrdas and Tulsīdās. These teachers churned out deeply moving devotional poems that caught the imagination of the general populace, whipping up fervent devotional sentiments among a large base of people at the grassroots. A large section of the *bhakti* devotionalism that we find during this period was Vaiṣṇava in orientation,[2] and although there were individuals of these movements who promoted devotion to Śiva or Devī, it was Viṣṇu or his various manifestations (such as Rāma, Kṛṣṇa or Narasiṃha) that became a major focus of *bhakti* poetry and object of devotional fervour. Chaitanya's movement finds its context in the *bhakti* movement in general and Vaiṣṇavism in particular. Besides, Gauḍīya Vaiṣṇavism has a lot of theological similarities to the various other regional Indian Vaiṣṇava movements and its literary roots can be traced back to courtly devotional poems of the twelfth and thirteenth centuries, but Chaitanya's rendition of *bhakti* uniquely stands out in terms of doctrine and practice.

In terms of the immediate socio-historical context, the Gauḍīya Vaiṣṇavism grew out of the town of Nabadwip, in the district of Nadia in West Bengal, India a hundred miles north of Calcutta. This town was a prominent urban educational centre during the fifteenth century, attracting students and scholars from various parts of the country to engage in the emerging scholarship of neologic (*navya-nyāya*).[3] During Chaitanya's time, this area was overshadowed by a priestly orthodoxy, which churned out stringent codes of conduct relating to ritual purity while it also practised left-hand tantra[4] involving ritual sex and consumption of "impure" substances like meat, blood, corpses and faeces. Amid these extremes, there was a small community of *bhakti* practitioners, but they were very small in numbers and practically had no social influence. They kept to themselves, sporadically congregating behind closed doors to sing and dance and study some sacred texts of their tradition.

The founder and his movement

Chaitanya was born as Visvambhar Mishra in March 1486, the tenth son of a priestly couple in Nabadvipa, and was raised with utmost care, as not only did all eight of his previous siblings die before him, but his immediate surviving brother left home to become an itinerant monk. According to his biographies, during his teens Visvambhar turned out to be a scholar of Sanskrit grammar and neo-logic, mastering these two prominent academic disciplines. After finishing his education at a very early age, he started his own educational institution and began enrolling students and during this phase of his career, he became well known for his scholasticism, and also his aversion and scorn towards the mystical devotion of Vaiṣṇavism that existed in the margins of his society. But young Visvambhar had an epiphany, and underwent a complete transformation during a trip to Gaya, where people from all over India came to do the final cremation rites of their parents. Going there to perform the last rites of his father, he met his *guru* Ishvara Puri who initiated him into the Vaiṣṇava

Figure 13.1 Chaitanya and his companions dancing, from an 1876 lithograph print, Calcutta Art Studio (photo courtesy British Library Online Gallery).

bhakti tradition giving him a secret *Kṛṣṇa-mantra*. On his return to Nabadvipa, the townsfolk saw a completely transformed Visvambhar and for the first time he found the Vaiṣṇava company attractive and would spend days and nights with them singing the names of Kṛṣṇa and dancing with them.

After he came back to Bengal, Visvambhar had also lost all interest in his academic pursuits and had somehow become more inclined to devotional mysticism found in verses of the Sanskrit text, the *Bhāgavata Purāṇa*. At this point his following began to grow, as did opposition to his burgeoning movement and at the age of twenty-four, he felt a tremendous urge to share his message of Kṛṣṇa-*bhakti* and experiences with the people of the Indian subcontinent. As he gauged the importance of respect accorded to monks in India, he took the decision to become a wandering monk himself in order to get a platform to spread his message. Accepting the vows of an itinerant ascetic he took the name Chaitanya and travelled the length and breadth of India on foot for six years, going from village to village and engaging people in the public chanting of the holy names of Kṛṣṇa, and especially two particular *mantras*.[5] After this phase of his career, he settled down in Jagannatha Puri, meditating on the activities of Kṛṣṇa mentioned in the *Bhāgavata Purāṇa* meanwhile having instructed his main disciples to compose texts on the various aspects of the school he was founding.

Central texts

The followers of Chaitanya – especially his six ascetic disciples in Vrindavan – were very prolific, and composed about fifty exhaustive exegetical and literary works furthering the ideas of the school. However, everything Chaitanya's followers ever wrote was based on one single text: the Bhāgavata Purāṇa, a devotional text which is said to have originated in Southern India. According to modern scholarship, this text was compiled sometime around the tenth century; the tradition however claims that it is much older, going back at least 5,000 years.[6] The main theme of the text is the redemptive power of pure love of God and it critiques religious ritualism on the one hand and pure scholasticism on the other. Divided into ten "books", each book of this work has specific stories about Kṛṣṇa or Viṣṇu and his intimate interactions with various devotees, highlighting the exalted position of personal devotion above any other processes of salvation.

The text claimed that Kṛṣṇa was *bhagavān svayam* (*Bhāgavata Purāṇa* 1.3.28, in Vyasa 1983: 19), "God Himself", but in his sweet personal and romantic form where he relinquished his majestic attitude of godhead-ness for the sake of enjoying loving relationships (*rasa*).[7] It further asserted that the other prominent conceptions of divinity found in the *Vedas* or the **Upaniṣads** – the impersonal Brahman (absolute reality, substratum of everything) or the indwelling *paramātman* (the supreme self within each being) that *jñānis* (seekers of knowledge) or *yogins* (mystic ascetics) strove for in their austerities and penances – were merely external manifestations of Kṛṣṇa the person. This text pointed out that Kṛṣṇa was not an ordinary human lover but the ultimate personification of God and all the other manifestations of God could not match up with the intensity of the intimacy found in this particular version. And in this schema, not only was this personal vision of god the sweetest (*madhura*), his amorous *līlās* and relationships (*śṛṅgāra*) were the most attractive.[8] Kṛṣṇa's apparent moral transgressions when he danced all night with his girlfriends were considered sacred and sweet by his devotees – in the text and in practice – for Kṛṣṇa was not only god as a little boy who stole butter, but a divine playboy stealing girls' clothes while they bathed, or a lover in the *rāsa-līlā* (circle dance) dancing his way into his devotees' hearts.

The essential core of this section eulogized his amorous dalliances with several rural girls (*gopīs*) of Vraja (*Bhāgavata Purāṇa* 1.1.20, in Vyasa 1983: 15),[9] especially with an unnamed heroine, described as his "best worshipper" or "Rādha" (*Bhāgavata Purāṇa* 10.30.28, in Vyasa 1983).[10] The zenith of the narrative was a nocturnal *rāsa-līlā*, where his numerous *gopīs* left behind everything they ever cared for – their homes, husbands and children – to be united with him. They found Kṛṣṇa hidden in the forest groves of Vraja on a beautiful autumn moonlit night, playing on his flute as if anticipating them. And when they came, Kṛṣṇa mystically expanded himself to be individually with each and every one of them, reciprocating their devotional act and dancing all night to their hearts' content. The *Bhāgavata* portrayed this particular activity of Kṛṣṇa to be the highest vision of godhead and represented the intense conjugal devotion of the *gopīs* as the pinnacle of spiritual perfection (Schweig 2005).

The Bhāgavata Purāṇa's sacred love-story of Rādha and Kṛṣṇa became increasingly popular in south Asia and the narrations of their esoteric erotic play (*līlā*)[11] not only attracted serious hermeneutical exegesis in the various Vaiṣṇava *bhakti* schools of Vedānta,[12] but also found widespread cultural expressions in south Asian literary, pictorial and performance arts.[13] After initiation and experiencing a spiritual transformation as mentioned earlier, Chaitanya asserted that the *Bhāgavata Purāṇa* was the best source of scriptural authority and the conclusive "ripe fruit" of the tree of the Vedic literatures. And though Chaitanya himself did not write anything except eight small verses summarizing his thoughts, he asked some of his disciples to compose explanations and commentaries based on the Bhāgavata to expound his theology. And writing they did: a large group of Chaitanya followers, began to compose books on dramaturgy, music, hagiography, liturgy and theology and composed about fifty major and hundreds of minor books that became a part of the Gauḍīya Vaiṣṇava canon. These books not only became the source of information on Chaitanya's life and legacy, but also gave his fledging movement a very sophisticated intellectual orientation and elaborate explanations of the basic tenets of Chaitanya's tradition.

The foundational tenets

The basic tenets of Gauḍīya Vaiṣṇavism are fairly simple and can be summarized under three categories: *saṃbandha* (inter-relationships), *abhidheya* (means/process) and *prayojana* (the aim). Although in a post-Chaitanya era his followers developed a much more sophisticated theology, this threefold explanation remained the basic framework to the various aspects of the thoughts that developed in this school. The first part, *saṃbandha*, dealt with the ontological status of Kṛṣṇa, and the inter-relations between him, the innumerable number of living entities (*jīvas*) and the rest of the inanimate creation (*prakriti*). *Abhidheya*, the second part concerned itself with *bhakti*, the means or the process: the realization of one's real position in the scheme of things necessitated action in one's true capacity and thus the tenets assumed that one who knew his real self would thus naturally start practising *bhakti*. Finally, the third part *Prayojana* refers to the idea that when an individual understood *saṃbandha* and engaged in *bhakti*, she would directly experience the final aim, *prema*, or pure love of God, transcending the constraints of the phenomenal world.

In terms of the basic ideas of *saṃbandha*, each and every living being is a transcendent person beyond her body, mind, senses, intelligence and ego, being an infinitesimally small part of Kṛṣṇa; her relationship to Kṛṣṇa is similar to that of a small spark to a blazing fire. In the entire creation, innumerable such living beings constantly transmigrate through the cycles of birth and death based on the laws of action and reaction (*karma*). Kṛṣṇa is both immanent within and transcendent from everything – simultaneously one with and different from his animate and inanimate creations. In this scheme of things, each conscious entity has the capacity to act independently and the reason individuals either suffer or enjoy in this world is due to their misidentification with their physical self, which is not much more than a temporary covering of their real self (*ātman*). Individuals especially suffer because of their forgetfulness of the timeless relationship they have with Kṛṣṇa in the spiritual world, where they can have unhindered enjoyment as they engage in Kṛṣṇa's intimate plays as his servant, friend, parent or lover. The spiritual world, Gauḍīya Vaiṣṇava texts describe, is a place where every step is a dance and every word a song; everything there, including particles of dust, are conscious, and everyone is always satiated and forever youthful, for time does not affect anything in that realm; each one of us is looking for this without knowing it (Krishnadasa & Dimock 1999: 992–1000).

This utopian alternative reality is not only a transcendent reality, but can also manifest within our phenomenal world for a sincere and qualified practitioner of *bhakti*. When a practitioner engages in *bhakti* transforming everything she does into a sacred act – "Kṛṣṇa-izing" her reality – she can get out of her "spiritual amnesia", release herself from bodily identification and revert back to her original state of loving God. The theologians of this school claim that when one rediscovers this lost love, it fulfils the craving she constantly feels in her heart in this world and has an ultimate loving reunion with Kṛṣṇa, fulfilling the prayojana or aim of Gauḍīya Vaiṣṇavism. But how would an individual practitioner achieve this in her life? How can one transform every act to "Kṛṣṇa-ize" one's reality? How do these tenets translate into practice?

Basic practices of Gauḍīya Vaiṣṇavism

One of the ways of harmonizing the activities of one's life, for instance, would imply offering one's food to Kṛṣṇa before consuming it and only accepting the remnants as his "grace" (*prasāda*). The majority of the practitioners abjures meat, fish and eggs and avoids pungent vegetables like onion and garlic. Ritual offering one's meal to Kṛṣṇa as if he were a guest or a family member makes sure that there is no bad *karma* incurred in the process of cooking. Since even vegetarian food, involves killing plants, Gauḍīya Vaiṣṇavas would consume food that causes minimum violence and has been first offered to Kṛṣṇa. Most of them would also avoid intoxicating substances that would alter the states of the mind, like alcohol or drugs, abjure gambling and restrict sexual relations within the sanctity of marriage. According to Gauḍīya Vaiṣṇavas, engaging in unrestricted sex, meat consumption and the like reinforces a bodily conception of life that eventually proves antithetical to their spiritual practices and aspirations.

Figure 13.2 Gaudiya Vaiṣṇavas dancing, Baruipur, December 2009 (photo © Travis Chilcott, used with permission).

But these practices are considered tertiary when it comes to worship of Kṛṣṇa, especially meditation on his names and activities. The names of Kṛṣṇa, set into certain *mantras*, are sometimes chanted softly (*japa*), when the practitioner is supposed to listen to his own chanting, and at other times celebrated through singing and dancing (*saṃkīrtana*). During these two kinds of chanting, it is considered that there is no difference between Kṛṣṇa and his names because on an absolute level there is no difference between God and his powers. Chanting or singing Kṛṣṇa's name, therefore, is the ultimate spiritual activity, where one directly associates with Kṛṣṇa and, if the attitude of meditation was right, it becomes akin to participating in Kṛṣṇa's dance with his beloved girlfriends.

The four other important aspects of practising *bhakti* include worshipping Kṛṣṇa's image with faith, staying in the company of other devotees of Kṛṣṇa, residing in a holy place of pilgrimage and hearing the narratives of the *Bhāgavata Purāṇa* (Rupa & Haberman 2003: 711–17). All these practices, which would immerse a devotee in thoughts about Kṛṣṇa, would inevitably help her to come out of the "spiritual amnesia" and remember her real position in the realm of Kṛṣṇa. And when one attained that level of perfection, one need not annihilate one's existence, as the Buddhists suggest, nor become one with the non-personal existence, as the non-dualistic schools of Hinduism offer, but rather continue to relish one's relation with Kṛṣṇa as one of his guardians, friends or lovers.

But all this may still leave us with a question: could not such remembrance and meditation on Kṛṣṇa be a personal affair? What was the need of such group public singing and dancing? For the Gauḍīya Vaiṣṇavas, much like Mahāyāna Buddhism's *bodhisattvas*, relinquishing one's elevated spiritual state for the sake of rekindling love for Kṛṣṇa in the hearts of others is seen as the highest expression of compassion (Krishnadasa & Dimock 1999: 558). One's own release from the phenomenal world was not of much consequence compared with saving others, and the best way to remind the maximum number of people would be to make the chanting of Kṛṣṇa's names a public affair. Not only did it ensure the group of practitioners' own remembrance of Kṛṣṇa and engagement with him, it also helped them to bring uninitiated members in touch with their tenets and practices.

Conclusion

Gauḍīya Vaiṣṇavism began to grow in popularity during and beyond Chaitanya's lifetime, and within 300 years this brand of Kṛṣṇa worship became especially powerful in Bengal and Vraj areas of northern India. In Bengal and nearby regions like Tripura it claimed a following of almost 8 million people, or approximately a fifth of the Bengali population (Chakravarti 1985), while developing similar importance in Vraja. It was a common sight in the cities and villages to see a number of people come out in the streets and sing and dance to the names of Kṛṣṇa, and to some extent it still is today. Especially during the latter half of the nineteenth century, some prominent and influential people in urban Bengal took up the leadership of this movement, and planned to transplant it beyond the shores of south Asia. In particular, Kedarnath Datta Bhaktivinoda (1838–1914), a Vaiṣṇava intellectual and a district magistrate in the colonial government, began to draw up plans to take Gauḍīya Vaiṣṇavism to the Western world (Chakravarti 1985; Bhatia 2011; J. D. Fuller 2005).

It took several decades before Bhaktivinoda's plan was fulfilled when his son, Bhaktisiddhanta Saraswati (1874–1937), began to send missionaries to Europe in the period between the two world wars. But it was one of Bhaktisiddhanta's disciples, Bhaktivedanta Swami (1896–1977), who achieved a major breakthrough in terms of bringing Gauḍīya Vaiṣṇavism to a popular level internationally after he founded the Hare Kṛṣṇa movement (International Society for Kṛṣṇa Consciousness, or ISKCON) during the 1960s. This movement attracted a lot of followers from the American counterculture, and later from the Indian diasporas, and continues the practices of Gauḍīya Vaiṣṇavism.

Whether it was a village in Bengal or downtown Manhattan, Gauḍīya Vaiṣṇavas have some core beliefs, values and practices: For them Kṛṣṇa is the supreme personal being, and each and every individual is a minute part of him, like sparks from a fire; the natural state of every being is to engage in his loving service, or *bhakti*. The best method for both relishing *bhakti* and giving it to others is through the processes of worshipping the icon of Kṛṣṇa, visiting or residing in holy places associated with him, hearing and reciting the *Bhāgavata Purāṇa*, being in the company of the devotees of Kṛṣṇa, and most importantly meditating on the holy names through soft chanting or group singing and dancing.

Notes

1. To begin with, it is difficult to define what the term "Hinduism" means or what makes one a Hindu. Hinduism, unlike Abrahamic traditions such as Judaism or Christianity, does not have a founder or one single text. Therefore it does not fit into the definition of "religion" in the technical sense of the term, but has come to be used as such since the nineteenth century. In this chapter, following most scholars in the field, I will consider Chaitanya Vaiṣṇavism a part of Hinduism. One of the major sixteenth-century biographers of this tradition, Krishnadasa Kaviraja, mentions the word "Hindu" several times in his central text, the *Chaitanya Charitamrita*, usually to separate the identity between the ruling Islamic groups of the time and the non-Muslims. Flood (1996: 177) observes that although Hinduism cannot be technically termed a religion before the nineteenth century, Vaiṣṇavism can be technically called so.
2. Vaiṣṇavas are worshippers of Viṣṇu who they understand to be the "supreme person". Viṣṇu is a deity of minor importance in the early Vedas, but with development of what we call Hinduism, he gained tremendous importance. Some recent scholarship has claimed that about 70 per cent of Hinduism is Vaiṣṇava, and although this figure needs to be verified, there is no doubt that it has a major pan-Indian presence. See Rosen (2006: 151–69).

3. For further discussion on the intellectual context of fifteenth-century Bengal, see De Kumar (1986: 1–25).
4. For a discussion on the practices of both right- and left-handed *tantra*, see White (2000).
5. These two *mantras* are: "Haraye Namaḥ Kṛṣṇa Yādavāya Namaḥ/Gopāla Govinda Rāma Śrī Madhusūdana" and "Hare Kṛṣṇa Hare Kṛṣṇa, Kṛṣṇa Kṛṣṇa Hare Hare / Hare Rāma Hare Rāma, Rāma Rāma Hare Hare".
6. For a discussion on the origins of *bhakti* in south India and the *Bhāgavata Purāṇa*, see Hardy (1983: 483–9).
7. *Rasa* does not have a fixed translation in English and can take up a variety of meanings, including sap, taste, flavour and humidity; this is different from *rāsa*, which is a circle dance. It is also important to note here that although Kṛṣṇa was well known for his part-human, part-divine character in the *Gītā* and the *Mahābhārata* centuries before this *Purāṇa*, this "romantic" aspect gathered prominence with the composition of the later *Purāṇas*. There are references to such erotic-sacred love in the works of the ninth-century Tamil̲ mystic Āṇṭāḷ, who had composed poems glorifying Kṛṣṇa imagining herself as a cowherd girl craving to marry Kṛṣṇa, and yet constantly in the pangs of separation.
8. The "sweetness" of Kṛṣṇa's līlas is perhaps best celebrated in the famous eight verses "Madhurāṣṭaka" by the sixteenth-century mystic Vallabha. See Raghavan (1963: 255).
9. Vraja or Vrindavana is a town about 100 miles north of Delhi, where Kṛṣṇa supposedly enacted his childhood and adolescent pastimes. See Haberman (1994).
10. The commentarial tradition identifies her as Rādhā, but the text itself mentions only "*ārādhitā*", meaning the best of Kṛṣṇa's worshippers. For further discussion see Schweig (2005).
11. Līlā is a spontaneous and joyful act, performed in "a state of rapt absorption comparable to that of an artist possessed by creative vision or to that of a child caught up in the delight of a game played for its own sake" (Dimock 1989; Hein 1995: 13).
12. Vedānta is one of the classical philosophical schools of Vedic orthodoxy and is related to the more ritualistic *Uttara-Mimāṁsā*. By the eighth or tenth century, Śaṅkara, a monist hermeneutic propounded the philosophy of oneness, "*advaita*", which caught the imagination of the Brahmanical intelligentsia. It asserted the ultimate ontological oneness of individual and the non-personal absolute reality, Brahman. In the centuries following Śaṅkara, several thinkers like Rāmānuja, Madhva, Vallabha and Chaitanya appeared critiquing his soteriology and worldview, providing an alternative "dualistic" system that gave prominence to the difference between a personal godhead (*īśvara*) and individuals (*jīva*) and the loving relation between them (*bhakti*). See Flood (1996: 224–50).
13. For some recent discussion on the pan-Indian nature of Kṛṣṇa since the tenth century, see Beck (2005) and Bryant (2007).

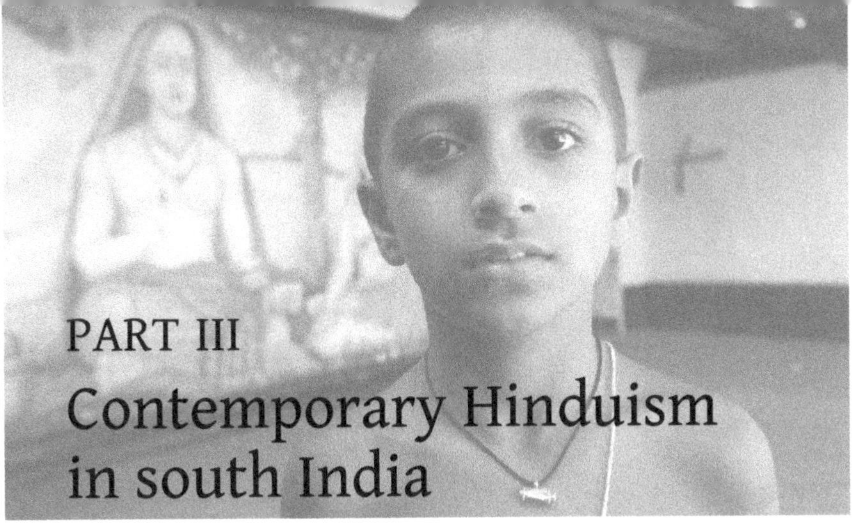

PART III
Contemporary Hinduism in south India

As much as the south of India is culturally very unique and different from the north, the diversity within the south is as prominent as it is in the north. There is a significant temple culture in the south. It is a land that was once buoyant with devotionalism that gave rise to many of the present Śaivite and Vaiṣṇavite temple traditions. Famous philosophers and religious reformers such as Śankara and Rāmānuja lived in these parts of the south. As we shall see, some parts of the south such as Kerala claimed to be "God's own land", and some of the temples such as Tirupati claimed to be "heaven on Earth". With such intense devotional background, the south offers us great opportunities to explore the variety of contemporary Hindu practice. We present here narratives of snake goddesses by Amy Allocco in Chapter 14. Weaving the narrative around a highly educated urban woman, she offers an insight into the significance of this worship for the society and women. Chapter 15, by George Pati, is on Nambūtiri Brāhmans and Ayyapan devotees, and offers us an insight into the rituals, beliefs and the devotional life of Kerala. In Chapter 16, Archana Venkatesan constructs her narrative on the sacred life of Āṇṭāḷ around the story of an elderly woman in Srivilliputtur, a small town in Tamilnadu. Following on from this, Afsar Mohammad (Chapter 17) narrates the festival of Brahmotsvam and the various daily rituals at Sri Venkateswara temple in Tirupati. Hinduism is not only about devotion, but it has also often provided impetus to political activism, as we find in the narrative about the Tamiḻ Tigers by William Harman (Chapter 18).

14. Snake goddess traditions in Tamilnadu

Amy L. Allocco

In the relative cool of the early morning a bustling crowd of women has already gathered in front of the grouping of stone snake statues (***nāga cilai*** or ***nāgakkal***) installed under a sacred tree in this Hindu goddess temple's open-air courtyard. Clad in colourful saris and carrying baskets and bags containing the assorted items necessary to perform their individual ritual worship ceremonies (*pūjā*), these women represent a wide spectrum of class and caste backgrounds. It is a Friday in the sultry month of **Āṭi**, the ritually heightened month that spans July to August and is most closely associated with worship of the Hindu Goddess in the south Indian state of Tamilnadu. Fridays are considered especially auspicious days to worship local goddesses in their many manifestations during Āṭi, and the temple thrums with ritual activity on this day every week of the festival. Here in Chennai, Tamilnadu's capital and India's fourth largest city, the Āṭi festival season has been celebrated in increasingly elaborate ways in recent years, and the popularity of the snake goddess in her multiple forms has undergone a corresponding growth as well.[1] The snake goddess is one among the goddess' forms and she, like other local goddesses, attracts the most devotional attention from female worshippers. Because Āṭi is understood as a time when the goddess is both particularly powerful and uniquely accessible to her devotees, women visit Chennai's snake goddess and other temples where stone snake images are available for worship in huge numbers during this period.[2]

Most of the women who make their way to this popular Hindu goddess temple this morning live nearby and come on foot, but some arrive by public bus or come by private car or scooter. Drawn by the goddess' reputation for relieving problems and granting wishes, they approach her with specific requests, as well as the desire for more generalized blessings for their families.[3] Before leaving her house each woman would have bathed, decorated her residence's entrance with an auspicious ritual diagram (***kōlam***), and performed at least a simple *pūjā* for the deities who grace her home shrine. Whether she had them ready at home or bought them from vendors outside the temple, by the time she approached the installation of stone snake images she would have assembled the requisite ritual offerings and substances for her worship. These items might include some or all of the following: milk, fresh flowers, bananas, incense sticks, a small earthen oil lamp, and turmeric and vermilion powders.[4] In the cramped space each woman selects one among the dozens of stone ***nāgas*** for her individualized worship and, seemingly unbothered by the crowd of women pressing around her, artfully arranges her offerings before the image with care and precision. She then pours small amounts of milk over as many of the snake images as she is able, in keeping with the belief that milk nourishes and pleases the *nāga*, who is symbolically thought to partake in this food offering.

This Friday morning Susheela, a highly educated scientist from the Madhva Brāhmin community who lives just up the street from the temple and is one of the goddess' most committed devotees, comes to the temple with offerings overflowing a sterling silver basket. She stops at one of the stalls flanking the temple to purchase fresh flowers, and selects several varieties of roses, large marigolds and a creamy string of fragrant jasmine blossoms. Upon entering the temple she stands on her tiptoes to see and be seen by the goddess (to have *darśan*) installed in the inner sanctum before joining the crowd of women assembled in front of the stone *nāgas* (Figure 14.1).[5] Susheela finds a spot in front of an image depicting two snakes intertwined, sets down her basket full of *pūjā* supplies, and begins her worship.[6] She slowly pours clear golden honey over the image, washes it with water, and then sends a cascade of milk down over the

Figure 14.1 Women engaged in worship activities at a grouping of stone snake images in the courtyard of a goddess temple in Chennai (photo by author). The abundance of flowers draped on top of these *nāgas* indicates the care devotees have taken in adorning them, as do the lamps and other offerings arrayed on the ledge in front of this grouping of images. Also visible are wooden cradles hanging from the tree; these are offered by women who wish to conceive.

black stone surface. This ritual bathing is a gesture of respect and devotion, and is an abbreviated version of a ceremony that is performed using a number of substances for enlivened divine images at many temples in India every day.

After dressing the *nāga* with a piece of silk brocade, Susheela adorns the image with the flower blossoms she has brought, nestling them in the folds of the gold-bordered fabric and in the sinuous curves of the two snakes. She balances a small bundle of sacred grass atop the snake stone, drapes a strand of jasmine along its edge, and lights some incense sticks, waving them in front of the *nāga* and fanning the perfumed smoke towards the image before inserting the sticks into a small banana at its base. Next to the banana she places some shiny green betel leaves with a silver rupee coin on top and a chunk of white camphor, which she lights. Murmuring prayers, Susheela bows before the camphor flame and touches it quickly three times, each time bringing its essence (warmth and light) to her eyes.

Next to her, a woman deftly coats a single coiled *nāga* with bright yellow turmeric powder before daubing its surface with vermilion dots. She, too, adorns the image with flowers and lights a camphor flame on a small brass plate, which she circles before the decorated stone snake. Susheela falls in behind this woman as they circumambulate the grouping of *nāga* stones three times, ducking down to pass beneath a large branch of the sacred *peepal* tree that towers above the assembled images. This low-hanging branch is laden with dozens of miniature wooden cradles, left as votive offerings by women who desire to be blessed with children, and is wrapped in yellow threads and cords tied there by women who wish to get married.[7]

After circling the tree and the stone snakes three times, Susheela makes her way to each of the other free-standing shrines in the temple. She spends a few minutes in prayer at the base of another sacred tree, which is located behind the temple's main sanctum. The tunnel-like roots at the base of this banyan tree are understood as the dwelling place of the temple's divine snake, considered to be the goddess in her reptilian form. Devotees and officials here say that due to the overwhelming crowds that have flocked to the temple in recent years, this snake rarely reveals herself to worshippers anymore and so the devout have to be content to reach between the wrought iron bars that protect the tree to leave their offerings at its foot. In addition to milk and flowers, eggs are often left here as food for the divine snake, who is thought to symbolically consume them. Some devotees hang paper garlands that they have strung together out of 108 folded pieces of paper inscribed with handwritten prayers; these dangle down from the tree's branches and flutter in the breeze as a tangible manifestation of individuals' *bhakti*, or devotion.

Nearby there is small shrine containing a single stone image of a cobra, which stands in for the divine snake thought to reside somewhere in the depths of the banyan's gnarled roots; Susheela arranges her last few flower blossoms in front of this *nāga* before completing her circumambulation of the temple's interior. Her final stop is the temple's inner sanctum, which she enters after purchasing a special ticket. Here the goddess' image is understood to be ***svayaṃbhū***, or self-manifest. The fact that it appeared spontaneously, without human intervention, distinguishes it from images which are sculpted by artisans and later enlivened by priests in complex rituals aimed at installing divine breath in them. The deity's self-manifest form is closely related to the temple's unique status among local goddess temples in this area of the city, and devotees regularly reference this feature in their attempts to describe to me why this goddess is particularly powerful and what motivates their devotional relationships with her.

Following Susheela as she carries out her worship at this urban local goddess temple early on an auspicious Friday morning in the Tamil̲ month of Āṭi offers us a window into some of the ways that female devotees approach the snake goddess in contemporary Hinduism. Still, the picture that has emerged thus far is only a partial one, and it leaves us with several important questions. One central question concerns the reasons underlying the worship of this goddess: why do women pray to the snake goddess? How do these female worshippers understand their relationships with this goddess? Moreover, why is the worship of snake goddesses a gendered religious practice, or one that is overwhelmingly the domain of Hindu women? Other questions relate to the wider repertoire of rituals devoted to the snake goddess: are there other ways in which devotees approach and honour her during the Āṭi festival season, and does she also receive worship throughout the year? Relying on examples drawn from ethnographic fieldwork carried out in Chennai over several periods between 2005 and 2011 and on women's own narratives about and articulations of their devotional relationships with the snake goddess, the subsequent sections of this chapter will offer some answers to these questions.

Gender in the worship of Tamil̲ snake goddesses

Here we will consider what might be gendered about contemporary snake goddess worship in Tamilnadu as well as why the city's educated and upwardly mobile are increasingly bringing their concerns before this deity. *Nāgas* have long been associated with fertility in belief, custom, and local mythology, and in contemporary south India they are primarily worshipped by women who wish to conceive.[8] Those who are believed to be affected by a negative condition called ***nāga dōṣam***, which literally means "snake blemish", also worship the snake goddess for relief from its afflictions.[9] *Nāga dōṣam* is diagnosed when an astrologer detects unfavourable planetary configurations in an individual's horoscope. This astrological malady – which my research shows disproportionately affects women in contemporary south India – is most often faulted for delayed marriage and infertility. Those who have been formally diagnosed with this horoscopic flaw (and even some who are facing problems arranging their marriages or conceiving and therefore believe they may have this condition) undertake the worship of snake images and make vows to snake goddesses in bids to alleviate their difficulties.

Indeed, stone snake images like the ones worshipped by Susheela in the example above and found under sacred trees in temple courtyards all over south India are offered by those afflicted by *nāga dōṣam*.[10] The astrologer who diagnosed the individual's **dōṣam** typically prescribes this ceremony and will recommend an astrologically favourable day on which to have the stone *nāga* installed and enlivened in a rite called **nāga pratiṣṭhā**. Once arrangements with the temple where the sculpture will be offered have been made, the stone image is immersed in water and then in grains for a period up to forty-eight days in order to purify it. The installation ceremony, which cost almost US$100 in 2007, is typically presided over by a male priest; I have witnessed these rites performed by members of the priestly Brāhmin caste, as well as non-Brāhmin ritual specialists. The priest places gems representing the nine planets of Hindu astrology under the snake stone and chants *mantras* that consecrate the image.[11] It is then decorated and adorned with flowers, a silk garment and sacred grasses, and the priest chants the requisite *mantras* to establish the deity's presence and kindle life-breath (**uyir**) in the image before opening its eyes with a small golden stick.[12] Now understood to be an embodiment of the divine, the *nāga* must be worshipped daily for an additional forty-eight days to complete the cycle of offerings that are thought to alleviate the donor's *nāga dōṣam*.

Whether an individual's astrologer has confirmed that the planetary positions in his or her horoscope signals *nāga dōṣam* or that person has other petitions to place before the snake goddess, individuals often choose to visit a particular temple because of its powerful reputation. Accounts of illnesses cured, marriages arranged and babies conceived circulate via word of mouth and motivate devotees to seek out new shrines. Others might visit a particular temple after reading a pamphlet featuring its myths and miracles or after happening upon an article in a devotional magazine that highlights the power of that particular site for mitigating the effects of *nāga dōṣam* and other astrological problems.

The temple pamphlet from Chennai's popular **Muṇṭakakkaṇṇi Ammaṉ Temple**, which explicitly credits worship at its cobra shrine with relief from *nāga dōṣam*, serves as one such example.[13] This short text, which is written in colloquial Tamiḻ, provides an expansive list of the goddess' special powers:

> This mother is known for curing one from pox, diseases, blindness, paralysis, and lameness. She also removes sorcery and evil spirits, *nāga dōṣam* and planetary defects, and helps the weak and poor to prosper. The holy water which is distributed here is a cure for all ailments. This temple is a powerful place to make vows and petitions. (Muṇṭakakkaṇṇi Ammaṉ Temple, n.d.)

Temple pamphlets and inexpensive Tamiḻ-language devotional magazines are widely read both by homemakers and working women in Chennai and this literature directly influences individual ritual practices and local beliefs about particular deities' special powers. Even a single copy of one of these magazines may pass through many hands in an office setting or circulate around an apartment building, making it hard to estimate how many individuals its articles about temples, deities and rituals might reach. What is clear is that this type of popular religious literature plays an important role in popularizing *nāga dōṣam* traditions, its ritual remedies and particular snake goddess temples. In 2006, for example, I was able to trace an influx of new devotees at a goddess temple in Chennai where I was conducting research to a particular article touting that site's power to relieve *nāga dōṣam* that had just been published in a devotional magazine. Many of the women I interviewed cited this article as the catalyst for their initial visit to the temple, demonstrating the extent to which this genre of religious literature is shaping the landscape of snake goddess and *nāga dōṣam* traditions in Tamilnadu today.

In addition to their principal connections with fertility and *nāga dōṣam*, snake goddesses are broadly understood as having power over a range of concerns that are especially important in the experience of contemporary Tamiḻ women. Female devotees frequently told me the snake goddess can answer their prayers for a successful marriage, safeguard the welfare of their children, and ensure the general health and well-being of their families. For these and other reasons, women vastly outnumber men among regular devotees of the snake goddess and it is safe to say that in south India, at least, women predominate in local goddess worship more generally.

That *nāga dōṣam* and its negative consequences primarily affect women and that the worship of snake goddesses is a gendered religious activity is corroborated by the traditional history (***talavaralāṟu***) of Muṇṭakakkaṇṇi Ammaṉ, the popular goddess whose temple pamphlet I referenced above. Written in Tamiḻ, this 200-page narrative devotes a long discussion to the goddess' ability to relieve a constellation of ill effects caused by astrological blemishes (*dōṣam*), explicitly links these undesirable effects with women, and recommends that women worship at Muṇṭakakkaṇṇi Ammaṉ's temple to secure a reprieve from them. Among the negative outcomes of *nāga dōṣam* for women are delayed marriages, diseases affecting her husband, his early death, the inability to conceive children (especially male children) or to deliver children who live full lifespans, and troubled family lives (Kēcikaṉ 1992: 107). The temple history states that Muṇṭakakkaṇṇi Ammaṉ appears in the form of a *nāga* and promises, "[T]he women who worship her and offer milk and eggs to the *nāga* in the anthill at the back of the temple will remove their *nāga dōṣam* and lead happy lives with their husbands and children" (Kēcikaṉ 1992: 108).

While the women who are devoted to the snake goddess entreat her perhaps most often to fulfil specific requests related to fertility, marriage, and childbirth, it is also the case that they approach her for more generalized blessings and prosperity. Further, males do figure among the snake goddess' devotees, especially at particular times of the year (such as during the goddess' festival season in Āṭi), in relation to a vow to secure a particular wish, or because of family participation in some ongoing ritual relationship with the snake goddess.

During my 2011 field research at snake goddess temples in Chennai I witnessed a young man with a freshly shaven head engaged in focused worship of a single stone *nāga* (Figure 14.2). His aesthetic sense was evident in the attention he paid to decorating the image with turmeric powder and vermilion dots and adorning it with a strand of sweet-smelling jasmine flowers. He carefully broke a coconut and laid its two halves before the *nāga*, and polished an apple before placing it between them. After his worship had concluded he told me that the snake goddess is his family's deity (***kulateyvam***), and that one member of his family takes responsibility for making offerings to the goddess every year to renew their bond with her and ensure their collective protection. He said that he had shaved his hair recently at another temple to thank the deity for helping him to pass his final exams and to earn his Master's degree in Engineering. To help smooth his transition into the working world and to acknowledge all that he had to be thankful for, this young man had agreed to undertake the snake goddess' worship on behalf of his family members this year. The specific request he was making of the goddess was that she bless him with a good first job in his chosen field; in addition, he prayed for his family's overall welfare, and asked that they remain free of illness and misfortune.

This young man's example serves as a counterpoint to my earlier claim that snake goddess worship is overwhelmingly the practice of women in contemporary Tamilnadu, as well as my contention that this deity is chiefly associated with fertility and the blessings of marriage and children that are most commonly sought by women. Although these generalizations are certainly accurate, no

Figure 14.2 *Nāga* image decorated by a young engineering graduate (photo by author). Notice how the application of turmeric causes the details carved into the snake stone's surface to be visible.

generalization can take account of all of the diversity that characterizes Hindu traditions. One of the strengths of ethnographic research is that it reveals the specific ways that everyday Hinduism defies categorical statements. Fieldwork over a long period of time at a particular temple suggests that goddesses may at times appeal to a new cohort of devotees and can take on new ritual "work" as the needs of worshippers shift.[14] To reflect some of this nuance in an essay like this, one can qualify such generalizations by offering additional cases that help us to understand the on-the-ground realities a bit better than simply sketching a broad picture might allow. Thus, while it is safe to say that the worship of the snake goddess in contemporary Tamilnadu is a gendered religious activity insofar as most of this deity's committed devotees, many of whom understand themselves as participating in reciprocal devotional relationships with the goddess, are female, this young man indicates that there are important exceptions which may hint at potential emerging directions or new patterns in her worship.

Rituals in repertoire: worshipping the snake goddess throughout the year

Our attention now shifts to the devotional relationships that many female devotees maintain with the snake goddess. These interactions are regarded as reciprocal because these local goddesses (and other Hindu deities) are often thought of as responsive and engaged agents who take part in a *bhakti* relationship with the humans who honour and worship them. While such relationships are certainly animated by an abiding devotion to and love for the deity, they are also often characterized by give and take: the devotee dedicates offerings, engages in ritual practices and does other things with the goal of pleasing the deity, and the deity is expected to bestow blessings on and fulfil the specific requests of the devotee.[15] It is common for an individual worshipper to make a vow (*vēṇṭutal* or *pirārttaṉai*) to formalize this devotional pact with the deity; such vows may be instrumental (that is, the vow serves as a means for the devotee to get something s/he wants), prophylactic (meaning that the vow is undertaken to ward off some undesirable occurrence, such as illness), or offered in thanksgiving (meaning that the vow is discharged in gratitude after a wish is fulfilled).

Because the kinds of requests that are usually associated with vows continue to be women's primary areas of concern – including the health, welfare, success and prosperity of her husband and her children – vows can be described as a gendered religious practice in Hindu traditions. Women may promise to observe their vow for a fixed period of time, such as from this month's new moon day until next month's, or indefinitely, as in the case of a woman who has vowed to sew beaded garments for the snake goddess every festival season as an ongoing gesture of thanksgiving for the good fortune she feels this deity has bestowed on her family.

Many of the vows that women dedicate to snake goddesses and other local forms of the Goddess are performed within the context of the Āṭi festival season.

During this period temples arrange special public rituals whose success is predicated on enthusiastic participation from the goddess' devotees. The most common ritual programme begins on Friday when participants have protective strings (**kāppu**) tied around their wrists to signal their festival vow and lasts until Sunday when a ritual feast is prepared and served to the goddess and her devotees. Ritual drummers, who preside over the weekend's ceremonies, build a temporary image of the goddess in a large, flower-draped vessel (**karakam**) on Friday, which is then worshipped, attended to, and taken out in procession around the neighbourhood over the next two days. Women come to the temple to cook **poṅkal** (a boiled rice and lentil mixture) over individual cow-dung fires, and many assist in cleaning and decorating the temple in preparation for the festivities.

Other more elaborate worship ceremonies are arranged by particular temples as per their traditions. For example, one tiny snake goddess temple where I conducted research annually sponsors a fire-walking ceremony where hundreds of devotees walk (or dance) across a bed of glowing embers as one kind of offering. These Āṭi festivals uniformly feature ritual drumming and possession, which allows the priests to communicate with the snake goddess while she is present in the body of her human host. In these dialogues the goddess' permission to conduct the festival is secured and she is asked to pronounce whether the arrangements are satisfactory to her; devotees may also ask for divination or for solutions to their problems from the goddess in her temporary human form. Some temples organize milk-pot processions in which a group of mostly female devotees set out in a procession through the streets surrounding the temple with pots of milk balanced on their heads. Upon their return to the temple each woman can pour the contents of her pot over the goddess' enlivened stone form with her own hands in an intimate bathing ritual that is on other days performed only by male priests. These weekend festivals conclude on Sunday when the goddess' ritual vessel is processed through the streets one last time before her presence is dismissed and it is ultimately immersed in the ocean or in a river.

Although the rituals that collectively comprise the Āṭi festival are on a large scale and public, and therefore among the most easily identifiable religious practices associated with snake goddesses in contemporary Chennai, these ubiquitous goddesses are honoured in more modest expressions of devotion beyond this festival season, as well. Many devotees attend to her shrines and anoint her *nāga* images throughout the year. They may undertake vows – whether of the instrumental, prophylactic or thanksgiving type – to circumambulate her temple a certain number of times, bring particular offerings to her temple for a set number of weeks, or recite sacred syllables and prayers before her image on specific days. Many women demonstrate their devotion to the snake goddess by gifting attractive and/or valuable items to her in the hope that these will please her. Saris are so frequently offered for this purpose that temples regularly auction off the goddess' excess clothing to raise funds for temple projects, such as the free midday meal programme that is common at many mid-sized and larger temples. The discussion of the repertoire of ritual practices dedicated to the snake goddess in

Tamilnadu provided here is intended to orient the reader to the multiple ways in which this deity may be approached and engaged with by her devotees both within and beyond the Āṭi festival. While the tempo of the *nāga* goddess' worship certainly accelerates during this season, rituals and vows to the goddess are performed and undertaken all year long and the deity and her devotees remain in a relationship marked by mutual responsiveness and reciprocity.

The snake goddess as "everything": protection, support and rewards in women's devotional relationships

In the final section of the chapter we turn to the stories of two female devotees of the snake goddess. Each of these women holds the goddess in high esteem as a consummately powerful but also benevolent and accessible deity, and considers herself extraordinarily fortunate to have been blessed by a life-changing boon that this goddess granted. Rajamma and Saraswati are hardly unique in this regard. Indeed, over the course of my field research I collected narratives from dozens of women who described how, as a result of their devotion to the snake goddess, they had their livelihoods restored, marriages secured, wishes to conceive and/or deliver a healthy baby fulfilled, and were (or a close family member was) healed of illness. Many of the women with whom I consulted told me that they kept the snake goddess foremost in their minds among the other forms of the Hindu goddess, whom they also worshipped on some occasions, and that they demonstrated their close relationship with her by visiting her temples often. I conducted much of my research in a temple-rich neighbourhood of the city, where three local snake goddess temples were located within easy walking distance. Many of the women I knew there made their way to these temples on Tuesdays, Fridays and Sundays – days special for the worship of the goddess in Tamilnadu – and lit small oil lamps, offered flowers and performed *pūjās* to demonstrate their reverence. They might bring specific requests before the goddess or simply ask for things in their lives to go smoothly: for their family members to be healthy, to do well in their studies, to get adequate jobs and for there to be enough to eat.

The story of a woman named Rajamma is illustrative of the sort of devotional relationships with the snake goddess that I am interested in highlighting here. In a 2005 interview Rajamma told me that she had long shared a special bond with the snake goddess whose temple was located on a tree-lined street near her home in one of Chennai's crowded lower-class settlements. The snake goddess regularly appeared in her dreams and sometimes materialized in her reptilian form at Rajamma's house to enjoy the milk and egg offerings that this ardent devotee made available on Fridays. Because of the deep affection she felt for this *nāga* goddess Rajamma would often volunteer her time at the temple, taking on tasks like sweeping and washing the ritual items used in *pūjā*.

Rajamma described how in 2003 she was hit on the head by a falling beam at the construction site where she was working as a day labourer. Despite the fact that she suffered from internal bleeding and severe dizziness after the accident, Rajamma narrated how the snake goddess had enabled her to avoid an operation and to fully recuperate after taking medication. "The female doctor I was seeing said, 'Whatever goddess you worship has saved you.' Now I am normal. I can carry weight again, like two pots of water. Now I can do all of my work. The goddess is my support [**tuṇai**]." In Rajamma's understanding it was a combination of the snake goddess' power and their close relationship that ultimately made possible what medical treatment could not have accomplished alone, namely her complete recovery without a costly and frightening surgical procedure. Rajamma believes that the snake goddess knew her as a worthy devotee who had selflessly served at the goddess' temple and dedicated herself to worshipping the goddess even though her means were limited. Their relationship was, in Rajamma's view, characterized by intimacy and reciprocity in that each of them cared for the other enough to both clearly perceive and effectively respond to the other's unique needs.

Saraswati's account, on the other hand, is part of a genre of miracle stories involving women who experienced fertility problems and later delivered healthy babies as a result of the snake goddess' blessings, and so underscores the primary association between snake goddesses and fertility.[16] Saraswati's narrative circulated among devotees at a well-known Chennai snake goddess temple where I carried out research, and I had heard this account from women there long before I interviewed its protagonist. A Brāhmin woman who suffered twelve years of childlessness, Saraswati had consulted a distinguished array of medical and religious specialists. In fact, the couple's doctor discovered that Saraswati's husband had both a low sperm count and poor sperm motility around the same time their astrologer diagnosed him with *nāga dōṣam*. They undertook a number of medical and ritual treatments, including regular offerings and worship at a local snake goddess temple, but still did not conceive.

As the years stretched on, the couple's doctor became increasingly insistent that they come to terms with the fact that a biological child would not be possible for them and that they consider adoption. Still they resisted adopting, believing instead that the snake goddess would eventually reward their faith in her with a baby. Since Saraswati's husband was the one with both the horoscopic and physiological problems, he diligently offered milk at the snake goddess' temple every day until his wife learned she was pregnant. Saraswati related her account to me with tears streaming down her face one afternoon at the temple while her young son napped at home. Determined to impress upon me how grateful they are to the snake goddess, whom they credit with fulfilling their most fervent desire, she repeated over and over, "The snake goddess is everything to us." Now seven years old, their son drinks a sip of holy water from this snake goddess' temple every day after his bath.

Rajamma's and Saraswati's narratives are a good way for us to conclude our examination of contemporary snake goddess traditions in south India because they offer us a sense of the very real reasons why Hindu devotees may invest their faith in a particular deity, whom they understand as responsive to their concerns and powerful enough to address their needs. The situations in which the snake goddess is thought to have the authority to intervene, viz., evaporating marriage prospects, infertility, and illness, are among those which Indian women find most anxiety-producing and difficult to navigate. Where *nāga dōṣam* serves as one interpretive framework to help those who are facing these challenges to explain their misfortunes, the vows and other religious practices that constitute the snake goddess' ritual repertoire offer ways to negotiate the attendant suffering and to move forward. Devotees report that in ordinary times they derive sustenance and satisfaction from their devotional relationships with the snake goddess and in times of distress they call on her to deliver them from illness and affliction. They frequently note that in addition to whatever medical treatments or other solutions they might also be pursuing, they also need the snake goddess' divine clout to help them find solutions to their difficulties.[17] Whether motivated by the miracle stories that circulate at her temples, the claims of devotional magazines and Tamiḻ-language religious materials, or solely by their own abiding faith in her efficacy, devotees contend that when they humbly bring their concerns before the snake goddess they often find that their prayers are answered. It is precisely because this goddess is understood to be accessible, compassionate and uniquely powerful that devotees enter into and maintain ongoing devotional relationships with her. As Susheela put it when explaining her dedication to the snake goddess to me, "somehow she entered my heart".

Acknowledgements

The ethnographic research and fieldwork on which this chapter draws has been supported by generous funding from Elon University's Hultquist Stipend and Summer Research Award; the American Institute of Indian Studies Junior Fellowship; Emory University's Fund for International Graduate Research; and Emory University's Graduate School of Arts and Sciences and its Graduate Division of Religion.

Notes

1. The expansion of snake goddess worship in contemporary Tamilnadu, as well as the increasing popularity of the Āṭi festival, are discussed at length in my PhD dissertation, "Snakes, Goddesses, and Anthills: Modern Challenges and Women's Ritual Responses in Contemporary South India" (2009, Emory University).
2. On the festivals that punctuate the month of Āṭi, see Hancock (1990: 212–19; 1999: 133–6) and Logan (1980: 175–214).
3. The literature on vows and votive offerings in Hindu traditions is vast. Some examples include McDaniel (2003); McGee (1987; 1992); Pearson (1996); Pintchman (2005); Raj and Harman (2006); Tewari (1991); Wadley (1983).
4. For a useful overview of Hindu worship, or *pūjā*, with special reference to south Indian traditions, see C. J. Fuller (2004: ch. 3).
5. The classic source on *darśan* (which also discusses the roles that images play in Hindu traditions) is Eck (1981).

6. Some of the particulars concerning *nāga* iconography may be found in Smith and Narasimhachary (1991), Rao (1990) and Zimmer ([1946] 1992).
7. Stork (1992) discusses cradle offerings and other votive practices intended to promote fertility.
8. Colonial-era sources focusing on south India that treat these topics include Dubois (1899), Elmore ([1913] 1984) and Thurston (1906). Particularly notable is a passage from Henry Whitehead's *The Village Gods of South India* (1921: 22), which demonstrates how observations that were recorded nearly a century ago continue to bear a close resemblance to the traditions and practices under discussion here: "The worship of serpents, especially the deadly cobra, is common all over south India. In one village of the Wynaad I came across a Mission school which was visited almost daily by a large cobra, which glided undisturbed and harmless through the school-room. Neither teachers nor pupils would have dared to kill it. Constantly they fed it with milk. In many towns and villages large slabs of stone with figures of cobras, often two cobras intertwined, carved in bas-relief are seen on a platform under a large tree. They are worshipped especially by women who want children."
9. Apart from my dissertation (Allocco 2009), which deals extensively with *nāga dōṣam*, the most focused and detailed source on this condition and its spectrum of harmful effects is Kapadia (1995: ch. 4, esp. 82–91).
10. Nugteren (2005) offers a comprehensive treatment of sacred trees in Indian literature and ritual systems and considers the links between their status and Indian environmental movements. Sacred trees and groves (and their potential links to religiously informed conservation) have received significant attention in recent scholarly literature; examples include Haberman (2010), Kent (2010), and Gold and Gujar (1989). A focused discussion of sacred trees in Tamilnadu can be found in Amirthalingam (1998, 1999).
11. For helpful overviews of the nine planets, or *navagrahas*, and Indian astrology, see Gansten (2009, 2010).
12. Eck (1981: 51–5) discusses the rites of consecration for Hindu images and briefly describes the culminating eye-opening ritual.
13. Waghorne discusses this temple in her chapter on new visual forms at urban Tamiḻ temples and the "gentrification" of the Tamiḻ goddess (2004: 150–70).
14. Here I am referencing that fact that this goddess belongs to a class of goddesses who have traditionally been associated with pox-related illnesses and who now deal with a much-expanded repertoire of afflictions and concerns. Other scholars who foreground change in Tamiḻ goddess traditions include Harman (2004, 2006), Craddock (1994, 2001) and Younger (1980, 2002). See also Ferrari (2010) on this theme in the worship of Śītalā in rural west Bengal.
15. The nature of these give-and-take relationships is at the heart of Raj and Harman's volume (2006).
16. See Dempsey and Raj's recent volume (2008) on miracle stories across south Asian traditions.
17. Discussions about the characteristic and well-established south Asian cultural practice of operating in two (or more) healing repertoires simultaneously can be found in, for example, Bellamy (2011), Flueckiger (2006), and Goslinga (2006).

15. Nambūtiris and Ayyappan devotees in Kerala

George Pati

Imagine ... as some of us go to bed at four in the morning after a long night of playing Xbox 360, or chatting with friends, or convening a fraternity meeting, or writing papers, some people on the other side of the globe wake up and take a bath in the bathing tank outside and perform daily rituals around this time. This remains true in the lives of both Nambūtiri[1] Brāhmans and Ayyappan devotees in Kerala, the southwestern state of peninsular India located between the mountain ranges of the Western Ghats and the Arabian Sea, occupying a total area of 24,148 square miles and with a coastline of 360 miles. Its geographical position and abundance of natural plant products add to its natural beauty and serenity, and Malayalis (people of Kerala), who speak Malayalam, popularly refer to it as "God's own country". Kerala's socio-religious and cultural matrix, an amalgam of native and foreign cultures and creeds, shapes its distinctive culture.

Hinduism, a way of life, can be observed in the day-to-day rituals and customs of the Hindus, including both Nambūtiri Brāhmans and Ayyappan devotees. Nambūtiri Brāhmans are those orthodox Brāhmans of Kerala, who occupy the highest position in the Kerala caste system. The Nambūtiris learn and practice Vedic rituals and adhere to principles of ritual purity. Ayyappan devotees are those Hindus from Kerala and elsewhere who express devotion towards Lord Ayyappan through worship and pilgrimage. As part of the pilgrimage and devotion, Ayyappan devotees engage in austerities and rituals. These rituals give order and meaning to the lives of those who perform them. More importantly, rituals transcend boundaries of time and space as they mirror devotion and social reality. In this broad context of rituals and devotional love, this chapter discusses the daily devotional life, rituals and beliefs of Nambūtiri Brāhmans and the Ayyappan devotees. Though distinct in their practices, beliefs, and rituals, both communities understand rituals as a way of transcending the boundaries between the physical and the spiritual, terrestrial and celestial as way of emphasizing love of divine and humans.

Nambūtiri Brāhmans of Kerala

Vedic Brāhmanism, ancient Dravidian religious beliefs and devotional traditions of the medieval period comprise the Hindu religious fabric of Kerala. Govindan Namboodiri highlights the literary world documenting the presence of Vedic Brāhmanism in Kerala. For example, **Kātyāyana**, the fourth century BCE grammarian, records that the works of the kingdoms of the south and the **Caṅkam** poets exhibit Aryan influence (Gopalakrishnan 1974); the **Cēra** kings patronized the Caṅkam poets, who were local Brāhmans. Additionally, Nambūtiris believe Kerala to be **Paraśurāma-kṣetram** ("land of Paraśurāma"), a great Brāhmin sage and warrior of the race of **Bhṛgu**, because he created the land of Kerala by throwing his axe from Gokarnam. They also argue that soon after the Jains and Buddhists arrived around the third century BCE, the first group of Brāhmans came to Kerala, conducting Vedic sacrifices as mentioned in the **Patittupāṭṭu**. Various other references attest to the presence of Brāhmin communities in Kerala before the widely accepted eighth century period: Kautilya's **Arthaśāstra** tells of the Vedic Brāhmin community, their organization and special customs, their skills of planning; the ***Mathavilāsaprahasana*** of Mahendravarma I and the *Avantisundari Kathasara* of Dandin Kanchi also detail the community. Based on ***Kēraḷamāhātmyam*** and ***Kēraḷōlpatti***, according to Kerala historians Keshavan Veluthat and T. K. Gangadharan, Paraśurāma created the land between Gokarnam and Kanyakumari and settled Brāhmans there in sixty-four ***grāmas***, or settlements (Veluthat 1978; Gangadharan 2003). E. M. S. Namboodiripad (1952) argues that all people of Kerala, including Nambūtiris and **Nāyars**, were originally from the same caste and that only after the arrival of the immigrant Brāhmans did caste stratification become a part of the Kerala socio-religious and political fabric.

While inquiring about the spread of Brāhmanical Hinduism in Kerala, Ravindran Namboodiri asserted the works of Śaṅkarācārya, the eighth-century philosopher, contributed to the spread of Brāhmanical Hinduism in Kerala by teaching Hindu philosophy to the Brāhmans. Śaṅkarācārya, a native of Kerala known for *advaita Vedānta* or non-dualism, contributed to the knowledge tradition of Hinduism. His father passed away when Śaṅkara was a child and, at the age of sixteen, he renounced the world and became a ***sannyāsi*** (an ascetic) under the tutelage of Govinda Bhatta on the banks of the river Narmada. Before renouncing, he promised to his mother that he would be with her during her last days, which he later fulfilled. Śaṅkarā travelled all over India engaging in philosophical debates, and wrote devotional hymns and ***bhāṣya*** (commentary) on several texts, most importantly the **Brahma Sūtra**. Śaṅkarā established that spiritual ignorance is caused by superimposing the self onto the self and that removing such superimposition enables understanding of the reality as a singular reality. That is, removing superimposition removes ignorance. For him, ***jñāna*** (knowledge) leads to *mokṣa* (liberation). He bases his arguments on the ideas of *tattvamasi* ("you are that") and ***aham brahmāsmi*** ("I am the absolute").

Even though he emphasized *jñāna*, he did not refute *bhakti* (devotion). For him, Brahman as an object of consciousness is both ***nirguṇa*** (Brahman without attributes) and ***saguṇa*** (Brahman with attributes).

Despite ongoing debates among historians and scholars regarding the origin and evolution of Nambūtiri Brāhmans, Brāhmans in Kerala can be divided into two broad categories: Tami<u>l</u> Brāhmans in Kerala, who maintain their distinct Tami<u>l</u> culture and tradition, and Nambūtiri Brāhmans, who are typically Keralite. More importantly, the caste system became established in Kerala, with Nambūtiris at the top of the hierarchy, which gave birth to caste distinction. The Hindu caste divisions were known as Nambūtiri, Nayar, and **Īzhava**. The **Vaiśya** caste (that of the traders) was not present in the Kerala caste system, but the Christian, Muslim and Īzhava traders took its place. Eventually, the Nambūtiris attained ritual and social supremacy because they controlled the temples and lived in surplus (T. M. Menon 2000: 783). Though Nambūtiris have assimilated well within the Kerala socio-religious fabric, their daily rituals, beliefs and customs are unique. These Nambūtiri Brāhmans distanced themselves from the rest of Indian Brāhmin community because of the practice of four ***ācārams*** prohibited to Nambūtiris, and sixty-four ***anācārams*** permitted elsewhere but prohibited to Brāhmans of Kerala (*ibid.*: 787–9). The four *ācārams* allowed include bathing with clothes on; Nambūtiri can be his own priest; Nambūtiri should not bow down to another; they need to wear only one sacred thread, even if they are married, and the eldest son alone should marry. Ravindran Namboodiri asserted that in contemporary Kerala, Nambūtiris who once enjoyed a privileged status in the socio-religious realm have lost their status and their number dwindles. However, some Nambūtiris still adhere to the ancient practices and maintain customs and rituals unique to their caste.

Deities, devotion, and daily worship (*pūjā*)

Payyanur, a rural town tucked into the lofty Ezhimala hills of northern Kerala, houses some of the earliest Nambūtiri settlements of Kerala. Payyanur serves as a nexus of religion and culture as the place abounds in ritual and performative traditions upheld by many Nambūtiri families. In Payyanur, one observes various Nambūtiri *illams* (joint households) situated in various settlements. *Kōṟōm*, a settlement within a five-kilometre radius of Payyanur, has several *illams* where Nambūtiris still preserve the Vedic rituals. *Illams*, though similar to Nayar ***taṟavātu*** (households) consist of patrilineal descendants of common ancestors. Left of the *Kōṟōm* grade school stands a couple of *illams* – namely, Velliyottu *illam*, where Govindan Namboodiri and his family reside, and Pulleri *illam*, where Ravindran Namboodiri and Unnikrishnan Namboodiri reside. Nambūtiris controlled ritual and temple Hinduism until the colonial period, when Sree Narayana Guru, a socio-religious reformer, challenged some of the temple ritual practices. Besides the use of Vedic hymns, complicated purificatory rituals and complex gestures derived from **Āgamic** and Tantric texts are performed during Nambūtiri rituals. The incorporation of tantric forms of worship with daily ritual practices makes Nambūtiri Brāhmans of Kerala distinct from pan-Indian Brāhmans. The Nambūtiri rituals adhere to the *Tantrasamuccaya* from around the fifteenth century and *Īśānaśivagurudevapaddhati* around the twelfth century, which deal with the rituals connected to seven important deities, including Viṣṇu, Śiva, **Śaṅkaranārāyaṇa**, Durgā, **Subrahmaṇya**, **Gaṇapati**, and **Śāsta** (Sastri 1990a, b; cf. Sarma 2009: 319–39). Such ritual practice integral to Nambūtiris transcends sectarian boundaries between Vaiṣṇava, Śaiva and other local deity sects in Kerala, giving the *Tantrasamuccaya* a prominent place among tantric texts from Kerala. Here, one can observe Tantrism completely embedded within the orthopraxy of *vaidika* traditions, as Gavin Flood contends (Flood 1996: 171). More importantly, Nambūtiri daily rituals represent an amalgamation of the Vedic and devotional traditions.

At home, by virtue of Brāhminhood, Nambūtiris must perform ***sandhyāvandanam***, ritualistic prayer, popularly known as ***ūkka***, at three critical times of the day: morning, noon and dusk. Traditionally, Nambūtiris performed *ūkka* three times a day – morning during *brahma muhūrtam*, the ambrosial hour before sunrise, at noon and dusk; but nowadays, due to changing lifestyle, they perform twice a day – at dawn and dusk. These extremely complex daily rituals demonstrate the level of discipline and devotion of these Nambūtiris as they represent an amalgamation of Vedic culture and **Āgamic** temple worship interspersed with devotional elements popularized during the medieval period. Although many younger and older generations of Nambūtiris hardly have any time in contemporary Kerala, some do find time to perform these rituals on a daily basis before going on to their daily routine.

Govindan Namboodiri and Unnikrishnan Namboodiri perform *ūkka* on a daily basis. Govindan Namboodiri begins his day at the ambrosial hour around 4 am, as he wakes up facing the east and slowly walks to the ***kuḷam*** (bathing tank; Figure 15.1), to take his morning ritual bath. Though the first step of purification of the body is washing himself in the bathing tank, it is followed by daily performance of ***prāṇayāma*** or breathing exercise to cleanse himself internally (T. M. Menon 2000: 256). At dawn, when the Nambūtiri begins his bath, he recites the ***gāyatrī*** *mantra* or basic prayer for a Brāhmin, facing the east; at noon, facing the sun; and at dusk, the west. *Ūkka* begins with the ***pūrvāngams*** or prologues including, ***ācamanam*** or cleansing of the sense organs, ***prokṣanam*** or internal cleansing done by taking water and sprinkling water on the face accompanied by the recitation of *mantras* with the sacred thread in the hand, and finally sprinkling water on the head before coming out of the water. After the *prokṣanam* follows ***mantrasnānam*** or the wash in holy water, chanting the *pranavam* (the cosmic sound *om*), and sprinkling water on the face after chanting *mantras* of *prokṣanam*. The ritual continues with ***jalaprāsanam***, the penitence ritual, done with water and acknowledging the sun god, ***arghyadānam***. As the Nambūtiri performs this ritual, he faces eastward at dawn and midday, and

Figure 15.1 A *kuḷam*, or bathing tank (photo by author).

westward at dusk. The posture involves aligning the feet together and clasping both hands to form a cup, keeping the thumb away from the palm, then taking water and reciting the *gāyatrī mantra*. The next act involves *pradakṣiṇā* or circumtreading, going round in one place, followed by ***tarpaṇam***, honouring the divine, the sages and ancestors, which consists of turning the right hand and proffering water. The Nambūtiri faces the north while performing the *tarpaṇam*, reciting three times, honouring the gods (*Ōm devamstarpyāmi*), the sages (*Ōm rsistarpyāmi*) and the forefathers (*Ōm pitramstarpyāmi*). This ritual of *tarpaṇam* after bathing remains an integral part of Nambūtiri belief. *Tarpaṇam* is followed by *japam*, which begins with the recitation of the *gāyatrī mantra* 108 times, followed by 108 recitations of the *Nārāyaṇam*, and 108 recitations of *Ōm Namah Śiva*, ***Devī Mahātmya Stutī*** and ***Śāsta Sahasranāmam***. The Nambūtiri comes to the household shrine known as ***tevāram*** in the *pūjā* room known as ***padiṅjāta***. The simultaneous worship of five deities known as ***pañcāyātana pūjā*** reinforces the ***smārta*** understanding of universality of the reality. Nambūtiris commonly practised the *pranavam, dasapranavam* or *gāyatrī pranavam*, followed by 108 recitations of *gāyatrī mantra*, and *punha pranavam*. However, *Śāsta Sahasranāmam* is done by devotees of Lord Ayyappan or Śāsta (whom I discuss in the next section). Some households, such as Tottasseri *illam* in Tiruvalla, offer prayers to Devī/**Bhagavatī**, as their *iṣṭadevatā* or personal god of choice. Once the recitations of hymns are over, *bhasmam* (ashes) and *candanam* (sandalwood paste) are applied on the hands and chest, as well as on the forehead as a mark of devotion. *Japam* is followed by ***upasthānam*** or prayers, which are different for dawn and dusk. The final act, *anthimudikkuka*, includes ***diśovandanam*** or paying obeisance to the directions by carrying the ***nilaviḷakku***, traditional floor lamp, first to the entrance of the house and then to the back door of the house; ***dhruvāsi*** or circumtreading seven times; and ***abhivādyam***, or paying respect to earth, by holding the base of one's ears with the opposite hands and bowing one's head down to earth.

One day, Govindan Namboodiri, after his ritual bath, went straight to the temple of Lord Ayyappan or Śāsta, where he performed *pūjā* consisting of lighting the lamp, offering fruits and flowers, making marks on the deity with turmeric and sandalwood paste. Once the Nambūtiri performs *pūjā* at the temple he comes back to his household *pūjā* room and performs *pūjā* to the deity in the household shrine. Only after performing these *pūjās* at the temple and home, does he have his breakfast. Devotees from nearby homes attend the morning worship at this temple as they go along their daily routine and receive *prasāda*, the offering offered by the priest. The offering, folded in a small piece of banana leaf, includes a few pieces of coconut, sandalwood paste, and a flower. Devotees receive the offering and then walk around the altar in a clockwise direction and exit the temple precinct, thus symbolically receiving the deity's grace and blessing. As soon as the devotee receives the *prasāda*, he or she applies the sandalwood paste on the forehead in one straight line and consumes the piece of coconut, reinforcing the mystical union between the deity and devotee. In essence, Nambūtiri rituals and beliefs represent Vedic ritual practices and devotional elements.

Closely affiliated with yet distinct from the worship of spirits is ***mantravādam***, exorcism, which is practised mostly by Brāhmans with the objective of propitiating and controlling the spirit by spells, incantations, and penances. These Nambūtiris, also known as Tantri, perform the functions of temple priest and ***mantravādin***, or exorcist (Flood 1996: 171). During such ritual, two types of deities are invoked: good spirits and bad spirits, of which **Kuttichātan** remains the most important. The method of worship in *mantravādam* involves *homams* (rituals) and *japams* (prayers), as in Śaiva and Vaiṣṇava traditions. This practice of exorcism can be associated with the Tantric tradition, which has become a predominant tradition of the Nambūtiri Brāhmans of Kerala, as in Tamilnadu it has become an integral part of temple culture (*ibid.*). Furthermore, ***kṣūdram***, working evil with the aid of low genii, was commonly performed in Kerala. In this ritual, an earthen pot containing human hair, flowers, charcoal, bones, and a small silver or copper plate inscribed with a mystical diagram, along with an effigy of the victim, was buried under the threshold of the house of the target person (Aiya 1999).

In these daily rituals and acts of devotion, Nambūtiris believe domestic space to be a microcosm of the macrocosm and that their daily ritual gives order and meaning to their life, establishing equilibrium with the merging of the individual soul with the universal soul. In addition, these rituals reinforce the importance of maintaining purity over pollution even to the extent that when Nambūtiris drink from a glass, they do not touch the rim of the glass, and they serve food on banana leaf – all to avoid pollution of any kind. Such practices highlight the imperative ritual purity from the Vedic period in contemporary globalizing Kerala.

Ayyappan devotees

Lord Ayyappan – also known as Hariharaputra, Śāsta or **Maṇikaṇṭan** (popularly referred as Śāstāv in Malayalam) – reinforces the idea of masculinity by vowing a strict code of celibacy. Despite various Hindu mythologies associated with Ayyappan's origin, Rama Varma Raja, a member of the Pandalam royal family who lived around the eighteenth century, chronicles his origin in the Sanskrit text ***Bhūtanāthopākhyā*** (Sekar 2009: 479–84).

Among the various mythologies, the famous myth of the Mohini is popularly associated with the birth of Ayyappan. According to the story, Viṣṇu took the form of Mohini when Śiva slew the demon Tripurasura and brought *mokṣa* to the universe. The *asuras* approached Viṣṇu to restrain Śiva's anger. On the advice of Narada, the sage Viṣṇu meditated upon Devi (goddess or feminine power) and gained the power to transform himself into a Mohini, and as such he enchanted Śiva. When irresistible Śiva impregnated the temporarily female Viṣṇu with his powerful semen, this union gave birth to Lord Ayyappan (O'Flaherty 1973). This Ayyappan was destined to kill the demoness Mahishi, in the form of a she-buffalo, sister of **Mahiṣāsura**, whom the goddess Durgā killed. Mahishi, wanting to retaliate her brother's killing, secured a boon from Lord Brahma that no one can slay her except the child of Viṣṇu and Śiva. Meanwhile, Mahishi, an embodiment of evil, went to the celestial realm of the *devas* and troubled them. They in turn requested Viṣṇu to intervene, and he did so in the form of an enchantress during the churning of the milky ocean. Viṣṇu as Mohini danced with seductive grace, swaying her body rhythmically in such a way that the asuras and the demons alike were charmed. The asuras, obsessed with the beauty of Mohini, were distracted from their objective of obtaining the ambrosia: they failed in their plan, and the *devas* consumed the ambrosia, saving the world. In this respect, Viṣṇu in the form of Mohini danced the dance of existence and sustenance, distributing the ambrosia among the *devas* and assuring them eternal existence. Śiva insisted on seeing the form of Viṣṇu and, overcome by lust, made love to Mohini, not realizing Mohini was Viṣṇu. As a result, Hariharaputra (son of Viṣṇu and Śiva) or Ayyappan was born from Viṣṇu's thigh. Both Śiva and Viṣṇu were ashamed; they left the child in a basket on the bank of river Pampa. It is believed that the childless Pandalam King Rajasekara found the child on the banks of the river, adopted it, and named him Maṇikaṇṭan (the one with a golden neck).

After some years, the Pandalam queen gave birth to her own child and jealousy grew over who would inherit the throne. The queen along with the court physician plotted for her own child: she informed the king that her illness could only be cured by tiger's milk. Ayyappan, an adolescent at that time, volunteered to make the arduous journey to the hill forest to get tiger milk. On his dangerous journey, he was helped by a Muslim named Vavar and a tribesman named Karrutta Swami. Despite goddess Ganga distracting him from his goal to acquire tiger's milk for his ailing mother, he mounted a tiger and went to Pandalam with tiger's milk, an act which revealed his divine identity. Maṇikaṇṭan reminded his father, King Rajasekara, that he had accomplished the goal for which he was created, that is, to kill the demoness. But before Maṇikaṇṭan departed, his father asked where he should construct a temple in his honour. In response Maṇikaṇṭan shot an arrow, which fell in Śabari, where the royal family then constructed the temple. He bid farewell to his adopted family and going back to the hill-forest on top of the mountain Śabarimala, he achieved his divine form, remaining an eternal celibate, whereupon several male devotees started to come on pilgrimage to worship him (Osella & Osella 2003: 729–54). More importantly, Ayyappan asserted that he would bless devotees who observed forty-one days of penance or *vratam*, led an austere lifestyle, and brought offerings of coconut and *ghī* (clarified butter) on their heads. From then on, Lord Ayyappan's image has been placed in the temple for *darśana*, sacred gazing by his devotees.

Śabarimala Ayyappan temple

Śabarimala **Śrī Śāsta Devasthānam**, built in Kerala style, remains the focus of devotion for the devotees of Lord Ayyappan. The temple, a space for harmony between the physical and the spiritual upholds the intrinsic themes of devotional movements of the medieval period: equality among all devotees in love of the divine. As a corollary, all devotees, mostly men, as a mark of brotherhood, without respect to caste, creed, or class, refer to each other as *Swami*, holy man. Such a mark of brotherhood can also be observed in the Muslim pilgrimage known as *hajj*.

The Śabarimala temple complex, situated in a plateau region surrounded by lush green tropical forest looking down towards the valley, comprises a main temple known as **Sannidhānam** (literally, "presence"). Here, to experience the presence of Lord Ayyappan is the final goal of a devotee. This temple has a copper-plated roof with four golden finials at the top, two *mantapams* or altars, and the *kodimaram* or flag staff. The image of Ayyappan within the *sanctum sanctorum* was originally carved out of stone but later replaced with one made of an amalgamation of five metals.

To the southwest of the main temple sits Gaṇeṣa's shrine, where pilgrims offer their prayers to Gaṇeṣa before they proceed to the Sannidhānam. To the left of Lord Ayyappan's temple, around a hundred metres away, Malikapurathamma's shrine is situated. Between the Sannidhānam and Malikapurathamma's shrine is the ***bhasmakuḷam*** or ash tank, where, after their exhausting trip on foot to Śabarimala, pilgrims take a ritual dip in the waters of the ash tank symbolic of spiritual sanctification.

Malikapurathamma's small temple houses the shrines of Bhagavatī and Karrutta Swami, and stands at the bottom of the ***patinēttāmpadi*** (eighteen sacred steps) as the guardian of the Sannidhānam. Devotees roll unbroken coconuts on the ground and offer prayers with other elements of worship. One of the interesting features of this temple is that the door of the shrine always remains closed. On the right side of Malikapurathamma temple are the shrines to snake gods, where some pilgrims perform ***sarppapāṭṭu*** (snake song) to please the snakes for protection from snakebites during their journey. Adjacent to the *patinēttāmpadi* is the shrine of Vavar, a Muslim, because of his close association with Lord Ayyappan.

Devotion and daily worship (*pūjā*)

While Ayyappan devotion has been prominent in Kerala, in the late twentieth century it spread to other parts of south India. On a daily basis, a devotee visits an Ayyappan temple to perform *pūjā* (Figure 15.2), an act of devotion which includes offering food, flowers, and prayers, singing of him, thinking of him, offering prayers, adorning him, serving him, and becoming one with the deity according to purāṇic theism. In Kerala, Ayyappan devotees practice devotion towards Ayyappan and take refuge in him by experiencing union with him. Such union with the deity remains the goal for devotional Hinduism.

Here the devotee perceives himself as the god's lover or wife, and the hope of winning a godlike husband remains the theme for songs women sing at home (C. J. Fuller 2004: 216). But the heightened hope of union with the deity finds much greater equality among those who make the annual pilgrimage to the temple.

Figure 15.2 An image of Śāsta (photo by author).

Śabarimala annual pilgrimage

Travelling on Indian railways to Kerala during December and January, one encounters thousands of men wearing black or ochre loincloths (*dhoti*) and black shirts, and chanting *Swāmiye śaraṇam Ayyappo* ("O Lord Ayyappan, you are our refuge"). These people are on their pilgrimage to the Śabarimala Ayyappan temple, which has become an integrating force among the culturally and linguistically diverse Hindus of India as large numbers of devotees from different regions annually visit during the month of *dhanu* (December to January) to participate in the festival of **Makaraviḷakku**, which occurs on the third day of the Malayalam month of *makaram* (January to February). This pilgrimage is performed by Ayyappan devotees in India and elsewhere. The pilgrims, mostly consisting of men, with a small number of prepubescent girls and post-menstrual women, prepare forty-one days in advance before they begin their journey. The male pilgrims are called "Ayyappan" and the female pilgrims are called "Malikappuram". The *advaita* concepts from the *Upaniṣads* – *tattvamasi*, *aham brahmāsmi* and *ayam ātma brahma* (this self is the absolute), promoted by Śaṅkarācārya, the eighth-century philosopher from Kerala – underpin the idea of pilgrimage to Śabarimala Ayyappan. Pilgrims gain the knowledge that leads to liberation, no matter how temporary it may be, and such realization enables a pilgrim to discern spiritual and worldly matter. Pilgrims travel forty-seven miles uphill to reach the temple, journeying through the hilly terrain and remembering the journey Ayyappan himself took. The pilgrimage involves three important stages: first, initiation to mark the beginning of the forty-one-day vow or *vratam*; second, performance of the *kettunira* ritual (ritual preparation of *irumudikettu*) when pilgrims set out on their pilgrimage; and finally, the climbing of the *patinēttāmpadi* or the sacred eighteen steps in Śabarimala.

Ayyappan devotees take their pilgrim vows and make their pilgrimage to the temple by preparing forty-one days in advance, the period known as *vratam*. The *maṇḍala pūjā*, usually performed beginning on the first day of the Malayalam month of *Vrischikam* (mid-November) and extending up to *Dhanu* (around 26 December), initiates a pilgrim. There are a few restrictions on who can go for pilgrimage, because Ayyappan is an ascetic: the preparatory process involves strict abstinence from sexual activity, no consumption of non-vegetarian food, sleeping on the floor, and wearing only black, ochre or dark blue loincloths, as well as a garland of *rudraksha*. These all emphasize asceticism, cutting ties with the world and society. During this time of preparation, pilgrims do not wear footwear, a practice which prepares them for the arduous journey to the hill; in addition, they perform group devotional rituals, known as *vellamkudi* (drinking water). They lead a simple lifestyle, praying three times a day and taking the name of Lord Ayyappan. While practising austerity, devotees wake up during the ambrosial hour (between 3am and 6am), take a bath and offer prayers to Ayyappan. One of the important aspects of devotion remains recitation of prayers, for example, reciting the 108 names of Lord Ayyappan beginning with

Om Śrī Dharma Śāstāve Namah, obeisance to Lord Ayyappan. Two of my informants, Shiju and Aneesh, who have made the pilgrimage to Śabarimala several times, consider this ritual conducted in the house of one of the pilgrims to be meaningful and spiritually empowering. Also, these pilgrims stated that the procession on the eve of the *maṇḍala pūja* is a significant aspect of the pilgrimage as it is intended for bringing the tiruaṅki (a decorated gold shawl) with which the image of Lord Ayyappan will be adorned on the last day of *maṇḍala pūja.*

The second ritual, *kettunira,* performed after the completion of the forty-one-day *vratam* consists of the *irumudikettal* ceremony, in which a cloth bag divided into two parts is prepared to carry offerings for the Lord and food for the pilgrim. During the *kettunira* ritual, a coconut is filled through one of its eyes with the sacred offering of *ghī* (*nei* in Malayalam). When I asked a pilgrim, he mentioned that the draining of the water from within the coconut symbolizes the draining of worldly attachment from the mind and filling it with spiritual desire. The front portion contains *pūjā* articles including a three-eyed coconut (*thenga*) filled with *nei, carpuram* (camphor), *ari* (unboiled rice), *pazham* (plantain), *aval* (flattened rice), *pori* (puffed rice), sandal paste, incense sticks, *vibhuti* (sacred ash), *kuṃkuṃ* (vermilion), ***maṅjalpodi*** (turmeric powder), ***śarkara*** (jaggery) and *kalkkandom* (candied sugar). The rear pouch of the *irumudikettu* contains edible items necessary for the pilgrim's personal nourishment during the journey to Śabarimala and back. The *irumudikettu* is tied and carried on the head in such a way that the portion carrying offerings for Lord Ayyappan comes in front and the part containing the edible items for the pilgrim comes at the rear. The *irumudikettu* symbolizes the two dimensions of humanity, spiritual and physical; it reminds the pilgrim that maintaining balance remains the goal of humans who strive to achieve freedom.

The journey to the Śabarimala temple in past years used to require trekking sixty kilometres on foot through the forest, but now allows taking public or private transport up to the banks of the river Pampa. Either way, the last phase of around 8 kilometres still requires climbing the mountain Nilimala on foot. Pilgrims stop at three spots in Erumeli at the two shrines of Lord Ayyappan, known as *Kochambalam* (small shrine) and *Valliambalam* (bigger shrine) and at the mosque of Vavar, where a Muslim priest blesses the pilgrims on their way. Here they engage in a ritualistic dance called the *petta-tullal* and worship at the shrines. *Petta-tullal* re-enacts the lore of Ayyappan slaying the Mahishi, the demoness having the form of a she-buffalo, for pilgrims popularly believe Erumeli received its name from the place where the demoness was killed. A pilgrim asserted that during *petta-tullal,* ritual transformation of the mind takes place: the lower stage of consciousness symbolized through Mahishi changes to the higher human consciousness of Lord Ayyappan. The pilgrim takes a ritual bath in the river Pampa and offers prayer to Lord Gaṇeṣa, the remover of obstacles, at the Gaṇeṣa temple, before setting out on the last league of the journey. While climbing the mountain on foot pilgrims chant and cry, *Swamiye śaraṇam ayyappo!*

The climbing of *patinēttāmpadi*, or the sacred eighteen steps before reaching the presence of Lord Ayyappan, marks the final phase of the journey. The eighteen steps symbolize the eighteen major obstacles a person must overcome in order to achieve self-realization. The first five steps represent the sense experiences; the next eight steps represent the eight blinding passions, namely, *kama* (desire), *krodha* (anger), *lobha* (greed), *moha* (illusory attachment), *mada* (haughtiness), ***mātsarya*** (rivalry), *dambha* (egotism) and ***asūya*** (jealousy); next, the three ***guṇas*** (qualities) – *sattva* (goodness), *rajas* (passion) and *tamas* (darkness); and the last two signify *avidya* (ignorance) and *vidya* (knowledge). Only those who have practised austerity and are carrying the *irumudikettu* are allowed to climb the eighteen steps. Once the pilgrims have climbed the eighteen steps, they arrive at the Sannidhānam, the presence of the deity. First they go towards the shrine of Lord Gaṇeṣa to invoke his presence, then they proceed southwards to the shrine of divine mother, Malikkapurathamma, where they roll a coconut around the shrine. Here, legend states, goddess Malikkapuratha is yearning to marry Lord Ayyappan. But being an eternal celibate, Ayyappan evades her plea by promising her that if there comes a time when first-time pilgrims cease to arrive, he would marry her. Devotees believe Malikkapuratha waits to see if new arrows are placed by first-time pilgrims; when she sees new arrows, she comes to her abode, dejected, and awaits the opportune time.

Throughout the pilgrimage, despite suffering, one develops love towards the deity, which finally culminates at the feet of Lord Ayyappan in breaking the butter-filled coconut (*nei thenga*), lighting the lamp and performing the *nei abhiṣekam*, or pouring the *nei* on the image of the Lord to mark the union between the devotee and the deity. Here, the *nei thenga* signifies the ***jīvātman***, or individual self, which is essentially free because of the fluid characteristic of *nei*. At this moment, a pilgrim experiences self-abnegation, even for a fleeting moment, a union essential to south Indian devotional traditions. In addition, ***tiruvābharaṇam*** (gold ornaments) are taken from Pandalam palace to Śabarimala to adorn the image of Lord Ayyappan on the festive occasion of Makaraviḷakku, a symbol highlighting the relationship between Pandalam palace and Lord Ayyappan. After the pilgrims have become one with the deity, they return to their homes and break another coconut to reincorporate into secular life by removing their ascetic attire and placing the garland of *rudraksha* in the *pūjā* room of their homes.

Through this pilgrimage a pilgrim in his householder stage temporarily practises a life of renunciation; in doing so he symbolically crosses over from the *saṃsāra*. The Śabarimala pilgrimage emphasizes the paradoxical relationship between householder and renouncer, forging transcendence in the everyday life of these pilgrim men. Therefore, making the pilgrimage to Śabarimala transcends time and space and transforms the devotee. As rites of passage and pilgrimages are ways of expressing Hindu identity and devotion, places and temples become central for a Hindu. Pilgrimage places serve as *tīrtha*, places of crossing over which attest to the idea of sacred geography transcending boundaries of space and time.

Conclusion

These Hindu communities of Kerala represent an amalgam of indigenous and other pan-Indian Hindu traditions through their beliefs and practices; particularly, they emphasize the wider south Indian devotional movements that have squarely influenced rituals and performances, all of which crosses the boundary between the sacred and the mundane, as well as time and space. More importantly, the rituals, customs and practices among the Nambūtiri Brāhmans and the Ayyappan devotees represent Kerala as a place where gods and humans play, a place where the complexity and diversity of Hindu traditions find expression through religious, aesthetic and sacred geography, attesting in a different way to the aphorism, "God's own country".

Acknowledgements

I wish to thank all those who have helped me in myriad ways in the process of writing this chapter, especially Govindan Namboodiri and Vasudevan *Kōṟōm* of Veliyottu Illam, Payyanur; Ravindran Namboodiri and Malayalam film actor P. V. Unnikrishnan Namboodiri of Pulleri Illam, Payyanur; Vasudevan Nampoothiri and Sarasvati Antarjanam of Thottasseri Illam, Tiruvalla; Sreedevi Antarjanam of Kaladi; and G. M. John, Shinoy Jesinth, K. R. Shiju and Aneesh Ravi. I acknowledge the assistance provided by Gino Issac.

Note

1. Nambūtiri, also written as Namboodiri, refers to the same exclusive high-caste Brāhmin of Kerala. While I am referring to names of Nambūtiris, I am using how it is spelt officially in their records: Namboodiri or Namboodiripad.

16. Ecstatic seeing: adorning and enjoying the body of the goddess

Archana Venkatesan

In a small town in south India was a very old woman, who lived in a small house that nestled the walls of the local temple. She spent most of her days on the tiny porch seated in a rickety chair observing the lazy pace of small-town life. She marked her long, endless days with waiting – eager for the moment when her beloved goddess and her consort would emerge from within the temple walls and stop before her house. She drank in the divine sight of their richly adorned bodies: her gorgeous crown, his dashing turban; her bright green parrot, his flashing discus; her sinuous form, his mysterious smile. She could recall from memory the vision of *her* gods, Viṣṇu and his bride, Āṇṭāḷ. Her sightless eyes followed their beautiful forms, even as they disappeared around the corner to continue their sojourn around town.

People around town said that there was no greater devotee of Āṇṭāḷ and Viṣṇu than this old woman, whom they revered as a matchless poet and scholar. They still speak in awed whispers of the poem she once addressed to Āṇṭāḷ pleading with her to end a formidable drought. "It rained the very next day, and for seven days thereafter. Such is the power of *our* Āṇṭāḷ!" the locals enthused. The old lady used to wave away such fanciful thinking: "Her grace is boundless and causeless!" she insisted. "I am just her vehicle" she often added for good measure.

So when I went to Srivilliputtur, this small south Indian town, in 2002, to learn more about Āṇṭāḷ, locals and the priests at the Āṇṭāḷ temple alike insisted that I meet the old woman: "Tiruvenkatammal will tell you everything you need to know about Āṇṭāḷ. There is none who enjoys Āṇṭāḷ as she does." So on a hot April afternoon accompanied by the priest and my video camera, I made my way to meet Tiruvenkatammal in her home. She was dressed in a simple widow's white sari and her wise old face was creased with wrinkles. She smiled a toothless smile and with girlish enthusiasm said, "So, you have come all the way from America to learn about our Āṇṭāḷ. What do you want to know from me?"

"Tell me her story", I said.

This is the story she told me.[1]

The story

After Viṣṇu rescued the goddess of the earth, **Bhū Devī**, from the clutches of an evil demon, he imparted to her vast knowledge. She learned of the universe, its cause, its end and its nature. But being compassion itself, when Bhū looked at the world and witnessed the suffering there, she was moved to intercede in some way. She wondered how she could ease their pain, and realized that the answer lay in the wisdom she had gained from Viṣṇu, who is the very seed of the world. She expressed the desire to share the wisdom she had acquired, and Viṣṇu in his infinite mercy agreed. He told Bhū that one day when the time was right, she would manifest on earth as a young girl, and through her experiences in the world show people the way out of the endless cycles of birth and death.

Aeons passed, and finally one day at the height of summer, a beautiful girl child, radiant as a thousand suns, dressed in splendid silks and adorned with jewels emerged from the earth. **Viṣṇucittaṉ**, a childless garland maker at the local Viṣṇu temple found her and took her home to raise as his child. He named her **Kōtai** and lavished affection upon her. She grew up hearing of the great exploits of Viṣṇu, and soon she was so completely in love with him that she resolved to marry him and no one else. So every morning she would take the garland her father had woven for Viṣṇu and unbeknownst to him wear it, imagining herself as Viṣṇu's bride. It went like this for many, many days until eventually, her father discovered her secret – some say it was because he found a long dark curly hair entwined in the garland – and scolded her for behaving in such a manner. You see, you cannot offer god something that you have already used. He quickly made another garland and offered it to Viṣṇu, but much to his surprise, Viṣṇu refused it. The garland kept slipping off the ink-black body of the slumbering icon. Was Viṣṇu punishing him or his daughter for transgressing the ritual laws of worship in such a flagrant manner? Viṣṇucittaṉ finally made his way home, and fell into a restless sleep. Then much to his shock, Viṣṇu appeared in a dream and demanded that from that day forward he *only* receive the garland after Kōtai had first worn it, because it exuded a special fragrance that he relished. From that day forward Kōtai would first wear the garland and then her father would offer it to Viṣṇu. This went on for several days, and Kōtai came to be known affectionately as ***cūṭikkoṭuttavaḷ***, or the girl who gave what she had worn.

Kōtai in the meantime continued to nurture her grand desire to marry only Viṣṇu. When she was playing with her friends, they would tease her about this secret love. Eventually, her desire became so unbearable that she undertook a special vow to win Viṣṇu as her husband. She gathered all her friends together for the vow, and she sang about it in her poem called the **Tiruppāvai**. When this did not achieve the result that she desired, she became so demented with longing that she prayed to **Kāma**, the god of love. She spoke to birds and to the rain clouds and asked them to take her messages of love to Viṣṇu. Kōtai dreamed that she married Viṣṇu in a grand ceremony that was attended by all the gods, but when she woke up, she was even more distraught to realize that the dream was false. She recorded these experiences in her long poem, the **Nācciyār Tirumoḻi**. This went on for several days, and Viṣṇucittaṉ began to despair for his daughter's welfare. Finally, Viṣṇu once again appeared to him in a dream and commanded him to bring Kōtai to the great temple in Srirangam, and that he would marry her there. Kōtai, decked in her bridal finery left with her father and several companions for Srirangam. But before entering the temple premises, the group stopped on the banks of the Kaveri to purify themselves in the sacred waters of the river. However, Kōtai remained inside her palanquin. When the group returned they were astonished to find it empty. Kōtai had disappeared and was nowhere to be found. Her father lamented that she had been stolen by the god, dark as the rain clouds. Viṣṇu appeared before him then to reveal that his daughter Kōtai was none other than Bhū Devī, the goddess earth, but because she had won him with such matchless love, she would be known henceforth as Āṇṭāḷ, she who rules.

What the story tells us

The story of Kōtai–Āṇṭāḷ began to circulate in south India around the tenth century among a south Indian sect known as the **Śrīvaiṣṇava**. Although Kōtai was a historical figure – she was a ninth-century poet, who composed two important poems – her story has been embroidered so lavishly that it is impossible to separate her history from her legend. What we do know about this extraordinary female poet is that she was part of a movement centred on ecstatic devotion (*bhakti*) that began around the sixth century in Tamiḻ-speaking south India. Around the tenth century, Kōtai (or Āṇṭāḷ as she came to be known more commonly) was inducted into a revered group of twelve Tamiḻ poet–saints known as the *āḻvār*. As the sole woman in this elite group of twelve poet–saints, she received singular attention, and by the late twelfth century was worshipped as a goddess and the embodiment of Bhū Devī. For the Śrīvaiṣṇavas, Āṇṭāḷ is not just a divinely inspired poet, but a divine being in human form. Thus over a span of approximately three centuries, Āṇṭāḷ is transformed from a poet who expresses devotion to god to becoming an object of devotion herself. This shift is readily apparent in Tiruvenkatammal's account, which begins and ends by affirming Āṇṭāḷ's divine status as Bhū Devī, while the fantastic elements of the Āṇṭāḷ story serve as a model for exemplary, passionate, and steadfast devotion.

Āṇṭāḷ's story, and the manner in which it was told to me by Tiruvenkatammal all those many years ago, offers the ideal entry point into the religious life of Śrīvaiṣṇavas, for it encapsulates several of their central concepts. The primacy of single-minded devotion, the disregard for normative ritual behaviour in the service of god, and the unity of the god and goddess, are ideas shared across many of Hinduism's theistic traditions. Thus, in elaborating the Śrīvaiṣṇava approach to some of these ideas, and by focusing specifically on this community's different ways of engaging with deity, we can begin to elucidate the rich and vibrant lives of Hinduism in practice.

For the Śrīvaiṣṇavas, the emotional relationship between the devotee and god is best articulated through the concept of ***anubhava***, or enjoyment. Although there is no Śrīvaiṣṇava doctrinal text that explicates *anubhava*, it dominates the landscape of oral memory. In the following pages, we will explore *anubhava* through the stories, poems and images of Āṇṭāḷ, reading them both as the sites of its production and as the *loci* of its consumption.

What is *anubhava*?

The word *anubhava* means experience, enjoyment or relish, and for Śrīvaiṣṇavas this enjoyment is special, for it is directed to Viṣṇu, his consorts and his most exemplary devotees, such as the *āḻvār* poets. *Anubhava* is activated on three major levels: poetic, narrative and ritual, and each of these enable the devotee to access an ecstatic experience of the divine. It is a means to understand god's unfathomable nature, to enter into his world of play, and to make manifest the divine presence on the terrestrial realms.

For the Śrīvaiṣṇava communities, the most perfect *anubhava* is the reciprocal one shared between Viṣṇu and his *āḻvār* devotees, the twelve poets who lived between the seventh and ninth centuries, and are enshrined as canonical figures for embodying such exemplary devotion. Their poems (which total approximately 4,000 verses) describe with great fervour the pain of unrequited love for Viṣṇu, and the boundless joy of momentary union with him. These poems of union and separation take various guises, ranging from impassioned love poems to abstract metaphysical musings. The experiences recorded in the poems are regarded by the Śrīvaiṣṇava communities as the poets' enjoyment (*anubhava*) of Viṣṇu, and are therefore read autobiographically. The poems thus become the source for the legends of the *āḻvār*, as they are forged into narrative arcs that provide context and nuance to the many compositions.

Our ninth-century poet Āṇṭāḷ is an excellent example of this phenomenon. In her two poems, the Tiruppāvai ("the sacred vow") and Nācciyār Tirumoḻi ("the lady's words"), Āṇṭāḷ imagines herself to be the beloved of Viṣṇu, rejoicing at their all too infrequent unions and despondent at their interminable separations. Āṇṭāḷ's compositions express the unending oscillations between union and separation in beautiful, poignant terms:

> O cool clouds, place the plea of this servant
> at the feet of the one with the beautiful lotus eyes
> that one who churned the ocean filled with conch.
> Beseech him to enter me for a single day
> and wipe away the vermilion smeared upon my breasts.
> Only then can I survive.
>
> (Nācciyār Tirumoḻi 8.7, in Venkatesan 2010: 169)

But for devotees like Tiruvenkatammal and countless other narrators before her, verses such as the one above are not simply beautiful words strung together. They describe a specific moment in her mystical quest for Viṣṇu, a moment of *anubhava* frozen in time and fixed in words. In other words, for Śrīvaiṣṇava devotees, Āṇṭāḷ in the full throes of her mystical yearning really did send the cool monsoon clouds with a message to her beloved. So when these poems are forged into her story, they are cast as petitions and love letters to Viṣṇu describing in painstaking detail a very real, tangible and corporeal experience. In this manner, the Āṇṭāḷ story fashioned from her words becomes another *anubhava*, a way for a devotee removed by space and time to enter into Āṇṭāḷ's life, and in doing so to enjoy *her* experience of Viṣṇu. This is an essential feature of how Tiruvenkatammal told me the Āṇṭāḷ story; in fact it was why I was directed to her by the locals of Srivilliputtur, because as I was reminded repeatedly, no one in that most sacred city of Āṇṭāḷ relished this mercurial poet–saint–goddess Āṇṭāḷ more. Tiruvenkatammal's enjoyment of Āṇṭāḷ expressed itself in the retelling of her story, in memorizing Āṇṭāḷ's poems, in composing her own verses of praise and devotion, and most deeply in the enjoyment of the divine body, both that of Āṇṭāḷ's and that of her beloved Viṣṇu. One might argue that for Śrīvaiṣṇavas, all *anubhavas* begin with enjoyment of the divine body, for it is the vision of that magical body and the yearning for that most precious sight, which stimulates *anubhava* at its most elemental level. It is to the peculiar and particular savouring of the divine that I turn next.

Service: seeing the divine body

For the lord
of the sweet fragrant groves of Māliruncōlai
I offered a hundred pots of butter
and yet another hundred brimming with sweet rice
Will the beautiful lord who rides on Garuḍa
not come to claim my offering?
(Nācciyār Tirumoḻi 9.6, in Venkatesan 2010: 172)

The priests of Āṇṭāḷ's temple in Srivilliputtur often recite the above verse from Āṇṭāḷ's Nācciyār Tirumoḻi, and by way of explanation, follow it up with a story of the pilgrimage to this most holy of sites by the great Śrīvaiṣṇava theologian, Rāmānuja (1017–1137ce, traditional dates).

The story goes like this. Rāmānuja was deeply attached to Āṇṭāḷ and would often fall into a swoon when he heard some of her beautiful verses. So great was his immersion and enjoyment of Āṇṭāḷ's love for Viṣṇu! He desired to worship her in her temple in Srivilliputtur, but as he prepared to undertake the journey, he recalled the above verse from Āṇṭāḷ's Nācciyār Tirumoḻi. Realizing that Āṇṭāḷ's vow to offer pots of butter and sweet rice to Viṣṇu had not been fulfilled, he resolved to rectify the oversight. On his way to Srivilliputtur, he travelled to Viṣṇu's mountain shrine of Maliruncolai, and offered the sweet rice and butter on Āṇṭāḷ's behalf. When he arrived at the temple in Srivilliputtur, the image of Āṇṭāḷ came alive, and she ran out with arms outstretched, greeting Rāmānuja as "Aṇṇā", or older brother, to honour his intervention on her behalf. To commemorate this extraordinary event, once a year the image of Rāmānuja is given pride of place beside Āṇṭāḷ in the innermost shrine of her temple.

This famous apocryphal story of Rāmānuja's visit to Srivilliputtur can be unpacked in several ways, but for our purposes we will focus on how it both elucidates and employs the concept of *anubhava* and its connection to the body of god (here, Āṇṭāḷ). On the most basic level, the tale seeks to reveal Rāmānuja's profound savouring of Āṇṭāḷ's poems and the intimate relationship with her that was its fruit. Rāmānuja, who systematized both Śrīvaiṣṇava theology and ritual, composed his several treatises and prose poems in Sanskrit. These texts make no mention of the Tamil̲ *āl̲vār* poems, nor do they reveal their influence. Yet stories such as the one above, passed down orally or embedded in written medieval commentaries suggest this foundational theologian's immense attachment, enjoyment and love for these Tamil̲ poems. In Śrīvaiṣṇava lore, Rāmānuja was particularly fond of Āṇṭāḷ, even earning him the epithet Tiruppāvai Jīyar (Master of Tiruppāvai). Against such a backdrop, the story of Rāmānuja's desire to fulfil Āṇṭāḷ's vow can be read as an expression of his *anubhava* of her poem and her life. To Rāmānuja, and indeed to countless devotees who follow, Āṇṭāḷ's promise in the Nācciyār Tirumol̲i is not a literary trope, employed for maximum poetic and emotional effect; rather it is an authentic record of a very real experience. It is Āṇṭāḷ's *anubhava* of Viṣṇu, and it is this *anubhava* that Rāmānuja relishes, and enjoys so deeply as to participate in it. Such complete involvement in the life and poetry of an exemplary devotee is not surprising if we recall that the word *bhakti* (ecstatic devotion) is derived from a word that also means to share and participate. It is perhaps this participatory impulse that motivates the Srivilliputtur priests to recount this story, and to invite the listener into the story of Āṇṭāḷ, Viṣṇu and Rāmānuja. The devotee–listener attends not to the fact that there was no temple to Āṇṭāḷ in Srivilliputtur in Rāmānuja's time; she does not wonder if Rāmānuja *really* went to the hills of Maliruncolai to fulfil Āṇṭāḷ's vow. Instead, through this story the listener comes to see Rāmānuja not as a stern philosopher and theologian, but as an exemplary devotee and a filial intimate of Āṇṭāḷ. The most immediate understanding of the Rāmānuja–Āṇṭāḷ story explicates the intertwined and interdependent relationships between philosopher and poet, between cerebral argumentation and visceral emotion, demonstrating the difference between the abstract contemplation of god/goddess nature, and the subjective, participatory savouring of divine nature. For the *āl̲vār* poets and for the Rāmānuja of the above story, *anubhava* of the divine was induced, encountered, experienced and mediated through the body of god.

Embodied in images of stone and metal, Viṣṇu and his consorts are ever-present and accessible to their devotees. And although each image in each temple is equally imbued with the divine essence, each image is also unique, endowed with its own individual histories, myths, legends and genealogies. For Śrīvaiṣṇavas, to see the divine form is to enjoy it in all its detailed particularity. Such seeing and appreciation of the image (*mūrti*) is often glossed by the Sanskrit word, *darśana*, where the devotee and divine gaze interlock in an intense communication of supplication and grace, of surrender and acceptance. As several scholars have pointed out, worship in the theistic Hindu traditions is itself glossed as *darśana*. One sees the gorgeously attired images of stone or metal (*mūrti*) ensconced in the heart of the temple not with the critical perspective of the art historian, but with a devotional eye.[2] The concept of devotional seeing and extravagant beholding is very much at the heart of the Śrīvaiṣṇava traditions as well, though it is slightly modified to accommodate a major theological concern, expressed beautifully in the Rāmānuja-Āṇṭāḷ story.[3]

Tamiḻ Śrīvaiṣṇavas speak of worship, of which seeing the god is a major element, as ***cēvai*** or service. Thus, most Śrīvaiṣṇava devotees speak of going to the temple not for *darśana* (seeing) but for *cēvai* (service). This semantic identification between the two words indicates something quite foundational: seeing the god, enjoying the body of god *is* service. Seeing is an act of loving worship, as the devotee engages her senses in absorbing and enjoying the body of god. Rāmānuja doesn't simply come to see Āṇṭāḷ at Srivilliputtur. He performs a service (offering the hundred pots of butter and sweet rice) to Viṣṇu at Maliruncolai to please Āṇṭāḷ, and as preparation for his vision of her. His reward for this loving *cēvai* is the spectacular vision of Āṇṭāḷ running to greet him as a dear, long-lost brother, and as such is immersed in the *anubhava* of her unbounded love.

Adornment: enjoying the divine body

Every August the Srivilliputtur temple celebrates a grand ten-day festival to mark Āṇṭāḷ's manifestation on Earth at this most sacred of sites. It is the temple's most important annual event, and draws devotees from all over south India, who often travel great distances for a chance to witness the several daily rituals and events. The festival is organized around Āṇṭāḷ's daily processions for which her mobile, bronze image of Āṇṭāḷ is dressed in distinctive ensembles, known as ***alaṅkāra*** (adornment) or ***tirukkōlam*** (divine form). It is to enjoy these gorgeous and imaginative *alaṅkāras* that devotees flock, immersing themselves in a rapturous savouring of the body of their beloved goddess. A glimpse of Āṇṭāḷ riding in her palanquin, or on a beautiful golden swan, elicits frequent gasps of wonder from the crowds: "Look, how beautiful our Āṇṭāḷ is today!" "The *alaṅkāra* is particularly pleasing!" "She looks like a blushing bride! Wait till Viṣṇu sees her." Such evocative, spontaneous utterances at the sight of Āṇṭāḷ's richly ornamented form recall Tiruvenkatammal's ever-eager desire to gaze upon the processing images, and further stress the mutually sustaining relationship of *anubhava* and the divine body, realized most accessibly in the exquisitely decorated temple icon. They equally recall Āṇṭāḷ's own transgressive act of adorning herself with the garland meant for Viṣṇu and his reciprocal savouring of Āṇṭāḷ's garland. In Āṇṭāḷ's story, the garland is the ornament, the adornment, the *alaṅkāra*, that remakes a young lovesick into the bride of god. In turn, the god is ornamented with *her* garland, the symbol of her *anubhava* and the result of her loving service (*cēvai*). So, it is to the related concepts of ***arcā*** (divine body) and *alaṅkāra* (adornment) and their connection to *anubhava* that we turn to next.

In Śrīvaiṣṇava theology there are five manifestations of deity, the first of which is the transcendent, abstract form.[4] The fifth form is the *arcā*, which is the form of god meant for worship. These icons of stone and bronze – of Viṣṇu, his consorts, the *āḻvārs* – enshrined in temples and sometimes in homes, receive elaborate ritual services and acts of devotion. Although the *arcā* is counted as the fifth form, it is not regarded as of lesser importance or value. Rather, it is quite the opposite because the *arcā* is conceptualized as imbued with a kind of "super-matter" known as ***śuddha sattva*** that comprises the abstract form of deity. Thus, the *arcā* – this material, human-made form – is also transcendent and supreme. In this form, the inconceivable, supreme, formless god (or in our case, goddess) is accessible to his/her devotees. Within such a framework, the *arcā* is not just a representation or a symbol of god, but is embodied divinity, filled with divine presence and comprised of divine matter. We have already seen this in the story of Rāmānuja and Āṇṭāḷ, where the image is envisioned as embodied in so far as she is able to move, speak and act.

The most common terms – ***divya rūpa*** (divine form) and ***tirumēṉi*** (divine body) – used by poets, lay persons and theologians alike, attest to this conviction that because the *arcā is* god, it is constituted of god's infinite virtues and auspicious qualities: his infinite beauty, his infinite mercy, his infinite grace. Lush fabrics and the dazzling jewels of *alaṅkāra* (adornment) become the visual language to express the inexpressible beauty of god. Just as a poem is made beautiful through the judicious use of the ornaments of metaphor and simile, *alaṅkāra* of the divine image, the *arcā*, aims to reveal the inconceivable beauty of god. And just as pondering the elusive images in a poem helps us unlock its many meanings, the contemplation and enjoyment of *alaṅkāra* enables the devotee to apprehend the unfathomable nature of god.

It is within such a rubric of *alaṅkāra* and *arcā* that the image of god incites acute feelings of ecstatic enjoyment (*anubhava*) in the devotee. Here the devotee upon seeing god is so supremely affected by the divine vision that it results in a spontaneous outpouring of feeling. While for some, such feeling may express itself in simple exultations at the beauty of god – "see how beautiful Āṇṭāḷ is" – for others, such as our old lady, Tiruvenkatammal or the *āḻvār* poets of yore, the *anubhava* crystallizes in poetry, and the poem became a record of their enjoyment of the god. It becomes what we may term, a verbal icon – an *arcā* in words. Just as the *arcā* is beautifully decorated with glittering gems and resplendent silks to approximate something of god's blinding beauty, so too does the *āḻvār* poem lovingly crafted with literary adornment seek to convey the poet's *anubhava* of Viṣṇu. The sculptor, metal-worker and temple priest use the language of stone, metal and jewels to manifest the body of god (*arcā*) that the poet creates through and in words. In both cases – literary and visual – the word for such adornment is *alaṅkāra*, and an example from Āṇṭāḷ's own poem will help us grasp the interpenetrating relationship of *alaṅkāra* and *anubhava* for the Śrīvaiṣṇavas.

In her jewel-like Tiruppāvai, Āṇṭāḷ imagines a group of young cowherd girls on a quest for Viṣṇu in his guise as the playful lover, Kṛṣṇa. In the nineteenth verse of this poem, the girls arrive at Kṛṣṇa's bedroom door, where he is presumably ensconced with his lovely wife, **Nappiṉṉai**. They address him as such:

The lamps are ablaze.

You laze upon this bed with its stout ivory legs
and five fine qualities
your broad chest draped in garlands of flowers
rests upon the breasts of Nappiṉṉai,
her hair entwined
with heavy blossoms.

Please answer us.

O lovely woman with large eyes
darkened with kohl

How much longer

will you prevent him
from rising?

We know,
you cannot bear to be apart

from your beloved

for a single instant

But this does not befit you:
It is unfair.

ēl ōr empāvāy[5] (Tiruppāvai 19, in Venkatesan 2010: 69)

The verse sets a captivating and vivid scene of Kṛṣṇa and his beloved in loving embrace. Rather than shying away from the details of such an intimate scene, the poet relishes the opportunity to crack open the door to the divine bedchamber. There, past glittering lamps, Kṛṣṇa wearing a garland of flowers lies on a luxurious bed with his head resting on the breasts of his dear wife, Nappiṉṉai. He is as fully her adornment as the delicate, fragrant blossoms that are entwined in her hair. Just so, she with her heavy, fragrant hair is his most perfect ornament.

Coiled like two serpents made of flowers, Kṛṣṇa and his beloved are inseparable, one entity in two bodies, each the adornment for the other. The girls' (and the reader's) enjoyment of this moment of divine union is so great that they are not content just to appreciate it from afar. Instead, they boldly demand to participate in it, declaring that it is unfair for Nappiṉṉai to monopolize Kṛṣṇa's affection. The *anubhava* is not an abstracted, objective, cerebral experience, but a visceral one that requires complete absorption. The *arcā* manifest as a verbal icon in the poem enables the poem's readers (and the questing girls) to relish the body of god not as (literary) artefact, but as embodied, corporeal and somatic.

The divine form in repose: *alaṅkāra* and *anubhava* at the Āṇṭāḷ Temple

I return now to the annual August festival at the Āṇṭāḷ temple of Srivilliputtur. This is the festival that celebrates Āṇṭāḷ's birth, and it is the largest and grandest function that the temple hosts. Conducted over ten long, frenetic days, the festival is an occasion for this tiny, out-of-the-way temple-town to become the centre of the universe. Locals dress in their best clothes and devotees from all over south India throng to visit the temple for a vision, a *cēvai* of Āṇṭāḷ. Ignoring the blistering heat, the unforgiving dust, and the cramped quarters, the crowds swell with each passing day, and the gathered devotees enter into a strange, ecstatic delirium on the festival's seventh day. On this, the seventh night of the festival, Āṇṭāḷ and Viṣṇu are in an *alaṅkāra* known as **Śayana Tirukkōlam**: the divine form of repose.

Figure 16.1 Āṇṭāḷ reclining (photo by author).

From the first moment that I arrived in Srivilliputtur in 2002, I had been told of this special *alaṅkāra*. Locals would dust off old photographs of past Śayana Tirukkōlams to share with me. Some of these sepia-toned photos frayed at the edges hid more than they revealed. Still others were glossy and in flashy colour, leaving nothing at all to the imagination. Holding these photos, the priests and locals would reminisce of this most special *alaṅkāra*, describing it with such detail and verve that I couldn't help but believe that Āṇṭāḷ and Viṣṇu were reclining in divine repose right before our very eyes. My appetite whet after hearing so many enthusiastic accounts of the Śayana Tirukkōlam, I was eager to experience it for myself. It didn't have to wait long; I had my chance in August 2002.

On the evening of the seventh day of the festival, the image of Āṇṭāḷ and Viṣṇu are taken in procession from the Srivilliputtur temple to a neighbouring local sixteenth-century Kṛṣṇa temple. Inside this small temple is a capacious main hall, at the end of which is a raised stone platform flanked by four large, unadorned pillars. The images of Āṇṭāḷ and Viṣṇu are placed on this raised platform facing north. Soon after, the priests tie a curtain around Āṇṭāḷ and Viṣṇu to obstruct the devotees' gaze as they ritually bathe the images and begin the painstaking process of *alaṅkāra*. During the long wait of several hours devotees mill around, visit the inner sanctum of the temple, sing devotional verses, gossip and find ways of passing the time. Finally, as word comes down from the priests that the curtain is to be lowered, people pack into the hall, which suddenly no longer seems spacious. Their eyes are riveted to the enclosed raised platform anxiously awaiting the moment that Āṇṭāḷ and Viṣṇu are revealed. When the

Figure 16.2 Āṇṭāḷ at her wedding (photo by author).

curtain is lowered around 8pm, and the priests wave a bright camphor flame to illuminate the resplendent forms of Āṇṭāḷ and Viṣṇu, the devotees gasp as if one, raise their arms in the air and call out Āṇṭāḷ's name. "One needs a thousand eyes to fully enjoy this", many enthusiastically declare.

Āṇṭāḷ and Viṣṇu are placed on a bed covered in silks and brocades. Āṇṭāḷ, sumptuously attired is seated in the pose of royal ease. Her left hand holds the parrot, while the right hand rests lightly and elegantly upon her raised right knee.[6] She faces forward, gazing outward toward the devotee. Viṣṇu reclines, left hand cradling the head that is placed upon Āṇṭāḷ's lap, his right hand holding up his mace, very much the king, but one whose face is turned away from his petitioners. At first blush this is a moment where the devotee is invited to peek into the bedroom of god to witness the bliss of divine union. This gorgeous and imaginative *alaṅkāra* immediately calls to mind the voyeuristic quest of the girls in the Tiruppāvai and their encounter with Kṛṣṇa and his wife in their bedroom in Tiruppāvai 19, the verse cited earlier. Though Viṣṇu is not quite lying on the breasts of Āṇṭāḷ here as in the Tiruppāvai verse, there is no question in the minds of either the devotees or the priests that they are witnessing an intensely intimate moment. In the Tiruppāvai, the girls intrude on just such a moment and beg to be allowed to participate equally in it. After attempting unsuccessfully to coerce the god into waking up, they turn their attention to Nappiṉṉai and accuse her of monopolizing Kṛṣṇa's attention.

Through this *alaṅkāra*, it would seem that the devotees have all entered into a Tiruppāvai-like scenario. They made their way to see this Kṛṣṇa temple and waited for several hours for the curtain to be lowered. And when it finally is, it is to find Viṣṇu reclining, his face turned away, asleep. So they direct their petitions to his consort.[7] The medieval commentaries on Tiruppāvai 19 stress exactly this point: that the girls in their enthusiasm to reach Kṛṣṇa failed to petition his wife first, forgetting that their success would be far greater with her intervention. The Śayana Tirukkōlam embodies this commentary. Here it is Āṇṭāḷ cast in the role of wife, a mediator who interacts with her devotees, hears their pleas, and intercedes on their behalf. Just as she had manifested out of the temple's inner sanctum to run out and greet Rāmānuja, here too she is the active agent in securing liberation for the devotees. The lord, transcendent and inaccessible, dreaming the worlds into existence, remains passive, engrossed in a deep *yogic* sleep. It might be said that what he creates, she mediates.

Āṇṭāḷ's primary role in this *alaṅkāra* is brought into stark relief when contrasted with the usual position of Śrī, Viṣṇu's primary consort. Śrī is always either at Viṣṇu's feet, ready in attendance, or adorning his chest. But Āṇṭāḷ, like Nappiṉṉai in Tiruppāvai 19, reverses the positions in this *alaṅkāra*. Now, the god lies on her chest (or as the case may be on her lap). She is not at his feet, the exemplary wife or devotee, looking to god, her husband for direction. Āṇṭāḷ is, as her name suggests, she who rules. She is the sovereign. Her gaze is directed outward, inviting the petitions of her devotees. The poetess Kōtai earned the name Āṇṭāḷ, she who rules primarily because she won the heart of Viṣṇu through an unswerving, single-minded passion. And for this, she is regarded as the paradigmatic devotee. In this *alaṅkāra*, Āṇṭāḷ becomes the vehicle of Viṣṇu's grace, the power through which he works, the means through which he mediates.

The Śayana Tirukkōlam depicts a moment that is erotically charged, and as such enforces the mutual inseparability of Viṣṇu and Āṇṭāḷ, just as in the Tiruppāvai verse cited above. Through this *alaṅkāra* she is cast not just as the active agent of Viṣṇu's grace, but the source of that grace as well. She straddles the private, inner world of love and the public, outer world of divine sovereignty.

The Śayana Tirukkōlam registers on many different levels – on one level it depicts Āṇṭāḷ's unique place in the Śrīvaiṣṇava universe – the intimacy that she has with the lord because she won his heart like no other. Devotees experience this intimacy of Āṇṭāḷ and Viṣṇu seeing in it the complementary nature of exemplary wife-hood and exemplary devotion. Lauded as she is for her passion, adored as she is for her extraordinary love for god, cherished as she is for the sweetness of her words, the path of Āṇṭāḷ's single minded devotion is not a path either open or recommended for devotees. It is in the savouring of *her* devotion, given form through the *alaṅkāra* of the Śayana Tirukkōlam, in the vicarious pleasure derived from seeing the intimate world of the god and goddess, and in surrendering to her ability to mediate that the devotee too can surrogately experience the divine.

The fruit of enjoyment: concluding thoughts

One of the first Āṇṭāḷ stories I heard from the locals of Srivilliputtur was during the celebration of the temple's annual spring festival in mid-April. Like the Rāmānuja story, this apocryphal tale too involved a Śrīvaiṣṇava luminary, the fourteenth-century philosopher and poet, **Vedānta Deśika** (c. 1268—1369 CE). There is no story that I heard during my frequent visits to Srivilliputtur that so lucidly captures the intersections of *anubhava, alaṅkāra*, and *arcā* for Tamil̲ Śrīvaiṣṇavas.

Deśika decided to make a pilgrimage to Srivilliputtur, the sacred site of Āṇṭāḷ's birth. His arrival coincided with the celebration of the temple's annual spring festival and despite observing a strict vow of silence he joined the crowds eager to see Āṇṭāḷ and Viṣṇu's unique *alaṅkāra*. The images of Āṇṭāḷ and Viṣṇu would be smeared with cool sandalwood and dressed in garments stitched together from soft, fragrant, fresh jasmine buds, all in a nod to the soaring temperatures of early summer. He waited silently alongside fellow travellers and devotees for the moment when the divine couple would turn on to his street. But nothing had prepared him for the vision that he beheld. As they moved slowly forward on their palanquin, his eyes thirstily drank in the intoxicating sweetness of Āṇṭāḷ's smile, the delicacy of her gracefully curving form, her long and lovely braid; his eyes lovingly roved over the serene face of her beloved,

Viṣṇu, pausing to enjoy his enigmatic smile, his regal form, his dashing turban of flowers. Emotion swelled in him and unable to squelch this rising ecstasy, Deśika broke his vow and his silence, and spontaneously composed this verse:

> You are the wish-fulfilling creeper
> in the grove of the clan of Viṣṇucittaṉ
> entwined around the sandalwood tree
> that is Raṅgarāja.[8]
> You are patience and compassion.
> You are another Śrī.
> Godā,[9]
> you are my only refuge
> I surrender to you.
>
> (Archana Venkatesan, unpublished translation)

Deśika continued in much the same vein for another twenty-eight exquisite verses of a poem in praise of Āṇṭāḷ called the **Godā Stuti**.

In this story, Deśika's poem is born from the vision of an extraordinary *alaṅkāra*. It is the result of such acute enjoyment that it transgresses ritual vows and laws, just as Āṇṭāḷ flouted the rules to adorn herself with Viṣṇu's garland, and Viṣṇu disregarded convention in adorning himself with what was a ritually polluted offering. That reciprocal enjoyment is the expression of the mutual dependence of god and devotee, god and consort. Like the Nappiṉṉai and Kṛṣṇa entwined in intimate embrace that Āṇṭāḷ imagined in her Tiruppāvai, for Deśika it is Āṇṭāḷ and Viṣṇu coiled together as creeper and tree. The images of bronze become images of words, and the poetry of Deśika transforms into the stories of Srivilliputtur, stringing together like the fragrant blossoms of a garland in an unbroken chain of infinite enjoyment.

Notes

1. This is a paraphrase of the story Tiruvenkatammal recounted to me in April 2002. It is neither a transcription nor a literal translation of her rather lengthy narration, which was embellished with several quotations from Āṇṭāḷ's poetry, Śrīvaiṣṇava hagiography and other scriptural sources. In this paraphrase, I have attempted to capture Tiruvenkatammal's engaging story-telling style.
2. Diana Eck's important book *Darśan* discusses the concept in great detail (Eck 1981). Richard H. Davis develops many of these ideas further in his discussion of the biography of Indian images, those that are both in worship and in museums within the context of what he calls the devotional eye (Davis 1997: 37–8).
3. Steven Hopkins (2007a) explores the concept of extravagant beholding.
4. The five forms are *para* (transcendent/supreme), *vyūha* (primary manifestations of Saṁkarṣaṇa, Pradyumna and Aniruddha, iconographically depicted as Viṣṇu reclining on the ocean of milk), *vibhava* (descents/terrestrial forms of the ten *avatāras* such as Rāma and Kṛṣṇa), *antaryāmin* (the in-dwelling, Viṣṇu who resides in the heart of his devotees) and *arcā* (the icon).

5. *Ēl ōr empāvāy* is the poem's refrain and also lends the poem its title, *Tiruppāvai* (Venkatesan 2010).
6. The effect of the seated posture is achieved through the use of detachable arms and feet made for the specific purpose. These are attached to the body of the god so as to produce a faux body, which is then draped with the yards of cloths so that the underlying form of the icon is no longer visible.
7. Around the seventeenth century, the *Śrīvaiṣṇava* community split into two major subsects, known as the Northern (Vaṭakalai) and Southern (Teṅkalai) schools. The fault lines were drawn in the fourteenth century as the sect's main teachers grappled with theological issues that were consolidated into eighteen major differences between the two. One of the major differences had to do with Viṣṇu's relationship to his consort, *Śrī*. Simply put, for the Northern school, *Śrī* is on par with Viṣṇu, while for the southern branch of *Śrīvaiṣṇavas*, she is subordinate to him (see Kumar 2000). However, such differences do not always translate into practice as is evident in the case of Āṇṭāḷ at her temple in Srivilliputtur. Although the Srivilliputtur temple belongs to the Southern branch, it is Āṇṭāḷ who is accorded supreme status here, and one might even go so far as to argue that she is the primary deity at the Srivilliputtur temple, referred to by locals as Āṇṭāḷ Kōvil (Āṇṭāḷ's Temple) or Nācciyār Tirumāḷikai (The Lady's Mansion).
8. Raṅgarāja is another name for Viṣṇu.
9. Godā is the Sanskrit form of the Tamiḻ name Kōtai.

17. The Sri Venkateswara temple in Tirupati

Afsar Mohammad

Behold! Yonder is the abode of Hari
That is the lofty holy Venkata hill;
That is the hill which is dear and precious sight to even Brahma and other devas;
That is the permanent residence of innumerable sages and saints;
Behold that holy hill
Bow down to that hill of bliss;
It is the choice resort of devas from heaven;
Behold the priceless sacred treasure of that hill
Behold the dazzling golden peaks;
Behold that embodiment of several Vedas
Behold the Venkatagiri, the seat of Kaivalya (salvation).
That is the hill which is Lord Sri Venkateswara's wealth;
That is quintessence of all conceivable wealth and treasure;
That hill is the holiest of the holies.

Composed by fifteenth-century Telugu poet Annamayya, this poem still echoes through the seven hills of Tirumala, which attract thousands of devotees each day from India and abroad. As described in the above verse, this place is surrounded by a huge mountain that extends for several miles. The deity that lives on this hill is popularly called "the God of Seven Hills". North Indians call the deity "Balaji"; for south Indians, the deity is Sri Venkateswara and "the God Venkata of the Seven Hills" (*Yedu kondala venakateswarudu* in the local language Telugu). Although Sri Venkateswara is considered an *avatāra* of Viṣṇu, and most of the practices and rituals at the temple reflect a tradition of Śrī Vaiṣṇavism, a distinctive sect of Vaiṣṇavism that highlights the worship of Śrī, the consort of Viṣṇu. The act of visiting Tirupati is an obligatory vow in return of some fulfilled wish. The sectarian differences among the Hindus blur when it comes to the devotion to Sri Venkateswara. Some Muslims regard the consort of Sri Venkateshwara, Bibi Nancharamma, as properly worshipped within their Muslim religion and visit the deity to perform worship or to fulfil their vows.

The life of Sri Venkateswara and his abode at Tirupati is an endless chain of multiple stories that encompass multiple traditions. His life is a constant source of devotion in various forms such as stories, devotional hymns, music and most importantly, various rituals that begin with daily worships and climax to a huge annual public festival called **Brāhmotsavam** (the "Festival of the Brahma" or the "Great Festival"), when more than 500,000 pilgrims visit Sri Venkateswara. Devotees tell Sri Venkateswara's life stories in many ways, and for each social group, or caste, his name represents a specific set of devotional patterns and ideals of everyday life. Who, then, is Sri Venkateswara? Why is his abode Tirupati, as described by Annamayya, "the holiest of holy" places? What roles do Sri Venkateswara and Tirupati play in the practices of contemporary south Asian religions, particularly Hindu traditions?

Sri Venkateswara and Tirupati

Most of the devotional hymns in Tirupati begin with the line "there is no God other than Venkatesha". Either Śrī Vaiṣṇavites or any sects of Hindus or non-Hindus who visit Tirupati strictly adhere to the worship of both Śrī and Venkateswara. As one pilgrim told me:

> All their senses are glued to Śrī and Venkateswara at once. Here is one place where both deity and his consort are treated equally. That's why it's always Sri Venkateswara together. Their sole purpose is to impress Sri Venkateswara and make him happy with their prayers and vows. For those who visit Tirumala, it's a new beginning of their life, an auspicious moment that protects them from all bad aspects in life.[1]

As a regularly recited devotional hymn in Sanskrit puts it: "*sadaa Venkatesham smaraami smaaraami*" ("I think of Venkatesha all the time").

Sri Venkateswara is known by many epithets. As the destroyer of sins and the giver of prosperity, Sri Venkateswara is called Śrīnivāsa, "the one in whom the Goddess of Prosperity, Śrī or Lakṣmī, dwells". He is also called Nārāyaṇa, (the creator and the destroyer), Perumal (the Great Lord), Malaiyappa (The Lord of the Hill) or Govinda (a name of Lord Kṛṣṇa). During the rituals at the temple, the devotees endlessly chant "Govindaa". The most popular name in Telugu is *yedu kondala venkanna* (the God of the Seven Hills). Most of the pilgrims make a vow to climb the hill chanting "Oh, God of the Seven Hills, Venkata Ramana, Govindaa ... Govindaa", an utterance that rings through the hills of Tirumala. Several legends about Sri Venkateswara connect him to the history and geography of these seven hills called Venkatadri, the mountain of **Vēṇkaṭa**.

Vēṇkaṭa is a specific name given to the manifestation of Viṣṇu at Tirupati. According to the **Vāyu Purāṇa**, *vem* means dire sins and *kata* is the protective power, and the utterance Vēṇkaṭa protects the devotees from all sins. The text Vāyu Purāṇa also provides another definition that the utterance Vēṇkaṭa has both nectar and affluence and for those who utter the word Vēṇkaṭa it brings both nectar and affluence (Kṛṣṇa 2000: 49). The word *Venkatam* first appears in the earliest Tamil̲ poetry from the early centuries of the Christian era, and in the Tamil̲ epic narrative Cilappadikaaram it became identified with Viṣṇu with "recognizable iconographic features", now visible in the image of Sri Venkateswara at Tirumala (Rao & Shulman 2005: 97).

Several stories describe what made Viṣṇu to land and settle in Tirupati. According to the *Brahmapurāṇa*, Viṣṇu wanted to take a walk outside the heaven (*vaikuṇṭham*) and Narada asked him to visit the hills of Tirupati. According to the *Bhaviṣyottara Purāṇa*, Viṣṇu came down to these hills at the request of several sages after austere *tapas*.[2] Viṣṇu, who descended upon the hills of Tirupati, never left for heaven, and he finally settled at Tirupati as his permanent home.

The divine and human manifestations of Venkateswara encompass a great variety. Thus, in a way, his life story is a blend of the ordinary and the extraordinary. Although most of the stories undoubtedly reiterate that Sri Venkateswara is a form of Viṣṇu, some scholars argue that he was originally Harihara, a blend of Śiva and Viṣṇu. According to N. Jagadeeshan, a south Indian historian, "it would appear that originally the image in the temple was only a Harihara, but

Figure 17.1 Moolavirat (Śrī Venkateswara) (photo courtesy of Radha Krishna, Tirupati, with permission).

later during Rāmānuja's time acquired specifically Vaiṣṇavite characteristics" (Jagadeeshan 1989: 182). Nevertheless, in contemporary Hinduism, the manifestation of Sri Venkateswara and the stories about his abode are popular for their Vaiṣṇavaite practices, and most of the devotees perceive him as an *avatāra* of Viṣṇu. However, for an ordinary devotee and pilgrim these distinctions are not significant. In their religious worldview, Sri Venkateswara is a more accessible deity than any other Hindu gods and goddesses. Devotees believe that just by reciting the name (***nāmasmaraṇa***) and by making simple vows, Sri Venkateswara will bestow his blessings upon them. The devotees recite his name as they climb his seven hills at Tirupati and declare their absolute submission by gifting their hair.

Gifting hair or tonsure, which is called ***muṇḍana*** in Sanskrit and Telugu, is a very popular ritual at Tirumala.[3] This ritual is connected to one of the most popular stories about Sri Venkateswara falling into a debt trap in order to make a dowry for his marriage with a local girl called Padmavati in Tirupati. Devotees who visit Tirupati believe that Sri Venkateswara is still paying the interest on the debt, and they give away their hair as a means to enable him to pay at least the interest.[4] For this reason, Sri Venkateswara is also called "a deity who lives on the interest paid by the devotees", ***vaḍḍī kāsula vāḍu*** in Telugu. Another local story about his marriage with a local Muslim girl Bibi Nancharamma is also popular in south India. However, it is also explained that the story about Bibi Nancharamma was a folk imagination during the times of conflicts between Hindus and Muslims in the medieval times (Deekshitulu 2010: 66). When compared to the devotion to Sri Venkateswara both among both Hindus and Muslims, it is not unusual that these stories are in wide circulation. Many manifestations of Sri Venkateswara reveal the personal aspect of devotion in the *bhakti* tradition and he remains the family deity irrespective of any religious and caste distinctions in India.

Śrī Vēṇkaṭa and Rāmānuja's *bhakti* tradition

The devotion and popularity of Sri Venkateswara results from the influence and intensity of the *bhakti* tradition in south India, particularly Śrī Vaiṣṇavism.[5] Most of the verses recited during various daily and special rituals for Sri Venkateswara inside the temple and outside the temple's surrounding environs reflect vernacular notions of the *bhakti* movement in south India along with the Sanskrit mode of Vaiṣṇava tradition. The mode of devotion to Sri Venkateswara in Tirupati is, to use the words of Gavin Flood, considered to be "the Lord as the transcendent cause and sustaining power of the cosmos, and, on the other, the southern Tamiḻ tradition of longing devotion to a personal Lord installed within specific temple icons" (Flood 1996: 135–6).

Though the term Śrī Vaiṣṇava occurs in the Tiruvenkatam (Tirupati) temple inscriptions as early as 966 CE, the Śrī Vaiṣṇava tradition of south India became systematized around the time of its most important teacher Rāmānuja (1017–1137ce). The teachings of Rāmānuja represent a powerful blend between the Sanskrit and vernacular traditions. Rāmānuja himself introduced many of the rituals and the schedules of worship at the temple in Tirupati. The influence of Rāmānuja as a theologian is profoundly visible in every aspect of the devotion to Sri Venkateswara and his abode Tirupati. As Sanjay Subrahmanyam observed:

> in the case of Tirupati, Rāmānuja is most closely linked with the Govindaraja shrine, reported in the *sthalapurāṇas* of the area to have been organized by him around the *utsavamūrti* that had earlier been moved there from Cidambaram, purportedly to escape the depredations of the fiercely Saivite Cola king, Kulottunga I (1070–1120).
> (Subrahmanyam 1995: 341–2)[6]

Theologically, Rāmānuja's ideas and practices represent a blend between Sanskrit and vernacular traditions, known as **ubhaya Vedānta** (Vedānta based on both Tamil̠ and Sanskritic traditions). His most important contribution to the history of Hindu theology is the idea of *viśiṣṭādvaita* or the qualified philosophy of the oneness of God which combines *advaita* (oneness of God) and *viśiṣṭa* (the special attributes of God).

It is to be emphasized that Rāmānuja's ideas of worship and devotional acts systematized the entire ritual sphere in the premises of the temple through his expositions on worship and devotional acts. Indeed, Rāmānuja initiated most of the rituals that are currently observed in the temple and its surroundings in accordance with his ideas of new theology which, in a sense, popularized Hinduism in southern India.

Rituals: daily and special

Thousands of devotees and pilgrims visit Sri Venkateswara not just for his *darśana* at some random time, but to have a *darśana* at a specific point of time during the day or on the special days. The pilgrims plan their visits according to the specific timings which they believe are important for the deity and they believe that visiting the deity during these specific moments makes their wishes come true. These timings and modalities for the regular and special services of worship were first initiated by a very specific school of Vaiṣṇavas, the Vaikhānasa, a system of worship named after a prominent sage Vikhanas to whom a text called *Śrī Vaikhānasa Bhagavat Śāstra* is attributed.[7] The text consists 400,000 Sanskrit verses which provide rules and codes to perform various services of worship and rituals in any Viṣṇu temple. Even the earliest stories of worship for Sri Venkateswara reflect a strong connection to the Vaikhānasa tradition and texts. The texts of the Vaikhānasa are said to be the earliest sources of the iconic worship of Viṣṇu. The Vaikhānasa tradition instructs that the worship should be performed six times a day beginning from early dawn to midnight. Each of these six rituals are called *sevās* (worship or service). The services are classified as daily, weekly and annual. While daily and weekly services are to continue the tradition of *nitya pūjā* (the constant worship), the annual service is the celebration of the key moment in the life of Sri Venkateswara that is called *Brahmotsav*, the great festival of Brahma.

Daily and weekly *sevās*

Early dawn rituals begin with a popular worship ***suprabhāta sevā***, the morning worship that begins at 2am. The deity is woken up, and milk, butter and sugar are offered. After one hour, the ***tōmāla sevā*** (cleaning and bathing ritual) is offered. This *sevā* is immediately followed by the ***koluvu***, which literally means holding the court. Along with several verses from Sanskrit, the descendants of the temple poet Annamayya recite the Telugu language hymns for Sri Venkateswara. During the *koluvu*, the deity is informed about his various sources of income. Most importantly, during this ritual both Sanskritic and vernacular literary traditions are blended and verses from various Sanskrit texts including *Varaha Stuti* and *Yati Raja Ślokas*, and verses from the Tamil̲ texts such as *Divya Prabandha* are recited.

Each day Sri Venkateswara receives three types of worship called ***sahasranāma arcana*** (reciting 1,000 names) and two types of *archana* (praise). After offering the incense and light, the priest recites 1,000 names of Sri Venkateswara. During the second type of *archana*, 108 names of Sri Venkateswara from the *Varāha purāṇa* are recited. After these two types of *archanas*, the ***sarvadarśana*** (the complete *darśana*) is allowed for all the devotees. The third type of *archana*, a regular worship, is followed after the *sarvadarśana*. All the day rituals come to an end with a night ritual called ***ekānta sevā***, which lasts about forty-five minutes, to put the deity to sleep. Then the temple doors are closed until the early dawn.

Along with these daily *sevās*, certain weekdays are hectic with special *sevās* such as ***viśēṣa pūjā*** (special worship) on Mondays, 108 golden lotuses worship on Tuesdays, the bathing of the deity with thousand pots of water on Wednesdays, special offering of food and flowers on Thursdays, ritual bath and offering new clothes on Fridays. During most of these rituals, many verses from Sanskrit and Tamil̲ are recited inside the temple whereas outside the temple, the environs resound with the Telugu verses of Annamayya.

Each day nearly 100,000 pilgrims visit Tirumala and participate in various rituals. During the weekend, particularly on Saturdays, the number increases as pilgrims arrive from various parts of India.

Brāhmotsavam (the festival of Brahma)

The annual festival is called Brāhmotsavam. It is told that Brahma, the creator of the universe, according to the Hindu mythology, came down to the earth and handed over the responsibility of redeeming the sins of the devotees to Sri Venkateswara on the first day of the New Moon in the month of *bhādrapada* in the Hindu calendar. The event was first celebrated for ten days, and later became a tradition. The day this festival marks is also the day that Brahma decided that Viṣṇu should remain on the hills of Tirumala throughout the **Kaliyuga** – the age of discord, strife and contentions – and the last of the four stages as narrated in the Hindu mythology. As Brahma ordained, it is the responsibility of Sri Venkateswara to remove the sins of discord, strife and contention on Earth. The celebration of the Annual festival Brāhmotsavam reinforces this idea of redeeming the sins and the continuation of the creation made possible by Brahma.

The annual Brāhmotsavam is now celebrated in the months of September and October. These two months are considered to be holiest of the entire calendar and each day is hectic with numerous rituals and devotional practices in Tirupati. In the month of September, Brāhmotsavam attracts several thousands of pilgrims and almost each day is a festival day in Tirupati. Every morning and evening, the highly decorated images of Venkateswara, Śrīdevī and Bhudevī are taken out in procession through the streets around the temple and then bathed in herbal waters. Each day different *vāhanas* (cars) are used to take out the procession. The car festival called **Rathotsavam** is a prominent ritual on the eighth

Figure 17.2 Temple procession (photo courtesy of Radhakrishna, Tirupati, with permission).

day. Car festival is an elaborate ritual where forty-four deities are invoked by reciting various verses. It is believed that whoever has a *darśana* of Venkatesa during this car festival is assured of ultimate liberation, or *moksha*. On the ninth and concluding day of the Brāhmotsavam, three main rituals of sprinkling holy turmeric (***cūrṇa***), the flag celebration (***dhwajaarohana***), and the celebration of flowers (***puṣpayāga***) will be performed. Each of these three rituals have a very specific purpose as the turmeric powder is said to represent Viṣṇu, the flag celebration is for the purpose of thanking the deities who made the festival a success, and finally the celebration of flowers is for wish fulfilment and for getting rid of any demerits.

Tirumala: "the heaven on Earth"

Tirumala, the actual abode of Sri Venkateswara, is popularly known as the "heaven on Earth" (**Bhooloka Vaikuntha**). Pilgrims who visit Tirupati each year to gift their hair (*muṇḍana*) unhesitatingly believe that they are at the steps of heaven. Because of its central deity Sri Venkateswara, Tirumala has a long history as a pilgrim site. Even the post-Sangam epic *cilappaṭikāram* mentions it as a pilgrim site. During the reign of the Vijayanagara kings, the shrine gained political importance specifically in the fourteenth century.[8] As Chris Fuller observed, this shrine is situated in a rather unimportant locality, but the immense popularity of the deity Venkateswara makes this locality a centre of Hindu pilgrimage now (C. J. Fuller 2004: 206). Among the Hindus in diaspora, the devotion to Sri Venkateswara goes to the extent of constructing replicas of Tirumala elsewhere, for instance Vēṇkaṭa temple in Pittsburgh, Pennsylvania, USA. However, the diaspora Hindus visit Tirupati to have a "real" *darśana* of Sri Venkateswara and to perform actual rituals such as *muṇḍana* in the "real" presence of Venkateswara. As one pilgrim told me, "we visit both Pittsburgh and Tirupati each year, but for every family function including weddings and rites of passage we visit Tirupati and we perform these rituals in the presence of 'real' Venkateswara".[9]

This idea of "real" form of Sri Venkateswara plays an important role in the devotion to Tirupati Venkateswara that makes the devotees to visit Tirupati each year. The temple poet Annamayya describes this experience of pilgrimage in one of his poems:

> Unmindful of the rains, surging crowds come from all directions,
> far and near,
> Wives, neighbours, kith and kin, well-wishers, all come crowding;
> Observing all vows, they come flocking from hundreds and thou-
> sands of miles
> To offer worship to you;

> Some come with their offerings tied in all sorts of bundles balanced
> on their heads
> Others come with their ladies decked in dazzling jewellery
> And with lots of money, riding on elephants and horses;
>
> Chieftains, kings, emperors rich and poor alike come from far
> And near to have your *darshan*, O lord of Venkatadri!
> (Annamayya, quoted in Ramesh 2000: 60)

This notion of a closer "*darshan*" (*darśana*) plays an important role in the devotional life of pilgrims. Though most of the villages have Viṣṇu temples either in one *avatāra* (incarnation) or another, visiting Tirupati has become a family tradition in modern times. Each pilgrim narrates a distinctive version of devotional experience and having a closer *darśana* is still a beginning of several key events, such as marriage, starting a business, schooling or a new employment in the life of a devotee. Participating or performing rituals in the presence of Sri Venkateswara makes a big difference to many devotees. For Vaiṣṇavites, Tirupati is one of the 108 *divya desas* (sacred sites for Vaiṣṇavites), and Tirumala is also known as the *Svayam vykta kshetra*, which means that the images in the temple were not sculpted by human hands, but they are self-revealed (***svayaṁ vyakta***). Although pilgrims that I spoke with have several reasons to justify their visit to Tirupati, this notion of the self-revealed images plays a significant role too.

In addition, as we can observe from the description of several rituals that most of the practices are directly or indirectly connected to certain specific narrative practices, which include singing hymns, telling stories and reciting directly from various texts.

Narrative practices: singing hymns and telling stories

As for many deities in Hinduism, the life of Sri Venkateswara is also told in many forms. Though several texts narrate the story of Sri Venkateswara, there are also stories that continue to circulate among the devotees and pilgrims. These stories take on more creative manifestations not only as expressed in folk-art forms, but also in the local popular culture such as movies, audio-visual narratives and devotional lyrics. These stories and hymns are significant for their role in popularizing the devotion to Sri Venkateswara. Including everyday conversations (what contemporary ethnographers call "conversational narratives"), devotees and pilgrims use several narrative devices to talk about their connection with Sri Venkateswara.[10] We learn more from these conversational narratives which explain very specific family and caste associations with Sri Venkateswara. Many of the lower castes and Muslim versions of devotion to Viṣṇu still remain unexplored, but these versions also show the impact of the *bhakti* movement in south India. During my visits to Tirumala on different occasions, I found that these caste groups weave several stories that connect their lives to the devotion to Viṣṇu. Most of these stories, they claim, passed down to them from their ancestors. As one Muslim pilgrim told me:

> We are following the tradition within our family. If you ask for the specific origins of this tradition, we won't be able to trace it or figure it out. We have just been continuing the practices for several generations and our children also continue it. We are as much devoted as any Brāhmin in this regard. [11]

Narrative plays an influential role in the expansion of devotion to Sri Venkateswara. This aspect has a sustained history both in literary and non-literary worlds. This aspect reaches its peak in the hymns composed by Annamayya who has now become an icon of ideal devotion to Sri Venkateswara. Along with describing the regular rituals and practices at Tirupati, the medieval temple poet Annamayya goes to the extent of "owning" the deity by "eroticizing" the devotion too:

> When I'm done being angry,
> Then I will make love.
> Right now, you should be glad
> I'm listening.
>
> You hug me, I hug you back
> You can see I'm still burning.
> I can't help it, god on the hill,
> if I'm engulfed in your passion.
>
> (Annamayya, quoted in Rao & Shulman 2005: 102)

As Rao and Shulman note, "we are overhearing a bedroom conversation conveyed to us by Annamayya" (*ibid.*).

The narrative practices centred on the devotion to Sri Venkateswara deal with diverse forms that range from folklore and classical to modern. Whereas several inscriptions refer to the story of Tirupati, many ***purāṇas*** including *Varaha, Garuḍa, Vāmana* and *Bhaviṣyottara* narrate the stories (***sthala mahima***) of this place. Most importantly, Srimad Anantarya, one of the disciples of Śrī Rāmānuja, wrote a text called Venkatesa Itihasa Mala (The Garland of the stories of Venkateswara), believed to be more than 900 years old. First published in Telugu, this was later translated into Hindi and English in 1971.

Within the realm of rituals and practices, the verses recited every morning during the daily worship refer to the larger tradition of Sri Venkateswara. These verses blend both Sanskrit and vernacular narrative practices that include the Vedas, Mahābhārata, the poetic tradition of the saint-poet Nammāḻvār and theologian Śrī Rāmānuja. Referring to Sanskrit texts as a part of narrating the life of Sri Venkateswara and the place story of Tirupati is a key component of the entire tradition. Referring to the significance of the Vengadam hills, the great poet Kamban, in his *Rāmāyaṇa*, describes:

> Commanding his armies under different leaders to proceed in different directions in search of Sītā, Sugrīva says to Hanumān – You will reach the cool Vengada Hill which is overgrown with forests full of bee-hives, which forms the boundary between the northern and the southern languages, which contains the Truth enshrined in the four Vedas and all the Sastras, which is the abode of all good deeds and which stands out as the eternal Satya.
>
> (Kamban, quoted in Ramesh 2000: 15)

In many classical Telugu texts we find a description of Tirupati and Sri Venkateswara. Sri Krishnadeva Raya, the great Vijayanagara emperor, provides a vivid description of the Venkata Hills, but the text itself opens with the homage to Sri Venkateswara:

> The pendant of Lakṣmī's necklace reflects Him;
> She is seen in the lovely Kausthubha gem.
> Their loving presence within
> Is now imaged outside, as it were,
> Shining through the divine bodies crystal-pure.
> To this Venkateswara, I bow in devotion.
>
> (Quoted in P. N. Kumar 2009)

Both Tirumala and Sri Venkateswara are endless sources for various stories and hymns in folklore. However, Sri Venkateswara holds a key position even in popular culture. Each year hundreds of video cassettes and CDs are released, Tirumala as a sacred place and Sri Venkateswara as a popular deity find a greater place in several movies and Tirumala – Tirupati becomes the centre of many folk performances and cultural activities throughout the year. Varieties of narratives are produced and transmitted through these activities.

Conclusion

The temple culture of Tirumala–Tirupati and the devotion to Sri Venkateswara has been undergoing radical changes for at least two decades. Most of the practices in and around the temple are now more inclusive, as the temple culture has begun to adapt certain administrative strategies that yield space for diverse caste groups and shared devotional practices. The growing devotion among lower caste groups within Hinduism, the endlessly increasing interest in the temple beyond south Asia, and the rise of tourism are now directly impacting the temple culture and the administration.

Regular daily services and programmes of the temple administration are now currently planned and supervised by a board of trustees of the Tirumala Tirupati Devasthanam (TTD), appointed by the government of Andhra Pradesh. Established in 1932, the TTD provides various services to the devotees. Not limited to several programmes on religious education, the Devasthanam continues to expand its activities to diverse social causes such as building hospitals, higher educational institutions, technological services and maintaining ecology.

As already mentioned, more devotional space is now being provided to lower-caste and other marginalized groups within the temple activities. However, this aspect of inclusivity and shared devotion is not uncommon in the folklore of Sri Venkateswara, and we find many stories that cross the religious and caste boundaries. The story of Bibi Nancharamma has already been a source of shared practices between Hindus and Muslims at least since the medieval times. In his 2004 essay, Richard A. Davis shows how this narrative offers insights into a shared devotion for Viṣṇu.[12]

Nevertheless, as Davis observed in his essay, there was an ongoing effort to "purify" shrines and festivals that are religiously shared across south Asia. Yet the shrine of Tirupati remains open to inclusive devotional practices. In 2007, the TTD introduced the innovative programme called "Dalit Govindam" under which the wedding ceremonies of Sri Venkateswara are being performed in certain Dalit neighbourhoods. During my visit on this occasion in 2007, one priest explained that

> it is not unusual in the temple of Tirumala to allow backward castes and Dalits to certain rituals, actually the morning rituals such as gifting food to Sri Venkateswara are even now performed by backward castes. In addition, even classical poets such as Annamayya or any other Vaiṣṇava respect Bibi Nancharamma as the consort of the deity.

It was also the year when the TTD chose 108 Dalit hamlets from five administrative divisions of each district to conduct this annual ritual that started with *Nityārchana* (daily worship) and *Sri Venkateswara Homam* (the fire ritual). The same year, in a far-reaching move, the TTD has decided to admit Dalits to its Vedic school, which trains students to become priests. However, most of these innovative programmes are also being criticized by Dalit groups as a process of the Hinduization of the Dalit caste groups and their neighbourhoods. Yet the popularity of Sri Venkateswara among the lower castes and the devotional practices for the deity still hold a greater prominence.

Most of these traditional and innovative programmes show the growing importance of the devotion to Sri Venkateswara and the centrality of Tirumala–Tirupati as a pilgrim centre in contemporary Hinduism. Tirumala–Tirupati reflects both the devotional aspects of tradition and modernity, the blend of Sanskrit and vernacular language practices in the making of Hinduism. Though the devotees and pilgrims who visit Tirumala–Tirupati worship Sri Venkateswara in general, the emphasis on the consorts of the deity makes this place a significant shrine. Most of the oral and written narratives tell the stories of the consorts of the deity, and describe their everyday life as lived on the hills of Tirumala–Tirupati. This aspect still emphasizes the significant role of Śrī in the life of Sri Venkateswara. Since the seven hills of Tirumala remain the centre of the major events in the life of Sri Venkateswara, the *darśana* of Śrī and Venkateswara at Tirumala takes on a central significance for their devotees too.

Notes

1. A conversation with Venakatamma, a forty-year-old pilgrim, 20 October 2006.
2. For more stories about the landing of Sri Venkateswara at Tirupati, see M. R. Rao (1982: 28–35) and Viraraghavacharya (1997: 21–30).
3. For more on the ritual of *muṇḍana*, see Bhardwaj (2003: 154).
4. For a detailed narration of this story, see Rao and Shulman (2005: 119).
5. For an understanding of Śrī Vaiṣṇavism, see Flood (1996: 103–147) and Narayanan (1994: 2).
6. For a detailed narration of this aspect, see M. R. Rao (1982: 50–51) and Viraraghavacharya (1997: 243).
7. For an understanding of the Vaikhānasa school of Śrī Vaiṣṇavism, see Flood (1996: 123).
8. For more on the economic aspect of the temple, see Stein (1960).
9. A conversation with Śrīnivasa, a thirty-year-old pilgrim from the USA, 22 October 2006.
10. For the relevance of "conversational narratives" see Prasad (2007: 19–20).
11. A conversation with Mastan Vali, a fifty-year-old pilgrim, 21 October 2006.
12. For a detailed version of this story in Srirangam, see Davis (2004). For a recent news report on the visits of Muslims to Tirumala, see Neelima (2010).

18. The militant ascetic traditions of India and Sri Lanka

William Harman

The notion of "militant Hinduism" might seem to the casual observer a bizarre contradiction. After all, Hinduism – as Western observers have portrayed it – has a reputation for tolerance. It is often associated in popular writings with a religious perspective that endorses pacifism. For example, in the year 2000 a group of the most influential American scholars of Hinduism signed an impassioned public petition decrying the fact that India had test-detonated three atomic explosives at Pokhran in northwest India. They deplored the fact that the government used Hindu religious terms and imagery to portray the nuclear tests. But the imagery was not exclusively Hindu: the tests were deliberately scheduled to coincide with the Buddha's birthday. The scholars' petition read, in part:

> We ... protest the use of religious imagery to sanctify the use of nuclear weapons in India. ... Hindus have used their tradition of non-violence to brilliant political effect ... The present use of Hindu imagery to valorize weapons designed only for mass destruction of human life is a travesty of such a tradition of peace. The use of such terms as "**Agni**" [god of fire], "**Pṛthvī**" [goddess of the earth], and "**Shakti Peeth**" [powerful location from which divine goddess energy emanates] to describe the Indian nuclear arsenal is a betrayal of what the Hindu tradition has contributed to the building of world peace.[1]

There is little doubt that Hinduism, Buddhism and Jainism, three major religions originating on the Indian subcontinent, are portrayed in their ideal forms as peace-loving traditions. Mahatma Gandhi's espousal of ***ahimsa*** ("non-violence") – a religious value he borrowed from Jainism – has perhaps become the most well-known term associated with pacifism's role in Indian political theory and in Ghandi's strategic approach to gaining political concessions through ***satyagraha***, a term loosely translated as "truth force" or "soul force". In addition, traditions associating the great Indian King Asoka (304–232 BCE) with Buddhist pacifism reinforce the somewhat distorted image of a bovine, pastoral, bucolic Indian history that supposedly followed Asoka's reign.

But we need not go far to discover clear evidences of militancy and martial predilections in Hindu practices. Standard iconic conventions depict Hindu deities replete with deadly weapons – swords, spears, chakras, bludgeons, bows and arrows. And the classic religious lifestyle of renunciation to which the good Hindu, especially males, should aspire, has at various points in Indian history been associated with militant violence. This was especially true between the fifteenth and nineteenth centuries, but remnants of that ethos linger.

I speak here of the Hindu "holy man", the renouncer known also as a *sannyāsi*. The terms *sādhu*, *yogi*, ***gosain*** and ***vairāghi*** are more specific elaborations of this category of people who have renounced or simply rejected the normal life of a working, married householder. Their lifestyles entail various forms of ascetic activity, some quite severe, others less so. A very small percentage of Indian men pursue this lifestyle. In principle, their goal is to achieve a spiritual awareness not available to people living ordinary work-a-day lives. That awareness emerges out of specific ascetic disciplines. Freedom from worldly concerns and emotional attachments permits, they maintain, a pursuit of goals that transcends earthly limits. Most live on alms and engage in meditation and prayer while wandering from one holy site to another. Certain groups, particularly those who follow a spiritual teacher or *guru*, practice a range of austerities in order to hone their spiritual consciousness. They will often defy conventional norms of respectable society by going naked, or nearly so. They may consume substances most folk find unsuitable, disreputable or unthinkable: in ritual contexts they consume their own faeces, alcohol, hashish, human flesh and mud, among other things. Others choose a diet of nothing but fruits or vegetables. They systematically push the limits of physical endurance, such as taking a vow to hold one arm high above the head for uninterrupted years at a time until the arm atrophies and the fingernails in its clinched fist grow through the hand and out the other side. Others will stand on one leg for months or years at a time, effectively becoming permanent cripples. The prosaic image of the ascetic who lies on a bed of nails pales in comparison with these long-term tasks of spiritual/physical endurance. Concern for physical injury or annihilation is considered a worldly concern, something well beneath men of the ascetic's spiritual stature. As ascetics who have "died to the world", their quest to overcome the fear of death, and death itself, is tested and confirmed in resolutely facing substantially daunting odds. Not unusual, for example, is an ascetic's vow to venture alone up into the treacherous winter snows of the Himalayas, clothed lightly, if at all, and with no supplies for survival. Such tests of endurance often involve embracing a frozen death on the sacred peaks associated with the quintessential ascetic deity, Śiva. Another such scenario, more typical of eighteenth- and nineteenth-century ascetics, involved marching barefoot and stark naked into battle against armour-clad military adversaries. Ascetics understand themselves to have moved beyond the consequences of inflicting or sustaining injury and death. They can act with impunity because standards for suffering and punishment are worldly conventions, and so do not apply to ascetics.

James Lochtefeld makes the case eloquently for a not-so-latent violent strain in Hindu history as it emerged in modern history in Muslim–Hindu tensions, focusing on a massive Hindu assault on a Muslim mosque in Ayodhya on 6 December 1992. He describes how a group of people, including assorted holy men, ascetics and *sādhus*, "managed to level the 430 year old structure in a little less that six hours" (Lochtefeld 1994: 587).

While the Vishva Hindu Parishad, a radically militant Hindu political party, was in the forefront of organizing this assault in Ayodhya, Lochtefeld observes that *sādhus* and *sannyāsis* were among the leaders of this violent attack:

> Aside from their role in forming the VHP's policy, ascetics are an important part of its membership. There were many ascetics in the crowd attempting to storm and destroy the disputed mosque both in October 1990 and in December 1992, and their presence lends religious respectability to the movement as a whole.
>
> (Lochtefeld 1994: 588)

Lochtefeld's association of Hindu ascetics with violence is by no means new. According to a personal communication from one of the directors of a college study-in-India programme, an American college student traveling alone in India in 2000, and interacting unwisely with ascetics, was apparently murdered by one of them (Rizzo 2000). In my limited experiences with ascetics I have always been advised by Indian companions to tread cautiously. It is wise, I am told, to avoid their displeasure. Their curses are feared. Because they are "dead to the world", many having literally presided over their own symbolic funerals, they are agents who answer to no accepted norms of worldly behaviour. Having renounced their family ties, their names and their past, they will generally not care to talk about their past. Who they once were no longer exists. By Indian case law they are no longer a legal entity, no longer able to claim or inherit property. Technically, they are beyond the official authority of the law. Though they operate in reference to conventions governing other ascetics and their *guru*, theirs is generally an antinomian perspective on the world: worldly ethical prescriptions are irrelevant. They are amoral rather than immoral.

They may lapse either into physical or verbal abuse at any moment – if they will speak to you at all. Their concern is not so much with holiness or sanctity or purity, but rather with that one element Gerardus Van der Leeuw long ago associated with the quintessential religious quest, which is the acquisition of power (Van der Leeuw 1967: esp. 23–52). Again, the issue is not worldly power, but a perceived spiritual/supernatural power that enables ascetics to be exempt from the limits and standards to which ordinary humans are inevitably bound.

Lochtefeld joins a growing number of scholars concerned with the logic and dynamics of militant and violent asceticism. J. N. Farquhar, writing in 1925, was one of the first Western scholars to address the issue openly and directly. He attributed militant asceticism to two factors: first, the reverence of ascetics for the frightful, intimidating Hindu deity **Bhairava**, a ferocious form of Śiva. In imitating the appearance of that deity, says Farquhar: "The *yogi* went naked, had his hair in a great matted cone on the top of his head, carried a sword in one hand and a cup of liquor in the other, and, if possible, he also wore a garland of human skulls hanging from his neck" (1925: 436). The second, more important factor was, he said, the necessity for Hindu *yogis*, *sādhus*, *sannyāsis*, *gosains* and *vairāghis* to protect themselves from the violent depredations of invading Islamic Sūfi fakirs. This second reason achieved wide explanatory power in the later work of W. G. Orr (1940). Orr attributed the beginnings of ascetic militancy to the Islamic invasions of the twelfth century, which brought into India large numbers of Muslim fakirs who had experience in warfare. They were supposed to have wreaked havoc among the peaceful Indian population, and especially among the unarmed ascetics. Predatory Muslims, said Orr, staked out sacred pilgrimage and bathing sites where they regularly ambushed the heathen, polytheistic Hindu ascetics. In response, Orr believes, the first order of ascetics, *yogis* or ***naths***, armed themselves for self-defence. Other ascetic groups followed their lead, discovering that doing so not only assured them greater safety, but a more secure supply of available food. Laypeople took much more seriously an armed ascetic's request for a handout since the reluctance to accommodate such implicit requests carried the potential of turning out very badly for non-compliant layfolk: a seventeenth-century south Asian version, perhaps, of "trick or treat".

David Lorenzen took up this issue in 1978 with considerably more sophistication. He emphasized a theatre of battle between Muslims and ascetics on which a competition for material wealth emerged as the basic factor catalysing the formation of militant ascetic Hindu groups. Still, he accepted the proposition that Hindu–Muslim enmity was the cause of ascetic violence, and that ascetics functioning as militants were able to control their destinies by brokering power and influence in the regions where they operated (Lorenzen 1978).

Whether there was any single impetus for militant asceticism will not be easy to determine in Indian history. We know that armed ascetics are mentioned in the seventh-century Sanskrit drama *Harṣacaritra,* and in the eleventh-century Sanskrit comedy *Prabhodhacandrodaya* (Lochtefeld 1994: 590), well before Islamic Sūfi ascetics presumably roamed central India in purportedly predatory and violent bands. Perhaps the most eloquent objection to this reading into India's past of a violent enmity between Muslim and Hindu emerges in the impressive work of William Pinch, who contends that an interpretation focusing on Hindu–Muslim enmity as an explanation of how India's ascetics adopted violence and militancy comes out of an anachronistic reading of history (Pinch 2006: 6–7). Pinch posits that during the sixteenth and seventeenth centuries, when bands of roving militant ascetics were common in northern India, the lines between Hindu and Muslim asceticism were indistinctly drawn. Later caricatures of the non-violent, victimized Hindu ascetic and of the violent, predatory Muslim worked to reinforce this constructed narrative of a defensive posture assumed by Hindu ascetics. The simple fact is that the historic facts do not seem to reinforce theories that fix on militant Hindu asceticism as a response to militant Islamic asceticism. For one thing, the most significant clashes between armed ascetic groups were instances of combat among two or more Hindu ascetic groups seeking to control land at holy shrines. It is also true that Hindu ascetics and Muslim fakirs fought together frequently in the eighteenth century in Calcutta against the East India Company (*ibid.*: 29). The first historically verifiable account of militant ascetic violence seems to have occurred in 1567 when the Emperor Akbar accidentally became embroiled in an impending skirmish between two Hindu ascetic groups armed to the teeth. The event is referred to by Farquhar, Orr, Lorenzen and Pinch. Pinch's description is the most detailed. He describes how an auspicious eclipse was occurring near the sacred riverside shrine of the deity Thaneswar, and how two groups of Śaiva ascetics were demanding the right to occupy prime land that would enable them to gain access to pilgrims coming to the festival and to the alms the pilgrims would surely dispense. Historians mention 500 *yogis* and about half that number of *sannyāsis*. Akbar sought to mediate the dispute in vain, and finally agreed to withdraw at a safe distance to watch the hand-to-hand, close-range slaughter. Hoping for a fair fight, he agreed to send some of his own men to fight on the side of the *sannyāsis*, who had, it seems, arrived first on the prized real estate. In the end, the *yogis* suffered grievously, and their leader was beheaded. "The Emperor greatly enjoyed the sight", says Pinch, taking his descriptions from four Persian sources (*ibid.*: 96–7).

As we follow the history of armed ascetic groups into the nineteenth century, we discover that they allied themselves in a dizzying array of shifting allegiances, fighting on the side of Muslim rulers, sometimes with the British, and sometimes quite independently. Anup Giri, one of the most successful *guru*–generals of an ascetic army, commanded between 5,000 and 9,000 naked ascetic soldiers.

I intend to argue in this chapter that the discipline associated with the ascetic life of these *yogis*, *sannyāsis*, *gosains* and others adopting the renunciatory life of Hinduism is a lifestyle that naturally gives rise to the possibility – though certainly not the inevitability – of militant violence. Circumstances contributing to the development of militant asceticism include an influential *guru* or leader who is willing to encourage vows and spiritually ascetic disciplines that take the form of militant activity. Areas in which the rule of law was lax, if not altogether absent, were most likely to foster these groups. And periods of serious famine or drought contributed to militant asceticism because young children were often donated to swell the ranks of ascetic militant groups when their families could not provide for them. As the size of communities grew, so did the need to insure security and food supplies also grow. An ability to use force in this context became a clear advantage.

We know that the ascetic, in turning his back on society, renounces normal life, "dying to the world". The ascetic pursues a deathless state in which his fierce and violent disciplines are designed to move him beyond the normal limits of pain, physical discomfort and mortality. In the Indian tradition, the human condition inevitably entails pain and suffering. What distinguishes the deities is the fact that they do not suffer. In torturing his body, and in learning to endure pain, the pain is transformed. It becomes the very means to conquer suffering. It becomes the source of masochistic pleasure as the ascetic demonstrates to himself and to others that he is well on his way to achieving immunity from the human categories of pain, suffering and vulnerability to the elements. Everyday Hindus thus venerate these ascetics, largely in proportion to the rigours their ascetic practices involve.[2]

Jeffrey Masson has proposed that the root of all asceticism is disgust with the world, and a depression that manifests frequently in masochism or aggression:

> I believe that the concern voiced ubiquitously by the ascetic in Indian literature – *vairāgya* or ***nirveda**, "world weariness" or "disgust"* – is an oblique reference to the affective disorder known as sadness when mild, depression when strong, and melancholia when severe. The most striking example of this phrase is one known to every Sanskritist: ... "On the very day that one conceives disgust for the world, on that very day should one set out to wander alone."
>
> (Masson 1976: 618)

Masson cites as his source *Jābālopaniṣad* IV, saying "I do not think that in this context 'depression' as a translation of *nirveda* or *vairagya* would be very far off", and moves to discuss depression as a form of internalized aggression (*ibid.*). It is a bit strange that Masson does not take up the subject of the militant ascetic, for so much of what he says is compatible with the phenomenon. Two examples:

1. In representing the ascetic as a masochist, Masson cites R. M. Loewenstein as follows: "By imagining or producing scenes of [his own] torture or punishment ... the masochist excludes the possibility of being tortured or punished in an unexpected or uncontrollable way" (Loewenstein 1957: 226). The ascetic, in other words, is intimately involved in conjuring forms of violence, usually of a masochistic nature as a way to protect himself and to enable his own spiritual achievements. As Ramdas Lamb has pointed out so clearly, the ascetic is defined by his vows, and those vows are almost always associated with a fierce discipline that implies violence or deprivations bordering on violence (Lamb 2006: 183).
2. Yet, says Masson, almost as an afterthought, "if the ascetic were to do to others what he does to himself, he would be a homicidal maniac rather

> than a saint". Thank goodness the preponderant majority of ascetics have chosen to engage in what Masson would label as masochist activity rather than the sadistic violence especially typical of the large groups of ascetic militants of the seventeenth and eighteenth centuries.

In discussing this phenomenon in psychoanalytic terms I risk appearing to minimize what many would term basic spiritual aspirations of asceticism. There is no doubt that ascetics, by virtue of their graduated vows, are dedicated to the notion of transcending the world in which they find themselves. In honing their bodies as fighting machines, by practising severe disciplines that produce hard bodies able to survive long periods without food or water and under severe stress, they do, in fact, transcend normal limits. But perhaps most important is that when they enter into battle deliberately handicapped, stark naked and barefoot, lacking any armour whatsoever, they face head-on the prospect both of encountering death and of conquering it by moving beyond it. The ascetic seeks to conquer death and to remain in that deathless state. As the *Hathayogapradīpika* would have it:

> 107. The yogi who has passed beyond all the states and is freed from all thoughts and who appears as if dead is liberated without doubt.
>
> 108. A yogi in Samadhi [a state of intense concentration] is not swallowed up by death; he is not affected by action; he cannot fall under the influence of others. ...
>
> 111. A yogi in Samādhi is not affected by heat or cold, pain or pleasure, honour or dishonour.
>
> 112. Verily, he is a liberated one, who is clear-minded, who is in the waking state, yet appears to be in sleep, devoid of inhalation and exhalation.
>
> 113. A yogi in Samādhi is not vulnerable to any weapons, not assailable by any persons, not subject to control by the use of magical incantations. (Svatmarama 1972: 82–3; cited by Pinch 2006: 14)

"For the *yogi*, the conquest of death (and by extension, the limitations of time and space) is an end in itself; it is the product of esoteric knowledge and practices, available to a select few" (Pinch 2006: 15). What better and more dramatic way to face down death and to move beyond it than to engage in mortal combat? It becomes a win–win situation for the ascetic. It does not matter if he dies. He is already dead to the world. If he conquers, he is confirmed in the deathless state he has already attained. And conquer these ascetics most certainly did. Their obvious fearlessness in the face of battle their opponents found unnerving. Many felt that ascetics had magical powers, supernatural strength that fortified them in combat. Indeed, many of the ascetics themselves felt this way. Masson suggests this in discussing the ***siddhis*** (special powers) ascetic disciplines are believed to produce:

> So what is it that the ascetic says? He says, "I am not anonymous, insignificant. I am important and central. I am not alone; I live in a world peopled with mythic figures. I am not powerless; I can create magic – I can fly, I can become big or small. I can remember my past births. I can know everything. I can go anywhere."
>
> (Masson 1976: 624)

We might be tempted to suppose that Hinduism's militant asceticism appears today only sporadically, as in the Ayodhya incident mentioned above. But I want to suggest that it still informs modern attitudes and strategies emerging from time to time in south Asia. My case in point focuses on the small island nation of Sri Lanka and the recent cataclysmic civil war waged there. Sri Lanka in the late 1970s and early 1980s saw the growth and development of a separatist army, predominantly Hindu, called the Liberation Tigers of Tamil̲ Eelam (LTTE), usually referred to simply as the Tamil̲ Tigers. That army, until quite recently, operated a remarkably spirited military insurgency against the Buddhist Sri Lankan government.[3] The Tigers claim the dubious distinction of having first designed and used to devastating effect the suicide bomber belt. One of the most distinguishing features of the Tamil̲ Tigers, a feature they share with the militant ascetic movements of northern India, is their sense of being able to accomplish remarkable feats in the face of unlikely circumstances, feats believed to be the direct result of their ascetic training, extraordinary discipline, and unwavering concentration and commitment. They became an organized group under their revered *guru* and preceptor Vellupillai Prabakaran in 1976. Prabakaran was a devoted Hindu and spoke glowingly of the ideals espoused by ascetic Hindu renouncers. With an army of about 8,000 at the pinnacle of their strength they faced down and won several convincing victories against the Sri Lankan government-armed forces of about 124,000. When the Indian army intervened on behalf of the Sri Lankan government, its overwhelming numbers and massive firepower suffered a humiliating defeat at the hands of the Tigers. The Tigers then went on to murder India's prime minister, Rajiv Gandhi, in a suicide bomber attack perpetrated by a woman. Another significant element of the Tamil̲ Tiger militia is the fact that women constituted nearly a quarter of their fighting force. Women endured the same disciplines and ascetic lifestyles as the men, and evoked a sense of wonderment and fear among male Sri Lankan soldiers who suspected bizarre supernatural capacities among women who could perform so effectively men's work of killing and destruction.

The Tamil̲ Tiger cause, many insist, is not religious, but rather a nationalist movement, secular by self-profession, committed to achieving self-determination for the twenty per cent Tamil̲ minority population of Sri Lanka. While the Tigers embrace no officially recognized tradition such as Hinduism, Christianity or Islam, they have forged a religious perspective on their struggle. It includes uniquely sacred rituals, a sacred terminology, sacred spaces, and a sacred doctrine based on a sacred narrative that extols the destiny of the Tamil̲ people and their culture. The Tamil̲ Tiger movement is shot through with religious imagery, and much of it draws on the assumptions of asceticism, sacrifice, discipline and achieving a state that elevates members above the entanglements of this world and above death itself.

Tamil̲ Tiger recruits went through a rigorous initiatory process in which they pledged absolute fealty and obedience to the leader/*guru* Prabhakaran, as is the case with many communities of Indian ascetics. Like the ascetic endurances of Indian renouncers, their physical training was difficult, and often involved long periods of isolation in wilderness tracts.[4] Recruits were required to adhere to vows of celibacy and abstention from alcohol, drugs and tobacco. Because there were both men and women in the cadres, celibacy proved to be the most challenging rule, and several recruits were executed because they were unable to conform to that directive (Narayan Swamy 2008: 204). After recruits joined the organization they were required to renounce contact with former acquaintances and family unless those contacts were for strategic ends. Tiger recruits signalled their commitment to the cause by donning the *kuppi* necklace, a vial of potent cyanide worn as a testament that they accepted their death, and would initiate it by biting into the vial when threatened by capture. It represented the death to which they aspired as potential sacrificial martyrs. With the *kuppi* they were able to achieve a death that guaranteed "life beyond" as a martyr (Schalk 1997: 74). Poems, songs and orations were common among Tamil̲ Tiger groups as they extolled the virtue of death by cyanide, a symbolism similar in the Hindu ascetic tradition to the ritualized funeral that marks the ascetic's entrance into the life of renunciation: in a formal funeral ceremony the renunciant watches as an effigy of himself burns on a makeshift funeral pyre, signalling that he has been cremated and is no longer alive to this world. And so, in the formal ceremony of bestowing on a person the *kuppi*, that person embraces his or her own death as inevitable, honourable, and pointing to a life beyond as a powerful martyr.

There is little doubt that the Tamil̲ Tigers developed an elaborate cult of martyrs based to no small degree on the model provided by the renunciatory tradition of the Hindu ascetic. The reverence for these martyrs, both dead and committed to death, invites comparison with India's ascetics:

> Prabhakaran, the leader of the LTTE, requested the people to venerate those who die in the battle for Eelam (The Tamil̲ nation) as *sannyāsis* (ascetics) who renounced their personal desires and transcended their egoistic existence for a common cause of higher virtue. (Chandrakanthan 2000: 164)

Tamil Tiger cadres whose deaths issue from conviction and commitment to the cause became deathless in popular perception. They were understood to have entered another state, much like *samādhi*, becoming minor deities. One of the remarkable features of the Tigers' ritual tradition was that of burying rather than cremating the remains of these deceased martyrs. The Tamil Tigers prized highly the burial grounds of the martyrs, which they understood to be temples where martyrs may be worshipped because their spirits remain there. Relatives who visited these burial sites engaged in dialogues with the "great heroes" (**Maveerar**) as they might in pleading with deities in a temple. In interviews with Christiana Natali, relatives of the deceased martyrs vehemently insisted that the burial areas were not conventional cemeteries. Rather, they insisted, these "resting places" (***tuvillum ilam***) are temples and therefore sources for those still living to achieve spiritual and inspirational invigoration (Natali 2007). It is significant that in the Indian tradition ascetics are among the few groups of people for whom burial is appropriate (Malamoud 1989: 65). Their graves are regarded as sources of divine protective power (Roberts 2005: 499).

The identification of these Maveerar with divine personages who have moved beyond death is quite explicit, claims Natali (2007). Stuart Blackburn documents the cults found in modern southwestern India that focus on the worship of commemorative stones erected to heroes who have died in defence of justice and righteousness. These figures are buried, not cremated, and their spirits return annually to visit and assist the living (Blackburn 1985). Roberts notes that the term "Bhairava" (a deity, you may recall, associated with the earliest of militant Indian ascetics) is used generically to designate the spirits inhabiting these hero stones, and that some of the stones are offered weapons such as spears, knives and billhooks (Roberts 2005: 500), the very instruments carried by militant ascetics into battle.

If the Tamil Tigers can be seen as ascetics, how can we place them into a larger frame of religious commitment and devotion?[5] They are definitive in denying a necessary commitment to Hinduism. I focus on the statement of commitment Tigers were required to adopt, a simple pledge of faith. Michael Roberts describes the "holy aim" (***putantiram***) of the Tigers, the loyalty oath that involved the reiteration of the credo that is widely proclaimed in many posters and publications: "The task [thirst] of the Tigers [is to achieve] Motherland Tamililam" (Roberts 2005: 496). Their demands in war always focused on a safe, separate territory in the north and east of Sri Lanka where Tamils and the Tamil language might flourish, apart from obstruction or oppression the Sri Lankan government might impose on Tamils and Tamil culture. In the mid-1950s the Sri Lankan government declared that Tamil could no longer be used in official government communication, and it imposed significant disadvantages on all Tamil speakers when it came to securing university admissions or positions in government service.

I propose, then, that the Tamil Tigers borrowed many of the features of Indian ascetics, but they did so in the cause of a deeply religious commitment to a movement larger than simple devotion to martyred spirits. The Tigers martyred themselves for the cause of the Tamil̲ language and the culture it transmits, and it is their devotion to that language that constitutes the basis of their commitment.

It is tempting to want to write off a commitment to the "Motherland" of Tamil̲ as something more mundane, and less lofty, than religious devotion. "Linguistic nationalism" might be more appealing to the analyst. Or perhaps we might prefer to call it a secular dedication of a people to the preservation of a homeland and a familiar culture and language. But I would argue against these minimalist explanations, fortified by the impressive case made by Sumati Ramaswamy (Ramaswamy 1997). She writes about the passionate dedication and devotion among Tamil̲s for their language and culture. It is a commitment shared by Indian as well as Sri Lankan Tamil̲s.

Tamil̲ speakers of India have faced an increasingly aggressive central government attempt to marginalize Tamil̲ language and culture by imposing the northern language of Hindi, often referred to by Tamil̲s with a sneer as "*antha vada moli*" ("that northern language"). The result has been dramatic: dozens of Tamil̲s have committed suicide for the sake of their devotion to the Tamil̲ language. Some have soaked themselves with gasoline and died in the flames. Others have died in hunger fasts or taken poison. Commemorative statues and hero stones have been erected in their memory, and in 1968 the ruling DMK party of Tamilnadu, which advocates the sacred quality of Tamil̲, began the annual celebration of Language Martyrs Day on 25 January. After one of the most dramatic self-immolations by a man named Chinnasami in 1965,

> several other young men followed in his footsteps and immolated themselves. Today, in various devotional tracts, their names are repeated, over and again, almost like a litany: Sivalingam, Aranganathan, Veerappan, Muthu, and Sarangapani. Three other young men ... died after consuming poison. ... The varying stories of all these young men have been narrativized in the devotional community to conform to the image of the selfless Tamil̲ martyr, overwriting individual aspirations or passions they might have had. Each of them, prior to death, professed his devotion to Tamil̲ and lamented Tamil̲'s fate at the hands of Hindi. Some left behind letters ... in which they proclaimed their deaths to be "in protest against the imposition of Hindi, and as a sacrifice at the altar of Tamil̲".
>
> (Ramaswamy 1997: 232–3)

But it takes more than martyrs to lay claim to a devotion that constitutes what we might call a religious consciousness. Tamil̲ as a language is consistently and self-consciously portrayed as a deity; in fact, as a mother goddess. And I am not simply talking about rhetorical flourishes, hyperbole, or metaphor. Iconographies of "Mother Tamil̲", the goddess, appear in religious drawings, posters and magazines. Her carved images can be found in many temples where devotees regularly pay her respect. An entire temple is dedicated to her in the Indian town of Karaikudi. One Tamil̲ poet from Sri Lanka invokes conventions from *bhakti* devotional poetry in praising Tamil̲ Tay (Mother Tamil̲):

> Like [our] mother, she gives us food;
> Like [our] father, she gives us learning.
> Like [our] spouse, she creates pleasure at home
> Like [our] child, she gives sweet words, pleasant to our ears.
>
> (Quoted in Pillai 1947: 86)

The thousands of poetic panegyrics composed in honour of this goddess describe her relations with other deities, such as Śiva, Murukan̲ and Meenakshi. Some claim her words to be more authoritative than the Vedas, and government officials running for office are always well advised to sponsor special *pūjās* for her at one of her altars, preferably in her temple in Karaikudi.

In summary, I have proposed that the example of the militant Hindu ascetic in India's history has served to inspire at least one militant ascetic movement beyond India's southern shores. The model of the militant Indian ascetic in Hinduism constitutes an inspiring example for the militant Tamil̲ Tiger movement of Sri Lanka. For both the Indian ascetic and the Tamil̲ Tiger, disciplined devotion to a cause represented by a deity and/or a divinized *guru* affords access to supernatural status. That status offers a path to immortality and to the eventual conquest of death itself. For both groups, physical discipline, resolutely taken vows, renunciation of sexuality and the normal life of the householder, combined with willingness to "face down" death in daunting feats of endurance and bravery – all constitute a means to achieving a definitive immortality.

Notes

1. The full text of the letter can be found in the RISA-L Archive at www.acusd.edu/theo/risa-l/archive/msg00782.html. Those interested in following the entire thread of the discussion should start with the thread listing "atomic bomb" in the RISA-L Archive, at www.acusd.edu/~lnelson/risa. See my full discussion of the implications of this letter in Harman (2000).
2. For images of sadhus, see http://forum.santabanta.com/showthread.htm?233336-The-Yogis-Of-India-And-Nepal (accessed June 2013).
3. The Sri Lankan government has termed the Tamil̲ Tigers a "terrorist" organization. The description remains a disputed one.
4. See Masson's (1976) comment on the isolation in which Hindu ascetics often choose to live. See Daniels's (2000) description of the arduous "penances" LTTE recruits experienced.
5. www.tamilnet.com is a newswire service focusing on news from a Tamil perspective, and associated images.

19. Afterword

P. Pratap Kumar

Here I want to reflect on some theoretical issues emanating from the materials we have presented in this volume. My purpose here is not to write a comprehensive essay on the theory and method in the study of Hinduism, but rather to highlight some issues that have significance for our scholarly pursuit. In the introduction, I have alluded to why text-based presentation of Hinduism is inadequate in offering a more realistic view of how Hinduism is practised throughout south Asia, as well as further afield. There is some parallel between how Indian history generally has been presented over the years and how Hinduism has come to be studied. We have all become used to studying Indian history through the British Imperial historians who divided it into three parts – Hindu India, Muslim India and British India. Therefore, when we read about Hinduism, it is all about that ancient Hindu India unlocked through ancient Sanskrit texts, as though Hinduism has stopped evolving after those texts were composed. The fact is that Hinduism continues to evolve to this day. Or, if evolution of Hinduism is admitted, it is generally presented as if it evolved from Veda to the popular, Vedic religion assimilating elements of regional traditions in the process. The model of how Christianity is understood vis-à-vis the Old Testament may also have been partly responsible for how other religions such as Hinduism have been approached. That is to say, for instance, to understand medieval Hindu traditions or various regional popular traditions, we need to go back to Vedas. In other words, all Hinduism is generally explained with reference to ancient Vedic traditions. This linear chronological approach has skewed our understanding of Hinduism and committed an injustice against the vernacular regional traditions. To assume that Hinduism evolved from top to bottom is not only a gross misunderstanding, but more importantly it undermines any attempt to explore alternative ways of seeing Hinduism. Even when regional temples, such as Madurai Meenakshi temple where Sundareswara and Meenakshi are worshipped, relate Sundareswara and Meenakshi to classical mythological figures of Śiva and Pārvatī, such reflections are only retrospectively done rather than the temple priests being conscious of such relations on a daily basis. Such relations are less important for their daily ritual.[1] Thus, instead of traversing through the vast regions of the Indian subcontinent and taking account of the local significance of those traditions, we have simplified our task of learning about Hinduism through texts that only allowed us to see it with tunnel vision. In this regard, this volume departs from the previous attempts to offer insights into Hinduism.

Thus, it is necessary to highlight two things about this book. The first point is the diversity of Hindu practice reflected through oral narratives. It is important to recognize that this diversity is not simply based on exploring different textual traditions, but rather different regional and vernacular traditions that are based on oral narratives. The roles oral narratives play in the shaping of diverse Hindu practices have been generally underestimated. I believe that it has to do with the rise of Vedānta based middle-class Hinduism that overestimated the role of texts in Hindu practice. What has complicated the situation in the academic study of Hinduism is that it was first presented to the West as an alternative spiritual practice exemplified in Vedānta through the erudition of *Swamis* such as Vivekananda. In that sense, Vedānta might have offered an alternative spirituality to the West. But studying Hinduism is and ought to be more than textual presentations of what might have been considered *par excellence*. Therefore, the second point that we need to emphasize is that the oral nature of the multiple narratives of Hinduism affords us an opportunity to describe Hinduism through ordinary people who practice their traditions rather than solely depend on the elite and the experts. Certainly, experts matter. However, over-reliance on their authoritative words not only takes us away from the ordinary folks that we come across on a daily basis, but also deprives us of the enormous diversity that exists in Hindu practice. In this volume, therefore, we focused on multiple regional narratives of Hindus that are deeply rooted in their oral transmission and in their lived context. The transmitters of these narratives are not necessarily experts or elite spokespersons of the various traditions, but rather ordinary folk who practice their traditions as passed down to them from their previous generations, be that in the diaspora context or in the south Asian context.

It is only in recent times that scholars began to pay serious attention to contemporary Hinduism dispersed in various regions of the subcontinent and the diaspora. It is not as if we do not have sufficient information on these diverse traditions both within the subcontinent and abroad. We have indeed reached a stage in our scholarly pursuit where we have an abundance of materials available to us today on diverse oral narratives from various regions on lived Hinduism. Scores of scholars not only from the mainstream religious studies discipline, but also from the related fields of social sciences, history, art, music, *inter alia*, have offered us in the last two decades both descriptive and analytical materials on the diverse traditions that we associate with Hinduism. As a result, today we are more knowledgeable about the diverse ritual, mythological and historical traditions of Hindus from various parts of India and abroad.

Furthermore, these are contemporary lived traditions that practising Hindus observe today. It is my conviction that we are now in a position to bring more enriched and diverse narratives of Hinduism to our students and also to share them with our colleagues not only in the field of Hinduism but also in the broader field of comparative religions. Bringing these diverse narratives may perhaps substantively change the way we have described and analysed Hinduism in the past primarily through texts. On a methodological and theoretical level this may also offer us both new challenges and opportunities to engage in redescribing Hinduism and reconceptualizing our definitions of it.

The idea in this volume is to focus on contemporary practice of Hinduism both in the subcontinent and abroad. It is not intended as an exhaustive attempt, but a moderate one that highlights the difference so that it prods us to think of ways in which we may bring coherence to that diversity. Here, by "coherence", I do not mean "unity". It is also not just for the sake of showing the difference, but also to underscore the dynamic and continuously changing character of Hinduism. Perhaps it is here that we fundamentally depart from the text-based representations as they have tended to freeze the dynamic traditions in time and space. By focusing on contemporary Hindu practice, we have the opportunity to describe it in its dynamic and vibrant context. This does not in any way minimize the value of text, but rather the context offers us the opportunity to make sense of the text and interpret it in ways that we have not done before. A good example would be to take a look at how diversely the Bhagavad Gītā has been read and interpreted in the modern context and not only through the lives of some eminent people of our time, such as Mahatma Gandhi and Robert Oppenheimer (to take two completely different individuals). Another example might be to consider the Mahābhārata play directed in our time by Peter Brooks, or consider the numerous enactments of the Rāmāyaṇa and the Mahābhārata, both on television and on the stage in the many villages of India. These many renderings of the old texts in our modern times are indeed the commentaries for many practising Hindus. If we freeze the interpretation of the Gītā or the Rāmāyaṇa through the classical commentaries, we miss the ingenious ways in which these ancient texts can speak to us today.

We also depart in some important ways from focusing mainly or only on the dominant traditions of the past, such as the Veda as the origin of Hinduism or the Vedānta as the quintessence of Hinduism. These texts and sources continue to be dominant and relevant in the lives of some modern groups belonging to new movements of Hinduism, as well as some orthopractic Hindus. Therefore, it is not in any way to underestimate the value of these sources of Hinduism even for modern times, but rather to move away from privileging them in our discourse on Hinduism. This is the fundamental methodological shift in this volume. There are many narratives that have been lost along the away in our telling of the story of Hinduism. Our tendency to tell the dominant narrative through textual traditions or through Brāhmanical intellectuals could miss how millions of Hindus outside those privileged circles make sense of being Hindu. As early as 1955 McKim Marriott brought to our attention something profound, but we do not seem to have paid attention to it. While documenting the lives of

Hindus in a small village called Kishan Garhi in Uttar Pradesh, he noticed something interesting. The landed castes rooted in their Brāhmanical version of Hinduism were celebrating the Gobardhan festival. As tradition has it, they would recall the significance of Kṛṣṇa as the cattle-giver or cattle-nourisher. But on the other side of the village the low-caste Hindus were also celebrating the very same festival. The difference is that they reversed the story. For them Kṛṣṇa was not cattle-nourisher, but the giver of cow dung. For them, being landless and with no cattle, it made no sense to think of Kṛṣṇa as cattle-giver, but since they were free to collect the cow dung on the fields so that they could dry it and use it as an alternative to firewood, it made abundant sense to think of Kṛṣṇa as the giver of cow dung. All they needed to do was to make a semantic twist on the word *gobardhan*. If we split the compound word *go* + *bardhan* in Sanskrit, we could translate it as *go* (cattle) + *bardhan/vardhan* (nourisher).[2] But the landless and casteless Hindus outside the village broke the compound word differently. First of all, for them the word is just another Hindi word and did not have its Sanskrit ruminations. So, they ended up breaking the compound as *gobar* (cow dung) + *dhan* (wealth). A semantic twist from a different cultural perspective can bring out a different narrative of Hinduism.

These narratives are manifold. But the dominant narrative of the Brāhmanical intellectuals can obfuscate them to the detriment of our complete appreciation of Hinduism. Fortunately, as indicated earlier, some scholars in the last couple of decades deviated from the beaten track and went in search of these peripheral narratives that are not only rich additions to the overall story of Hinduism, but also provide us with important links to the past. To give some idea of this, let me call our attention to some such scholars. While some of us were most busy reading texts and interpreting Hinduism through them, Diana Eck goes off on a detour, as it were, to Benares, and calls our attention to another way of "seeing" (*darśana*) Hinduism, as if lifting its philosophical veil.

In an important sense, the narratives of Hinduism that we have included in this volume are counter to any attempt to impose a single origin theory for Hinduism, or to suggest that there is a single essence of Hinduism overall. My task as the editor is not to discover in these diverse narratives some over-arching and abiding unity, but rather to relate them in a coherent way so that they neither lose their narrative integrity and autonomy in telling their visions of Hinduism, nor lead us into the blind alley of assumptions that all these narratives lead us to the same destination.

Hinduism has been called polytheism, pantheism, pan-en-theism, henotheism, kata-henotheism, and so on and so forth. The attempt of all these to view Hinduism as a unified system did not yield the desired result, but instead the diverse traditions that we associate with Hinduism continue to evolve as we become increasingly aware of their global context. When Hinduism was inaugurated into the family of "world religions" as a late-comer long after Buddhism, whatever might have been the intention of such inclusion, the three key notions that defined religion – a Christian notion of God, a single text as scripture and a clearly laid-out doctrine – came under enormous pressure. Hinduism could not be defined as religion under any of these key notions. If Hinduism could not be defined as religion under the normative concepts, then should we ask the question whether there is religion in India in the first place? Or should we rather ask what could possibly be meant by the term "Hindu"? Those who tried to answer the former question tended to argue that there is no such term as "religion" in Indian languages, but there are ritual and mythological traditions and ethical views, and these could be subsumed under the word "*dharma*" (moral order); others suggested "*mata*" or "*matam*" (opinion), the terms generally used in places like Tamilnadu and Andhra Pradesh. These cultural responses may not adequately deal with the theoretical deployment of the concept "religion". Perhaps if we apply this view of the meaning and intention of the term "Hindu" in the systemic concept "Hinduism" then we might find some resolution to our predicament.

My own sense is that instead of treating the term "Hindu" as a systemic concept that unifies everything that exists in India, we might see it as a relational notion that relates various autonomous cultural traditions. Attempts at unity have generally been from a top-down approach, in our case through the Brāhmanical intellectual traditions as the criteria. But a relational notion need not project such hierarchical order but can simply enable us to see the relationships between traditions. Such relationships are not intended to offer unity at the expense of diversity, nor to trace all things to a single origin, but to connect traditions in order that they cohere.

When we look at the history of Indian culture, it is this relational coherence that enabled different traditions to coexist without competing, instead quietly absorbing each other's ideas and ways of doing things, and yet remaining neutral units. From Buddhists, Jains and Sāṃkhya-Yoga teachers to earlier Upaniṣadic teachers, they all have quietly assimilated ideas from one another and yet remained autonomously recognizable units of intellectual traditions. The Mariamman worshippers in the south and Kālī worshippers in the north have quietly assimilated ideas from the Brāhmanical myths, and the Brāhmanical ritual traditions quietly absorbed various regional beliefs into the various temple rituals. All of this assimilation process that went on for millennia did not result in a single religious tradition but rather remained a mosaic of worldviews, connected by their seamlessness.

Hindu is the word that we use in this volume to relate these seamless traditions that do not pretend to a common ancestry, nor deny that they have criss-crossed each other at one time or another. Instead of viewing the idea of Hindu as a unitary concept, it might be more analytically fruitful if we accept it as a federal notion. This would be in line with my above argument in favour of Hinduism as a relational notion. In any event, the deployment of the notion of Hindu and Hinduism has been both political and pragmatic. Even Swami Vivekananda in his lecture at the Parliament of World Religions deployed the term Hinduism pragmatically. Today, academics and the lay community, outsiders and insiders, use the term. This volume is therefore not averse to the term, but we see its ability to relate diverse traditions more than its ability to offer an essential unity – be it philosophical or historical.

Representing Hinduism has generally been a contested project. It not only abounds in theoretical and methodological problems; it also brings political and social issues to the fore. Many scholars have debated the issue of representing Hinduism. The debates generally centred around the issues of diversity versus unity, insider versus outsider, Brāhmanical versus non-Brāhmanical or, to put it in the old-fashioned way, classical versus popular or literate versus non-literate. Let me clarify that this book is not about juxtaposing the issues, but rather, on the one hand, it aims to go beyond them, and on the other it aims to fill the gaps that were left ignored for too long. Having made that clear, let me also submit that scholars generally agree that Brāhmanical texts and their perspectives have been privileged in the representations of Hinduism to the detriment of ignoring the vast plethora of regional traditions that include both Brāhmanical and non-Brāhmanical, both urban and rural. There exists enormous diversity not only in the subcontinent, but also in the last 150 (and more) years of diasporic inventive attempts to preserve Hinduism in many lands far away from India. The diaspora Hindus have created traditions that are often incomparable with the place of their origins. In closing, therefore, it is to appreciate this diversity and inventiveness of regional narratives that I invite readers. I do hope that the readers will have enjoyed reading these various narratives as much as I have enjoyed relating them to each other in this volume.

Notes

1. C. J. Fuller (2004: 190) refers to three important festivals observed for Meenakshi in the Madurai temple (Adi Mulaikkottu festival, July–August; Navarātri festival, September–October; Kolatta festival, October–November), and points out the following: "In none of the three festivals is there any explicit ritual reference to the Sanskrit myths of Śiva and Parvati."
2. In Hindi, the Sanskrit letter "v" changes to "b".

Glossary

abhiṣeka: anointing by pouring *ghī*; the ritual of worship by pouring libations on the statue of the deity

abhivādyam: paying respect to earth

ācamanam: cleansing of sense organs

ācārams: normative practices

Ādi Granth: sacred text of the Sikh religion

ādivāsi: tribal group

advait: "non-duality" (Sanskrit: *advaita*)

Āgamic: belonging to the Āgama ritual texts

Agni: god of fire

aham brahmāsmi: I am the absolute

ahimsa: non-violence

Akshar: the second highest existential reality in BAPS devotionalism; also, the abode of Purushottam

Akshar Guru: the one who takes the aspirant from darkness into light; in BAPS, the one who helps to cleanse the *ātman* so that it can be in eternal devotion to Purushottam

akshar-rupa: the state of "becoming like Akshar"

alaṅkāra: adornment or ornamentation; in the context of Chapter 16, it refers to the adornment of the images of deity

Allah: name of God in Islam

āḻvār: refers to the twelve canonized saints of the Śrīvaiṣṇavas

Amavāsya: new moon day

Amil: subcategory of Sindhis, often endogamous, comprising professionals and government workers

anācārams: prohibitions

Annakūṭa: The festival that marks the occasion when Kṛṣṇa assumed the form of Mount Govardhan and accepted food offerings from the resident of Braj

antardṛṣṭi: introspection

anubhava: enjoyment or experience

Anurāg Sāgar: one of the two sacred texts of the Kabīrpanthis

āratī: ritual in which small oil lamps sitting on metal plates are lit and waved in front of the images of deities to the accompaniment of communal devotional singing

arcā: one of the five forms of Viṣṇu, and specifically the images (stone, bronze or of other materials) that are in worship

arghyadānam: offering of water

Arthaśāstra: an ancient social and economic treatise attributed to Kautilya

Arya Samaj: a nineteenth-century reform movement

āsana: a small mat or rug on which to sit

āśram: an area or compound in which a religious leader lives and teaches his students, who often live with him; a shelter or hermitage

asūya: jealousy

Āṭi: the fourth Tamil̲ month, which runs from mid-July to mid-August

ātman: eternal self or soul that is subject to rebirth; can be freed from rebirth in BAPS through the guidance of Guru

atmagnan: knowledge of self (Sanskrit: *ātma jñāna*)

ātmanivedana: self-surrender

avatāra: incarnation or manifestation (anglicized spelling: avatar)

Baigā: ritual officiant

bel: (*Aegle marmelos*) exotic fruit

Bhagavad Gītā: part of the Mahābhārata story, a dialogue between Kṛṣṇa and Arjuna

Bhāgavata Purāṇa: sacred text of the Vaiṣṇavas

Bhagavatī: Goddess

Bhagvān/Bhagwan: literally, "lord"; same as Purushottam; often written as God or Lord in English

bhagwā: God's colour

Bhai: literally brother Guru (teacher); in north India it is a respectable way of addressing a teacher

Bhaiband: subcategory of Sindhis, often endogamous, comprising business people

Bhairava: a ferocious form of Śiva

bhajan: devotional or religious song

bhakt: a devotee of God (Sanskrit: Bhakta)

bhakti saṃpradāya: devotional communities

bhakti: ecstatic devotion to a personal deity

bhārūḍ: an allegorical poem that depicts a human character, animal or event in such a way that it bears a spiritual as well as worldly meaning

bhasmakuḷam: ash tank

bhāṣya: commentary

bhāva: devotional state of mind

bhog darśana: the sixth *seeing/visualization*; a snack is offered to Kṛṣṇa prior to his departure for the pastures

Bhooloka Vaikuntha (Telugu): heaven on earth (Sanskrit spelling: Bhūloka Vaikuṇṭha)

Bhṛgu: an ancient Brāhman race

Bhū Devī: the goddess of the earth and Viṣṇu's secondary consort

Bhūtanāthopākhyā: a text regarding the origin of Ayyappan

Bījak: one of the two sacred texts of the Kabīrpanthis

Brahma Sūtras: a text that offers the most authoritative encapsulation of the Upaniṣads

Brāhman: generic category used to refer to the ritual specialists (alternative spelling: Brāhmin)

Brahmotsava: the festival of the Brahma, or the "Great Festival"

Caṅkam: refers to both the genre of literature and the period (early centuries of the Common Era) during which such poetry was developed in the south

Cēra: ancient dynasty of kings in Kerala

cēvai: service; specifically, ritual service

Chamār: person of an untouchable caste (leather-workers)

chamara sevā: literally "fan-service"; refers to the ritual offered to the image of the deity by waving the fan in front of the deity

chelā: disciple

Cheti Chand: festival unique to Sindhi Hindus

cūrṇa: powder

cūṭikkoṭuttavaḷ: "she who gave what she had worn"; an epithet of Āṇṭāḷ

dar khāne: eating of rich food on previous night of *tīj* by Hindu women

dargahs: shrines

darśana/darśan: viewing (e.g. of Kṛṣṇa); gazing at a deity/object of devotion with the desire for a return gaze

Devī Mahātmya Stutī: hymn for the glory of the Goddess

Dharti Mātā: Mother Earth

Ḍholīpaṭiya: A courtyard in the *Nathdwara haveli* where devotees can buy flowers as offerings to Srinathji

dhruvāsi: ritual of circumtreading seven times

dhwajaarohana: flag festival (Sanskrit: dhvajārōhaṇa)

diṇḍī: a group of pilgrims who band together in order to undertake a pilgrimage

diśovandanam: obeisance to the four directions

Divāli: festival of lights

divya rūpa: divine form

Ḍolotsava: swing festival

dōṣam: blemish, flaw, or defect, especially associated with unfavourable planetary arrangements in an individual's horoscope

dūlaiharu: brides

Durgā: Hindu goddess

dvait: literally, "duality"; dualist philosophy (Sanskrit: *dvaita*)

ekānta sevā: night ritual to put the deity to sleep

fakir: roaming ascetic

Gaṇapati/Gaṇeṣa: son of Śiva/remover of obstacles

garbha griha: inner sanctum of a temple where *mūrtis* are consecrated

Garuḍa: vehicle of Viṣṇu; also used as a short form for the text Garuḍa Purāṇa

gāyatrī: prayer performed facing the sun

ghaṇṭi: small bell

ghāri: Indian spicy cake

ghī: clarified butter (anglicized spelling: ghee)

Godā Stuti: "praise to Goda"; a verse composition by Vedānta Deśika that celebrates Āṇṭāḷ as the beloved wife of Viṣṇu

Gopīnāth: eldest son of Vallabhācārya

gopīs: milk maidens, devotees of Kṛṣṇa

gosain: category of people who have renounced or simply rejected the normal life of a working, married householder

grāmas: settlements, villages

guṇas: qualities

gurdwāra: Sikh temple

Gurmukhi: script in which Sikh Scripture is written

guru: leader, guide, one who takes the aspirant from darkness into light

Guru Granth Sāhib: Sikh scripture

guru paraṃparā: lineage of teachers

Guru Pūrṇimā: full moon in month of Ashadh or June–July

gvāl darśana: the third *darśana*; viewing of Kṛṣṇa while he takes his cows to graze

Hanumān: monkey-faced god, depicted as the ideal devotee of Rāmā

Hari: an epithet of Viṣṇu

Harijan: untouchable caste; also known as "Scheduled Caste"

Hariyālī Amāvasyā: festival that occurs during July and August to mark the coming of the monsoons

havan: ritual offering to the sacred fire; an ancient Vedic ritual popularized in the modern period

havelī: the term used in the Puṣṭi Mārga to refer to the multi-storeyed residences that acts as temples for Kṛṣṇa

Holī: spring festival devoted to Kṛṣṇa

iṣṭadevatā: personal god of choice

Īzhava: one of three ancient castes of Kerala

jai stambh: flag pole

jalaprāsanam: penitence ritual

jalebi: Indian sweet

jānave: the sacred thread traditionally worn by the three highest castes

jhandi: a flag commemorating a Hindu deity

jīva: enduring self

jīvātman: individual self (literally "living soul")

jñāna: knowledge

jñāna-yoga: path of knowledge

jyotirliṅga: *liṅga* of light, manifestation of Śiva

Kabīr: north Indian devotional poet

Kabīrhā: central Indian local dialect term for Panthi

Kabīrpanth: one of the low caste religious groups in central India

Kālī kī Mātā: Mother Kālī

Kālī: one of several forms of the Great Goddess; she represents the ferocious and dangerous side of the goddess when she kills the demons; in her more benevolent form she appears as Durgā

Kaliyuga: according to the Hindu calendar, Kaliyuga is the age of discord and strife

Kāma: the god of love and desire

kāppu: a protective turmeric-rubbed ritual thread tied around the wrists of vow-keepers

karakam: ritual vessel, usually decorated with flowers, into which the goddess is temporarily installed in the context of the Āṭi festival

karma: literally, action and/or work; the cosmic law of cause and effect

Karva Chauth: festival of fasting

kathā: religious discourse or sermon

Kātyāyana: fourth century BCE grammarian

kāvaḍi: a dance performed in honour of Murukaṉ

Kēraḷamāhātmyam: an ancient mythological text about Kerala

Kēraḷōlpatti: an ancient text about Kerala's origins

kīrtan: in Marathi usage, a type of performance that involves communal singing and the exhortation of a spiritual or philosophical message by the leader; in some other regions this refers to communal singing only

kōlam: an auspicious ritual drawing, traditionally created out of rice flour, which women draw daily in front of the entrances to their homes

koluvu: court (Telugu); also refers to the offering of service to Lord Venkateswara;

Kōtai: poet who composed the Tiruppāvai and Nācciyār Tirumoḻi, and comes to be known as Āṇṭāḷ

Kṛṣṇa: incarnation of God Viṣṇu

Kṣatriya: person of warrior caste

kṣūdram: evil spirit

kuḷam: bathing tank

kulateyvam: one's family or lineage deity, who is understood as protective of the family and whom members of that family are obligated to worship on specific occasions

Kumārī: virgin, daughter, an unmarried girl also refers to the epithet of the Goddess, as in Kanyākumārī

kuṃkuṃ: red powder used for the dot on the forehead and also to smear on the images of the deities

kurtā: long, loose-fitting Indian-style shirt

kusaṅg: bad company or influence

Kuttichātan: deity invoked during exorcism

Lakṣmī: goddess of prosperity, wife of Viṣṇu

Lāl Darvāzā: One of the entrances to the inner sanctum of the *haveli* in Nathdwara. It literally means the "door to the beloved"

līlās: divine pastimes of Kṛṣṇa

liṅgam: Śiva's creative aspect, symbolized by his phallus

Lohana: general classification of caste among Sindhi Hindus

mādhurya bhāva: intense yearning

Mahābhārata: one of the two epics of Hinduism, the other one being the Rāmāyaṇa

maharāj: in Marathi usage, the title of a Vārkarī spiritual leader who performs kīrtans, initiates new members into the tradition, and advises a group of devotees. Less technically, *maharāj* is a term of extreme respect, used especially by Vārkarīs toward each other while on pilgrimage

mahārāja: descendant of Vallabhācārya; although the word *mahārāja* means "king", it is a special title for the descendants of the founder of the sect

Mahiṣāsura: buffalo demon

Mahotsavam: the annual great festival of a temple

Mai: mother

Makaraviḷakku: festival that occurs on the third day of the Malayalam month of *makaram* (January to February)

mālā: rosary beads

Mānas: short for *Rāmcharitmānas*

manasī sevā: Refers, in the Puṣṭi Mārga, to the mental state needed to maintain complete absorption in Kṛṣṇa

maṇḍala: sacred diagram drawn for ritual purposes

maṇḍapa: sanctified ground

mandir: temple

maṇgala darśana: the first *darśana*, generally occurring before sunrise

Maṇikaṇṭan: another epithet of Ayyappan

maṅjalpodi: turmeric powder

mānsī pūjā: mentally offering devotion to Guru and Bhagwan

mantrasnānam: bathing in the holy water

mantravādam: exorcism

mantravādin: exorcist

Manusmṛti: the book of Hindu codes of law

Māriyamman: (also spelled as Mariamman) non-Brāhmanical goddess popular in south Indian villages

maryādā: rules and regulations

mātā (or **mātājī**): mother

Mathavilāsaprahasana: an ancient text attributed to Mahendravarma I

mātsarya: rivalry

māulī: literally, "mother"; used figuratively to address the Vārkarī saint Jñāndev's role as the "mother" of the tradition (Marathi)

Maveerar: great heroes (Tamiḻ)

melā: carnival, festival

milnā: to meet

mokṣa: liberation (*moksh* in Hindi)

mudrā: symbolic hand gesture

muṇḍana: tonsure

Muṇṭakakkaṇṇi Ammaṉ Temple: pronounced colloquially as "Mundakkanni", a popular local goddess temple in Chennai where the deity's stone image is understood to be *svayambhū* ("self-manifest")

mūrti: image of a Hindu deity, often utilized in worship

Nācciyār Tirumoḻi: The Lady's Words. Āṇṭāḷ's second composition, consisting of 143 verses in fourteen sections

nāga: snake; *nāgas* are understood as divine in Indian traditions and are imaged as goddesses who are particularly connected with fertility in Tamilnadu

nāga cilai: a stone snake sculpture carved by an artisan and offered by a devotee suffering from an astrological defect, typically *nāga dōṣam*, in a remedial ritual intended to diminish this malignant condition

nāga dōṣam: literally "snake blemish"; a negative astrological condition that is commonly thought to result from having killed or harmed a snake, whether in this or a previous life, and which is primarily faulted for delayed marriage and infertility

nāgakkal: a stone snake sculpture carved by an artisan and offered by a devotee suffering from an astrological defect, typically *nāga dōṣam*, in a remedial ritual intended to diminish this malignant condition

nāga pratiṣṭhā: an enlivening ceremony designed to consecrate an image and instil or kindle "life" (*uyir*) and "breath" in it

nakṣatra: regions in the sky through which the moon passes during its orbit

nāmasmaraṇa: chanting the names

Nambūtiri: a subcaste of Brāhmans in Kerala state

Nappiṉṉai: Kṛṣṇa's cowherd wife and an important character in the Tiruppāvai

Nārāyaṇa: one of many names of Viṣṇu

nāsto: snack food

Naths: a particular tradition of ascetics

navagraha: the nine planets of Hindu astrology

Nāyars: a subcaste of Brāhmans

nilaviḷakku: traditional floor lamp

nirguṇa: without attributes (refers to Brahman/absolute reality)

Nirmalas: heterodox Sikhs

nirveda: disgust

nitya pūjā: daily worship

padiṅjāta: prayer room

pādukās: representations of the Vārkarī saints' sandals, nowadays usually made of silver, which are revered as physical manifestations of the saints' continuing presence

pajāma: comfortable, loose-fitting Indian-style trousers

pakhvāj: a two-headed drum suspended from the neck and played with the fingers and hands, commonly used in Vārkarī *bhajans* and *kīrtans*

pālkhī: literally, the palanquin that holds a Vārkarī saint's *pādukās* and is carried to Pandharpur during Vārkarī pilgrimages; also used loosely to connote the groups of pilgrims who become attached to and accompany the palanquin on its journey

pān: mixture of betel leaf and spices

pañcāṅga: calendar based on the movements of the sun and the moon

pañcāyātana pūjā: worship of five deities

pandits: leaders in ritual life

Panthi: sect, group

Paraśurāma-kṣetram: Kerala as a land of Paraśurāma, an ancient sage

patinēttāmpadi: eighteen sacred steps (in Malayalam language)

Patittupāṭṭu: ancient text found in Kerala

pīr: title of a Sūfi master

pirārttaṉai: a petitionary prayer offered in the hope of receiving some benefit from the deity

poṅkal: a boiled rice and lentil mixture that women often cook and offer at goddess temples before bringing the cooked dish home to be consumed as a blessed substance

pradakṣiṇā: clockwise circumambulation around a sacred site and/or sacred object(s), e.g. *mūrti*

praṇām: gesture of respect made by bringing the palms of both hands together, raising them to the level of one's face, and bowing slightly

prāṇayāma: breathing exercise

prārthnā: prayer

prasād/prasāda: food that has been offered to the deities and is then returned to devotees as a form of divine blessing

prokṣanam: internal cleansing

Pṛthvī: goddess of the earth

pūjā: temple or domestic ritual; the act of honouring, making offerings to, and worshipping a deity or deities; a key component of *bhakti* Hinduism

pūjā koṭhā: worship room

pūjāri: temple priest

purāṇa: a genre of texts identified as mythological narratives, e.g. Bhāgavata Purāṇa

Pūrṇimā: full moon day

purohit: Brāhmin priest

Purushottam: the highest existential reality in BAPS devotionalism; the creator of all, the all-doer; in BAPS, Purushottam manifested in the form of Sahajanand Swami from 1781–1829; Purushottam is served by Akshar

pūrvāngams: preparatory rituals (prologues)

puṣpayāga: the ritual of flowers

Puṣṭi Mārga Vaiṣṇavite bhakti community popular in Gujarat and Rajasthan

putantiram: holy aim (Tamiḻ)

qalandar: honorific term in Sufism

Qur'an: Islamic scripture

ratha: chariot

rājbhog darśana: the fourth *darśana*; viewing of Kṛṣṇa with food offerings before he is laid to sleep

Rāma: incarnation of God Viṣṇu

Rāmānuja: the eleventh/twelfth century teacher of the Śrīvaiṣṇavas, responsible for developing a new philosophical system

Rāmāyaṇa: one of the two great epics of Hindus, the other being the Mahābhārata

Ramayan: short for *Rāmcharitmānas*

Rāmcharitmānas: Hindi rendering of the Sanskrit Rāmāyaṇa, attributed to Tulsīdās

Rāmlīla: festival of Rāma, popular in northern India

Rāmnāmi Samāj: one of the low-caste religious groups in central India

raṅga pūja: ritual directed towards the deity Hanumān

rāsa līlā: circle dance of Kṛṣṇa with the *gopīs*

Rathotsavam: festival of chariots

rudraksha: dark brown beads used as an aid in meditation

sādhanā: practice

sādhu: monk, male renunciate

saguṇa: with attributes (refers to Brahman/absolute reality)

sahasranāma arcana: the chanting of thousand names

Śaiva: of or relating to the worship of Śiva; the form of Hinduism devoted primarily to the worship of Śiva

samādhi: in Marathi usage, a state of ecstatic absorption that a person achieves while meditating, or the act of intentionally allowing one's body to die while absorbed in such a state, or the memorial site of a saint's death; also resting place, grave

samāj: community

Samnyāsa Upaniṣads: a genre of Upaniṣads that emphasize the ascetic practice

saṃpradāya: denomination, sect, Hindu sub-tradition, sectarian followers

saṃsāra: cycle of rebirth (i.e. birth and death and rebirth)

saṁskāra: ceremony, especially rite of passage

Sanatana Dharma Maha Sabha: a Hindu organization established in the nineteenth century in northern India

sandhyā āratī: the seventh *darśana*, marking Kṛṣṇa's return home from the pastures with an offering of lamps in the evening

sandhyāvandanam: rituals performed three times during the day

Śaṅkarācārya: eighth-century philosopher

Śaṅkaranārāyaṇa: deity with aspects of both Śiva and Viṣṇu

Sannidhānam: a temple, meaning "presence of the deity" (Ayyappan)

sannyāsi: renouncer, an ascetic

sant-kavi: a term that describes the Vārkarī saints, who are understood to be both exemplary human beings and outstanding poets, conveying their religious teachings through poetic compositions

santo: Gujarati plural for male renunciate; same as *sādhus*

śaraṇam: refuge

śarkara: jaggery, a traditional unrefined whole cane sugar

sarppapāṭṭu: snake song

sarvadarśana: complete vision (Sanskrit)

sarvātmabhāva: The term use in the Puṣṭi Mārga to refer to the state of complete absorption in Kṛṣṇa

Śāsta: another name of Lord Ayyappan

Śāsta Sahasranāmam: hymn of the thousand names of Ayyappa

satī: Hindu practice of burning alive of the widow with the husband's body

Satnāmi Samāj: one of the low-caste religious groups in central India

satsang (satsangh): literally, "a community of truth"; people who gather together in fellowship to remember God

satsangi (satsanghi): one who follows a specific devotional teaching

satyagraha: truth force (a term coined by Mahatma Gandhi)

śayan āratī: the eighth and final *darśana*; viewing of Kṛṣṇa after dusk

Śayana Tirukkōlam: the attitude of divine repose; the special adornment performed annually on the seventh night of the Āṇṭāḷ temple's most important festival

sevā: the path of devotional service to Kṛṣṇa as defined in the Puṣṭi Mārga

sevā praṇālī: manuals of service

sevak: one who volunteers work and resources

Shakti Peeth: location of power

Śiva: one of the three great Gods in Hinduism (anglicized version: Shiva)

shūdra: lowest of the four castes

siddhis: special powers

Sītā: wife of god Rāma

smārta: follower of Smṛti texts (also refers to a Brāhmin subcaste in southern India)

Ṣoḍaśagranthaḥ: sixteen Sanskrit treatises belonging to the school of Vallabha

śrāddha: ancestor rituals, rituals to honour the recently dead

Śrī Śāsta Devasthānam: organization that takes care of the Ayyappan worship

Śrīnāthjī: principal image of Kṛṣṇa worshipped by members of the Puṣṭi Mārga

Śrīvaiṣṇava: a primarily south Indian sect that worships Viṣṇu and his consort Śrī. They also acknowledge Tamil̲ compositions of the *āl̲vār* and the Sanskrit Vedas as the twin sources of their tradition

śṛṅgār darśana: the second *darśana*; decorated viewing (of Kṛṣṇa)

sthala mahima: the miracle/significance of the place

Subrahmaṇya: son of Śiva

śuddha sattva: the special, divine substance that permeates the image of god in worship

Sūfi: Islamic ascetic or follower of Sūfi sect of Islam

suprabhāta sevā: morning service or worship

sūtarfeṇī: Indian sweet

svarūpa: term used to refer to images of Kṛṣṇa in the Puṣṭi Mārga

svatantra: independent

svayaṁ vyakta: self-revealed

svayambhū: literally, "self-manifest"; an image of a deity (whether humanlike or featureless) that arises "naturally", through divine agency

Swami: a Hindu monk

ṭāḷ: a pair of small, simple brass hand-cymbals tied on opposite ends of a strap and worn around the neck, to be played as rhythmic accompaniment for bhajans and kīrtans at Vārkarī events (Marathi)

talavaralāṟu: the traditional history of a place, particularly a temple; an account focused on a temple and its deity that also includes local myths

Tamil̲: A south Indian classical language, distinctive from Sanskrit and with a continuous literary tradition dating to at least the first century CE

tanujā sevā: In the Puṣṭi Mārga, the use of physical effort in the service of Kṛṣṇa

tapas: literally, "heat"; austerity and penance

taṟavātu: households

tarpaṇam: offering to gods, sages and forefathers

tēr: chariot

tevāram: household shrine

thāḷ: plate with vegetarian food items to be offered to *mūrtis*

tīj: women's celebration

Tijri: Sindhi Hindu festival

ṭīkā: red dot on the forehead

tīrtha: pilgrimage place (literally "place of crossing over")

tiruaṅki: a decorated gold shawl

tirukkālam: daily schedule of sacred hours

tirukkōlam: divine form (Tamil̲)

tirumēṉi: divine body; the phrase often used by Śrīvaiṣṇava commentators to describe the body of god

Tiruppāvai: "The Sacred Vow", Āṇṭāḷ's thirty-verse composition

tiruvābharaṇam: gold ornaments

tithi: stages of the moon's waxing and waning

tivārī: triple-arched galleries

tōmāla sevā: the purification service (Tamil̲)

tonhā: males who are said to have powers

tonhī: females who are said to have powers

tulsī: a type of plant, a variety of basil that is sacred to the Hindu deity Viṣṇu

tuṇai: support, help, protector, refuge; this term often refers to the role one's chosen deity plays in his/her life

tuvillum ilam: resting places

ubhaya Vedānta: Vedānta based on both Tamil̲ and Sanskrit traditions

ūkka: daily ritual

upākū: boundary

upanayana: initiation ceremony for young boys involving investing them with a sacred thread

Upaniṣads: philosophical texts of the Vedas

upasthānam: prayers relevant for morning or evening

utsavamūrti: processional icon

utthāpan darśana: the fifth *darśana*; viewing of Kṛṣṇa when is being woken up in the morning

uyir: life, essence, spirit (Tamil̲)

vaḍḍī kāsula vāḍu: the person who pays interest on money (Telugu)

vāhana: "vehicle", the animal associated with a Hindu deity

Vaikhānasa: a system of worship named after a prominent sage Vikhanas (Sanskrit)

vaikuṇṭha: heaven; the term the *sādhus* use to describe their religious experiences of meeting God in the world

vairāghi: an ascetic

Vaiṣṇava: of or relating to the worship of Viṣṇu; the form of Hinduism devoted primarily to the worship of Viṣṇu

Vaiśya: caste of traders

Vallabha Saṃpradāya: Vallabha community

Vallabhācārya: founder of a Vaiṣṇava tradition popular in Gujarat and Rajasthan

vārī: a long walking pilgrimage (Marathi), especially one of the four annual walking pilgrimages to the temple of Viṭṭhal in Pandharpur (southern Maharashtra); the largest and most prominent *vārī* occurs in the month of Āṣāḍh (June/July)

Vārkarī: literally, "one who does *vārī* or pilgrimage" (Marathi); in its strictest sense, a Vārkarī is someone who takes a vow with a *maharāj* to make the pilgrimage to Pandharpur annually, to eat only a vegetarian diet, to wear a necklace of *tulsī* beads and to speak the truth; in a common and less technical sense, a Vārkarī is simply someone who makes the pilgrimage to Pandharpur, regardless of vows or religious affiliation

Vārtā Sāhitya: religious tales related to Vallabha and his devotees

vātsalya bhāva: motherly tenderness, affection

Vāyu Purāṇa: mythological text detailing the origin of creation and the various ages in the evolution of time

Vedānta: philosophical system, otherwise known as Later Mīmāṃsā

Vedānta Deśika: fourteenth-century Śrīvaiṣṇava theologian, poet and philosopher, and author of *Godā Stuti*

vēl: Murukan̲'s weapon

Vēṇkaṭa: Tamil̲ and Telugu name for Lord Venkateswara; because of the mythological narrative about Lord Viṣṇu appearing on the hills of Veṇkaṭa, he is known in the temple built on the hill as Lord Vēṇkaṭa

vēṇṭutal: a vow or request that a devotee brings before a deity

vīṇā: in colloquial Marathi usage, the name of a hollow wooden instrument with between one and four strings that is plucked to maintain a tuning pitch for a Vārkarī singer; in northern India, the one-stringed version of this instrument is called an *ektār*; this simple Vārkarī instrument should not be confused with the more sophisticated *vīṇā* that is used in Indian classical music

visarjan: disposal

viśēṣa pūjā: special service or worship

Viṣṇu: one of Hinduism's major deities; often depicted with a conch and discus, and is associated with rain and fertility

Viṣṇucittaṉ: tradition believes him to be Āṇṭāḷ's father; he was also a Tamiḻ poet and a devotee of Viṣṇu

vittajā sevā: In the Puṣṭi Mārga, use of one's wealth in the service of Kṛṣṇa

Viṭṭhalnāth: Younger son of Vallabhācārya and Gopīnāth's younger brother

Yaśodā: wife of Nanda, cowherd chieftain

yihi: customary wedding ceremony practised primarily by the Newars (the original inhabitants of Kathmandu)

yogi: an ascetic

Bibliography

Aiya, V. N. 1999. *The Travancore State Manual*, vol. 1. Thiruvananthapuram: Kerala Gazetteer's Department.
Aiyar, N. 1939. *Origin and Early History of Śaivism in South India*. Madras: University of Madras.
Allen, M. R. 1984. *The Cult of Kumari: Virgin Worship in Nepal*. Kathmandu: Institute of Nepal and Asian Studies.
Allocco, A. L. 2009. "Snakes, Goddesses, and Anthills: Modern Challenges and Women's Ritual Responses in Contemporary South India". PhD dissertation, Emory University.
Ambalal, A. 1995. *Kṛṣṇa as Shrinathji*. Allahabad: Mapin Publications.
Amirthalingam, M. 1998. "Sthala Vrikshas of Tamilnadu". In *The Ecological Traditions of Tamilnadu*, N. Krishnan & J. Prabhakaran (eds), 83–100. Chennai: CPR Environment Educational Centre.
Amirthalingam, M. 1999. "Sacred Trees of Tamilnadu". *Eco News* 4(4): 12–16.
Ansari, S. F. D. 2005. *Life After Partition: Migration, Community and Strife in Sindh, 1947-1962*. Oxford: Oxford University Press.
Arunachalam, S. P. 1924. "The Worship of Muruka". *Journal of RAS (Ceylon)* 29(77): 234–61.
Babb, L. 1984. "Indigenous Feminism in a Modern Hindu Sect". *Signs* 9(3): 399–416.
Barz, R. 1992. *The Bhakti Sect of Vallabhaācarya*. New Delhi: Munshiram Manoharlal Publishers.
Baumann, M., B. Luchesi & A. Wilke (eds) 2003. *Tempel und Tami̲len in zweiter Heimat. Hindus aus Sri Lanka im deutschsprachigen und skandinavischen Raum*. Würzburg: Ergon Press.
Baumer, R. V. M. & J. R. Brandon 1993. *Sanskrit Drama in Performance*. Delhi: Motilal Banarsidass.
Beck, G. L. 2005. *Alternative Kṛṣṇas: Regional and Vernacular Variations on a Hindu Deity*. Albany, NY: SUNY Press.
Bellamy, C. 2011. *The Powerful Ephemeral: Everyday Healing in an Ambiguously Islamic Place*. Berkeley, CA: University of California Press.
Bennett, P. 1990. "In Nanda Baba's House: The Devotional Experience in Puṣṭi Mārgi Temples". In *Divine Passions: The Social Construction of Emotion in India*, O. M. Lynch (ed.), 183–212. Berkeley, CA: University of California Press.
Bennett, P. 1993. *The Path of Grace: Social Organisation and Temple Worship in a Vaiṣṇava Sect*. Delhi: Hindustan Publishing Corporation.
Bhagavad Gītā 2008. *The Bhagavad Gītā*, L. L. Patton (trans.). New York: Penguin.
Bharati, A. [1961] 2006. "Death Beyond Death: The Ochre Robe". In *The Life of Hinduism*, J. S. Hawley & V. Narayanan (eds), 76–87. Berkeley, CA: University of California Press.
Bhardwaj, S. M. 2003. *Hindu Places of Pilgrimage in India*. New Delhi: Munshiram Manoharlal Publishers.
Bhatia, V. 2011. *Devotional Traditions and National Culture: Recovering Gaudiya Vaishnavism in Colonial Bengal*. Ann Arbor, MI: ProQuest (University of Michigan Dissertation series).

Bhutanese Refugees 2010. "Bhutanese Refugees: The Story of a Forgotten People". 12 March, www.bhutaneserefugees.com (accessed 30 November 2012).
Bilimoria, P. 1989. *Hinduism in Australia: Mandala for the Gods*. Melbourne: Spectrum Publications.
Blackburn, S. H. 1985. "Death and Deification: Folk Cults in Hinduism". *History of Religions* 24(3): 255–74.
Brereton, B. 1985. "The Experience of Indentureship: 1845–1917". See La Guerre (1985), 21–33.
Brereton, B. 1996. *An Introduction to the History of Trinidad and Tobago*. Oxford: Heinemann Education.
Bromley, D. G. & L. Shinn (eds) 1989. *Kṛṣṇa Consciousness in the West*. Lewisburg, PA: Bucknell University Press.
Brooks, C. R. 1990. "Hare Kṛṣṇa, Radhe Shyam: The Cross-Cultural Dynamics of Mystical Emotions in Brindaban". In *Divine Passions: The Social Construction of Emotion in India*, O. M. Lynch (ed.), 264–81. Delhi: Oxford University Press.
Bryant, E. F. 2007. *Kṛṣṇa: A Sourcebook*. Oxford: Oxford University Press.
Bryant, E. J. 2003. *Kṛṣṇa: The Beautiful Legend of God*. London: Penguin.
Campbell, C. 1985. "The East Indian Revolt against Missionary Education". See La Guerre (1985).
Carter, J. R. (ed.) 1979. *Religiousness in Sri Lanka*. Colombo: Marga Institute.
Cartman, J. 1957. *Hinduism in Ceylon*. Colombo: Gunasena.
Chakravarti, N. S. 1927–37. *Gommatsara Karma-Kanda*, J. L. Jaini assisted by B. S. Prasada (ed., intro., trans., commentary). Lucknow: Central Jaina Publication House.
Chakravarti, R. 1985. *Vaishnavism in Bengal, 1486-1900*. Calcutta: Sanskrit Pustak Bhandar.
Chandrakanthan, A. J. V. 2000. "Eelam Tamil̲ Nationalism: An Inside View". In *Sri Lankan Tamil̲ Nationalism: Its Origins and Development in the 19th and 20th Centuries*, J. A. Wilson (ed.), 157–75. London: Hurst Press.
Cherian, P. J. 2000. *William Logan's Malabar Manual*. Thiruvananthapuram: Kerala Gazetteer's Department.
Clothey, F. 1982. "Chronometry, Cosmology and the Festival Calendar of the Murukan̲ Cult". In G. R. Welbon & G. E. Yocum (eds), *Religious Festivals in South India and Sri Lanka*, 157–88. Delhi: Manohar.
Coon, E. 2010. "Nepal Style: Rites of Passage". *Hinduism Today* (July–September): 4.
Coward, H. G., J. R. Hinnells & R. B. Williams (eds) 2000. *The South Asian Religious Diaspora in Britain, Canada, and the United States*. Albany, NY: SUNY Press.
Craddock, N. E. 1994. "Anthills, Split Mothers, and Sacrifice: Conceptions of Female Power in the Mariyamman Tradition". PhD dissertation, University of California, Berkeley.
Craddock, N. E. 2001. "Reconstructing the Split Goddess as Śakti in a Tamil̲ Village". In *Seeking Mahādevī: Constructing the Identities of the Hindu Great Goddess*, T. Pintchman (ed.), 145–69. Albany, NY: SUNY Press.
Cutler, N. 1979. *Consider Our Vow: Translation of Tiruppāvai and Tiruvempāvai into English*. Madurai: Muttu Patippakam.
Cutler, N. 1987. *Songs of Experience: The Poetics of Tamil̲ Devotion*. Bloomington, IN: Indiana University Press.
Danda, A. K. 1977. *Chhattisgarh: An Area Study*. Calcutta: Anthropological Survey of India.
Daniels, E. V. 1996. *Charred Lullabies: Essays in an Anthropography of Violence*. Princeton, NJ: Princeton University Press.
Davis, R. A. 2004. "Muslim Princess in the Temples of Vishnu". *International Journal of Hindu Studies*, 8(1–3): 137–56.
Davis, R. H. 1997. *Lives of Indian Images*. Princeton, NJ: Princeton University Press.
De, S. K. 1986. *Early History of the Vaisnava Faith and Movement in Bengal: From Sanskrit and Bengali Sources*. Calcutta: Firma KLM.
Deekshitulu, R. 2010. "Preamble of Amukta Malyada". *Swati Weekly* (1 September): 66.

Dehejia, V. 1988. *Slaves of the Lord: Path of the Tamil Saints*. New Delhi: Munshiram Manoharlal.
Dehejia, V. 1990. *Āṇṭāḷ and Her Path of Love*. Albany, NY: SUNY Press.
Deleury, G. A. [1960] 1994. *The Cult of Viṭhobā*. Pune: Deccan College, Postgraduate and Research Institute.
Dempsey, C. G. & S. J. Raj 2008. *Miracle as Modern Conundrum in South Asian Religious Traditions*. Albany, NY: SUNY Press.
DeNapoli, A. E. 2009. "Beyond Brāhmanical Asceticism: Recent and Emerging Models of Female Hindu Asceticisms in South Asia". *Religion Compass* **3**: 1–19 (doi: 10.1111/j.1749-8171.2009.00172.x).
DeNapoli, A. E. 2009. "Duty, Destiny, and Devotion in the Oral Life Narratives of Female *Sadhus* in Rajasthan". *Asian Ethnology* 68(1): 81–109.
Denton, L. T. 2004. *Female Ascetics in Hinduism*. Albany, NY: SUNY Press.
Dhere, R. C. 2011. *The Rise of a Folk God: Viṭṭhal of Pandharpur*, A. Feldhaus (trans.). New York: Oxford University Press.
Dhungel, R. K. 1999. "Nepalese Immigrants in the United States of America". *Contributions to Nepalese Studies* 26(1): 119–34.
Dimock, E. C. J. 1989. "Līlā". *History of Religions* 29(2): 159–73.
Doniger, W. (trans.) 1991. *The Laws of Manu*. New York: Penguin.
Dube, S. 1998. *Untouchable Pasts: Religion, Identity, and Power among a Central India Community, 1780–1950*. Albany, NY: SUNY Press.
Dubois, J. A. 1899. *Hindu Manners, Customs and Ceremonies*. Oxford: Clarendon Press.
Dwyer, R. 1996. "Caste, Religion, and Sect in Gujarat: Followers of Vallabhacharya and Swaminarayan". In *Desh Pardesh: The South Asian Presence in Britain*, R. Ballard (ed.), 165–73. Delhi: B. R. Publications.
Ebaugh, H. R. & J. S. Chafetz 2000. *Religion and the New Immigrants: Continuities and Adaptations in Immigrant Congregations*. Walnut Creek, CA: AltaMira Press.
Eck, D. L. 1981. *Darśan: Seeing the Divine Image in India*, 3rd edn. New York: Columbia University Press.
Eliade, M. 1959.*The Sacred & the Profance*. New York: Harcourt, Brace & World.
Elmore, W.T. [1913] 1984. *Dravidian Gods in Modern Hinduism*. New Delhi: Asian Educational Services.
Engblom, P. 1987. "Introduction". In *Palkhi*, P. Engblom (trans.), 1–30. Albany, NY: SUNY Press.
Entwistle, A. 1987. *Braj: Centre for Kṛṣṇa Pilgrimage* . Groningen: Egbert Forsten.
Eschmann, A. 1976. *The Cult of Jagannatha and the Regional Tradition of Orissa*. Heidelberg: University of Heidelberg.
Farquhar, J. N. 1925. "The Fighting Ascetics of India". *Bulletin of the John Rylands Library*, 9: 431–52.
Ferrari, F. M. 2010. "Old Rituals for New Threats: Possession and Healing in the Cult of Śītalā". In *Ritual Matters: Dynamic Dimensions in Practice*, C. Brosius & U. Hüsken (eds), 144–71. London: Routledge.
Flood, G. 1996. *An Introduction to Hinduism*. Cambridge: Cambridge University Press.
Flood, G. 2004. *The Ascetic Self: Subjectivity, Memory, and Tradition*. Cambridge: Cambridge University Press.
Flueckiger, J. B. 2006. *In Amma's Healing Room: Gender and Vernacular Islam in South India*. Bloomington, IN: Indiana University Press.
French, H. 1974. *The Swan's Wide Waters: Ramakrishna and Western Culture*. Port Washington, NY: Kennikat Press.
Fuchs, S. 1960. *The Gond and Bhumia of Eastern Mandla*. Bombay: Asia Publishing House.
Fuchs, S. 1975. *The Divine Hierarchy*. New York: Columbia University Press.
Fuller, C. J. 2004. *The Camphor Flame: Popular Hinduism and Society in India*. Princeton, NJ: Princeton University Press.
Fuller, J. D. 2005. "Religion, Class, and Power: Bhaktivinode Thakur and the Transformation

of Religious Authority among the Gaudiya Vaishnavas in Nineteenth-Century Bengal". PhD dissertation, University of Pennsylvania.

Gajwani, S. L. 2000. *A Sufi Galaxy: Sufi Qalandar Hazrat Qutab Ali Shah, His Spiritual Successors and Select Disciples - Sufi Saints of the Present Times*. Ulhas Nagar: H. M. Damodar.

Gangadharan, T. K. 2003. *Evolution of Kerala History and Culture*. Calicut: Calicut University Press.

Gansten, M. 2009. "Astrologers". *Brill's Encyclopedia of Hinduism*, K. A. Jacobsen (ed.), vol. III, 217–21. Leiden: Brill.

Gansten, M. 2009. "*Navagrahas*". *Brill's Encyclopedia of Hinduism*, vol. I, K. A. Jacobsen (ed.), 645–52. Leiden: Brill.

Gansten, M. 2010. "Astrology and Astronomy (*Jyotiṣa*)". *Brill's Encyclopedia of Hinduism*, K. A. Jacobsen (ed.), vol. II, 281–94. Leiden: Brill.

Garlington, W. 1984. "Baha'i Conversion in Malwa, Central India". In *From Iran East and West: Studies in Baha'i and Baha'i History*, vol. 2, 157–85. Los Angeles, CA: Kalimat Press.

Gaston, A.-M. 1997. *Kṛṣṇa's Musicians: Music and Music-Making in the Nathdwara Temple, Rajasthan*. New Delhi: Manohar Publishers.

Gerrit de Kruijf, J. 2006. *Guyana Junction Globalisation, Localisation, and the Production of East Indianness*. Amsterdam: Rozenberg Publishers.

Gold, A. G. & B. R. Gujar. 1989. "Of Gods, Trees and Boundaries: Divine Conservation in Rajasthan". *Asian Folklore Studies*, 48: 211–29.

Gold, A. G. 1989. "The Once and Future Yogi: Sentiments and Signs in the Tale of a Renouncer-King". *The Journal of Asian Studies* 48(4): 770–86.

Gold, A. G.(trans.) 1992. *A Carnival of Parting: The Tales of King Bharthari and King Gopi Chand as Sung and Told by Madhu Natisar Nath of Ghatiyali*. Berkeley, CA: University of California Press.

Goldberg, P. 2010. *American Veda: From Emerson and the Beatles to Yoga and Meditation-How Indian Spirituality Changed the West*. Bourbon, IN: Harmony Publishing.

Gopalakrishnan, P. K. 1974. *Keralatinte Samskarika Charitram*. Thiruvananthapuram: State Institute of Languages.

Goslinga, G. M. 2006. "The Ethnography of a South Indian God: Virgin Birth, Spirit Possession, and the Prose of the Modern World". PhD dissertation, University of California, Santa Cruz.

Grant, L. 2009. "High Level Example Set *Jhandi* Backlash". *Trinidad Guardian* (24 May), http://guardian.co.tt/commentary/columnist/2009/05/24/high-level-example-set-jhandi-backlash.

Gross, R. L. 1992. *The Sadhus of India*. Jaipur: Rawat Publications.

Gutschow, N. 1996. "The Astamatrka and Navadurga of Bhaktapur: Notions about 'Place' and 'Territory'". In *Wild Goddesses in India and Nepal*, A. Michaels, C. Vogelsanger & A. Wilke (eds), 191–216. New York: Peter Lang.

Haberman, D. L. 1994. *Journey Through the Twelve Forests: An Encounter With Kṛṣṇa*. New York: Oxford University Press.

Haberman, D. L. 2010. "Faces in the Trees". *Journal for the Study of Religion, Nature and Culture* 4(2): 173–90.

Hancock, M. E. 1990. "Women at Work: Ritual and Cultural Identity Among Smarta Brahmans of Madras". PhD Dissertation, University of Pennsylvania.

Hancock, M. E. 1999. *Womanhood in the Making: Domestic Ritual and Public Culture in Urban South India*. Boulder, CO: Westview Press.

Hardy, F. 1983. *Viraha-Bhakti: The Early History of Krishna Devotion in South India*. Delhi: Oxford University Press.

Harman, W. 2000. "Speaking About Hinduism ... and Speaking Against It". *Journal of the American Academy of Religion* 68(4): 733–40.

Harman, W. P. 2004. "Taming the Fever Goddess: Transforming a Tradition in Southern India". *Manushi*, 140 (January–February): 2–13.

Harman, W. P. 2006. "Negotiating Relationships with the Goddess". In *Dealing with Deities: The Ritual Vow in South Asia*, S. J. Raj & W. P. Harman (eds), 25–41. Albany, NY: SUNY Press.

Svatmarama. 1972. *Hathayogapradīpika of Svatmarama, Commentary of Jyotsna*. Madras: Theosophical Society.

Hausner, S. L. 2007. *Wandering with the Sadhus: Ascetics in the Hindu Himalayas*. Bloomington, IN: Indiana University Press.

Hawley, J. H. & M. Juergensmeyer 1988. *Songs of the Saints of India*. New York: Oxford University Press.

Hawley, J. S. & D. M. Wulff. 1996. *Devī: Goddesses of India*. Berkeley, CA: University of California Press.

Hawley, J. S. 2009. *Memory of Love: Sūrdās Sings to Kṛṣṇa*. Oxford: Oxford University Press.

Hebbar, B. N. 2005. *The Sri Krishna Temple at Udupi*. Springfield, VA: Nataraj Books.

Hein, N. 1995. *Līla: The Gods at Play - Līla in South Asia*. New York: Oxford University Press.

Hiltebeitel, A. & K. M. Erndl (eds) 2000. *Is the Goddess a Feminist? The Politics of South Asian Goddesses*. New York: New York University Press.

Hinnells, J. R. (ed.) 2007. *Religious Reconstruction in the South Asian Diasporas: From One Generation to Another (Migration, Minorities and Citizenship)*. Basingstoke: Palgrave Macmillan.

Hopkins, S. P. 2002. *Singing the Body of God: The Hymns of Vedāntadeśika in Their South Indian Tradition*. New York: Oxford University Press.

Hopkins, S. P. 2007a. "Extravagant Beholding: Love, Ideal Bodies, and Particularity". *History of Religions* 47(1): 1–50.

Hopkins, S. P. 2007b. *An Ornament for Jewels: Love Poems for the Lord of Gods by Vedāntadeśika*. New York: Oxford University Press.

Hudson, D. 1996. "Āṇṭāḷ's Desire". *Vaiṣṇavi: Women and the Worship of Kṛṣṇa*, S. J. Rosen (ed.), 171–211. New Delhi: Motilal Banarasidass.

Hutter, M. 2012. "'Half Mandir and Half Gurudwara': Three Local Hindu Communities in Manila, Jakarta, and Cologne". *Numen* 59(4): 344–65.

Jackson, C. 1994. *Vedānta for the West: The Ramakrishna Movement in the United States*. Bloomington, IN: Indiana University Press.

Jacobsen, K. A. 2003. "Settling in Cold Climate: Tamil Hindus in Norway". In *Tempel und Tamilen in zweiter Heimat. Hindus aus Sri Lanka im deutschsprachigen und skandinavischen Raum*, M. Baumann, B. Luchesi & A. Wilke (eds), 363–77. Würzburg: Ergon Press.

Jacobsen, K. A. & P. Kumar (eds) 2004. *South Asians in Diaspora: Histories and Religious Traditions*. Leiden: Brill.

Jacobsen, K. A. 2004. "Establishing Ritual Space in the Hindu Diaspora in Norway". In *South Asians in the Diaspora: Histories and Religious Traditions*, K. A. Jacobsen & P. Kumar (eds), 134–48. Leiden: Brill.

Jacobsen, K. A. 2006. "Hindu Processions, Diaspora and Religious Pluralism". In *Religious Pluralism and the Diaspora*, P. Pratap Kumar (ed.), 163–73. Leiden: Brill.

Jacobsen, K. A. 2008a. "Processions, Public Space and Sacred Space in the South Asian Diasporas in Norway". In *South Asian Religions on Display: Religious Processions in South Asia and in the Diaspora*, K. A. Jacobsen (ed.), 191–204. London: Routledge.

Jacobsen, K. A. 2008b. "Creating Sri Lankan Tamil Catholic Space in the South Asian Diaspora in Norway". In *South Asian Christian Diaspora: Invisible Diaspora in Europe and North America*, K. A. Jacobsen & S. J. Raj (eds), 117–32. Aldershot: Ashgate.

Jacobsen, K. A. 2009a. "Introduction". In *Brill's Encyclopedia of Hinduism*, K. A. Jacobsen (ed.), vol. I, xxxiii–xliii. Brill: Leiden.

Jacobsen, K. A. 2009b. "Establishing Tamil Ritual Space: A Comparative Analysis of the Ritualization of the Traditions of the Tamil Hindus and the Tamil Roman Catholics in Norway". In *Journal of Religion in Europe* 2(2): 180–98.

Jacobsen, K. A. 2010. "Leadership Structures and Government Regulation of Hinduism in Norway". *Finnish Journal of Ethnicity and Migration* 5(2): 39–46.

Jacobsen, K. A. 2011a. "Hinduismen i Norge". In *Verdensreligioner i Norge*, 3rd edn, K. A. Jacobsen. (ed.). 76–127. Oslo: Norwegian University Press.

Jacobsen, K. A. 2011b. "Institutionalization of Sikhism in Norway: Community Growth and Generational Transfer". In K. A. Jacobsen & K. Myrvold (eds), *Sikhs in Europe: Migration, Identities and Representations*, 19–36. Farnham: Ashgate.

Jacobsen, K. A. & K. Myrvold (eds) 2012. *Sikhs across Borders: Transnational Practices among European Sikhs*. London: Continuum.

Jacobsen, K. A. 2013a. *Pilgrimage in the Hindu Tradition: Salvific Space*. London: Routledge.

Jacobsen, K. A. 2013b. "Aramuga Navalar". In *Brill's Encyclopedia of Hinduism*, K. A. Jacobsen (ed.), vol. V. Forthcoming. Leiden: Brill.

Jagadeeshan, N. 1989. *Collected Papers on Tamiḻ Vaishnavism*. Madurai: Ennes Publications.

Jankie, A. 2011. "Moonilal, Protesters Blocked at School in *Jhandi* March". *Trinidad Express* (6 February), www.trinidadexpress.com/news/Moonilal__protesters_blocked_at_school_in_*jhandi*_march-115406864.html (accessed 23 February 2012).

Jha, J. C. 1985. "The Indian Heritage in Trinidad". See La Guerre (1985).

Jindel, R. 1976. *Culture of a Sacred Town: A Sociological Study of Nathdwara*. Bombay: Popular Prakashan.

Jones, A. K. 2002. *Politics in Sindh, 1907–1940: Muslim Identity and the Demand for Pakistan*. Oxford: Oxford University Press.

Kapadia, K. 1995. *Siva and Her Sisters: Gender, Caste, and Class in Rural South India*. Boulder, CO: Westview Press.

Karve, I. 1988. "'On the Road': A Maharashtrian Pilgrimage". In *The Experience of Hinduism: Essays on Religion in Maharashtra*, E. Zelliot & M. Berntsen (eds), 143–73. Albany, NY: SUNY Press.

Keay, J. 2000. *India: A History*. New York: Atlantic Monthly Press.

Kēcikaṉ, P. 1992. *Nalan Tarum Nāyaki Aṉṉai Muṇṭakakkaṇṇi*. Chennai: Arulmiku Mundaka Kanni Amman Tirukkoyil.

Kent, E. F. 2010. "A Road Runs Through It: Changing Meanings in a Sacred Grove in Tiruvannamalai, Tamilnadu". *Journal for the Study of Religion, Nature and Culture* 4(2): 213–31.

Keune, J. 2011. *Eknāth Remembered and Reformed: Bhakti, Brahmans and Untouchables in Marathi Historiography*. PhD Dissertation, Columbia University.

Keune, J. 2012. "*Eknāth*", in *Brill's Encyclopedia of Hinduism*, K.A. Jocobsen (ed.), 218-26. Leiden: Brill.

Keune, J. & C. L. Novetzke 2011. "Vārkarī". In *Brill's Encyclopedia of Hinduism*, vol. 3, K. A. Jacobsen (ed.), 617–26. Leiden: Brill.

Khan, A. 2004. *Callaloo Nation: Metaphors of Race and Religious Identity among South Asians in Trinidad*. Durham, NC: Duke University Press.

Khandelwal, M. R. 2004. *Women in Ochre Robes: Gendering Hindu Renunciation*. Albany, NY: SUNY Press.

Khandelwal, M. R. 2009. "Research on Hindu Women's Renunciation Today: State of the Field". *Religion Compass* 3(6): 1003–14 (doi: 10.1111/j.1749.8171.2009.00184.x)

Khandelwal, M., S. L. Hausner & A. G. Gold (eds) 2006. *Women's Renunciation in South Asia: Nuns, Yoginis, Saints, and Singers*. Basingstoke: Palgrave Macmillan.

Kim, H. H. 2007. "'Edifice Complex': Swaminarayan Bodies and Buildings in the Diaspora". In *Gujaratis in the West: Evolving Identities in Contemporary Society*, A. Mukadam and S. Mawani (eds), 59–78. Newcastle upon Tyne: Cambridge Scholars Publishing.

Kim, H. H. 2009. "Public Engagement and Personal Desires: BAPS Swaminarayan Temples and their Contribution to the Discourses on Religion". *International Journal of Hindu Studies* 13(3): 357–90.

Kinsley, D. R. 1986. *Hindu Goddesses: Divisions of the Divine Feminine in the Hindu Religious Tradition*. Berkeley, CA: University of California Press.

Kīrtankār, P. (ed.) 1994. *Utsav Darśan - Kīrtan Mālā* . Nathdwara: Śrīmadvallabh Aṣṭasakhā Smṛti Trust.
Klass, M. 1961. *East Indians in Trinidad: A Study of Cultural Persistence*. New York: Columbia University Press.
Knott, K. 1986. *Hinduism in Leeds: A Study of Religious Practice in the Indian Hindu Community and in Hindu-Related Groups*. Leeds: University of Leeds.
Kṛṣṇa, N. 2000. *Balaji-Venkateshwara, Lord of Tirumala-Tirupati: An Introduction*. Mumbai: Vakils, Feffer & Simons.
Krishnadasa, K. G. & E. C. Dimock 1999. *Chaitanya Caritamrta of Krishnadasa Kaviraja: A Translation and Commentary*. Cambridge, MA: Harvard University Press.
Kuiper, F. B. J. 2004. "The Worship of the Jarjara on the Stage" *Indo-Iranian Journal* 16(4): 406–10.
Kulke, H. & G.-D. Sontheimer (eds) 2001. *Hinduism Reconsidered*. New Delhi: Manohar.
Kumar, N. & P. Raghuram (eds) 2003. *South Asian Women in the Diaspora*. Oxford: Berg.
Kumar, P. N. 2009. "Preamble of Amukta Malyada". *Muse India* (July–August), www.museindia.com/viewarticle.asp?myr=2009&issid=26&id=1602.
Kumar, P. P 2009. "Introducing Hinduism in Practice". In *Religions in Focus: New Approaches to Tradition and Contemporary Practices*, G. Harvey (ed.), 257–71. London: Equinox.
Kumar, P. Pratap (2000) *The Goddess Lakshmi in South Indian Vaishnavism*. Oxford: Oxford University Press.
Kumar, P. Pratap. (ed.) 2006. *Religious Pluralism and the Diaspora*. Leiden: Brill.
Kumar, P. Pratap. 2010. "Introducing Hinduism: The Master Narrative – A Critical Review of Textbooks on Hinduism" *Religious Studies Review* 36(2): 115–24.
Kumar, P. P. 2013. *Hinduism and the Diaspora: A South African Narrative*. Jaipur, India: Rawat Publications.
La Guerre, J. (ed.) 1985. *Calcutta to Caroni: The East Indians of Trinidad*. St Augustine: University of the West Indies.
Lamb, R. 2002. *Rapt in the Name: The Ramnamis, Ramnam, and Untouchable Religion in Central India*. Albany, NY: SUNY Press.
Lamb, R. 2006. "Monastic Vows and the Ramananda Sampraday". In *Dealing with Deities: The Ritual Vow in South Asia*, S. J. Raj & W. Harman (eds), 165–83. Albany, NY: SUNY Press.
Lamb, R. 2008. "Devotion, Renunciation, and Rebirth in the Ramananda Sampraday". *Crosscurrents* 57(4): 578–90.
Lamb, R. 2010. "India: Past and Present". In *Encyclopedia of 21st Century Anthropology*, J. Birx (ed.), 725–35. Thousand Oaks, CA: Sage Publications.
Lari, S. Z. 1994. *A History of Sindh*. Karachi: Oxford University Press.
Leonard, K. I. 1997. *The South Asian Americans*. Westport, CT: Greenwood Press.
Lidova, N. 1996. *Drama and Ritual of Early Hinduism*. Delhi: Motilal Banarsidass.
Llewellyn, J. E. (ed.) 2005. *Defining Hinduism: A Reader*. New York: Routledge.
Lochtefeld, J. G. 1994. "The Vishva Hindu Parishad and the Roots of Hindu Militancy". *Journal of the American Academy of Religion* 62(2): 587–602.
Loewenstein, R. M. 1957. "A Contribution to the Psychoanalytic Theory of Masochism". *Journal of the American Psychological Association*, V: 197–234.
Logan, P. 1980. "Domestic Worship and the Festival Cycle in the South Indian City of Madurai". PhD dissertation, University of Manchester.
Long, J. D. 2007. *A Vision for Hinduism: Beyond Hindu Nationalism*. London: I. B. Tauris.
Lorenzen D. 1978. "Warrior Ascetics in Indian History". *Journal of the American Oriental Society*, 98: 61–75.
Lutgendorf, P. 1991. *The Life of a Text, Performing the Ramcaritmanas of Tulsidas*. Berkeley, CA: University of California Press.
Lyons, T. 2004. *The Artists of Nathdwara: The Practice of Painting in Rajasthan*. Bloomington, IN: Indian University Press.

MacPhail, J. 2008. "The Indians Are Coming". *Hinduism Today* (July–September): 54–5.
Maharaj, Viṭṭhalnāth. (ed.) 1937. *Śrīdvārakadhīś sevā Śṛṅgār Praṇālī*. Kankaroli: Kankaroli Vidyā Vibhāg.
Mahipati & J. E. Abbott [1927] 1997. *The Life of Eknāth = Śrī Eknāth Charitra, Translated from the Bhaktalīlāmṛta*. Delhi: Motilal Banarsidass.
Mahipati & J. E. Abbott [1930] 1980. *Life of Tukaram: Translation from Mahipati's Bhaktalilamrita, Chapters 25 to 40*. Delhi: Motilal Banarsidass.
Malamoud, C. 1989. *Cuire le mond. Rite et pensée dans l'Inde ancienne*. Paris: La Découverte.
Malcolm, J. 2001. *A Memoir of Central India including Malwa and Adjoining Provinces*, 2 vols. New Delhi: Aryan Books International.
Mangru, B. 1987. *Benevolent Neutrality*. Hertford: Hansib.
Manuel, P. 2000. *East Indian Music in the West-Indies: Tan-Singing, Chutney, and the Making of Indo-Caribbean Culture*. Philadelphia, PA: Temple University Press.
Markovits, C. 2000. *The Global World of Indian Merchants, 1750–1947: Traders of Sind from Bukhara to Panama*. Cambridge Studies in Indian History and Society no. 6. Cambridge: Cambridge University Press.
Marriot, M. 1955. "Little Communities in an Indigenous Civilization". In M. Marriot (ed.) *Village India: Studies in the Little Community*, 171–222. Chicago, IL: University of Chicago Press.
Martin, J. L. 1982. "The Cycle of festivals at Parthasarathi". In *Religious Festivals in South India and Sri Lanka*, G. R. Welbon & G. E. Yocum (eds), 51–76. Delhi: Manohar.
Martin, N. 2000. "North Indian Hindi Devotional Literature". In *The Blackwell Companion to Hinduism*, G. Flood (ed.), 182–98. Malden, MA: Blackwell.
Masson, J. M. 1976. "The Psychology of the Ascetic". *Journal of Asian Studies*, XXXV (4): 611–25.
Mayer, A. C. 1961. *Peasants in the Pacific: A Study of Fiji Indian Rural Society*. London: Routledge & Kegan Paul.
McDaniel, J. 1989. *The Madness of the Saints: Ecstatic Religion in Bengal*. Chicago, IL: University of Chicago Press.
McDaniel, J. 2003. *Making Virtuous Daughters and Wives: An Introduction to Women's Brata Rituals in Bengali Folk Religion*. Albany, NY: SUNY Press.
McGee, M. 1987. "Feasting and Fasting: The *Vrata* Tradition and Its Significance for Hindu Women". ThD dissertation, Harvard University.
McGee, M. 1992. "Desired Fruits: Motive and Intention in the Votive Rites of Hindu Women". In *Roles and Rituals for Hindu Women*, J. Leslie (ed.), 71–88. Delhi: Motilal Banarsidass.
McGuire, M. 2008. *Lived Religion. Faith and Practice in Everyday Life*. Oxford: Oxford University Press.
Mehta, T. 1999. *Sanskrit Play Production in Ancient India*. Delhi: Motilal Banarsidass.
Menon, K. D. 2009. *Everyday Nationalism: Women of the Hindu Right in India*. Philadelphia, PA: University of Pennsylvania Press.
Menon, T. M. (ed.) 2000. *A Handbook of Kerala*, vols 1–2. Trivandrum: International School of Dravidian Linguistics.
Michaels, A. 2008. *Siva in Trouble: Festivals and Rituals at the Pasupatinatha Temple of Deopatan*. New York: Oxford University Press.
Mines, D. 2009. *Caste in India*. Ann Arbor, MI: Association of Asian Studies.
Mishra, P. K. 2002. *South Asian Diaspora in North America: An Annotated Bibliography*. New Delhi: Kalinga Publications.
Misir, P. 2006. *Cultural Identity and Creolization in National Unity: The Multiethnic Caribbean*. New York: University Press of America.
Mohapatra, G. 1982. *Jagannatha in History & Religious Traditions of Orissa*. Calcutta: Punthi Pustak.
Mokashi, D. B. 1987. *Palkhi: An Indian Pilgrimage*, P. Engblom (trans.). Albany, NY: SUNY Press.
Mukhi, S. S. 2000. *Doing the Desi Thing: Performing Indianness in New York City*. New York: Garland Publishing.

Muṇṭakakkaṇṇi Ammaṉ Temple. n.d. *Aruḷmiku Muṇṭakakkaṇṇiyammaṉ Tirukkōyil Tala Varalāṟṟuc Curukkam*. Chennai: Neat Printers.

Muthanna, I. M. 1982. *People of India in North America*. Bangalore: Lotus Printers.

Nabokov, I. 2000. *Religion Against the Self: An Ethnography of Tamil̲ Rituals*. New York: Oxford University Press.

Namboodiripad, E. M. S. 1952. *The National Question of Kerala*. Bombay: People's Publication House.

Narain, K. 2004. *The Philosophy of the Vallabha School of Vedānta*. Varanasi: Indological Research Center.

Narasimha C. N. C. V. (trans.) 1987. *Venkatachala Ithihasamala of Srimad Anantarya*. Tirupati: Tirumala Tirupati Devasthanams.

Narayan Swamy, M. R. 2008. *Inside an Elusive Mind: Prabhakaran*, 6th edn. Colombo: Yapa Publications.

Narayanan, K. 1989. *Storytellers, Saints, and Scoundrels: Folk Narrative in Hindu Religious Teaching*. Philadelphia, PA: University of Pennsylvania Press.

Narayanan, V. 1987. *The Way and the Goal: Expressions of Devotion in Early Śrīvaiṣṇava Commentary*. Washington, DC: Institute for Vaiṣṇava Studies.

Narayanan, V. 1994. *The Vernacular Veda: Revelation, Recital and Ritual*. Columbia, SC: University of South Carolina Press.

Narsimha Reddy, D. 1983. *A Study of Some Minor Temple Festivals According to Pancaratra and Vaikhanasa Agamas*. Tirupati: Padmasri Publications.

Natali, C. 2007. "Building Cemeteries, Constructing Identities: Funerary Practices and Nationalist Discourse among the Tamil̲ Tigers of Sri Lanka". Paper presented 11 May, University of Sussex, Brighton. www.basas.org.uk/conference05/natali,%20cristiana.pdf.

National Ramlila Committee 1977. *Ramlilaverhaal en program 1977*. Paramaribo: National Ramlila Committee.

Neelima, P. 2010. "Muslims Celebrate Ugadi at Kadapa Temple". *The Times of India* (17 March), http://articles.timesofindia.indiatimes.com/2010-03-17/hyderabad/28116165_1_tirumala-temple-offer-prayers-lord-venkateswara (accessed 30 November 2012).

Nepali, G. S. 1988. *The Newars: An Ethno-Sociological Study of a Himalayan Community*. Kathmandu: Himalayan Booksellers.

Nugteren, A. 2005. *Belief, Bounty, and Beauty: Rituals around Sacred Trees in India*. Leiden: Brill.

O'Flaherty, W. D. 1973. *Asceticism and Eroticism in the Mythology of Siva*. Oxford: Oxford University Press.

Oberoi, H. 1994. *The Construction of Religious Boundaries: Culture, Identity and Diversity in the Sikh Tradition*. Oxford: Oxford University Press.

Oddie, G. A. 1977. *Religion in South Asia: Religious Conversion and Revival Movements in South Asia in Medieval and Modern Times*. Columbia, MO: South Asia Books.

Odorico & H. Yule 2002. *The Travels of Friar Odoric*. Grand Rapids, MI: Eerdmans.

Olivelle, P. (trans.) 1992. *Samnyasa Upanishads*. Oxford: Oxford University Press.

Olivelle, P. 2004. "Rhetoric and Reality: Women's Agency in the Dharmśāstras". In *Encounters with the Word: Essays to Honour Aloysius Piers*, R. Crusz, M. Fernando & A. Tilakaratne (eds), 489–505. Colombo: Ecumenical Institute for Study and Dialogue.

Orr, W. G. 1940. "Armed Religious Ascetics in Northern India". *Bulletin of the John Rylands Library*, 24: 81–100.

Orsi, R. 2003. "Is the Study of Lived Religion Irrelevant to the World We Live in?" *Journal for the Scientific Study of Religion* 42(2): 169–74.

Orsi, R. 2005. *Between Heaven and Earth: The Religious Worlds People Make and the Scholars who Study Them*. Princeton, NJ: Princeton University Press.

Osella, F. & C. Osella. 2003. "'Ayyappan Saranam': Masculinity and the Sabarimala Pilgrimage in Kerala". *Journal of the Royal Anthropological Institute* 9(4): 729–54.

Parmar, S. 1972. *Folklore of Madhya Pradesh*. New Delhi: National Book Trust.

Parry, J. 1994. *Death in Banaras*. Cambridge: Cambridge University Press.
Parry, J. H. 1981. *The Age of Reconnaissance: Discovery, Exploration, and Settlement, 1450-1650*. Berkeley, CA: University of California Press.
Pathamanathan, S. 1990. "Murukaṉ the Diviner Child: The Kantacuvami Temple at Nallur". In *Lanka: Tidsskrift om Lankesisk Kultur*, 80–102. Aalborg: Nordic Migration Conference.
Pearson, A. M. 1996. *"Because it Gives Me Peace of Mind": Rituals Fasts in the Religious Lives of Hindu Women*. Albany, NY: SUNY Press.
Pillai, Velayutam. 1947. *Moliyaraci*. Madras: South India Saiva Siddhantha Works.
Pinch, W. 2006. *Warrior Ascetics and Indian Empires*. Cambridge: Cambridge University Press.
Pintchman, T. (ed.) 2001. *Seeking Mahādevī: Constructing the Identities of the Hindu Great Goddess*. Albany, NY: SUNY Press.
Pintchman, T. (ed.) 2007. *Women's Lives, Women's Rituals in the Hindu Tradition*. New York: Oxford University Press.
Pintchman, T. 1994. *The Rise of the Goddess in the Hindu Tradition*. Albany, NY: SUNY Press.
Pintchman, T. 2005. *Guests at God's Wedding: Celebrating Kartik Among the Women of Benares*. Albany, NY: SUNY Press.
Prasad L, 2007. *The Poetics of Conduct: Oral Narratives and Moral Being in a South Indian Town*. New York: Columbia University Press.
Primiano, L. N. 1995. "Vernacular Religion and the Search for Method in Religious Folklife". *Western Folklore* 54(1): 37–56.
Purkayastha, B. 2005. *Negotiating Ethnicity: Second-Generation South Asian Americans Traverse a Transnational World*. New Brunswick, NJ: Rutgers University Press.
Radhakrishnan, S. 1927. *The Hindu View of Life*. London: Macmillan.
Raghavan, V. 1963. *Prayers, Praises and Psalms: Selections from the Vedas, Upanishads, Epics, Gita, Puranas, Agamas, Tantras, Kavyas and the Writings of the Acharyas and Others*. Madras: G. A. Natesan.
Raghoebier, R. 1987. *Sanskritiki Baten. Bijdragen tot de kennis van de Hindostaanse Cultuur in Suriname*. Paramaribo: Ministerie an Onderwijs, Wetenschap en Cultuur, Afdeling Cultuurstudies.
Raj, S. J. & W. P. Harman (eds) 2006. *Dealing with Deities: The Ritual Vow in South Asia*. Albany, NY: SUNY Press.
Ramachandra, R., G. Narayanan & A. Ramachandran 2005. *History of Medieval Kerala*. New Delhi: Pragati.
Ramanujan, A. K. 1993. *Hymns for the Drowning*. New York: Penguin.
Ramaswamy, S. 1997. *Passions of the Tongue: Language Devotion in Tamiḻ India, 1891-1970*. Berkeley, CA: University of California Press.
Ramchandra, N. (ed.) 1989. *Puṣṭipath praṇālikā*. Jodhpur: Śrī Subodhinī Prakāśan Maṇḍal.
Ramesan, N. 1981. *The Tirumala Temple*. Tirupati: Tirumala Tirupati Devasthanams.
Ramesh, M. S. 1997. *108 Vaishnavite Divya Desams*, vol V. Tirupati: Tirumala Tirupati Devasthanams.
Ramesh, M. S. 2000. *The Festivals and Rituals at Tirumala Temple*. Chennai: T. R. Publications.
Ramey, S. 2008. *Hindu, Sufi, or Sikh: Contested Practices and Identifications of Sindhi Hindus in India and Beyond*. Basingstoke: Palgrave Macmillan.
Rao, M. R. 1982. *Temples of Tirumala, Tirupati and Tiruchanur*. Tirupati: Tirumala Tirupati Devasthanams.
Rao, N. & D. Shulman 2005. *God on the Hill: Temple Poems from Tirupati*. New York: Oxford University Press.
Rao, S. K. R. 1990. *Pratima-Kosha: A Descriptive Glossary of Indian Iconography*, 6 vols. Bangalore: I. B. H. Prakashana for Kalpatharu Research Academy.
Rao, V. 2002. *Living Traditions in Contemporary Contexts: The Madhva Matha of Udupi*. New Delhi: Orient Longman.

Redington, J. 2000. *The Grace of Lord Kṛṣṇa: The Sixteen Verse-Treatises of Vallabhācarya*. Delhi: Sri Satguru Publications.
Rizzo, R. 2000. "Study Abroad Student Killed while Traveling". *The GW Hatchet* (24 January), www.gwhatchet.com/2000/01/24/study-abroad-student-killed-while-traveling (accessed 30 November 2012).
Roberts, M. 2005. "Tamil̲ Tiger 'Martyrs:' Regenerating Divine Potency". *Studies in Conflict and Terrorism*, 28: 493–514.
Rosen, S. 2006. *Essential Hinduism*. Westport, CT: Praeger.
Rukmani, T. S. 2001. *Hindu Diaspora: Global Perspectives*. Delhi: Munshiram Manoharlal.
Rupa, G. & D. L. Haberman 2003. *The Bhaktirasamrtasindhu of Rupa Gosvamin*. New Delhi: Indira Gandhi National Centre for the Arts.
Russell, R. V. & H. Lal 1916. "Gond". In their *The Tribes and Castes of the Central Provinces of India*, vol. 3, 38–143. London: Oxford University Press.
Ryan, S. 1999. *The Jhandi and the Cross: The Clash of Cultures in Post-Creole Trinidad and Tobago*. Trinidad: Institute of Social and Economic Research, University of the West Indies.
Sadhu Amrutvijaydas (trans.) 2005. *Swamini Vato: Spiritual Teachings of AksharBrahman Gunatitanand Swami*. Ahmedabad: Swaminarayan Aksharpith.
Sadhu Amrutvijaydas 2007. *100 Years of BAPS: Foundation-Formation-Fruition*. Ahmedabad: Swaminarayan Aksharpith.
Sadhu Anandswarupdas 2004. "Infinite Glory of Akshar". *Enlightening Essays* (22 October), www.Swaminarayan.org/essays/2004/2210.htm (accessed 5 November 2010).
Sadhu Mukundcharandas 2007. *Hindu Rites and Rituals: Sentiments, Sacraments and Symbols*. Ahmedabad: Swaminarayan Aksharpith.
Saha, S. 2004. "Creating a Community of Grace: A History of the Puṣṭi Mārga in Northern and Western India, 1493–1905". PhD thesis, University of Ottawa.
Saha, S. 2006. "Creating a Community of Grace: The Social and Theological world of the Puṣṭi Mārga". *Bulletin of the School of Oriental and African Studies* 69(2): 225–42.
Said, E. 1978. *Orientalism*. New York, Pantheon Books.
Samaroo, B. 1985. "Politics and Afro-Indian Relations in Trinidad". See La Guerre (1985).
Sarma, D. 2003. *An Introduction to Mādhva Vedānta*. Aldershot: Ashgate.
Sarma, D. 2005. *Epistemology and the Limitations of Philosophical Inquiry: Doctrine in Mādhva Vedānta*. Oxford: Routledge Curzon.
Sarma, S. A. S. 2009. "The Eclectic *Paddhatis* of Kerala". *Indologica Taurinensia*, 35: 319–39.
Sastri, T. G. (ed.) 1990a. *Īśānaśivagurudevapaddhati of Īśānaśivagurudeva*, 4 vols. Delhi: Bharatiya Vidya Prakashan.
Sastri, T. G. (ed.) 1990b. *Tantrasamuccaya*, N. P. Unni (intro.). Delhi: Nag Publishers.
Sastry, Sadhu S. 1981. *Tirupati Sri Venkateswara*. Tirupati: Tirumala Tirupati Devasthanams.
Schalk, P. 1997. "Resistance and Martyrdom in the Process of State Formation of Tamil̲ilam". In *Martyrdom and Political Resistance*, J. Pettigrew (ed.), 61–84. Amsterdam: VU University Press.
Schweig, G. M. 2005. *Dance of Divine Love: The Rāsa Līlā of Kṛṣna from the Bhāgavata Purāṇa, India's Classic Sacred Love Story*. Princeton, NJ: Princeton University Press.
Sekar, R. 2009. "Ayyappan". In *Brill's Encyclopedia of Hinduism*, vol. I, K. A. Jacobsen (ed.), 479–84. Leiden: Brill.
Shankar, L. D. & R. Srik 1998. *A Part, Yet Apart: South Asians in America*. Philadelphia, PA: Temple University Press.
Shankarananda, S. 2005. "Confessions of a Western Hindu" *Hinduism Today* (October–December), www.hinduismtoday.com/modules/smartsection/item.php?itemid=1371 (accessed 11 December 2012).
Sharma, A. 1988. *Sati: Historical and Phenomenological Essays*. Delhi: Motilal Banarsidass.
Sharma, B. N. K. 1981. *History of the Dvaita School of Vedānta and Its Literature*. Delhi: Motilal Banarsidass.

Sharma, B. N. K. 1986. *Philosophy of Sri Madhvācārya*. Delhi: Motilal Banarsidass.
Shastri, A. V. (trans.) 2002. *The Sanskar Vidhi: English Translation*. New Delhi: Sarvadeshik Arya Pratinidhi Sabha.
Shiksapatri [1826] 1992. *Shiksapatri: A Code of Conduct*. Ahmedabad: Swaminarayan Aksharpith.
Shukla, H. L. 1995. *Chhattisgarh Rediscovered*. New Delhi: Aryan Books International.
Sinclair-Brull, W. 1997. *Female Ascetics*. Richmond: Curzon Press.
Singh, K. 1988. *Bloodstained Tombs: The Muharram Massacre of 1884*. London: Macmillan.
Singh, R. P. B. 1993. "Cosmic Layout of the Hindu Sacred City, Varanasi (Benares)". *Architecture and Behaviour* 9(2): 239–50.
Shivji, R. 1931. *Śrī Vallabhpuṣṭiprakāś*. Bombay: Lakshmivenkateswar Press.
Smith, D. 1982. "Festivals in the Pancaratra Literature". In *Religious Festivals in South India and Sri Lanka*, G. R. Welbon & G. E. Yocum (eds), 27–49. Delhi: Manohar.
Smith, H. D. & M. Narasimhachary 1991. *Handbook of Hindu Gods, Goddesses and Saints*. Delhi: Sundeep Prakashan.
Stein, B. 1960. "The Economic Function of a Medieval South Indian Temple". *Journal of Asian Studies*, 19: 163–76.
Stork, H. 1992. "Mothering Rituals in Tamilnadu: Some Magico-Religious Beliefs". In *Roles and Rituals for Hindu Women*, J. Leslie (ed.), 89–105. Delhi: Motilal Banarsidass.
Subrahmanyam, S. 1995. "An Eastern El Dorado: The Tirumala–Tirupati Temple Complex in Early European Views and Ambitions, 1540–1660". In *Syllables of Sky: Studies in South Indian Civilization*, D. Shulman (ed.), 341–2. Delhi: Oxford University Press.
Suseendirarajah, S. 1979. "Religiousness in the Shaiva village". In *Religiousness in Sri Lanka*, J. R. Carter (ed.), 175–89. Colombo: Marga Institute.
Taylor, P. 2001. *Dance: Religion, Identity and Cultural Difference in the Caribbean*. Bloomington, IN: Indiana University Press.
Tewari, L. G. 1991. *A Splendor of Worship: Women's Fasts, Rituals, Stories and Art*. New Delhi: Manohar.
Thakur, U. T. 1959. *Sindhi Culture*. University of Bombay Publications Sociology Series no. 9. Bombay: University of Bombay.
Thapan, A. R. 2002. *Sindhi Diaspora in Manila, Hong Kong, and Jakarta*. Manila: Ateneo de Manila University Press.
Thomasson, F. 2009. *A History of Theatre in Guyana, 1800–2000*. Hertford: Hansib.
Thompson, E. J. 1928. *Suttee: A Historical and Philosophical Enquiry into the Hindu Rite of Widow-Burning*. Boston, MA: Houghton Mifflin.
Thurston, E. 1906. *Ethnographic Notes on Southern India*, 2 vols. Madras: Government Press.
Tinker, H. 1993. *A New System of Slavery: The Export of Indian Labour overseas 1830–1920*, 2nd edn. London: Hansib.
Toffin, G. 1992. "The Indra Jatra of Kathmandu as a Royal Festival: Past and Present". *Contributions to Nepalese Studies* 19(1): 74–92.
Toomey, P. 1994. *Food from the Mouth of Kṛṣṇa*. Delhi: Hindustan Publishing Corporation.
Tranum, S. 2004. "Board Disallows Hindu Symbols". *Sun Sentinel* (15 January), http://articles.sun-sentinel.com/2004-01-15/news/0401150127_1_hindus-flags-symbols (accessed 26 June 2010).
Tulpule, S. G. 1979. *Classical Marāṭhī Literature: From the Beginning to A.D.1818*. Wiesbaden: Harrassowitz.
Vachanamrut [1819–29] 2006. *Vachanamrut: Spiritual Discourses on Bhagwan Swaminarayan*, Sadhus of BAPS Swaminarayan Sanstha (trans.). Ahmedabad: Swaminarayan Aksharpith.
Vallely, A. 2002. *Guardians of the Transcendent: An Ethnography of a Jain Ascetic Community*. Toronto: University of Toronto Press.
Van der Leeuw, G. 1967. *Religion in Essence and Manifestation*, vol. 1. Gloucester, MA: Peter Smith.
Vedic Upaasnaa 1986. *Vedic Upaasnaa*. Trinidad: Arya Pratinidhi Sabha of Trinidad.

Veluthat, K. 1978. *The Brahman Settlements in Kerala: Historical Studies*. Calicut: Sandhya Publishers.
Venkatesan, A. 2007. "Who Stole the Garland of Love? Āṇṭāḷ Stories in the Śrīvaiṣṇava Tradition". *Journal of Vaiṣṇava Studies* 15(2): 189–206.
Venkatesan, A. 2010. *The Secret Garland: Āṇṭāḷ's Tiruppāvai* and *Nācciyār Tirumoḻi*. New York: Oxford University Press.
Verdia, H. S. 1982. *Religion and Social Structure in a Sacred Town: Nathdwara*. New Delhi: Researchco Publications.
Vergati, A. [1995] 2002. *Gods, Men and Territory: Society and Culture in Kathmandu Valley*. New Delhi: Manohar.
Vertovec, S. 1992. *Hindu Trinidad*. London: Macmillan.
Vertovec, S. 2000. *The Hindu Diaspora: Comparative Patterns*. London: Routledge.
Viraraghavacharya, T. K. T. 1997. *History of Tirupati*, vol. I. Tirupati: Tirumala Tirupati Devasthanams.
Vyasa, Ś. 1983. *Śrīmadbhāgavatapurāṇam*, S. J. Lal (ed.). Delhi: Motilal Banarsidass.
Wadley, S. S. 1983. "Vrats: Transformers of Destiny". In *Karma: An Anthropological Inquiry*, E. V. Daniel & C. F. Keyes (eds), 147–62. Berkeley, CA: University of California Press.
Waghorne, J. P. 2004. *Diaspora of the Gods: Modern Hindu Temples in an Urban Middle-Class World*. New York: Oxford University Press.
Walcott, D. 1992. *The Antilles, Fragments of Epic Memory*. New York: Farrar, Straus & Giroux.
Warrier, M. 2005. *Hindu Selves in a Modern World: Guru Faith in the Mata Amritanandamayi Mission*. New York: Routledge.
Welbon, G. R. & G. E. Yocum (eds) 1983. *Religious Festivals in South India and Sri Lanka*. Delhi: Manohar.
White, D. G. 2000. *Tantra in Practice*. Princeton, NJ: Princeton University Press.
Whitehead, H. 1921. *The Village Gods of South India*. Kolkata: Association Press.
Williams, R. B. 1988. *Religions of Immigrants from India and Pakistan: New Threads in the American Tapestry*. Cambridge: Cambridge University Press.
Williams, R. B. 2001. *An Introduction to Swaminarayan Hinduism*. Cambridge: Cambridge University Press.
Williamson, L. 2010. *Transcendent in America: Hindu-Inspired Meditation Movements as New Religion*. New York: New York University Press.
Woodward, R. D. 2006. *Indo-European Sacred Space, Vedic and Roman Cult*. Urbana, IL: Board of Trustees of the University of Illinois.
Youngblood, M. D. 2003. "The Vārkarīs". *Critical Asian Studies* 35(2): 287–300.
Younger, P. 1980. "A Temple Festival of Māriyammaṉ". *Journal of the American Academy of Religion* 48(4): 493–517.
Younger, P. 2002. *Playing Host to Deity: Festival Religion in South Indian Tradition*. Oxford: Oxford University Press.
Younger, P. 2010. *New Homelands: Hindu Communities in Mauritius, Guyana, Trinidad, South Africa, Fiji and East Africa*. New York: Oxford University Press.
Zelliot, E. 1987. "A Historical Introduction to the Warkari Movement". In *Palkhi*, P. C. Engblom (ed.), 31–53. Albany, NY: SUNY Press.
Zimmer, H. [1946] 1992. *Myths and Symbols in Indian Art and Civilization*, J. Campbell (ed.). Bollingen Series no. VI. Princeton, NJ: Princeton University Press.

Websites

http://prabhuguptara.blogspot.com/2006/07/update-on-indo-caribbean-custom-of.html
www.boloji.com/dances/00109.htm
www.yogamag.net/archives/1996/bmar96/tantric.shtml
www.boloji.com/dances/00109.htm

Contributors

Amy L. Allocco is Assistant Professor of Religious Studies at Elon University in North Carolina, USA. She specializes in performance and ritual studies, and has developed a particular interest in gender and women's religious roles and practices. She is co-editing (with Brian K. Pennington) a book entitled *Ritual Innovation in South Asian Traditions*, is the author of several book chapters and has published an article in *Method and Theory in the Study of Religion*.

Michael Baltutis is Assistant Professor of South Asian Religions at the University of Wisconsin, Oshkosh. His research deals with the relationships between text and practice in classical and contemporary ritual performances in India and Nepal, focusing on the Indrajatra festival of contemporary Kathmandu. His recent publications include "Renovating Bhairav: Fierce Gods, Divine Agency, and Local Power in Kathmandu" (*International Journal of Hindu Studies*, 2009) and "Reinventing Orthopraxy and Practising Worldly Dharma: Vasu and Aśoka in Book Fourteen of the Mahābhārata" (*International Journal of Hindu Studies*, 2011).

Antoinette E. DeNapoli has taught at the University of Wyoming in Laramie and Grinnell College in Grinnell, Iowa. She has held teaching fellowships from the Andrew W. Mellon Foundation and Emory's Graduate School of Arts and Sciences, and research and language fellowships from the American Institute of Indian Studies. She focuses on a female expression of vernacular asceticism in Rajasthan, India, and has published several articles in distinguished academic journals. She is currently working on a book entitled *Real Sadhus Sing to God: Gender, Asceticism, and Vernacular Religion in Rajasthan*.

Abhishek Ghosh is an instructor in Asian classics at Garaham School and a doctoral fellow in the South Asian Department at the University of Chicago. He has an MSt in the study of religion from the University of Oxford, and his present research focuses on the contemporary Bengali Vaiṣṇava guru, Bhaktivinode and his theological engagement with the modern world.

William Harman is the former chair of the Department of Philosophy and Religion at DePauw University and former department head at the University of Tennessee in Chattanooga. He has written *The Sacred Marriage of a Hindu Goddess* (1990, rev. 1994), edited *Religion in Tamilnadu: Beginnings of a Discussion* (1971) and, with S. Raj, edited *Dealing with Deities: The Ritual Vow in South Asia* (2006). His recent work is on the Tamil̲ Tiger insurgency in Sri Lanka, Hindu temple miracles, identity of a Hindu goddess, personal devotion and spirit possession in Hinduism, and the performance of ritual jokes in a festival in India.

Knut A. Jacobsen is Professor in the History of Religions at the University of Bergen, Norway. He has published widely on religions in south Asia and in the south Asian diasporas, and is the editor-in-chief of the five-volume *Brill's Encyclopedia of Hinduism* (2009–13).

Jon Keune received a PhD from Columbia University and is a postdoctoral fellow in the Centre for Modern Indian Studies (CeMIS) at the University of Göttingen in Germany. His research focuses on historiography and religion in Maharashtra between 1600 and the present, particularly in relation to bhakti and caste.

Hanna H. Kim is Assistant Professor of Cultural Anthropology at Adelphi University, New York. Her research focuses on the anthropology of religion, and, in particular, how religious movements are rich sites for exploring the discourses on religion and their influence on devotees and their publics alike. Recent articles include "Public Engagement and Personal Desires: BAPS Swaminarayan Temples and their Contributions to the Discourses on Religion" (*International Journal of Hindu Studies*, 2009).

P. Pratap Kumar is Professor Emeritus of Hindu Studies and Comparative Religions at the University of KwaZulu Natal, Durban, South Africa. He is the author of several books and scholarly articles. His publications include *The Goddess Lakṣmī in South Indian Vaishnavism* (1997, 2000) and *Hinduism and the Diaspora* (2013).

Ramdas Lamb is an Associate Professor of Religion at the University of Hawai'i. From 1969 to 1978, he was a Hindu *sādhu* (renunciant) in northern India. Since 1991, he has been teaching at University of Hawai'i. His academic research focuses on Hindu asceticism as well as on the religious traditions and movements of central India.

Jeffery D. Long is Professor of Religion and Asian Studies at Elizabethtown College in Elizabethtown, Pennsylvania. He is the author of *A Vision for Hinduism: Beyond Hindu Nationalism* (2007), *Jainism: An Introduction* (2009) and the *Historical Dictionary of Hinduism* (2011), as well as a variety of articles, papers and book reviews.

Afsar Mohammad teaches at the University of Texas at Austin. He specializes in Hinduism and Islam in south India, Telugu language and literature, saints and *yogis*, and pilgrimage in south Asia. He is a well-known poet and literary critic in his home language Telugu, and has published extensively and won national acclaim as a poet in India. He has published in distinguished journals.

George Pati is Associate Professor of South Asian Religions in the Department of Theology, Valparaiso University, where he also holds the Surjit Patheja Chair in World Religions and Ethics. He teaches on Indian religions and cultures, and Hinduism. His primary research and teaching interests are in historical study of south Asian religions, with special emphasis on Kerala, south India. His current research focuses specifically on the mediation of religion in modern Kerala through texts, traditions and theatrical performances.

Steven W. Ramey is an Associate Professor in the Department of Religious Studies at the University of Alabama, where he also directs the Asian studies programme. His research on Sindhi Hindus has been published in *Hindu, Sufi, or Sikh: Contested Practices and Identifications of Sindhi Hindus in India and Beyond* (2008).

Indrani Rampersad is a Senior Research Fellow in Ramlila at The University of Trinidad and Tobago. She has worked as an educator and journalist. She is Trinidad and Tobago's first state-recognized female Hindu priest.

Shandip Saha is Assistant Professor of Religious Studies at Athabasca University in Edmonton, Canada. His primary research has been on the patronage of the Vallabha Saṃpradāya and other north Indian religious devotional communities under the Delhi Sultanate and the Mughal Empire. His other research interests focus on religion and globalization and the relationship between religion and immigration in Canada.

Deepak Shimkhada taught courses in Asian religions at Claremont McKenna College. He retired from the College in 2008, and is now an adjunct professor for the School of Religion at Claremont Graduate University. He is a published author of several edited volumes and numerous book chapters and journal papers. His most recent edited books are *The Constant and Changing Faces of the Goddess: Goddess Traditions of Asia* (reissued 2009) and *Nepal: Nostalgia and Modernity* (2011).

Archana Venkatesan is Associate Professor of Comparative Literature and Religious Studies at the University of California, Davis. She is the author of *The Secret Garland: Āṇṭāḷ's Tiruppāvai and Nācciyār Tirumoḻi* (2010), and *A Hundred Measures of Time: Nammāḻvār's Tiruviruttan* (Penguin Classics, forthcoming in 2014). Her research focuses on Tamiḻ Vaiṣṇava devotional literature, and its interface with performance and visual cultures in Tamiḻ country.

Paul Younger is Professor Emeritus at McMaster University in Hamilton, Ontario. His current research interest is in the Hindu communities formed in diasporic locations. His most recent book is *New Homelands: Hindu Communities in Mauritius, Guyana, Trinidad, South Africa, Fiji and East Africa* (2010).

Index